FIVE HUNDRED YEARS OF LGBTQIA+ HISTORY IN WESTERN NICARAGUA

VICTORIA GONZÁLEZ-RIVERA

FIVE HUNDRED YEARS OF LGBTQIA+ HISTORY IN WESTERN NICARAGUA

THE UNIVERSITY OF ARIZONA PRESS
TUCSON

The University of Arizona Press
www.uapress.arizona.edu

We respectfully acknowledge the University of Arizona is on the land and territories of Indigenous peoples. Today, Arizona is home to twenty-two federally recognized tribes, with Tucson being home to the O'odham and the Yaqui. Committed to diversity and inclusion, the University strives to build sustainable relationships with sovereign Native Nations and Indigenous communities through education offerings, partnerships, and community service.

© 2024 by The Arizona Board of Regents
All rights reserved. Published 2024

ISBN-13: 978-0-8165-4280-2 (hardcover)
ISBN-13: 978-0-8165-5351-8 (ebook)

Cover design by Leigh McDonald
Cover photograph: Market scene at Granada, Nicaragua, 1909. Courtesy of National Photo Company Collection (Library of Congress)
Typeset by Leigh McDonald in Warnock Pro 10.5/14 and Rift (display)

Publication of this book is made possible in part by the proceeds of a permanent endowment created with the assistance of a Challenge Grant from the National Endowment for the Humanities, a federal agency.

Library of Congress Cataloging-in-Publication Data
Names: González-Rivera, Victoria, 1969– author.
Title: Five hundred years of LGBTQIA+ history in western Nicaragua / Victoria González-Rivera.
Description: Tucson : University of Arizona Press, 2024. | Includes bibliographical references and index.
Identifiers: LCCN 2023056398 (print) | LCCN 2023056399 (ebook) | ISBN 9780816542802 (hardcover) | ISBN 9780816553518 (ebook)
Subjects: LCSH: Sexual minorities—Nicaragua—History. | Gender identity—Nicaragua—History. | Indians of Central America—Sexual behavior—Nicaragua—History.
Classification: LCC HQ73.3.N5 G669 2024 (print) | LCC HQ73.3.N5 (ebook) | DDC 306.76097285—dc23/eng/20240124
LC record available at https://lccn.loc.gov/2023056398
LC ebook record available at https://lccn.loc.gov/2023056399

Printed in the United States of America
♾ This paper meets the requirements of ANSI/NISO Z39.48-1992 (Permanence of Paper).

This book is dedicated to my children, Raquel, Lucía, and Paulo,

and to Nena, researcher and sister extraordinaire.

CONTENTS

Acknowledgments		*ix*
	INTRODUCTION	3
1.	SODOMITES, CUYLONES, AND COCHONES: THE COLONIAL PERIOD	21
2.	"VERY DELICATE MEN" AND "QUEER" FILIBUSTERS: THE NINETEENTH CENTURY	66
3.	THE MODERN NATION-STATE, FEMINISM, AND THE MODERN WOMAN: THE EARLY TWENTIETH CENTURY	119
4.	POETRY AND PERSECUTION: THE SOMOZA DICTATORSHIP, 1936–1979	189
	CONCLUSION	253
Notes		*257*
Bibliography		*293*
Index		*323*

ACKNOWLEDGMENTS

Originally this book was going to cover only the twentieth century. My longtime collaborator and friend Karen Kampwirth (a political scientist) and I were going to write about the last one hundred years or so of western Nicaragua's LGBTQIA+ history. But then I came across a treasure trove of documents going back to the colonial period, and the material became too much for one single book. Our manuscript thus became two separate single-authored books, with mine covering the period from the late 1400s to the 1979 Sandinista revolution and Karen's covering the late twentieth century and the early twenty-first.

I wish to thank Karen for working with me during many years on this project. Writing with another person is doubly hard, but the recompense is also doubled. If it hadn't been for Karen, I probably would have given up on this project given the many crises that took place during the last few years. Knowing that she was writing under incredibly difficult circumstances inspired me to keep writing. Additionally, she was the one who insisted on obtaining the financing so that our book could exist in Spanish. I have learned so much from her and value her friendship enormously.

This book would not have been possible without the labor of generations of extraordinary journalists who wrote the first draft of Nicaraguan history. I also must thank the many archivists and librarians in Nicaragua and elsewhere, especially those at the Instituto de Historia de Nicaragua y Centroamérica and those at the Endangered Archives Programme, the Archivo Nacional de Nicaragua, the Biblioteca Roberto Incer Barquero at the Banco Central de Nicaragua, and the Biblioteca Enrique Bolaños. Without these archivists' work, the sources used in this book would not exist. I am of course also indebted to all the people who over the years have granted me interviews, among them Hilda Scott.

The list of those who have gifted me their support and friendship over the many years I have devoted to this book is very long, and it is hard to find the appropriate words to thank so many.

I especially wish to thank the following individuals, whom I have listed in alphabetical order, for sharing with me their valuable time, opinions, and knowledge: Alicia Ivonne Estrada, Amaral Arévalo, Ana Criquillon, Ana Quirós, Ana Victoria Portocarrero, Amy Bank, Aynn Setright, Bernard Gordillo Brockmann, Camilo Antillón, Carlos Fernando Chamorro, Celina Gallardo, Circles Robinson, Claire Huang Kinsley, Clara Murguialday, Claudia Rueda, Cynthia Enloe, David Rocha, Deena González, Donald Casco, Dora María Tellez, Eddy Kühl, Engel Ortega, Erick Blandón, Erika Blum, Eugenia Rodríguez Sáenz, Florence Babb, Gabriel Pérez, Geni Gómez, Gerardo Urbina (q.e.p.d.), Héctor Carrillo, Helen Alfaro, Helen Dixon, Helena Ramos, Irene Agudelo, Jeff Gould, John McKiernan-González, Jorge Fontdevila, Julián Guevara, Juan Pablo Gómez, Justin Wolfe, Karina Alma, Kitty Madden, Las Venancias, Leisy Abrego, Lupita Sequeira (q.e.p.d.), Margaret Power, Margaret Randall, Margarita Vannini, María Teresa Blandón, Maricruz Carrasco, Marvin Mayorga, Mary Bolt González, Matilde Córdoba, Nohelia Talavera, Nadine Jubb, Nancy Martin, Nicole Hayward, Nohelia Talavera, Rosibel Blandón, Soili Buska, Sylvia Torres, Suyapa Portillo Villeda, Turid Hagene, and Vondel Gámez. And, of course, Elyla.

I am also indebted with many of my high school and college friends who have showered me with love and support throughout the years.

I would also like to thank those who have invited me to present my work and have demonstrated an interest in this project. I especially appreciated the opportunity to participate in the 2018 Summer Institute on Women's Suffrage funded by the National Endowment for the Humanities at Carthage College. It was an important space in which to dig deeper into the connections between first-wave feminism, gender, and sexuality. My sincere thanks go out to the following organizers and participants: Stephanie Mitchell, Patricia Harms, Victor Macías-González, Lucy Grinnell, Indi Valobra, Claudia Montero, Augusto Espiritu, Ana Lau, and Asunción Lavrín. At the University of Michigan, I am very grateful to Eimeel Castillo, Sueann Caulfield, and Larry La Fountain for their suggestions and questions regarding my research. In San Diego, I wish to thank Marina Dillingham for giving me the opportunity to speak about my research. I am also grateful for Kori Pacyniak's support.

San Diego State University assisted me with a Critical Thinking Grant in 2018, a mini grant in 2015, and a sabbatical in 2022–23, and for that I am grateful. The American Council of Learned Societies (ACLS) supported this project with a collaborative grant in 2017–18, which allowed me to dedicate that entire year to this project. This grant also made the translation of the book into Spanish possible. I wish to thank the ACLS staff, especially Rachel Bernard, Matthew Goldfeder, Anna Marchese, Cindy Mueller, and Tami Shaloum, for their generosity and patience.

I also wish to thank editor-in-chief Kristen Buckles at the University of Arizona Press for her patience and encouragement as well as all the other individuals who helped bring this version of the book to fruition: assistant editor Elizabeth Wilder; art director Leigh McDonald; marketing manager Abby Mogollón; editorial, design, and production manager Amanda Krause; copyeditor Rebekah Slonim; and the anonymous reviewers who gave me feedback on my manuscript.

My colleagues at San Diego State University (SDSU) have been amazing. I especially wish to thank Esther Rothblum, Bertha Hernández, Coral McFarland Thuet, Leilani Grajeda Higley, Kim Price, Huma Ahmed Ghosh, Anne Donadey, Walter Penrose, Chuck Goehring, David Kamper, Joanna Brooks, Norma Iglesias, María Ibarra, Adelaida Del Castillo, Roberto Hernández, Michael Domínguez, Irene Lara, Mark Wheeler, Cheryl O'Brien, Ronnee Schreiber, Oliva Espín, Doreen Mattingly, Andrés Aguilar, Andy Wiese, and Kate Swanson. I also would like to thank my students, particularly Tiana Vargas and Alejandra González.

Finally, I want to thank my family, since they mean everything to me. They have been my biggest cheerleaders. Lucía, Paulo, Raquel, and Oscar have supported me in every way. My sister Paula was also key to this project since she assisted me extensively with my research. This book would not exist without her help. My mother, Kathy Hoyt, gave me feedback on the manuscript and was only a phone call away when I had random questions that I knew only she could answer. I am very lucky to have her in my life. I also want to acknowledge the boundless faith my aunt Victoria Morales Vargas has in me and the never-ending praise she has had for this book. Due to her remarkable memory and life journey, she has been a font of knowledge that I have relied on extensively for decades. I truly don't know how to thank her for everything she has given me. Jerónima and Dora Úbeda have also granted me love and support for decades. I don't know what I would have done without them. I must also acknowledge the support I have always received from my brother Bayardo Paul. I am also grateful to others in my family: my brother Bayardo, Michael, Ceci, Moises, Marie, Dee Dee, and many others. I am overwhelmed with gratitude.

FIVE HUNDRED YEARS OF LGBTQIA+ HISTORY IN WESTERN NICARAGUA

INTRODUCTION

¿Que sos, Nicaragua, para dolerme tanto?
—GIOCONDA BELLI

IN THE sixteenth century, Spaniards justified the brutality of the conquest to themselves by claiming that they were saving the residents of what is now Nicaragua from the sins of cannibalism, human sacrifice, idolatry, nonmarital sex, and sodomy. It is therefore not surprising that Spanish conquistadors sometimes used attack dogs to dismember and kill Indigenous people suspected of same-sex sexual practices.[1] But even powerful Spanish conquistadors like Andrés Caballero (a good friend and possibly a lover of the Spanish colonial governor Francisco de Castañeda) fell victims to the Spanish Crown's insistence on policing sexual relations between men. In 1536 Caballero was burned at the stake for the crime of sodomy in the colonial city of León Viejo, located about twenty miles from the Pacific Ocean.[2] The circumstances that led Caballero to such a violent fate—which I document in chapter 1—shed light on the intersection between Spanish colonial power, gender, and sexuality on Nicaragua's Pacific coast and the long-standing repercussions of the Inquisition.

Outsiders like Andrés Caballero preyed on Nicaragua because of their interest in its unique geography and natural resources, or for geopolitical reasons. Caballero's fellow sixteenth-century Spanish conquistadors, the nineteenth-century U.S. filibuster William Walker and his twelve thousand followers,[3] and later the U.S. Marines during the early twentieth century all focused not only on obtaining political and economic control of Nicaragua but also on controlling Nicaraguan gender and sexuality. Nicaraguans, meanwhile, have sometimes responded to foreign threats with moral panic, seeing foreigners as sexually (and therefore morally) suspect and calling into doubt the patriotism of Nicaraguan women and LGBTQIA+ Nicaraguans believed to have been influenced by foreigners. The attempts at sex and gender regulation by outsiders, and the sometimes-panicked responses of elite and non-elite Nicaraguans to those attempts, emerge repeatedly as themes over the course of centuries, with different nuances each time.

This book, which centers gender and sexuality in western Nicaragua, is by necessity one that also centers foreign intervention. Three hundred years of Spanish colonization and multiple U.S. military occupations in the nineteenth and twentieth centuries certainly wreaked havoc on Nicaragua. But what is most relevant here is that colonialism and U.S. intervention were often justified in ways that referenced gender and sexuality and had short- and long-term outcomes that were also gendered and sexed. Moreover, the inevitable resistance to colonialism and U.S. imperialism was often about "refusing the favor"[4] of having Spanish and/or U.S. gender and sexuality norms imposed on the local populations.

This story is sometimes messy and at times might appear to be counterintuitive for contemporary readers. It is a heartbreaking story. But it is necessary to counteract the academic and popular dominant narratives about the LGBTQIA+ history of western Nicaragua (inside and outside Nicaragua), which are often ahistorical. In some of these narratives the notion is put forth that LGBTQIA+ individuals did not exist in Nicaragua prior to the late twentieth century and that homosexuality and gender diversity are foreign imports. Other narratives maintain that LGBTQIA+ Nicaraguans have been more marginal *and* marginalized than LGBTQIA+ folks in wealthier countries.

Ahistorical and inaccurate narratives have served the political purposes of those Nicaraguans who, as the ideological heirs to colonization and imperialism, have sought to persecute and punish LGBTQIA+ Nicaraguans. The narratives have also served the interests of those non-Nicaraguans who continue to perceive and portray *all Nicaraguans* as backward and inferior, or maybe just as a little bit inferior or "inferior light."

In this book I have documented a Nicaraguan LGBTQIA+ past that is complex and nuanced. I highlight continuities and discontinuities over almost five centuries and argue that Indigenous survivance—"the union of active [Indigenous] survival and resistance to cultural dominance"— has sometimes prevailed, despite the best efforts of colonizers, the Catholic Church, and local elites.[5] I argue that, in fact, the LGBTQIA+ history of western Nicaragua is a profoundly Indigenous history that is often missed due to the emphasis on the official mestizo nationalisms that have prevailed in the twentieth and twenty-first centuries.[6] The concept of survivance is useful because it refers to "Native survivance . . . [as] an active sense of presence over absence, deracination, and oblivion in history; survivance is the obvious continuance of stories, not a mere reaction . . . Survivance stories are renunciations of state dominance."[7] Documenting Indigenous survivance as we slowly piece together western Nicaraguan's LGBTQIA+ histories means rethinking not only what constitutes Indigenous and LGBTQIA+ histories of that region but also what constitutes the broader history of Nicaragua such that it eventually includes all Nicaraguans.

Nicaragua was covered extensively by the U.S. press in the late 1840s and early 1850s, when thousands of U.S. Americans traveled through Nicaragua to join the gold rush in California. Nicaragua received even more attention in 1855 when William Walker, a white U.S. American filibuster, invited thousands of U.S. settlers to join him as he declared himself president of this small country and proceeded to reinstate slavery, which had been outlawed decades earlier. Nicaragua was in the U.S. news *again* when U.S. Marines were unable to defeat the anti-imperialist general Augusto C. Sandino in 1927 and anti-intervention groups in the United States demanded a withdrawal of U.S. troops.[8] Decades later, in 1979, the entire world turned its attention to Nicaragua as a small group of leftist guerrillas was able to defeat the U.S.-financed right-wing Somoza dictatorship. Nicaragua was discussed daily in U.S. television and newspapers during the 1980s, which documented the progression of the U.S.-sponsored Contra War against the Nicaraguan Sandinista revolution. The eventual defeat of the Sandinistas at the polls in 1990 and the peaceful transfer of power to a nonfeminist neoliberal woman president left many in shock. After that, most of the outside world stopped paying attention to Nicaragua. Apparently, there was nothing there to see.

Surprising many, Nicaragua developed the most visible feminist, gay, and lesbian movements in Central America in the early 1990s. Then Daniel Ortega, the former Sandinista leader, came back to power in 2006 with an antifeminist yet somewhat pro-LGBT agenda.[9] After establishing a pact with his former political and economic enemies, Ortega was ready to rule Nicaragua for an extended period. Things became complicated, however, in April 2018 when Sandinista supporters, the police, and eventually masked paramilitaries clashed with protesters against the government.

Nicaragua is very much at a crossroads, making this a particularly important historical moment to document western Nicaragua's LGBTQIA+ history. No one has ever attempted to tell this story, in part because many have assumed there is no story to be told, or that the story is not very interesting. The assumption is either that Nicaraguans have been too poor to care about anything beyond "bread and butter" issues and/or that LGBTQIA+ Nicaraguans are the product of "global queering," a mere reflection of what happens in the so-called Global North. A third and equally problematic assumption has been that the history of LGBTQIA+ Nicaraguans is just one of oppression, unlike the history of LGBTQIA+ individuals in more "developed" nations, where they get to have agency and all the contradictions human agency entails. This book dispels these myths and replaces them with a comprehensive narrative that revisits the *long durée* of western Nicaraguan history in a manner that underscores gender and sexuality.

Like many other works that claim to be about Nicaragua, this book is predominantly about urban populations on Nicaragua's Pacific coast, the area that was most highly populated when the Spanish colonized the region and the area where most Nicaraguans still live. I find it very important to label the book in a way that reflects this reality. This does not mean that rural peoples or that other regions, such as the central and Caribbean regions, do not merit inclusion, but rather that there are fewer sources to document the LGBTQIA+ history of other populations in Nicaragua, particularly in the earlier periods I study. There are also space and time limitations. Most saliently, this book does not address the history of Nicaragua's Caribbean Coast, a vast geographical region with a very different history from that of western and central Nicaragua, one that would require hundreds of additional pages to address.

While the Spanish conquistadors claimed all of Nicaragua for the Spanish Crown in the late 1490s, they were actually only able to conquer and colonize the western area of Nicaragua in the 1500s, and the central area years later. It was the British, and not the Spanish, who would become the primary colonizing force in the Nicaraguan Caribbean, starting in the 1620s. The British were the ones who brought enslaved Africans to Nicaragua's Caribbean region, although the initial individuals of African ancestry who settled permanently on Nicaragua's Caribbean Coast were freedom seekers known at the time as "runaway slaves." This meant that the Caribbean Coast, like the Pacific and central regions, initially developed with Indigenous, African, and European populations. However, the unique dynamics of each region resulted in very different ethnic/racial categories and power dynamics.

As discussed in chapter 2, the Nicaraguan nation-state (controlled by those who privileged lighter-skinned mestizos over Indigenous and Afro-Nicaraguans) forcibly took over the Caribbean Coast in the 1800s. Tragically, the mestizo racism against Caribbean Indigenous and Creole populations that justified that takeover still exists today. While the LGBTQIA+ history of Nicaragua's Caribbean Coast is not addressed in this book, and the LGBTQIA+ history of rural regions in the Pacific and central regions is discussed only minimally due to the lack of sources, I have sought to build a narrative about Nicaragua's Pacific coast that does not reproduce the racism that is at the core of the Nicaraguan nation-state.[10]

SEXUALITY, GENDER, AND LANGUAGE IN NICARAGUAN HISTORY

Spanish colonial authorities sought to punish those they believed to be guilty of what they considered to be the crime (and sin) of sodomy, and they called those who committed it *sodomitas, someticos,* or *sodometicos*. Not surprisingly, given that the country's legal system has its roots in the colonial period, as recently as 2008, Nicaraguan law forbade "scandalous relations between people of the same sex" using exactly the same word: sodomy (*sodomía*). *Pecado nefando* (nefarious sin) was another Spanish term used by colonial authorities, a term they brought with them from Europe. But there are also occasional references in the colonial record to a Nahuat word, *cuylon* (sometimes spelled *cuilon*), which, according to the Spanish, referred to a man who had sex with another man among Indigenous peoples in western Nicaragua. The existence of the word suggests that at least some of the Nahuat-speaking Indigenous residents of what is now the Pacific coast of Nicaragua, members of a group known as Nicarao, thought of men who had sex with men as a category apart. Alternatively, this usage of the word could have been a simplified Spanish interpretation of a more complex Indigenous lived experience. We also do not know if Nicaraos used the word *cuylon* in derogatory ways, or if it was simply a descriptive term. An additional question that remains unanswered is whether other Indigenous groups in the area, like the Chorotegas, had terms in their own language that were comparable to *cuylon*.

Historical evidence suggests that the Nahuat word *cuylon* evolved over time into the ubiquitous Nicaraguan Spanish word *cochón*, a word that for much of the twentieth and twenty-first centuries was typically used in a derogatory fashion. It has now been reclaimed by LGBTQIA+ activists, but it continues to be used by others in Nicaragua, usually as an insult for men who have sex with other men. Women who have sex with other women are often called *cochonas*.

In the twenty-first century, the terms *cochón* and *cochona* are commonly used in Nicaragua, along with other terms such as *lesbiana, gay, bisexual, trans, queer,* and *cuir*. One of the most common umbrella terms used by LGBTQIA+ activists is the term *diversidad sexual*, a term that encompasses gender and sexual diversity. This term has been widely adopted, and LGBTQIA+ individuals will sometimes refer to themselves as being *sexualmente diversos, diversos, diversas,* or *de la diversidad*.

In this book I use the umbrella terms *LGBTQIA+* and *sexual diversity* interchangeably, even when referring to people who lived hundreds of years ago, when neither of these terms existed. It is impossible to avoid the anachronistic usage of terms, but I have made every effort to document the lives of people in the past as accurately as possible. The most difficult decision regarding terminology was deciding what term to use in English for those individuals whose lived experience did not correspond to the Spanish/Catholic gender binary. When referring to individuals alive before the mid-twentieth century, I use the term *trans* in the broadest way possible to refer to individuals who might have identified as trans had the term existed at the time or had they lived in contemporary times. However, if I am referring to individuals who are currently alive or those who had the opportunity to go on the record with a preferred word, I use the term/s they prefer. For earlier periods I usually use the umbrella term *LGBTQIA+* to refer to individuals who today might call themselves gender-fluid, nonbinary, asexual, and/or intersex. It is important to point out that I do not use the terms *berdache*, *two-spirit*, *third gender*, or *Muxes*. There is no evidence to postulate that any of these terms make sense historically in Nicaragua.

THE LITERATURE ON PRE-1979 LGBTQIA+ HISTORY

Many Nicaraguan writers have briefly described moments or individuals in Nicaragua's pre-1979 LGBTQIA+ history. Erick Blandón and David Rocha, however, are the only two scholars who have written more than a few pages on the subject. Blandón and Rocha have written the only books that address Nicaragua's pre-1979 LGBTQIA+ history, albeit from cultural studies and/or literary perspectives. Blandón's *Barroco descalzo*, published in 2003, is a magisterial "cultural genealogy" that "investigates . . . the limits of what is considered 'culture,' what is excluded from the hegemonic concept of the national, what 'interrupts' the official history, [and] the inconvenient or the immeasurable."[11] It is within this cultural genealogy that Blandón sought to "understand what is the place of anomalous sexualities in the hegemonic culture."[12] While Blandón's book is not a chronological LGBTQIA+ history, *Barroco descalzo* is foundational, for it addresses homosexuality in the colonial period as well as its presence and absence in different historical instances of "popular" and dominant culture.

Rocha's book, *Crónicas de la ciudad*, published in 2019, is also a groundbreaking text that defies categorization.[13] It is history, fiction, poetry, and cultural studies, but most of all it is a love letter to Managua and Managua's LGBTQ+ population. Rocha writes: "This work is for the *locas* from yesterday, the current ones, the future ones and the urban *locas* who were born and who will be born in this Managua full of fugitive spaces."[14] His book constitutes the first "gay" history of Managua, focusing on the years between 1968 and 1972. Building on the Argentine activist and anthropologist Nestor Perlongher's work, Rocha created a cartography of Managua to map sexual subjectivities based on oral interviews, ethnography, archival research, and participant observation. Like Blandón's work, Rocha's is heavily informed by theory and a critical interpretation of the lived experience (whether their own or that of their fellow Nicaraguans) of the Sandinista revolution. In that sense, Blandón's and Rocha's books are crucial to understanding not only Nicaragua's pre-1979 LGBTQIA+ history but also Nicaragua's postrevolutionary LGBTQIA+ history. They are indeed foundational, and my work builds on theirs.

METHODOLOGY

Between 1990 and 2023, I spent over three years in Nicaragua, conducting participant observation, dozens of interviews, and substantial archival research at the Archivo Nacional de Nicaragua (National Archive of Nicaragua), the Instituto de Historia de Nicaragua y Centroamérica (the Institute of Nicaraguan and Central American History), the newspaper *La Prensa*, the Biblioteca del Banco Central (the Library of the Central Bank), and multiple privately held collections in Nicaragua. I also conducted extensive research online at the Biblioteca Enrique Bolaños (the Enrique Bolaños Library) and the British Library's Endangered Archives. Additionally, I visited the Bancroft Library in Berkeley and the National Archives in Washington, D.C. Over the course of my research for other projects, I encountered snippets of Nicaragua's LGBTQIA+ history, and I knew that the topic deserved a book of its own. I have devoted the last decade specifically to this project.

OVERVIEW OF THE BOOK

The chapters in this book are organized chronologically. In chapter 1, titled "Sodomites, Cuylones, and Cochones: The Colonial Period," I document the Spanish persecution of "sodomites" in western Nicaragua and the Spanish imposition of Catholic, heteronormative structures on the diverse Indigenous populations they colonized. I also address the colonial obsession with the stigmatization of those they considered to be the "passive" partners in sex between men, which resulted in their "discovery" of the Nahua cuylon. The limited colonial sources available do not reveal whether or not the Spanish interpreted the term *cuylon* accurately. However, I agree with earlier scholars, among them Jorge Eduardo Arellano and Erick Blandón, who believe the Nahuat term *cuylon* eventually became the well-known term *cochón*, which the writer David Rocha defines as being "used to designate the public and feminized face of homosexuality in our context."[15] Ironically, while the Spanish wanted to know how Indigenous peoples in Nicaragua "punished" the men who were "passive" sexual partners, implying feminine characteristics for these men, the one man we know for sure they burned at the stake for sodomy, Andrés Caballero, was never described as feminine.

In this chapter I also argue that, among some Indigenous Nahuat-speaking populations on the Pacific, there appears to have been a strong connection between femininity and local commerce. I contend that cisgender women and individuals who today might identify as trans women played an important economic role in the open-air Indigenous markets called *tiangues*—markets that, in precolonial times, did not allow the presence of any local men. This dynamic helps to explain the continued economic presence of trans women in many open-air markets, the greater visibility of trans women vis-à-vis trans men in western Nicaragua, and the relative tolerance Nicaraguans as a whole reported having toward trans individuals in the workplace in a 2016 survey (65 percent felt comfortable working with a trans individual; only 55 percent of U.S. respondents in a 2018 survey said the same).

The connection between Indigeneity, markets, and gender dissidence is one that continues to permeate western Nicaraguans' imaginaries. Its power is such that it helps explain why anti-LGBTQIA+ discrimination in Nicaragua is so often classist and racist, and *not only* homophobic and transphobic. On the other hand, I contend that the continued presence of trans women in open-air markets points to a long-standing Indigenous cultural and economic resistance.

Chapter 2, titled "'Very Delicate Men' and 'Queer' Filibusters: The Nineteenth Century," addresses the aftermath of Nicaraguan independence in the nineteenth century. This chapter documents the heteronormative vision that postcolonial elites sought to enforce on subaltern Nicaraguans. In particular, I address the constant elite efforts to "modernize" open-air markets while they simultaneously accepted the persistence of LGBTQIA+ occupational segregation. I also address the Euroamerican filibuster William Walker's 1855 white supremacist "imperial quest"[16] in Nicaragua from a perspective that emphasizes gender and sexuality. Walker (1824–60), called "the most distinguished of all American Soldiers of Fortune" in 1911,[17] was sometimes labeled "queer" by some of his contemporaries. The reception Walker and his quest received by fellow white U.S. Americans may be considered an example of a scenario the U.S.-based philosopher Jasbir K. Puar has described in more recent time periods: that "some homosexual subjects are complicit with heterosexual nationalist formations rather than inherently or automatically excluded from or opposed to them."[18] Indeed, Puar's insights are useful to understanding Walker: "the ascendancy of heteronormativity . . . is not tethered to heterosexuals."[19]

In chapter 3, "The Modern Nation-State, Feminism, and the Modern Woman: The Early Twentieth Century," I argue that while elites in Nicaragua favored "modernization," they balked at the so-called modern woman. In particular, political, religious, economic, and literary elites were terrified of women gaining too many rights, rights that a burgeoning first-wave feminist movement demanded. Men in power were particularly fearful of gender dissidence resulting from women voting, being elected to office, and playing sports. I argue that elite homophobic and transphobic discourse during this period had two significant consequences. The first was the increased persecution of lesbians, gender-fluid, and nonbinary individuals, "masculine" women, "feminine" men, and transgender men and women. The second was that elites disrupted (but did not eliminate) the long-standing connection, made in western Nicaraguans' historical imaginary, between Indigenous populations, homosexuality, and gender dissidence, by attempting to promote a new link: one between LGBTQIA+ populations and U.S. military intervention.

In chapter 4, "Poetry and Persecution: The Somoza Dictatorship, 1936–1979," I examine the lives of LGBTQIA+ individuals under the Somoza family dictatorship, the longest dictatorship in Latin American history. The dictatorship's longevity is typically explained in terms of the violence of the National Guard and the Somoza family's alliance with the

United States. However, the story is more complicated than that because Somocista rule was consolidated, in part, by the incorporation of subaltern groups into the Somozas' clientelistic networks. This does not mean that the Somozas promoted LGBTQIA+ rights. Indeed, they lengthened the sentences for those convicted of sodomy, and their National Guard harassed and persecuted working-class gay men, working-class trans women, and trans sex workers. However, the Somozas were sometimes libertarian—some would say they were opportunists. Just as they gave employment and leadership opportunities to some middle-class and working-class cis women who supported them politically, they sometimes tolerated homosexuality and incorporated some gay, lesbian, bisexual, and transgender Somocistas into their clientelistic networks. Moreover, they also tolerated an LGBTQIA+ nightlife in the late 1960s and early 1970s, as part of Managua's urban sexual world.

Some pro-Somoza individuals who engaged in discreet (and sometimes not-so-discreet) LGBTQIA+ relationships were accepted by the Somozas and their supporters, as long as they did not publicly disrupt heteronormative gender relations or question the dictatorship. That was the case of the entrepreneur and business owner Carmelo Aguirre (1931–71). This case in particular stands out because Carmelo was raised as a girl and lived his adult life very publicly as a man, marrying a woman (although not formally allowed by Nicaraguan law) and raising many children. The life story of La Caimana, as Carmelo was known, is particularly useful to contemporary debates in the United States, Nicaragua, and elsewhere over the contradictions created by lobbying for specific lesbian, gay, bisexual, and transgender rights (like marriage or adoption) without simultaneously advocating for a radical transformation of patriarchy or a more democratic society, contradictions understood as homonormativity. Indeed, La Caimana was able to live his life as a man in part because he embraced hegemonic masculinity and supported a right-wing dictatorship. Here we can see that "homonormativity can be read as a formation complicit with and invited into the biopolitical valorization of life in its inhabitation and reproduction of heteronormative norms."[20]

In this chapter, I compare La Caimana with La Sebastiana (1940–2016). The latter was a well-known figure in pre-earthquake Managua for the fruit drinks she sold and for her appearances in patron saint festivals in towns across the country, where she was often proclaimed queen of the festival. But homophobia and transphobia eventually took a toll: she turned to alcohol and ended up nearly homeless. The contrast between La Caimana and La Sebastiana highlights the nuances of Nicaragua's transgender traditions, drawing attention to issues of gender and class. Far from marginal, many remember the two as exemplifying life in the capital during the mid-twentieth century, and so they are the subjects of novels, poetry, and theater, which inform my interpretations, along with archival evidence and oral histories.

INDIGENEITY, OPEN-AIR MARKETS, GENDER, POWER, AND SEXUALITY: NICARAGUA AND MEXICO

Although my analysis is not a comparative one, I must point out that western Nicaragua is not the only region of the Americas with a tradition of women-*only* open-air Indigenous markets. There is at least one other: the southeast region of Oaxaca, specifically the area that encompasses the Zapotec cities of Tehuantepec and Juchitán. Could these two traditions be somehow related? In the case of Nicaragua, the assumption has been that since the terms *tiangue* and *cuylon* are both Nahua words, then the Nahuat-speaking Nicarao peoples would have been the ones to have had this tradition, which is in fact what the Spanish noted in their chronicles. But there is no evidence to connect the Zapotec communities of Oaxaca to the Nicaraos of Nicaragua. The Zapotec and the Nicaraos did not even share a linguistic tradition.

The Nicarao most likely traveled to Nicaragua from central Mexico hundreds of years before the Spanish arrived in Nicaragua. And Nahuatl-speaking groups like the Mexicas (Aztecs), whom the Nicarao were presumably related to, historically did not have a tradition of women-only markets.[21] It is possible that the Nicaraos could have borrowed the tradition of women-only markets from the Zapotecs or another Indigenous group. The Nicarao could have even borrowed it from their Chorotega neighbors (a point I discuss later in more detail), who did share a linguistic heritage with Zapotec communities, or they could have come up with it on their own. For now, its origins will have to remain a mystery. But the way in which the Zapotec market tradition was described by nineteenth-century travelers and tourists was eerily similar to the way in which the Nicarao markets were described by the Spanish in the sixteenth century.

In Nicaragua, the Spanish wrote that "no one from town—who is a man—can enter the tiangues."[22] In the case of Oaxaca, the Prussian adventurer Gustavus Ferdinand Von Tempsky (1828–68) visited Tehuantepec in 1854 and noted:

> In the middle of the square is situated a large roofed building, without walls ... Here, more than a thousand women congregate daily, to sell and buy ... No man is allowed to sell anything in that market: the trade is entirely monopolised by women.[23]

In 1899 another traveler, the controversial white U.S. American anthropologist Frederick Starr (1858–1933), wrote of the area: "There is an interesting commerce carried out in Juave towns by Zapotec traders of Juchitán. As might be expected, this is entirely in the hands of women."[24] He continued: "The great market of Tehuantepec is one of the busiest and most attractive in the republic, but all the sellers under the roof are women. It is claimed that no man would venture to sell there, or—if he did—that the women would drive him away."[25]

Like the nineteenth-century foreign travelers in Mexico (and others since then), the Spanish in Nicaragua (and others since then), seemed intrigued by the possibility that women's work in the markets might have contributed to relations between heterosexual cis men and cis women that were more egalitarian than European and Euroamerican ones. In the case of Nicaragua, however, the Spanish concluded that the relations between Nicarao men and women were complex: on the one hand, although most Nicarao men had only one legitimate wife, the caciques (all of whom were men) often had concubines, the concubines were often enslaved, and only women were sex workers. On the other hand, the Nicarao had at least one female god, women handled all local commerce, and at least on one feast day married women could have sex with whomever they wanted.[26] What to make of this situation?

One of the most famous Nicaraguan writers of the twentieth century, Pablo Antonio Cuadra (1912–2002), wrote extensively about the Nicaraos and the other major Indigenous group in western Nicaragua at the time of the conquest, the Chorotegas, an Oto-Manguean speaking group that had arrived earlier, also from Mexico, but was unrelated to the Mexicas. Cuadra wrote about the traditions of these two groups as he sought to capture what it meant to be Nicaraguan. Describing relations between heterosexual cis men and cis women in the precolonial period, in a chapter titled "The Indian We Carry Inside," Cuadra noted that, according to the Spanish soldier and chronicler Gonzalo Fernández de Oviedo y Valdés (1478–1557), the Chorotegas were "very bossed around and subject to the will and wants of their women." The Nicarao men, on the other hand, were "very in charge of their women and they tell them what to do and have them as subjects."[27] How exactly Oviedo reached this conclusion we will never know, although the Nicaraguan historian Manuel Moncada Fonseca has written that "contrary to what Oviedo argued, this other chronicler [Antonio de Herrera y Tordesillas (1559–1625)] believed that [among the Nicarao] the husbands were subjects to their women, who, when they got angry, would kick them out of the house, would hit them, and force them to serve them."[28] Making matters more intriguing, Herrera y Tordesillas never set foot in the Americas. Comments on the ways in which Indigenous cis men and cis women interacted were also present in the writings of the anthropologist Frederick Starr mentioned earlier, who wrote that "the women of Tehuantepec are certainly the heads of their houses; the men occupy but an inferior position."[29]

Despite the many similarities described thus far, the differences between Oaxaca and western Nicaragua carry more weight, especially as the twentieth century wore on. In the case of Oaxaca, the Mexican muralist Diego Rivera famously painted images of Indigenous women from the Tehuantepec region, a place he first visited in the 1920s. Frida Kahlo, Rivera's wife and a painter in her own right, often dressed in the style of Zapotec women. While the goal might have been to draw attention to the plight of marginalized peoples and to right the wrongs of the colonial period, the Mexican elite's obsession with Indigenous peoples and their "authenticity" created a tourist rush to the area.[30] The photographs of Graciela Iturbide in the late 1970s brought even more attention to Zapotec women in the region. In the case of Nicaragua, no such thing happened with regard to Indigenous women on the Pacific coast. And the reasons for that are critical ones to keep in mind.

In the 1920s, 1930s, and 1940s, Mexico was going through great postrevolutionary social and political upheaval. At this time, the "social-scientific paradigm" of *indigenismo*, in which "the Indian" was posited as "both a national ideal and a national problem," was taking hold in society.[31] Nicaragua, meanwhile, was dealing with a military occupation by the United States, followed by a right-wing dictatorship. Perhaps more importantly, however, is the fact that during the colonial period the western region of Nicaragua being addressed in this book was the center of Spanish colonial power in Nicaragua. This meant that, unlike Oaxaca, most Indigenous peoples in western Nicaragua lost their original languages early on during the colonial period. Indeed, by the twentieth century, only a few pockets of Indigenous communities in western Nicaragua were even recognized as such by the state: mainly the communities of Jalteva (in Granada), Sutiava (in León), and Monimbó (in Masaya).[32] Nicaragua's twentieth-century elites proclaimed the triumph of *mestizaje* (racial mixing between Spaniards and Indigenous peoples) in the region. For them there was no "authenticity" to be sought—and there were no visible markers of Indigeneity, hence the title of Cuadra's chapter: "The Indian We Carry *Inside*" (my emphasis). It is also crucial to note that while the open-air Zapotec markets in Oaxaca were still women-only spaces in the late nineteenth century, in Nicaragua tiangues had been opened to everyone in the early sixteenth century.

Those are the main reasons why Nicaragua's women-only markets have not drawn as much interest among tourists and academics as those in Mexico and why a comparison like the one I am making has not been made before. But there is another significant reason: the "discovery," exoticization, and objectification of the Oaxacan Indigenous Muxe (Muxe') community of Juchitán by whites and mestizos.

There is no doubt that sexual and gender diversity has been longstanding in Oaxaca. The 1578 *Vocabulary in Zapotec Language* by the Spanish Catholic friar/conquistador Juan de Cordova included several translated terms that alluded to a diversity of experiences and potential LGBTQIA+ identities. Among those terms were "puto sometico con hombre" and "ombre afeminado en el parecer o tratar."[33] What is unique to Oaxaca and specifically to Juchitán is that Zapotec cis women there have a historical and prominent role in local commerce *and* that there is significant tolerance and acceptance of "third gender" individuals knowns as Muxes who also play a significant role in local commerce alongside cis women.[34] Both of these groups have been exoticized by outsiders who have projected labels like "matriarchal society" and "gay paradise" onto Juchitán and its peoples when the reality is more complex than that.[35]

In the case of western Nicaragua, women-*only* open-air markets are a thing of the past, although many twentieth and twenty-first century scholars have written about Nicaragua's high number of women-headed households (when compared to other countries) and working-class women's extensive participation in the informal economy, especially in local commerce. The term *matriarchal* is sometimes applied to market women, usually by Nicaraguan politicians who seek favor with this important voting block. What is notable is that the association of women and femininity with local commerce still permeates popular culture, as I expand on later in the book. And the presence of self-identified trans women in contemporary open-air markets is usually tolerated and often accepted.

Before the category of trans became widespread in Nicaragua in the early twenty-first century, the most common label for someone who today might identify as a trans woman was cochón. Others might have simply said they were women. There has been no widespread public discussion in Nicaragua of a "hybrid gender" or "third gender" as there has been in Mexico. And what I call an Indigenous tiangue "tradition" is not generally perceived as such. Moreover, making a connection between women-only Indigenous open-air markets and trans gender dissidence in Nicaragua is novel. I hope my work lays a foundation for others to continue to explore this connection.

In 2002 the U.S. anthropologist Lynn Stephen wrote that

> the various sexual roles, relationships, and identities that characterize contemporary rural Oaxaca suggest that instead of trying to look historically for the roots of "homosexuality," "heterosexuality," or even the concept of "sexuality," we should look at how different indigenous systems of gender interacted with shifting discourses of Spanish colonialism, nationalism, and popular culture to redefine gendered spaces and the sexual behavior within them. Clear differences between elites and those on the margins of Mexican society underscore the importance of divisions by class and status.[36]

I have heeded this call in my historical research on western Nicaragua, adding U.S. imperialism to the mix as well a consideration of the enslavement of Africans and the ongoing anti-Black racism against the many Afro-descendant Nicaraguans on the Pacific coast.

I have also heeded the U.S. anthropologist Miranda Stockett's warning regarding the most common ways in which scholars have cataloged gender and power among Indigenous peoples in preconquest Mesoamerica. Stockett argues that we should avoid grasping on too tightly to the "gender hierarchy" and "gender complementarity" models, which are usually considered mutually exclusive. She suggests we avoid grand narratives altogether, for they may fail to account for variability and difference.[37] These models would certainly fail to address the contradictions and the nuance in/within gender and sexuality among the Nicarao as well other Indigenous groups in Nicaragua.

Additionally, it is important to note that, from a contemporary perspective, many would like to think that women working outside the home (in commerce, no less!) must lead directly to women holding political and economic power equal to men in a society, or to the vague concept of women's "empowerment." But this is not necessarily the case. My contention that women-only Indigenous markets played out in similar *and* different ways in two separate Mesoamerican locations points to the need to stay focused on the local nuances in order to best document our collective past.

While I cannot attend to the many nuances that exist in the Oaxacan context, I must circle back to women and markets in western Nicaragua and add yet another layer of complexity. It turns out that although the Spanish only mentioned that the Nicarao markets were women's domain, other markets in the Pacific region appear to have also had either an exclusive or a predominant presence of women. This is commonly understood to be the case of the Masaya markets, which presumably were Oto-Manguean Chorotega ones. A 1963 article on Masaya, for instance, noted: "the Indian woman goes to the market. . . . [S]he carries a basket with fruit and flowers . . . She has risen early . . . to sit like her ancestors did . . . in the Tiangue."[38]

If indeed Chorotega Indigenous markets in Nicaragua were women-only spaces, there is a slight possibility that they were connected in some way centuries ago to the Zapotec markets of Oaxaca, since both groups spoke Oto-Manguean languages. It might also make sense that women had an important economic role in Chorotega markets, given that some scholars have argued that they had important political roles in Mangue communities.[39] That the Chorotegan markets were called tiangues, a

Nahua word, could mean that Indigenous communities in the region were multilingual, since they lived in such proximity to each other. It could also reflect the importance that Nahuatl acquired after the conquest (and perhaps even before) throughout Mesoamerica as a lingua franca. Once they are fully addressed, these unanswered questions might lead us to a more accurate understanding not only of western Nicaragua but also of an entire region.

CONCLUSION

This book addresses how historical events (particularly Spanish colonialism, U.S. imperialism, and right-wing dictatorship) have shaped—and been shaped by—western Nicaraguans' gendered, sexed, and racialized identities and imaginaries. Given the period being discussed, doing so requires an intersectional approach that focuses extensively on Indigenous peoples. In fact, I contend that anti-Indigenous racism in particular has made it very difficult to document western Nicaragua's history of sexual and gender diversity. And vice versa, the erasure of western Nicaragua's LGBTQIA+ history has facilitated a narrative where Indigenous peoples on the Pacific coast have been homogenized, objectified, dehumanized, compared to animals, and sometimes even declared extinct. In other words, homophobia and transphobia have made it difficult to document fully and accurately Nicaragua's Indigenous history, while racism has made it hard to even see LGBTQIA+ individuals (many of whom were Indigenous) in Nicaragua's past. When Nicaraguan history is seen through the lens of an exultant and totalizing mestizaje, we miss Indigenous (and Afro-Nicaraguan) history, and we miss Nicaragua's LGBTQIA+ history.[40] This book hopes to make a dent in that hegemonic narrative.

SODOMITES, CUYLONES, AND COCHONES

The Colonial Period

THE INDIGENOUS ancestors of modern-day Nicaraguans most likely arrived in waves dating thousands of years ago. By the 1400s, groups of people distinct from each other lived in what today is Nicaragua and called it home. They were not a monolith. They spoke different languages and had different customs. They also had different religions. Then, after the arrival of the Spanish in 1502, they all became known as Indians, despite their differences, and all were considered by the Spanish to be inferior to Catholic Europeans. Although many of these Indigenous people died over the course of the conquest and the colonial period, quite a few survived, and their direct descendants are alive today in Nicaragua and elsewhere, since the Spanish sold thousands of Indigenous Nicaraguans they had enslaved throughout South America.

The Spanish were new to the region. What differentiated them from previous people who had arrived in these lands was that the Spanish attempted to conquer and convert all the people they encountered in the area and were eventually quite successful. Moreover, unlike the Indigenous peoples who preceded them, the Spanish wanted to exploit the land, the people, and the flora and fauna of Nicaragua on behalf of individuals who never intended to live in Nicaragua: the king and queen of Spain. Additionally, while the Native inhabitants sought to live off the land through the work of their own hands, the Spanish did not seek such lifestyle. The Spanish sought to make a profit by appropriating Native lands and enslaving Native peoples and peoples from Africa.

Indigenous peoples in Nicaragua were already familiar with slavery because some of them enslaved other Indigenous peoples, sometimes sacrificing them for religious reasons. However, slavery under the Spanish was more widespread and more permanent in nature. The complicated legal system crafted to justify and enforce the enslavement of Africans in the Americas was a transatlantic one that had profit and prestige as its primary goals. Slavery under the Spanish, unlike that of earlier times, was an important economic tool that also allowed the Spanish to strengthen the racial hierarchy that privileged the Spaniards' perceived whiteness and "purity of blood" (*limpieza de sangre*) over the perceived racial impurity of everyone else, particularly Africans (whom they associated with Islam) and Jews (whom they also despised—despite the fact that many Spaniards in the Americas had Jewish and/or Muslim ancestors).

Initially, all Native peoples who resisted the Spanish could, according to Spanish law, be enslaved. Later, in the mid-sixteenth century, the enslavement of Indigenous people was formally abolished, but Spaniards continued to informally enslave Native individuals in myriad ways. The enslavement of people from Africa and those of African ancestry, on the other hand, while legal from the beginning, became more prevalent throughout Latin America after the enslavement of Indigenous peoples formally ended, and remained legal through the end of the colonial period.

For enslaved Africans, the law specified that enslaved status be passed on from enslaved African mothers (or enslaved mothers of African ancestry) to their children. This was the case for Nicaragua's Pacific and central regions, the areas addressed in this book, as well as for Nicaragua's Caribbean Coast, which was colonized by the British. The so-called law of the womb ensured that no European/white woman would ever give birth to an enslaved human being, and that European/white enslavers would benefit from the sexual abuse of the women they enslaved. That said, the children of enslaved African men and free women of any racial and ethnic background were legally free, as were those enslaved children and adults who had been manumitted or who had been able to purchase their freedom. Generally, freedom seekers (those who "escaped from their owners") were in violation of the colonial laws (created by the enslavers themselves) and were still considered to be enslaved by the colonial governments.

Over the course of the colonial period, the Spanish brought with them thousands of enslaved Africans to Nicaragua's Pacific coast and central region. The presence of Africans, although often overlooked in history books and in the national imaginary, was crucial to the formation of Spanish-speaking Nicaraguan society as it developed over the last five hundred years. Over time, most Indigenous and Afro-Nicaraguans living on the Pacific and central regions, along with many Spaniards, mixed, producing western Nicaragua's contemporary mixed-race peoples.

Most of what we know about precolonial Indigenous societies in Nicaragua and the Africans who arrived enslaved by the Spanish we know through documents written by the Spanish themselves. In other words, we must use the words of enslavers and conquerors to tell the stories of the people they enslaved and conquered. This is highly problematic, to say the least. But it is an enterprise that must be engaged in if we are to tell this story at all. Later in the chapter, I address the problems inherent in the use of colonial sources as I document specific events.

In addition to taking great care when using colonial sources, we must be careful not to romanticize Indigenous life before the arrival of the Spanish, or African life before the Middle Passage, since doing so diminishes Indigenous and African agency. Thus, it is important to emphasize that I am not arguing that before the arrival of the Spanish in Nicaragua Indigenous peoples had not experienced inequality of different sorts. As noted already, some Indigenous peoples in Nicaragua enslaved others before the arrival of the Spanish. Indeed, humans were bought and sold by women market sellers in the open-air markets called tiangues. Moreover, most Indigenous groups in the area appear to have been stratified by class and gender before the arrival of the Spanish in the early sixteenth century. Similar class stratification presumably existed in the areas of West and Central Africa that were raided by enslavers.

While we know hardly anything about gender relations among the enslaved Africans brought specifically to Nicaragua, available documents suggest that women and men were not considered fully equal in Nicaragua's Indigenous precolonial society. For example, it appears that precolonial Indigenous women did not have access to the priesthood. Moreover, there is no evidence of male sex workers, only female ones. And only men could have multiple spouses, a practice called polygyny. Nonetheless, there is no evidence to suggest that before the conquest male gods were more important than female gods, nor is there any evidence to suggest that women were considered inherently inferior to men. Additionally, women were not sequestered in their homes, and they played important economic roles in society. Finally, policing women's sexuality does not appear to have been paramount for Indigenous Nicaraguans.

The arrival of the Spanish did not bode well for Indigenous women. In addition to being enslaved, they were forced to convert to Catholicism, a religion that heavily privileged men over women. Moreover, their sexuality was now suspect at every turn, and their reproduction, like that of enslaved African women, inevitably benefited their so-called masters.

The arrival of the Spanish also did not bode well for Indigenous men. In addition to being enslaved, their sexual lives became more prescribed after the conquest, because the Spanish believed that only sex between a man and his wife was legitimate and that all other sexual expressions were sinful and/or criminal. Moreover, although Catholicism privileged men over women, it privileged Spanish men over Indigenous men. This meant, among other things, that most Indigenous men (as well as men of African or Jewish origin, and all women), were denied the opportunity to become priests, understood to be God's representatives on earth.

We must not underestimate the role of Christianity in the conquest of Latin America and the role Catholicism in particular played in cementing a Spanish/Christian patriarchal cultural model in colonial Nicaragua. The new, seemingly unending rules that governed almost every aspect of everyday life seemed strange and unjust to Indigenous peoples. To add insult to injury, the new laws and expectations were applied unevenly and unfairly. Indeed, at the heart of the new cultural model was a profound hypocrisy, criticized by many from the very beginning, including some Catholic priests themselves.

During the three hundred years of Spanish colonialism that Nicaragua was subjected to, the hegemonic classes sought to normalize their dominance of the majority and the inequalities that sustained that dominance. Not surprisingly, the class, gender, religious, and racial inequalities that made colonialism possible intersected with one another in such a way as to make it impossible to imagine one type of inequality existing without the other. Moreover, the colonial period depended on heteronormativity (understood as the implicit and explicit expectations of heterosexuality as well as the concomitant legal and religious apparatus that ensured heterosexuality was normative) to regulate both sexuality and gender.

Such was the contestation of colonialism and its underlying inequalities, that elites often resorted to severe institutional punishments for those who dared to defy their oppression. The legal system created by the Spanish to support their rule was far-reaching, complex, and often inhumane. However, the law did allow non-elites, including those who were enslaved, some legal rights, which they quite frequently went to court to defend.

The fact that there was no separation between church and state during the colonial period meant that the line separating a (Catholic) sin from a crime was sometimes nonexistent. Under these circumstances, an individual who engaged in sex outside of marriage, for instance, could be prosecuted and punished with a prison sentence and eventually also go to hell. Moreover, it meant that colonial elites who did not hold religious posts were, in theory, as heavily involved in policing subaltern bodies as priests were. Colonial authorities thus became routinely involved in burning at the stake those convicted of "Judaizing" and "sodomy." Eventually, after independence, being Jewish and/or having Jewish ancestors ceased to be a sin/crime. But engaging in same-sex sexual relations continued to be a punishable offense until recently in Nicaragua.

Heteronormativity (heterosexuality as norm), women's subordination to men, and the official persecution and prosecution of "sodomites" (which I argue is a colonial tradition) are the three pillars upon which the modern Nicaraguan heterostate rests. This chapter sheds light on these three processes as well as the interstices that individuals and groups carved for themselves during the colonial period in western Nicaragua. I document the experiences of the very few LGBTQIA+ individuals who are named in the historical record before 1821 and briefly describe the development of homosocial (single-sex) spaces as well as the legal apparatus used to persecute those who engaged in, or were suspected of engaging in, same-sex relations. Additionally, I tackle the problematic nature of colonial sources as well as the invention of Indigenous "sodomy" by the Spanish and its transformation into the contemporary "cochón." Furthermore, I put forth the argument that Nicaragua's contemporary transgender community has Indigenous precolonial roots. This chapter offers an overview of the sexual and gender dynamics of the colonial period, for it is impossible to understand contemporary sexual and gender politics in Nicaragua without it.

CONSTRUCTING A COLONIAL HETEROSEXUALITY

Christopher Columbus himself arrived in what is today known as Nicaragua in 1502. Seventeen years later, the Spanish began the physical conquest and colonization of the Indigenous peoples of the country's Pacific region in earnest. In addition to taking over Native lands, the Spanish initially enslaved Nicaragua's Indigenous peoples, forcing them to work for free in Nicaragua on their encomiendas[1] and then selling thousands of them to conquistadors in other parts of Latin America, most often Peru, to work in the mines.[2]

Along with enslavement and disease came the spiritual conquest of Indigenous peoples through the imposition of Catholicism. Catholicism brought about many unwelcome changes in the lives of Native peoples. One of these changes had to do with the ways in which the meaning of marriage and sex changed after the conquest. Marriage between a man and a woman among Indigenous peoples of western Nicaragua predated the arrival of the Spanish, but there is no evidence to suggest that before the conquest sex outside a heterosexual marriage was a punishable offense for a husband, *unless* he had sex with another man's wife. Moreover, there is some evidence that, at least among some Indigenous people in the region, men *and* women could have premarital sex without punishment, and that under certain circumstances couples were able to dissolve their marital relationships and begin new ones, possibilities not entertained by Catholicism. Pascual de Andagoya (c. 1498–1548), a Spaniard who arrived in Nicaragua with the expedition of the infamous conquistador and eventual governor Pedrarias Dávila (1440–1531), wrote the following about the Indigenous peoples he encountered on Nicaragua's Pacific coast:

> There were many beautiful women and their parents [*padres*] had the custom, once they were young women ready for marriage, of sending

them off to earn money for their wedding: and that is how they ended up all over the land earning money publicly;³ and once they had their trousseau ready for their home ... they would return to the home of their parents and they were married.⁴

We do not know if it is indeed true that some Indigenous parents sent their daughters off to engage in sex work before marriage so that the young women could earn enough to have the items needed to establish their own homes. But another Spanish chronicler, Gonzalo Fernández de Oviedo y Valdés (1478–1557), usually referred to simply as Oviedo, coincides in noting that premarital sex was sometimes accepted and even preferred. Oviedo, who was in Nicaragua between 1527 and 1529, wrote fifty volumes on the Americas. In his writings on Nicaragua, he included the transcript from a study commissioned by Pedrarias Dávila, Nicaragua's governor between 1528 and 1531.⁵ The study was conducted by Fray Francisco de Bobadilla in 1528 to ascertain the extent to which Indigenous peoples in Nicaragua had been indoctrinated. For this purpose, Bobadilla, with the help of three interpreters, interrogated twenty Indigenous peoples, presumably all men, and Oviedo published the questions asked and the answers given in his *Historia general y natural de las Indias*. According to an Indigenous man interviewed by Bobadilla and cited by Oviedo, before marriage, Indigenous parents in Nicaragua would reveal whether or not their daughters were virgins. If the husband, after having been told his bride was a virgin, decided that his wife was not a virgin after all, he had the right to return her to her home, "and the husband was free" to remarry. But if, before marriage, the future husband did not mind that she was sexually experienced, the couple would marry without a problem, "because there are many [men] who prefer the corrupt ones to the virgins."⁶

Even though Andagoya, Oviedo, and Bobadilla most likely interacted with each other in Nicaragua in 1528, or later, in the Dominican Republic, in the case of Andagoya and Oviedo, it is unlikely that Andagoya and Oviedo/Bobadilla were talking about the same group of Indigenous peoples. If young women were expected to earn money in exchange for sex prior to marriage, then none of the young women would have been "virgins" before marriage, contradicting Bobadilla's informant. It is probably the case, then, that the chroniclers were actually describing different

Indigenous groups. This conclusion is supported by Oviedo himself, who, noting the diversity among Indigenous peoples in the region, stated that "since the tongues and customs of the people are diverse, so are their songs, dances, and other many things."[7] And it is possible, with regard to Indigenous women's premarital transactional sex, that what the Spanish understood as prostitution and corruption was something understood in altogether different ways by Indigenous people themselves.

North American anthropologist Holly Wardlow warns us that Western constructions of prostitution and sex work are not always useful in understanding the wide variety of ways in which individuals relate to the practice of having sex in exchange for something. She also notes that even the language we use is problematic. The term *prostitution* has historically implied a moral judgment, but the term *sex work* has its own problems:

> While the category sex work fruitfully invites approaches that focus on labor issues rather than on moral status, it can be critiqued as the compulsion to salvage women's morality by labeling what they do as "work," an activity that in the West is inherently virtuous and that is associated with industriousness, productivity, efficiency, and so forth. In other words, according to our [North American] Protestant ethic, work is always the saving grace; if the woman is engaged in work, even if it is on her back, then it must be okay.[8]

I would like to put forth the possibility that, in the case of precolonial western Nicaragua, women's premarital sex with men "all over the land" might have had multiple purposes and meanings. In other words, could these young women have been having sex with multiple men for reasons beyond acquiring a trousseau? Wardlow's research shows that women engage in "sex work" or "prostitution" for a variety of motives, not all of them having to do with making money. There is also, of course, the possibility of ritual sex practices. And some of these practices are in fact described by the Spanish. For instance, according to the Spanish chronicler Antonio de Herrera y Tordesillas (1559–1626), "[married women] would be allowed to [have sex] with other men [who were not their husbands] during certain holidays."[9] Other chroniclers wrote down similar accounts, making it highly likely that ritual sex did occur among some Indigenous groups.

While an in-depth discussion of sex work before the arrival of the Spanish and during the colonial period is beyond the scope of this book, I discuss it here, however minimally, because the trope of prostitution is one that has haunted Nicaraguan history since the conquest. Moreover, it is one that intersects with LGBTQIA+ history, as discussed in later chapters.

It is crucial to stress that while we contemplate the possibility of multiple meanings for Indigenous women's engagement in sex work or prostitution, for the Spanish there was only one possible interpretation: sexual and moral corruption. For the Spanish, as for the Catholic hierarchy, any sex outside of marriage was considered a sin, for both men and women. Moreover, marriage (between a man and a woman only) was a sacrament, understood as a relationship that ended only when one of the spouses died.

It bears repeating that Indigenous people had different sexual traditions from those of the Spanish, and they understood them differently. Even after the conquest, Native populations did not understand and/or accept certain Catholic concepts that were central to Spanish understandings of sexuality, like sin, perhaps because they did not imagine life on earth as an all-out war between good and evil, nor did they necessarily believe in the afterlife as a more important state than the here and now. The U.S. historian Pete Sigal, in his work on Maya peoples, argues that

> In order to understand the sixteenth-century Catholic concept of sin, one must take into account three vital points. First, sin required some notion of free will . . . Second, confessing one's sins was based on the presumption that the individual would try not to sin again. Third, one had to confess one's sins before death, or one would risk purgatory and hell . . . [But t]he Maya concept of the underworld and the Christian concept of hell were not synonymous . . .
>
> The friars [at first] did not understand that Maya mental processes made the people interpret sin in a different manner; it was not a case of simple misunderstanding . . . [Moreover] the Maya did not see Catholicism and traditional Maya religion as mutually exclusive. . . .[10]

U.S. historian Louise Burkhart reached similar conclusions about the Mexicas in her work, for they too did not have a perfect equivalent to the Spanish concept of sin or hell. The Spanish had to use an approximation, *tlacacolli*, for sin, but *tlacacolli* could mean anything from "conscious moral transgressions to judicially defined crimes to accidental or unintentional damage."[11]

We know less about the Catholic concept of sin in relation to Native peoples in western Nicaragua because there is less colonial documentation for Nicaragua than there is for Guatemala or Mexico. Nonetheless, it seems logical to extend the argument about Guatemala and Mexico to Nicaragua since Catholic priests dealt similarly with Indigenous peoples throughout Mesoamerica, suggesting they encountered similar problems. Moreover, as noted earlier, some Nicaraguan Indigenous peoples on the Pacific were culturally related to the Indigenous people of Mexico, a fact the Spanish themselves noted.[12]

What we do know about precolonial Indigenous religious and spiritual beliefs on Nicaragua's Pacific coast is mostly gleaned from the interrogations conducted by Fray Bobadilla. The following exchange took place between Bobadilla and an Indigenous religious leader in his sixties, Tazoteyda, who, when asked if he was Christian, responded that he was not:

FRIAR: Would you like to be one?

INDIGENOUS MAN: No; I am old already. Why should I become a Christian?

FRIAR: Because you will receive many goods in this life if you were one, and in the other one where we all must remain; and to the contrary, if you are not one, a bad life and work here, and there in the company of the devil, who, if you were Catholic, you would not see or fear.

INDIGENOUS MAN: I am old and I am not a cacique so I don't need to be Christian.[13]

Oviedo noted in reference to Tazoteyda that "in the end, no matter how much Father Bobadilla preached to him and admonished him, he never wanted to be a Christian."[14] Clearly, this one individual felt that Christianity was irrelevant to his life, even when threatened with eternal damnation, demonstrating that some, if not many, Nicaraguan Indigenous peoples refused to accept even the most basic Catholic teachings.

Indigenous peoples in Nicaragua had their own strongly held beliefs, which Tazoteyda expanded on, at Bobadilla's urging:

FRIAR: When the Indians die, where do they go?

INDIGENOUS MAN: They go underground, and those who die in the war of those who have had a good life, go up, where Tamagastad and Cipattoval are.

FRIAR: First you said that you did not know where they are; how can you say now that those who die in war of those who had a good life go up with them?

INDIGENOUS MAN: Where the sun rises, we call up.

FRIAR: The Indians who go below, what life do they have there?

INDIGENOUS MAN: They are buried and there is nothing more.[15]

As we can see in Tazoteyda's answer, there was a world of difference between the Catholic belief in the afterlife and the way in which Tazoteyda understood death and what happened to regular people after they died. There were also significant discrepancies in their understandings of God and the devil. Commenting on this issue, Oviedo concluded that "here in . . . Nicaragua they use different names for their gods, and with each name they say 'teot,' which means 'god,' and they even call the devil teot."[16]

Since the Catholic concepts of sin, hell, damnation, and the devil were so important to Spanish understandings of sex, it is crucial to underscore that a multiplicity of sometimes contradictory spiritual beliefs coexisted in Nicaragua during the early colonial period. Even years after conversion, most Indigenous peoples probably did not fully adopt the Spanish way of viewing sex and sexuality. This coincides with what scholars have found elsewhere throughout Mesoamerica. Historian Pete Sigal, for instance, argues in his work on Mexico that "the process of cultural assimilation was slower and less consistent than scholars have assumed."[17] Sigal argues something similar when examining Maya communities in Guatemala, where he found, in response to colonization, a high degree of hybridization.[18]

Precolonial Indigenous attitudes toward sex, albeit not monolithic, were perhaps more practical than those of the Spanish, since the latter had a very difficult time enforcing their own rules among their own people, even among Spanish priests and Spanish officials, who were tasked with their implementation and who were expected to model proper behavior. At times the Catholic Church became quite vicious in its attempts to enforce religious orthodoxy. One of the institutions created to keep the faithful in check was the Inquisition. Meant to root out heresy, the Inquisition vigorously persecuted individuals who practiced other religions, questioned Catholic doctrine, or had nonmarital sexual relations. Thus, individuals who were accused of engaging in bigamy, adultery, and "sodomy," among other sexual practices that were not considered normative, were sometimes prosecuted by the Inquisition and even killed for crimes/sins they may or may not have committed.

While the Inquisition was not formally instituted in New Spain and the Kingdom of Guatemala/Captaincy General of Guatemala (which included Nicaragua) until 1571, inquisitorial-like powers were given to Spanish authorities throughout the isthmus much earlier. In 1568, for instance, in the Nicaraguan city of León there was a "Process against Nicolás, a Genoese master/teacher [*maestre*], for having misinterpreted the biblical passage regarding what God prohibited Adam in paradise."[19] Much earlier, in 1543, Spanish authorities had acted against a dozen individuals, three for witchcraft, two for blasphemy, one for perjury, and six for cohabitation (*amancebados*).[20] Even earlier, in the 1530s, we find documentation for the prosecution of Andrés Caballero and another man, both burned alive at the stake for sodomy, also in León. Over two centuries later, in 1786, two additional men were formally prosecuted by the Inquisition for sodomy. Joseph Manuel Virto and Joseph Gregorio Ibarra, known as "Los Chepes," "were processed in Rivas for being tainted by the nefarious sin against nature."[21]

Not everyone who was found guilty of a crime was sentenced to death. A variety of punishments were available for the authorities to mete out, among them fines, floggings, exile, and prison time. For instance, Fernando Bachicao (also known as Hernando Machicao) was found guilty of blasphemy on March 12, 1530. His initial sentence, "to be chained at his feet for thirty days in a public jail," was subsequently commuted to having to purchase and donate "fifteen pounds of wax . . . to burn before the blessed Sacrament on Holy Thursday and Good Friday from the moment they enclose the Lord to when they unlock him."[22] Meanwhile, another man, Alonso de León, was found guilty in 1542, under Governor Rodrigo de Contreras, of defamation of character after stating repeatedly that the (Spanish) women of León were all "whores" (*putas*) and their husbands "cuckolds." De León's punishment was "perpetual banishment from these provinces of Nicaragua, that he not enter, under penalty of death" in addition to "around 100 public lashes on his back."[23] As can be seen from the discrepancy between these two sentences, the punishment a person received appears to have been influenced by factors other than the severity of the crime, an issue I will return to later in this chapter when I discuss the life and death of Andrés Caballero in more detail.

In 1571 Indigenous peoples were excluded from the jurisdiction of the Inquisition.[24] Among other considerations, the church and the Crown apparently realized that the additional violence and fear created by the Inquisition could be financially counterproductive, particularly with the rapid decline of Indigenous populations due to disease. Indigenous peoples were still expected to comply with Catholic doctrine but would not be punished through the "regular" Inquisition.[25] Everybody else, including enslaved Africans, however, remained under the jurisdiction of the Inquisition, which lasted in Central America until independence in the early nineteenth century.

AN ISSUE OF SOURCES: NICARAGUA'S "SODOM AND GOMORRAH"

The Franciscan friar Juan de Torquemada (c. 1562–1624) wrote extensively about the Americas in his book *Monarquía indiana*, published in 1615 and reprinted in 1723. While it appears that he never visited Nicaragua, he wrote about Nicaragua in his book, presumably basing his information on the descriptions of another Franciscan friar, Toribio Benavente (c. 1491–1565), known as Motolinía. Motolinía traveled to Nicaragua between 1527 and 1529.

One of Torquemada's most well-known descriptions of Nicaragua is a story that appears to combine elements of two separate passages from the Christian Bible. The Nicaraguan geographer Jaime Incer Barquero quotes "an almost biblical passage on the destruction of the town" known as Imbita or Mabitia or Imabite located next to the colonial city of León founded by the conquistador Hernández de Córdoba (c. 1475–1526):

> Towards the right of the city of this Lagoon ... it all was very populated by Natural Indians, and suddenly, in one night it flooded, and many souls perished, because this was one of the most populated areas of the entire earth. It is said to have flooded like that ... because they took many more women than their predecessors did, and because of other grave sins, which were committed there; because since the Inhabitants

abounded in maintenance (since the land was very fertile, like another Sodom), the inhabitants of it gave themselves to idleness, and there are vices, and perished like another Gomorrah and Sodom. Today, the Natural Indians, in their songs, mourn this and tell how they perished for their sins.[26]

Imbita was one of the major cities in the region before the arrival of the Spanish.[27] Gil González Dávila (1480–1526), one of the earliest Spanish conquerors, visited the town around 1522.[28] It is unclear how and when exactly it is that the town flooded. The city must have been renamed after the inundation took place since the name Imabite in old Chorotegan (an Oto-Manguean Indigenous language spoken at the time) meant "swallowed by the waters."[29] The name was a popular one for encomiendas, which reveals there must have been many people living in or near Imbita when the Spanish arrived. U.S. scholar Patrick S. Werner noted that "in the Tasación of 1548 there were at least seven encomiendas that included the word Imabite or Mabite or Mabitio or something similar in its name."[30]

The fact that this account feels so familiar to contemporary readers acquainted with the biblical stories of Sodom and Gomorrah and Noah's ark makes it suspect.[31] It points to the many problems inherent in using colonial sources to document the history of Native peoples. What makes this story, whether true or not, so problematic is that it coincided with the message the Spanish wanted to promote about Indigenous peoples to justify their conquest.

Two of the many Indigenous sexual behaviors that the Spanish disapproved of were adultery and sodomy, and promising to eliminate those practices helped the Spanish justify the violence inherent in the colonial process. Moreover, the story about Imbita was probably told in direct response to a question about whether Indigenous peoples in the area had ever known the world to flood, an important question, since the Spanish wanted validation for events described in their holy book. The Spanish would often question Nicaraguan Indigenous peoples about catastrophic flooding, possibly to figure out how they had survived the flood that led Noah to build his ark. Oviedo recorded the following exchange Fray Bobadilla had with an Indigenous man known as Misesboy:

FRIAR: Do you know or have you heard if after the world was made, if it was lost or not?

MISESBOY: I heard my parents say that a long time ago it had been lost due to water, and that that was already in the past.[32]

The problematic nature of colonial sources is one that has been widely addressed by scholars elsewhere.[33] The consensus is that one must be suspicious of colonial sources, given their intrinsic biases, and we must be particularly wary of self-serving accounts such as the one above. The Nicaraguan scholar Erick Blandón addresses this very issue in his work on colonial Nicaragua, referring specifically to the interrogations of Fray Bobadilla, financed by Governor Pedrarias Dávila:

> We must bear in mind that the document that has come down to us is only known in the language of the empire, Spanish; and that there is no way of knowing what the Indians' answers were in their original language ... we only have the version contaminated by the point of view of the interrogators and of ... Oviedo who, according to [the contemporary scholar] Jorge Eduardo Arellano, "considered the Indian not fully rational, morally imperfect, satanic and worthy of being treated like a beast."[34]

It is useful to also know that the study conducted by Fray Bobadilla was a politically partisan one, meant to discredit specific Spaniards who were enemies of Fray Bobadilla's dear friend, Governor Pedrarias Dávila. The governor had been accused by the Spanish conquistadors Gil González Dávila, Francisco Fernández, and Diego López de Salceda of not doing his job properly because he had been lagging in the number of Indigenous baptisms. González Dávila, Fernández, and López de Salceda, his rivals, bragged about the tens of thousands of baptisms they had conducted. In his defense, Governor Pedrarias Dávila argued that those conversions had had minimal effect and sent Bobadilla to prove it. Meanwhile, Bobadilla had his own objective: to baptize even more Indigenous peoples than Governor Pedrarias Dávila's enemies. In six months, Bobadilla baptized almost three hundred Indigenous individuals a day![35] Fray Bobadilla's political and religious motives and biases underscore the problematic nature of the interrogations themselves, their translation, and their transcription.

THE LIFE AND DEATH OF ANDRÉS CABALLERO: THE MYSTERY OF THE GOVERNOR AND "THE CITY'S BIGGEST SODOMITE"

Andrés Caballero (also spelled Cavallero), a Spaniard, was a friend and possibly a lover of Governor Francisco de Castañeda (hereafter Francisco Castañeda). According to the U.S. scholar Patrick S. Werner, Caballero "entered Nicaragua with the army of Francisco Hernández [de Cordoba] in 1524" and "took part in all the events of the early colony: he paid the forced repartimientos for a garrison and to fight the Chondales in Nueva Segovia; his name appears in the everyday documents of the colony."[36] According to the Nicaraguan scholar José Argüello Gómez, Caballero's name appeared on the list of the first distribution of gold that took place among the conquistadors in León.[37] Caballero also appears in many legal documents of that era as a witness or as someone directly involved in legal struggles over power and honor in what was an extremely litigious society. At the time there were 150 "Spanish 'vecinos,' one hundred of whom were owners of encomiendas" living in the colonial city of León, the seat of the Spanish colonial government.[38] Caballero was clearly part of the Spanish elite of León, for in 1530 he was named Town Council member (*Regidor de Cabildo*).[39] The prolific Nicaraguan scholar Jorge Eduardo Arellano wrote the following about Caballero:

> [One case that] ocurred in León Viejo in 1536, was that of the homosexual Andrés Caballero, burned alive by order of the mayor Diego de Tapia, long before the Inquisition was formally founded. Caballero was an intimate friend of Francisco de Castañeda—Pedraria's successor in the governorship—in whose house, next to Caballero's, there was . . . a door where they could communicate.[40]

Pedrarias had been the first colonial governor named by the Spanish Crown in Nicaragua. Francisco Castañeda became interim governor after Pedrarias died; Castañeda held that position from approximately March 1531 to 1535/36. This position was eventually occupied by Pedrarias's son-in-law, Rodrigo de Contreras, between 1536 and 1542. After serving almost six years as interim governor, it appears that Castañeda, who had many enemies, was accused of corruption and multiple abuses of power and, instead of facing trial, disappeared.[41]

Francisco Castañeda was actively involved in the sale of enslaved Indigenous peoples during his tenure. U.S. geographer Linda A. Newson noted that during the 1530s, he "controlled the issuance of export licenses. As such he purchased slaves cheaply, and by issuing licenses only to buyers who would accept his highly inflated prices, he forced up the price of slaves."[42] It appears that Castañeda also participated in the day-to-day operations of the sale and export of enslaved peoples. In 1533 he sailed from Nicaragua with seven hundred Indigenous peoples on five ships, presumably to deliver them in person to their new enslavers in Panama or Peru.[43]

All the early governors of Nicaragua are remembered as vicious, cruel, and inhumane in their treatment of Indigenous peoples and fiercely competitive with other Spaniards over who could acquire encomiendas, who could enrich themselves the most, and who would hold power.[44] Their cruelty was also directed toward anyone who criticized them for such behavior, including Spaniards, and culminated in the infamous assassination of Fray Bartolomé de las Casas's friend, Bishop Antonio Valdivieso (b. 1495), in 1550.[45]

This period was fictionalized in the 1995 novel *El burdel de las Pedrarias* by the Nicaraguan novelist Ricardo Pasos Marciaq. In the novel, Pasos Marciaq focuses extensively on the sexual abuse and the sexual exchange of Indigenous peoples that took place during the early 1500s at the hands of the hypocritical and corrupt Spanish women and men (including priests) who colonized Nicaragua. According to the contemporary scholar Francisco Rodríguez, in the novel, "sexuality is dehumanized and becomes... a monotonous mechanism of violence... [The novel] presents the dehumanization of the Conquest... in order to question and reject that process of imposition."[46]

Pasos Marciaq writes about Andrés Caballero in the novel, describing him as "the city's biggest sodomite"[47] and describes "homosexual orgies" that included Caballero and other Spanish conquistadors, among them "the bailiff Luis Daza [and] the forger [of signatures] Pedro Casas, who sleep in the house of governor Castañeda, when his wife [Ana Estacia Cornejo] is not there."[48] Colonial sources show that, indeed, witnesses at the time claimed that Governor Castañeda's male friends, including Caballero, spent the night at Castañeda's home when his wife was away, and that the *licenciado* Castañeda had a particularly strong friendship with Caballero. The mayor of León, Diego Núñez de Mercado, in a petition presented to the Council of Indies regarding the governor's conduct, testified in 1541 that

> Andrés Caballero . . . had a very close friendship with said licenciado and . . . they ate together many times and . . . doña Ana, the wife of said licenciado, would leave . . . and she was gone for a few days and during that time said Andrés Caballero always went in and out of the house of said licenciado and said licenciado always said very good things about said Andrés Caballero.[49]

Castañeda was such good friends with Caballero that when the latter was fined six gold pesos for an unnamed offense, Caballero ended up not having to pay the fine as a result of Castañeda's intervention. Caballero was on a list of Castañeda's friends who had failed to pay fines they owed the Crown and the city. The list was provided by Martín Martín Breño, the city of León's notary, in a letter attesting to Castañeda's corruption.[50]

In the small Spanish world of colonial Nicaragua, few things remained private. Multiple sources explicitly note that Caballero was known to engage in sex with men. Diego Núñez de Mercado refers to Caballero's homosexuality by three different names. He refers to it as a "nefarious sin," a "nefarious sin against nature," and "sodomy," while calling Caballero "sometico" (contraction of *sodometico*) and "stained with the nefarious sin against nature."[51] In that same petition Núñez de Mercado went on to label Castañeda a "bad Christian" who brought to his house people, including a priest, for lewd activities:

> Said licenciado was such a bad Christian and had such little conscience that . . . he gathered people in his house . . . for other knavery and lust . . . together in close friendships and conversation with a Friar of Mercy who calls himself Friar Ornardo de Lima Díaz, the worst Christian and dishonest life and most public committer of fornication and other ugly crimes and more bad examples that had never been seen in these parts and with this one and with . . . Andrés Caballero who was informed by the nefarious sin that he was later burned for, always had his friendship and conversation.

Another witness of that period, Benito de Prado, recalled in a declaration the following regarding Castañeda and Andrés Caballero:

> ... [the] licenciado Castañeda many times ... having favored an Andrés Caballero who he had imprisoned for submission [*sometico*?] ... since the crime was notorious and could not be concealed, he was imprisoned a second time, and while he was imprisoned to burn the said Andrés Caballero, this witness heard said licenciado Castañeda say if Andrés Caballero had died a man I would free him because he is my friend and I love him well.[52]

Prado's declaration raises more questions than answers in the original Spanish (see footnote). What is clear is that Prado overheard Castañeda say that Caballero was his friend *as Caballero awaited death*. It is also clear that Caballero was imprisoned twice for the same crime, the second time right before his burning, which presumably happened in León's central plaza, right across the street from Castañeda's house, which was next to Caballero's. The "notorious" crime that Caballero could not "conceal" was having sex with men. But the next few lines are unclear. Was the part about a man in reference to Castañeda or Caballero? Did Castañeda mean to say, "If only I had been a [brave] man I would have freed him"? Or did he mean "if Caballero had been a man, I would have freed him"? Or maybe what Castañeda meant was "if only Caballero had killed a man, I would have been able to free him." Presumably Castañeda was governor when Caballero was killed (if Prado actually overheard Castañeda while Caballero was waiting to be burned). But if so, why did Castañeda not free him? Perhaps (if Castañeda had indeed already fled Nicaragua in 1535) it was alcalde Diego de Tapia who sentenced Caballero to death, as the scholar Jorge Eduardo Arellano argues. Or did Castañeda himself sentence his friend to death? If the latter is true, why did Castañeda do it? What follows is the story I have been able to piece together given the available sources.

In 1536 the notary Alvar García stated in a written certification that the treasurer Pedro de los Ríos had sued Castañeda over a very long list of offenses. One of them was that "said licenciado [Castañeda] ... did not burn Andrés Caballero in time."[53] In other words, Castañeda had shown preferential treatment toward Caballero, and de los Ríos was not taking it anymore. At the time it was well known that Castañeda played favorites, like many other men in power did. The notary Diego Sánchez wrote that he believed Castañeda "towards some acted justly and towards others he did not." As proof, Sánchez noted that "said licenciado Castañeda held the Treasurer Pedro de los Ríos and the Mayor Diego Núñez de Mercado in prison for a long time without an accusation and without them knowing the cause of their imprisonment."[54]

Diego Núñez in his petition argued that "two or three years before the said Andrés Caballero was burned, he [Caballero] was accused of the said sin before the said licenciado [Castañeda], which was public and known that there was a great deal of information and that notwithstanding [the vast amount of information] said licenciado set him free and removed the witnesses from the case and made them retract their statements."[55] Diego Núñez was convinced that "if said licenciado had not favored [Caballero] this witness [Núñez himself] is sure that they would have burned him the year before."[56] Castañeda actually had an entire network of quid pro quo friends. And he needed them badly, because his enemies, which included Pedrarias Dávila's entire family, were very powerful. Castañeda had saved Caballero's life once, and in return, Caballero had lied under oath whenever necessary as a witness against Castañeda's enemies. Diego Sánchez, who appears to have been an eyewitness to Caballero's burning (as many Spaniards probably were), said that Caballero actually apologized, *while on his way to be burned,* for false statements Caballero had made against Sánchez:

> ... the said licenciado Castañeda against the people he did not like made [up] evidence and ... some of the things that the witnesses said did not happen like they said they did because he brought a certain case against this witness [Sánchez] and presented some witnesses, among them Andrés Caballero, who they burned and who, at the time they took him out to burn, he asked this witness [Sánchez] for forgiveness for what he had said against him.[57]

Despite the transactional component of their relationship, it does appear that Castañeda and Caballero were true friends. They spent a lot of time together eating and drinking, often alone, and Castañeda publicly proclaimed that Caballero was his friend. According to Diego Núñez they had become friends when Pedrarias was still governor, once Caballero chose to side with Castañeda against Pedrarias in what was a very well-known feud.[58]

In 1537 Castañeda wrote a letter to the king of Spain from Santo Domingo, in what is now the Dominican Republic, explaining why he had left Nicaragua in such a hurry. He told the king that he had to leave because he was sick, and his doctors had recommended he return to Spain. And he would have returned to Spain, he wrote, but he did not have access to a ship to go back home. The only ship available was on its way to Peru, so he took it. Castañeda did not say what many already knew, which is that he had powerful friends in Peru, among them the conquistador Francisco Pizarro himself.[59]

Castañeda did confide in the king that he feared for his life, since the treasurer Pedro de los Ríos and the alcalde Diego Núñez wanted him dead. Castañeda then begged the king to grant him the opportunity to leave Santo Domingo and defend himself in person against the accusations being made against him by Governor Contreras (Pedrarias's son-in-law) and his men.

In his defense, Castañeda argued that he had always obeyed the king's laws and had been a good ruler. Proof of that was that

> during the six or seven year of the administration of said justice in Nicaragua there were and occured fewer crimes than in the times of other governors and justices [and] for this [reason] there was no need to punish [anyone], nor did he punish any man with the death penalty or mutilation of limbs or lashes or shame ... except for two men that he ordered be burned and they were burned for the nefarious sin.[60]

Castañeda in this letter takes full responsibility for the deaths of Andrés Caballero and that of a man who remains unnamed. But if Castañeda sentenced Caballero, why did Jorge Eduardo Arellano state that the alcalde Diego de Tapia was the responsible party?

Diego Núñez, who, like Diego de Tapia, was also an alcalde, is the presumed source for Jorge Eduardo Arellano's take on this issue since Núñez stated in 1541 that Diego de Tapia was the one who sentenced Caballero to death: "they burned said Andrés Caballero for being a sodomite sentenced by the Mayor Diego de Tapia."[61]

To solve this enigma, it is important to remember what the historian José Mejía Lacayo has told us about the way in which the colonies were administered. Mejía Lacayo has documented how, in the mid-1520s, "with the intention of cutting expenses and increasing income, [the Spanish king] Carlos V complicated the administration of Nicaragua by having overlapping authorities, which caused serious jurisdictional conflicts between officials."[62] Mejía Lacayo argued that after these administrative changes were enacted there was a great deal of confusion because a rather large group was charged with governing the colony. In part because of this administrative peculiarity, we might never know how Caballero's sentence was reached or whether or not Castañeda could have done something to prevent Caballero's death. Another Nicaraguan scholar, Eduardo Pérez Valle, wrote that "for unknown reasons, Castañeda's protection [of Caballero] ceased."[63] It is definitely possible that Castañeda's power was waning with the ascendancy of Rodrigo de Contreras. We simply do not know. Ultimately, I believe Jorge Eduardo Arellano's analysis might be correct: that Caballero having sex with men, while considered a criminal offense that merited the death penalty, was in this particular case, simply a "pretext" and that "in the end, for political reasons, he was burned alive."[64]

There is a final twist to the relationship between Castañeda and Caballero. The notary Diego Sánchez said that, after Caballero died, Castañeda sent proxies to Caballero's estate sale ("almodena de los bienes") "so that they could get a few things for him."[65] Part of the punishment for convicted sodomites was the confiscation of all their property. Was Castañeda trying to benefit financially from Caballero's death by getting a few discounted items? Was he trying to get back items he had loaned to Caballero? Was he trying to get back items that might incriminate him? Or was he perhaps simply wanting a keepsake to remember a dear friend? Did Castañeda send a proxy because he was already in Santo Domingo? Could it be that Castañeda imprisoned his friend and then left, leaving the final decision regarding Caballero's death to be made by Diego de Tapia?

Even though we do not have enough evidence to answer all our questions, the life and death of Andrés Caballero matter for several different reasons. He is one of the few individuals found in the legal documents for the early colonial period who today would be considered a member of the LGBTQIA+ community. Because he was the friend and possible lover of an embattled governor, Caballero was relatively easy to find in the colonial archive. Someone with a lesser status might not have been found, which is probably why we know nothing about the other man who was also sentenced to death for sodomy. Caballero is also important because, to our knowledge, he is the first named man burned at the stake for sodomy in Nicaragua. This practice was common elsewhere at the time. The scholar Federico Garza Carvajal notes that "inquests conducted in Andalusia and in New Spain resulted in the burning of some seventy-five men and the interrogation of some five hundred other individuals within a period of 130 years."[66] Additionally, the documents available on Caballero help uncover the existence of private homosocial spaces where men would/could engage in sexual relationships. House parties such as the ones supposedly held at Castañeda's and Caballero's homes would continue to come under scrutiny during the colonial period. This was especially the case during the decades leading up to independence when the Crown attempted to gain more control over its colonial subjects through the Bourbon Reforms, a topic covered briefly later on in this chapter.

Caballero's life story is also crucial because it laid the foundation for a series of links made in the Nicaraguan national imaginary regarding homosexuality. It is not a coincidence that the Caballero "case" contained the typical elements that would come to define homosexuality in late twentieth-century Nicaragua. Despite the existing association between Indigeneity and gender/sexual dissidence, homosexuality came to be understood in some circles as an urban phenomenon, associated with politically corrupt (and sometimes foreign) elites. By examining Caballero's life and death we come to realize that "modern" Nicaraguan understandings of homosexuality have deep colonial underpinnings.

CAPTAIN MARTÍN ESTETE: "WASN'T MADE TO BE A CAPTAIN OR A MAN, AND HAS MANY DEFECTS THAT CAPTAINS SHOULDN'T HAVE"

While Andrés Caballero was, to my knowledge, one of only two early conquistadors convicted of sodomy, there were others who were informally accused of having sex with men, even if they were never charged.

One of those men was Governor Castañeda. Another was Captain Martín Estete, "Pedrarias' right hand."[67] In 1971 the Nicaraguan scholar Eduardo Pérez Valle spent eighteen months investigating the accusations and intimations of homosexuality against Castañeda and Estete, colonial rivals. Pérez Valle found enough evidence to argue that the documents, although sometimes vague, given the subject, "inspire strong suspicions."[68] Castañeda himself was one of the people who accused Estete of being the type of person who "only spent time lying down and [doing] other dirty things, setting bad examples."[69] The assumption here is that he was accused of having sex with men since it was the only behavior that would have gone unnamed. Pérez Valle went on to note that another conquistador, "Rodrigo Pérez . . . has quite revealing phrases: according to him, Estete 'wasn't made to be a captain or a man, and has many defects that captains shouldn't have.'"[70]

The insinuations against Estete were different from the accusations against Caballero. Caballero, it must be noted, was never accused of being feminine or "unmanly," even though he was, it appears, unmarried. In Estete's case, a great deal of emphasis was placed on him not being manly enough to be a captain, to lead his troops, or even be a good soldier in the fight against Native Americans (although there is evidence that he sometimes was incredibly cruel toward Indigenous peoples on a personal level). A witness in the 1529 case noted that Estete "was not meant to be a captain . . . because he is very careless and lazy in War." The witness also said that in the seventeen years that Estete had been in Nicaragua, his incompetence was such that he had never been seen with a sword at his side.[71]

Given the limited sources, we will perhaps never know what happened to Martín Estete. What we do know is that he started out initially as Governor Pedrarias's "servant," married to a woman who served Pedrarias' wife. That he had friends in high places perhaps explains why he was not formally accused of sodomy.[72]

Estete's life story allows us to see glimpses into what life might have been like for men who were rumored to be sodomites *and* not manly enough. Both Caballero's and Estete's cases also reveal a great deal about the privileges associated with being a Spanish man in early colonial Nicaragua. Indeed, their stories can shed light on what Garza Carvajal calls the "links between the politics of empire and perceptions of manliness."[73] Garza Carvajal has found that in seventeenth century Mexico, colonial officials displayed a particular sense of repulsion for the effeminate sodomite, a phenomenon often infused with images of anthropophagy, human sacrifices, the diabolical, cancer—[74]

I have not yet found enough evidence to fully discuss the "discursive mechanisms of colonial rule"[75] in relation to "effeminate sodomites" in colonial Nicaragua, but presumably I would encounter myriad colonial contradictions. One of those contradictions is that the only men specifically named in Nicaragua's historical record as sodomites or potential sodomites were all Spanish conquistadors even though the Spanish justified their conquest of the Americas in part as an effort to eliminate the "nefarious sin" from the region, all along arguing or implying that Native peoples were more prone to sodomy than the Spanish. The next sections examine in greater detail what the Spanish chroniclers had to say about Indigenous peoples and sodomy before turning to a discussion on the control of sexuality after the Bourbon Reforms.

"CORRUPTED BY THAT SIN"

When they arrived in the so-called New World, the Spanish had sodomy on their minds. In fact, sodomy, along with cannibalism and human sacrifice, were three of the main Indigenous practices the Spanish highlighted when justifying the colonization of Native peoples (along with "idolatry" and all nonmarital heterosex), as explained by Fray Bartolomé de las Casas, the renowned Dominican friar who visited Nicaragua in the 1530s.[76] Thus, one of the first questions Spanish conquistadors and priests asked Indigenous people in the Americas when they arrived in the "New World" was a version of "how do you punish sodomites here?" Back home in the Peninsula, the Spanish had just witnessed their king and queen pass the 1497 Pragmática de los Reyes Católicos acerca de los reos de pecado nefando, "the first Spanish anti-sodomy law of the modern period."[77] While not the first anti-sodomy law in Spain, this law renewed Spanish persecution of sodomites. It was the Pragmática that turned the previous punishment for sodomy, the death penalty, into death by fire, preceded by torture.[78]

Nowhere in the Americas did the Spanish find a system to rival their own when it came to the persecution of sodomites. The Spanish saw this as additional evidence of their superiority over Indigenous peoples. So the conquerors proceeded to build a colonial infrastructure from scratch to punish those individuals whom they thought were sodomites, in the name of God and the Catholic monarchs of Spain. The process was complex and involved everything from making sure Indigenous peoples and everyone else knew that "sodomy" was a punishable sin/crime, to encouraging them to reveal homosexual desires and practices during confession, to eventually naming Inquisitors, and hiring people to prepare the wood and the stake with which "sodomites" would be burned.

The official state-sponsored persecution of sodomites in Nicaragua can and should be considered a colonial tradition. This tradition is best symbolized not only by the flames engulfing a man tied with ropes to a stake but also by the attack dogs that the Spanish brought with them and which were sometimes used to maul and eat Indigenous peoples believed to be "corrupted by that sin."[79] This horrific punishment was depicted in Theodore de Bry's 1594 engraving "Valboa throws some Indians, who had committed the terrible sin of sodomy, to the dogs to be torn apart."[80]

WHAT PRACTICES DID THE SPANISH DESCRIBE?

There is no doubt that the sexual practices of Indigenous people in Nicaragua before the conquest were varied, given the ethnic diversity among them, and included practices that the Spanish could easily label "sodomy." But the lens through which the Spanish viewed sexuality was not the same lens used by Indigenous people. In this section of the chapter, I explore some colonial accounts of nonheteronormative sexualities in Nicaragua.

The most well-known colonial accounts of Indigenous sexual practices in Nicaragua are those of two Spanish priests, Fray Francisco de Bobadilla and Fray Bartolomé de las Casas, along with those of one very prolific apologist for the Spanish conquest, Gonzalo Fernández de Oviedo, the official chronicler of the Indies. Fray Bobadilla is the one who famously asked an Indigenous Nicarao man of Nahua descent, in what today is the department of Rivas, "What punishment do you give to the one who is a puto, the one you call cuylon, if he is the patient one?"—and wrote this down as the answer: "The young men stone him and do him harm and call him a scoundrel, and sometimes they die from the harm that is done to them."[81] So that readers understood exactly what he and Bobadilla were referring to, Oviedo made sure to note: "they call the sodomite cuylon."[82]

Erick Blandón argues that it is not surprising that some of these Spaniards had sodomy on their mind. He notes that Bobadilla, as a Mercedarian priest, was possibly stigmatized himself as a sodomite due to his religious order:

> The initiative of the Mercedarian friar . . . to find out the punishments that were inflicted on the cuylon or passive [individual] among the Nicaragua, implies a personal anxiety [over this] which could have been motivated by the stigma that, in the XVI century, the members of that order carried in Spain due to their reputation as sodomites. The fame that followed the friars of la Merced led several of its members before the court of the Inquisition that when it started to investigate, starting in 1525, the practices of sodomy . . . it discovered—according to B. Bussel Thompson and J. K. Walsh—in the Convent of la Merced in Valencia [Spain] "a nest" of sodomites.[83]

Such was the reputation of this order of priests that in Spain they mocked the Mercedarians with the rhyme: "When you see a friar of la Merced, put your ass against the wall."[84]

Given the problematic nature of colonial sources, it is difficult to know whether it is true that young men sometimes stoned "passive" *cuylones* to death in what today is the region of Rivas before the arrival of the Spanish. But it is significant to note that the Indigenous informant at no point suggested that there was a formal venue, process, or institution to punish cuylones. Moreover, he did not mention the involvement of adults in the policing or punishment of cuylones. In their punishment their gods were not involved and neither were their priests; there were no fines, no prison time, no confiscations, no enslavement, no torture, no burning at the stake, no being eaten alive by dogs, no need to wear distinctive clothing or tattoos; there was no banishment, no formal death sentence, no equivalent to "conversion therapy," no threats of eternal damnation, no need for the cuylones to repent, or confess their sin, or promise to never sin again in order to achieve salvation. If what Bobadilla wrote down is true, the "punishment" is horrific and heartbreaking, but it amounted to society turning a blind eye to male youth who took it upon themselves to bully, humiliate, physically injure, and sometimes kill men who were presumably their neighbors, friends, and relatives. It was mob violence, but it did not appear to be a policy that was formally backed by the religious and political elites. All of that would change for the worse after the arrival of the Spanish.

Another Indigenous practice recorded by Oviedo had to do with cross-dressing or *travestismo*. Oviedo witnessed during a dance that there were "up to sixty people, all of them men, and among them some made women, all painted and with much and beautiful plumage."[85] Cross-dressing was considered suspect by many Spaniards, as explained by Las Casas, who had traveled to Nicaragua several times and sought to give a different point of view:

> certain Spaniards found in a certain corner of one of the said provinces ["of Nicaragua, Honduras, and immediate countries"] three men dressed in women's clothing, who for that alone they judged to be corrupted by that sin, and without more evidence ["y no por mas probanza"] they then threw them to the dogs that they had with them, which tore them to pieces and ate them alive, as if they were their judges. But it could have been that they were not for that, but rather that it was not for women, and that it was a custom among those people that they wear women's clothing, to give notice of their defect, since they needed to attend to doing women's tasks and exercises, as some nations did.[86]

We will never know if Las Casas was correct in his hypotheses. Historian Pete Sigal, however, forcefully argues that Las Casas "engaged in tortured mental gymnastics" to explain certain practices among Indigenous peoples and that he "compared the Indigenous peoples of the Americas to the classical civilizations of the West. The effeminate, cross-dressed sodomites became eunuchs [in Las Casas's imagination], injured in some way and thus unable to complete their roles as men in warrior societies."[87] It is important to keep Sigal's analysis in mind in this discussion of Las Casas, but I must also stress that the analysis that Sigal presents in "The Cuiloni, the Patlache, and the Abominable Sin: Homosexualities in Early

Colonial Nahua Society" is specifically about Mexico (a land with many more archival sources). In the case of Nicaragua, there are simply not enough sources to know more than what is written on the page by Las Casas on this topic.

THE INVENTION OF INDIGENOUS SODOMY IN NICARAGUA: "WHAT PUNISHMENT DO YOU GIVE TO THE ONE WHO IS A PUTO, THE ONE YOU CALL CUYLON, IF HE IS THE PATIENT ONE?"

Since the Spanish were committed to promoting a virile version of masculinity, they were particularly concerned with the punishment of feminine men, whom they considered to be the "patient" or "passive" partners in sexual encounters between men. When Bobadilla interrogated an Indigenous man and asked him, "What punishment do you give to the one who is a puto, the one you call cuylon, if he is the patient one?" the Spanish gave birth to the Nicaraguan *cochón* as a concept. I agree with Erick Blandón, who states that "in [Bobadilla's] interrogation we find the birth certificate for the 'cochón' as a subject worthy of ridicule."[88] While we do not know who exactly was included under the category of cuylon, it appears that the Spanish concluded that men who had sex with other men were all called cuylones. But the Spanish were primarily interested in punishing the behavior of the partner whom they perceived to be feminine, thus contributing to an eventual narrowing of the category of cuylon.

The colonial category of the cuylon, which I argue later in this chapter turned into the contemporary cochón, privileged the masculine over the feminine, making it difficult to separate homophobia from sexism. In the Spanish imaginary, the category of cuylon was predicated on a gender binary and the belief that sex required penetration of one feminine or feminized individual by a masculine one, that the act of penetrating made a person "active," and that the act of being penetrated made a person "passive."

It is my contention that while there were a variety of preconquest Indigenous same-sex sexual practices, the Spanish colonial enterprise imposed Indigenous "sodomy" as a single legal, moral, and religious category, promoting the cuylon as its most visible and maligned symbol.

The reason for this was that the Spanish focused their attention on the individual that they felt most resembled the Spanish "sodomite." The cuylon-turned-cochón then became well-known throughout the Western academic world in the 1990s in large part through the ethnographic work of Roger Lancaster, a U.S. anthropologist who wrote extensively about the cochón in late twentieth-century Nicaragua.[89]

I have only found the term *cuylon* twice in Spanish colonial documents on Nicaragua. Nonetheless, the Nahua term *cuiloni* (and its variations) is used several times by other Spanish chroniclers in other parts of New Spain, and its use and meaning in Mexico have been extensively addressed by the historian Pete Sigal. It is important to point out that, while Sigal's discussion of the term *cuiloni* is important to the history of Mexico, it is not necessarily a fit for Nicaragua. While there are some obvious linguistic and cultural continuities between the Nahuas in Mexico and the Nahuas in Nicaragua, the latter arrived in Nicaragua possibly hundreds of years before the Spanish conquest. For that and other reasons, Sigal's arguments on Nahua populations in Mexico are not automatically applicable to Nicaragua.

USE OF THE TERM COCHÓN/A

There is a great deal of confusion regarding the term *cochón*, a word used exclusively in Nicaragua to refer to homosexual/gay men (or lesbians in the feminine version of the term, *cochona*). Some scholars have argued that it has French origins, because it is spelled like the French word for pig. Others have argued that it derives from the word *colchón*, which in Spanish means mattress, but there is no evidence to support either position.[90] As Erick Blandón argues, "the use of mattresses is relatively new ... Even at the beginning of the 20th century, the majority of Nicaraguans slept on leather beds, on mats [*petates*], in hammocks, or on canvas folding beds [*tijeras de lona*]."[91] Like Blandón, I agree with Jorge Eduardo Arellano, who, along with the Nicaraguan linguist Carlos Mántica (1935–2020), concludes that the term has Nahua origins.[92] However, Mántica and Arellano disagree on which Nahua word evolved into *cochón*. In the classic text *El habla nicaragüense*, Carlos Mántica argues that *cochón* comes from the Nahua *cotzoani*.[93] Meanwhile, Arellano argues that it comes from the Nahua word *cuylon* (also spelled cuilon).[94] I concur with Arellano that it derives from the word *cuylon* since that was the word used by Oviedo in Nicaragua.

Although it makes historical and linguistic sense to argue that the word *cochón* comes from the word *cuylon*, the term leads us to yet another mystery in western Nicaragua's LGBTQIA+ history: Why is the word *cochón* not found in any of the written records of the colonial period or the nineteenth century? Presumably it took many years for the word *cuylon* to become *cochón*, and there was a period when both words coexisted. So why is the word *cuylon* also not found in the period after the early 1500s? I believe there are several reasons for the absence beyond the fact that most people throughout the colonial and early national periods did not read or write. First, a Nahuat word would not have been a word used frequently by the Spanish if they had a Spanish synonym readily available, which they did: the word *sodomita*. That *cuylon/cochón* was not used commonly by the Spanish probably led it to be absent from documents written by the Spanish (in Spanish), or by anyone else for that matter. Here I must reiterate that Indigenous languages on Nicaragua's Pacific coast (unlike the situation in parts of Mexico and Nicaragua's Caribbean Coast) did not survive the conquest, making it that more difficult to document Indigenous terminology. Moreover, since not all Indigenous peoples in Nicaragua were of Nahua origin (not even in western Nicaragua), *cochón* initially would not have even necessarily been a word understood by all Native peoples in the region. Additionally, the word *cochón* was probably a slang term, like it is today, preventing it from making its way into formal Spanish writing. The process through which the term spread throughout western Nicaragua and became the preferred (usually derogatory) term for a gay man (or lesbian in the case of *cochona*) will probably remain an enigma. Nonetheless, we can still document its earliest uses.

According to the sources available, the word *cochón* first appeared in writing during the early twentieth century. It appears in a letter written to Vice President Bartolomé Martínez (1873–1936) in the early 1920s.[95] In the letter, an Indigenous ally of Martínez from Matagalpa refers to Colonel Domingo Portillo, a man "in charge of wooing the Indigenous vote away from Martínez . . ." as a "dirty cochón, there he has Marcelino Aguilar and several other indios in jail . . . shameless man . . . vulgar cochón, pot-bellied, weak."[96]

The term *cochón* was also used in "Chinfonía Burguesa," which was first published as a poem in 1931 and then rewritten for the stage in 1939. The poem was written by two of Nicaragua's most well-known poets, Joaquín Pasos Argüello (1914–47) and José Coronel Urtecho (1906–94), and was, according to the U.S. scholar Vicky Unruh, a "farcical performance manifesto."[97] It has been called "a penetrating satire of the life of the bourgeoisie of the colonial city of Granada, birthplace of the vanguard movement."[98] Although used to refer to a musical instrument, and not a person, the meaning of the word *cochón* in the poem, given the overtly sexual nature of the piece, is most likely "homosexual":

> *I dance to the whirligig*
> *to the cochón sound of my violin*
> *or to the violent sound of my wind instrument.*
> *But I love above all my pianola,*
> *my pianola Manola.*[99]

The word *cocheche*, which is a variation of *cochón*, is not very common in contemporary Nicaragua, but I have found it used in print in the 1930s. In the following quotation, "La Pilar," a street vendor in Managua, rhymes in order to sell her merchandise:

> *Here comes the fruit almibar . . .*
> *for the whores!*
> *I bring a sweet milk delicacy . . . For the cocheches!*
> *Here are the cashew sweets*
> *For the cabrones!*[100]

The word *cochón* was also used to refer to Colonel Crisanto Sacasa, a man active in the wars for independence and the postindependence political conflict that permeated Nicaragua. He was called a cochón for military actions he took during the 1820s in notes added to a poem written by the priest José Desiderio de la Quadra (b. 1779/86–1849). The poem was probably written in the 1820s, and although it circulated widely at the time, it was not published until July 15, 1876, in the newspaper *La Tertulia*. It was then reprinted over a hundred years after it was first published, with the note calling Sacasa "cochón," in the 1971 *Revista Conservadora*.[101]

However, nobody appears to know who wrote the notes or when the notes were written.[102] In other words, this use of the word *cochón* in the notes accompanying the poem could, in theory, date to the late 1870s or to 1971 or to any year in between. I believe it is significant because it exemplifies the other twentieth-century meaning of *cochón*, which is to be cowardly.

Jorge Eduardo Arellano stresses that the word *cochón* has "two fundamental meanings: homosexual and cowardly," which were recorded in 1948 by Alfonso Valle in the exhaustive *Diccionario del habla nicaragüense*.[103] The use of the term as a synonym for *coward* is evident in the work of the U.S./Nicaraguan historian Francisco J. Barbosa (1969–2022). Barbosa documented the student protests against the Somoza dictatorship of July 23, 1959, in which students called the National Guard members *cochones*.[104] How the term came to have these two meanings is yet another mystery that remains to be solved.

WOMEN AND SODOMY

That the politically powerful and those accused of crimes were more likely to make it into colonial records than others helps explain, in part, the overwhelming absence of women in the historical archives. But the absence of women is also explained by the Spanish conceptualization of women's sexual relationships with other women as potentially less common and less problematic, since "real" sex was often understood to involve penile penetration. The contemporary Spanish historian Alejandra Palafox has written that when

> Faced with an active, powerful, and on occasions uncontrollable masculine sexuality, in accordance with the prevailing ideal of virility, women were stripped of their sexuality, being seen as beings devoid of desires. This conception promoted less social control and concern about possible sexual encounters between women, which resulted in the masculinization of sodomy.[105]

The Spanish colonizers might have cared less about lesbianism than male homosexuality, but they did mention it in their writings as a concern.

For instance, Friar Gregorio García (1556–1627), who spent twelve years in the Americas but did not visit Nicaragua, mentions women in his *Origen de los Indios de el Nuevo Mundo e Indias Occidentales*, which was first published in 1607: "In Leviticus itself it was a law that the one who committed the nefarious sin should die. The Indians of New Spain kept that law . . . and executed it with great rigor . . . and the punishment itself was applied to the woman who slept with another, because it was also against nature."[106] There is no evidence that women who had sex with other women were killed in precolonial Nicaragua. Nor have I found evidence that any women were murdered at the stake for "sodomy" in colonial Nicaragua. However, the Spanish did investigate women in other parts of their empire for engaging in what was sometimes called a "bad friendship," as was a case documented by the British/U.S. scholar Stephanie Kirk in Mexico during the late 1700s. In that particular case, a young nun, María Josefa Ildefonsa de San Juan Bautista, was questioned by the Inquisition in part over an illicit "friendship" she had with a woman who worked as a servant, María Gertrudis Rodríguez.[107] In the investigation of María Josefa, the available sources did not reveal the ultimate outcome, but she was definitely not burned at the stake as so many Mexican men convicted of sodomy were.[108] In cases like this one, it appears that harsh punishment tended to hinge on whether or not a prosthetic device was used and whether the individuals involved "appeared to want to be men."[109] Since these were not issues raised in this investigation, a severe punishment was most likely avoided.[110]

Examples of female homoeroticism in convents during the early modern period such as the one documented in Mexico by Stephanie Kirk have been found throughout the Catholic world. The most famous case of all, however, is probably that of Sor Juana Ines de la Cruz (1648–95), the Mexican poet and scholar who got in trouble with the church hierarchy for a variety of behaviors considered to be unbecoming for a religious woman. Among other things, Sor Juana wrote feminist and what could be considered erotic same-sex poems. The quality of her writing earned her fame during her lifetime, and today she is remembered as colonial Latin America's best woman writer.[111]

What is important to note about these Mexican examples, is that, on the one hand, because all nuns at the time were cloistered, female convents were among the few strictly homosocial spaces available to women during the colonial era.[112] On the other hand, however, female convents did not exist in places like Nicaragua, which were far away from the colonial centers of power. The lack of convents in Nicaragua curtailed homosocial opportunities for women who might have wished to remain unmarried, live in a community of women, earn their own living in an "honorable" way, and live away from their families. Also worth noting is that the Spanish disrupted what might have been the most important precolonial homosocial space that existed for women, the open-air markets discussed below.

TIANGUES AS WOMEN'S DOMAIN AND THE ECONOMIC CENTER OF AN INDIGENOUS TRANSGENDER TRADITION

According to colonial sources, precolonial Indigenous open-air markets on Nicaragua's Pacific coast were women's and young people's domain. Some will no doubt point to the writings of Fray Nemesio de la Concepción Zapata as evidence for this:

> In Nicaragua it was not the woman, but the man, who swept the house and lit the fire. The woman was mainly in charge there of going to sell what the man earned from hunting, fishing, agriculture, or industry. Commerce was reserved for women and the rest of the jobs were for men.[113]

However, Fray Nemesio never existed. He was invented by Rafael Bolívar Coronado (1884–1924), a Venezuelan who wrote under multiple pseudonyms (some say up to six hundred different ones) in order to write fraudulent colonial documents for a living.[114]

It appears that Bolívar Coronado copied from Oviedo, who stated in his *Historia general de las Indias*:

> The men are in charge of providing the house itself with the work of the field and agriculture and hunting and fishing, and women with dealings and merchandise; but before the husband leaves the house, he has to leave it swept and light the fire, and then he takes his weapons and goes to the fields to do his work, or to fish or hunt, or do what he knows and has to exercise.[115]

Oviedo also wrote (citing Bobadilla's interrogation of an Indigenous man):

> no one from the town—who is a man—can enter the tianguez—which is the market square—to buy or sell or do anything else, nor stop to look at it from the outside; and if he looks at it, they scold him. And if he enters, they beat him up, and they would consider anyone [any man] who was there or passed by a scoundrel. But all the women go to the tianguez with their merchandise, and men and women can also enter if they are from other towns and foreigners in the said tianguez and markets without penalty; but this custom is not general to outsiders everywhere but among allies and friendly confederates; and to the said markets all kinds of women go, *and even boys/young men [muchachos]—if they have not slept with women*.[116] There they sell slaves, gold, blankets, corn, fish, rabbits, and many birds and everything else that is traded and sold or bought among us from what we have and what is on earth and is brought from other parts.[117]

On the one hand, it appears that women oversaw local commerce. On the other hand, men were prevented from entering into the local markets, or tiangues, a situation that appears to have been unique to that region of Nicaragua. Women's control of the precolonial markets became common knowledge after it was popularized by twentieth-century Nicaraguan intellectuals like Pablo Antonio Cuadra (1912–2002): "Both Oviedo and Bobadilla say that among the Nicaraguas only women were allowed to trade in the tiangue or market."[118] In 1976, the engineer Enrique Bolaños Geyer (1928–2021), who would rule as president of Nicaragua between 2002 and 2007, gave a speech at Masaya's open-air market, also noting the important economic legacy this precolonial tradition had left Nicaraguans:

> The Chroniclers of the Indies say that men were not allowed to enter the Aboriginal market. In the tiangues only women were in charge. And I think they continue to rule, because, although we are now allowed to enter, their Matriarchy is in plain sight in Masaya. This "Commercial Center Under Roof," "the biggest and most popular in Nicaragua," "the oldest of our communal institutions," is the productive seat of the Matriarchy.[119]

The Nicaraguan scholar Manuel Fernández Vílches further notes that women's economic role in the markets "has remained recognizable in tradition, up to the present."[120]

I wish to propose that at least some of western Nicaragua's contemporary communities of transgender women have their origins in the precolonial period. In other words, a rereading of the colonial evidence suggests the presence of individuals in preconquest Nicaraguan tiangues who, if they were alive today, might identify as transgender women. As noted above, Indigenous markets, which were traditionally the exclusive domain of local women, allowed, in addition to women and girls, only "muchachos if they have not slept with women" to enter. One can interpret that to mean prepubescent boys. Or one can interpret it to *also* mean individuals who today might identify as transgender women. This interpretation makes sense in light of contemporary western Nicaraguan history. Open-air markets in western Nicaragua today and throughout the twentieth century have been not only the center of working-class cisgender women's productivity but also the center of working-class transgender women's economic productivity. How else can we explain the long-standing economic presence of transgender women in Nicaragua's open-air markets *if not by* linking it to the precolonial tradition that allowed "muchachos" to be there (presumably working as market sellers) as long as "they had not slept with women"?

It is important to point out that I am not arguing for a third gender or berdache tradition in Nicaragua, for there is no evidence for that. I am suggesting instead that we reinterpret the link between markets, women, and femininity. In doing so we will find that sales and local commerce were conceived of as feminine enterprises. This helps explain why so many working-class cis and trans women still today seek employment as saleswomen in open-air markets or as street vendors located near markets or associated with markets on Nicaragua's Pacific coast.

That relatively large numbers of self-identified transgender women work as sellers in open-air markets or as street vendors in western Nicaragua today is a known fact. Proof of that is that in 2016, when ANIT, the Nicaraguan Association of Transgender Women (Asociación Nicaragüense de Transgénero), conducted a "survey regarding transgender individuals' perceptions on discrimination in the department of Managua," they interviewed many of their 202 survey participants at the Huembes market, the Oriental market, and the Iván Montenegro market, all open-air markets.[121] Sometimes market jobs are the only jobs available to them, as Ludwika Vega, president of ANIT, noted in 2017: "Trans women continue to work in beauty salons, markets, they are the kitchen helpers in the comiderías, some are waitresses. None of them are sitting in an office because when they want to enter formal companies, the doors are closed to them."[122] In spite of the rampant employment discrimination that Vega correctly pointed out, a 2016 poll showed that "65% of Nicaraguans confess that they feel comfortable working with a trans person, compared to 20.1% who say they are against it."[123] This statistic compared favorably with a 2018 survey in the United States that found that "fifty-five percent of those surveyed expressed no preference about their coworkers' sexuality or gender expression."[124]

The association made between selling food items in particular (in open-air markets, small street restaurants known as *comiderías*, or in the streets) and femininity (trans or not) has been so strong in western Nicaragua that the country's most simultaneously famous (he had 4.31 million YouTube subscribers in 2022) and infamous (due to the violently sexist, homophobic, and overall offensive nature of his jokes) contemporary comedian and YouTuber used this theme as a frequent premise for his show. In one of his YouTube shows called "Agapito Díaz y la melcocha a peso," José Ramón Quintanilla, known as JR, of the group INN, capitalized on the assumption that western Nicaraguans would find a male food vendor who appeared "feminine," a familiar, nonthreatening figure, and would be more likely to buy from this individual than from a male heterosexual "masculine" food vendor.[125] In fact, this version of the episode, which had been watched over 5.1 times in 2022, is about two men selling homemade *melcochas* (individual sweets) in the streets of a neighborhood in Managua. The feminine vendor, it turns out, is simply "faking" femininity to be a successful salesperson. This strategy helped him sell his melcochas. The masculine vendor, meanwhile, whose name is Agapito, had not sold a single one. When the two meet, the feminine salesperson decides to teach Agapito how to act in a feminine way in order to sell his melcochas. The plan works, and all goes well until Agapito is the target of sexual harassment by one of his male customers. The episode is offensive because it perpetuates stereotypes and uses derogatory language. But the episode is also fascinating, because the successful *melcocha* vendor explains to Agapito that femininity (which he calls "style" and "technique") is a skill that can be learned and that has economic value:

> The thing is you have to have style to sell . . . I'll explain. I studied marketing for a semester . . . there you learn sales techniques. Because to offer a product you have to sell it well. You have to know how to sell it. Do you understand me now? . . . to begin with, you have to have the style . . . do you understand me now? You have to have the style . . . you have to walk with style . . . look closely at me . . . you have to move . . . let go . . .

Once Agapito "gets it" his teacher tells him, "You are a good student. Amazing!"[126]

For a presumably heterosexual man to say that he learned femininity as a "technique" in what presumably was a postsecondary marketing course is supposed to be funny, given the everyday experience many Nicaraguans have of purchasing food items from transgender women vendors, most of whom are denied higher levels of schooling.[127] It is also supposed to sound strangely "sophisticated" when contrasted to Agapito's "ignorant" masculine rural Indigenous persona, which is symbolized by the machete he carries at his side.

The choice of the melcocha is a throwback to earlier times in Nicaragua, when most food products sold in the streets were homemade. It is meant to evoke nostalgia for the past, but also for Nicaragua, since many of INN's Nicaraguan YouTube viewers presumably lived outside Nicaragua and Nicaraguan melcochas are not easy to find elsewhere. JR felt the need to let people know, in writing on the YouTube page, that "the melcocha is a traditional sweet in my country, a handmade candy," most likely in response to the many non-Nicaraguans asking in the comment section, "What is a melcocha?" Saying "my country" instead of Nicaragua, is meant to emphasize JR's connection to Nicaragua and the national "authenticity" of his comedy, and it seemed to work, based on the thirty-five thousand likes and the nine hundred mostly positive comments the video received in 2022. But the figure of the feminine vendor is also meant to provoke nostalgia and a sense of national identity. It is my contention that the video "worked" because Nicaraguans recognized the feminine vendor as "authentic" and even as "one of our own." What made it "funny" to some people is that in the end it was all a farce, a case of mistaken identity, a performance of femininity, and thus a backdrop for homophobic jokes, homophobic stereotypes, and the ever-present threat of violence against men who are not "real" men. But it is my contention that the homophobic jokes, and the ever-so-brief moments that humanize male femininity as a marketing "strategy," would not work at all if there were not a long-standing transgender tradition in Nicaragua's markets that is recognized by most Nicaraguans as still alive today.[128]

My analysis of INN's comedy coincides with that of the U.S. scholar John Petrus, who has argued that

> I generally hold that INN's representations affirm normative masculinities, misogyny, and classism. However, I am not content with classifying the program as a simple reproducer of the violence of the patriarchy. I would like to read against the grain of the obvious in the format and content of the program in order to reveal the constructiveness of sexual expression and to critique the hegemonic gender ideology. In fact, there are episodes in which the male is ridiculed. The program serves as an alternative archive that allows us to think about the popular sexual imaginary: the masculinities and femininities present there.[129]

I would like to add that the "alternative archive" is also a historical one, a point Petrus alluded to when he stated that "the LGBTQIA+ characters [los personajes de la diversidad sexual] represented on iNN are tied to local stereotypes—for better or worse—not to internationally accepted and recognized 'positive' images of gays and lesbians."[130] Appropriately, given that his work is not meant to be historical, Petrus concluded that "the program captures certain attitudes and expressions of the moment, but also adjusts to the changes in the national hegemonic ideology on these same attitudes and expressions."[131] My research demonstrates that in spite of the inevitable changes in understandings of gender expression, gender identity, and sexuality over time, contemporary understandings of gender and sexuality in Nicaragua performed by comedians like JR/INN can reveal strong ties to long-standing traditions.

THE BISHOP VS. THE GOVERNOR: HOUSE PARTIES, FANDANGOS, AND THE BOURBON REFORMS

Although the Spanish generally agreed on the basics, such as the prosecution of sexual relations between men, sexual relations between women, and the subordination of women, the devil was in the details, and thus, there was no one Spanish colonial moral vision to be implemented in Nicaragua. Spanish elites were mired in conflict over whose moral vision would prevail, and these conflicts were often between representatives of the church and those of the Crown, although in theory there was no separation between church and state. Sometimes it was difficult to differentiate between moral conflicts and those over power, meaning that alliances could change quickly and outcomes were not always predictable. So, while Spanish elites generally agreed that they needed to have control over the sexual lives of everyone around them, including other Spaniards, they sometimes could not reach a consensus over who would be in charge and who would benefit financially from such an enterprise. Elites also had a hard time deciding which rules they themselves were going to follow and which Spaniards had the right to tell the others in their social class how to live their lives.

In the decades leading up to independence, the Spanish Crown put forth a series of reforms, known as the Bourbon Reforms, throughout the American colonies. These were meant to make the colonies more financially "efficient" (i.e., produce greater profit for Spain). They also meant to tighten existing regulations and create new regulations to govern people's daily lives. Some of the new laws sought to encourage individuals to marry their "equals," even though the Spanish had previously not shared with other European colonial powers an obsession with preventing miscegenation. One significant goal of the Bourbon Reforms in some areas of Latin America, notably Mexico, as documented by the U.S. historian William B. Taylor and others, was the Crown's attempt to wrestle power away from the Catholic Church. This led to several crucial and possibly unintended consequences. One of them was that it destabilized the religious legitimacy upon which the colonial system rested. Another was that it led approximately 10 percent of priests to support Mexico's independence from Spain.[132]

In the case of Nicaragua, the U.S. historian Cory L. Schott has done an excellent job at documenting some of the conflicts among the Spanish elites against the backdrop of the Bourbon Reforms. In particular, he highlights the clashes between Governor Domingo Cabello y Robles (hereafter Governor Cabello) and Bishop Juan Carlos Vílchez y Carrera in the 1760s and 1770s. Schott writes:

> The policies implemented during this time offered unequal prospects to social groups (e.g., Indians, merchants, soldiers, and farmers), state and non-state institutions (e.g., the Church, town councils, merchant guilds, and regional governments), and individuals to reconfigure traditional local power arrangements. This process, however, produced new conflicts ... I argue Nicaragua's relative isolation from the rest of the Spanish world allowed for the already complex and unwieldy process to become even more difficult. Thus, the majority of the reforms introduced over the eighteenth century remained poorly implemented ... I examine how vague (and sometimes contradictory) decrees from Spain provided opportunities for new expressions of local power ... I examine the effect that new laws limiting the power of the Church had on local officials and members of the clergy. For example, new ordinances concerning the regulation of private gatherings and dances provoked a major conflict between two pillars of local rule: the bishop and the governor.[133]

Cabello, a Spaniard born in Spain, became governor in 1764 and remained in his post until 1776. Vílchez y Carrera, on the other hand, came from a wealthy (Spanish) Nicaraguan family and, having been named bishop in 1763, before Cabello's arrival, was initially welcoming. The honeymoon stage did not last long. Schott notes that "the underlying causes of the disputes [between the two] stemmed from confusion over legal definitions and the application of authority over a wide variety of issues ranging from public decency to the treatment of Indians."[134] Of particular interest to us is the conflict over what constituted public decency and the measures taken to assure such goal. Schott notes:

> A few weeks after his arrival, the governor hosted a party in early January for the elite [*gente principal*] of the city in the episcopal palace to celebrate the Feast of the Epiphany. According to various testimonies,

including the governor's, the festivities included various dances called "fandangos" that lasted well into the night. Little did the governor know that by hosting a party he would be stumbling into a local controversy with years in the making. Some days later ... at ... mass ... the vicar ... posted and read aloud a new decree from Bishop Vílchez. The Bishop's decree stated that anyone who attended private parties where "lewd, shameful, and indecent acts" occurred ... would be subject to excommunication from the Catholic Church.[135]

The original documents, which are housed in the General Archive of Central America, describe what happened at these private parties and were transcribed from the Spanish by Schott. Here is a brief description of which behaviors were under attack:

> The public and scandalous sins that they perform in dances and fandangos ... where women, married men and single ones convene ... in which dishonest and provocative acts, such as holding hands, the men, and the women with impure gestures hugging and kissing each other, the faces with such liberty, that even the vulgar people are scandalized ... mixing women and men drinking alcohol, and spending the whole night in this disorder.[136]

The bishop proceeded to ban all types of private social gatherings, and the governor pushed back, suing the bishop. The case made it all the way to the authorities at the Audiencia in Guatemala, and eventually, in 1767, the ruling came out in favor of the governor. Governor Cabello had continuously argued that he would prosecute those who broke the law but that there were no laws broken simply by dancing. The courts agreed with him, thus contributing to the confusion over who had moral authority over Spain's colonial subjects and slightly decreasing the power of the Catholic Church in Nicaragua.

The complaints over "indecent" behavior happening among consenting adults in the privacy of their own homes take us back to the events that led to the death of Andrés Caballero. While we do not know if men were dancing with other men or whether women were kissing other women at the elite parties hosted by Governor Cabello, we do know that such parties would exist later on and that the right of LGBTQIA+

Nicaraguans to freely assemble in their own homes is a hard-won right, as documented by the U.S. political scientist Karen Kampwirth, among others.[137]

The most famous LGBTQIA+ private party in the history of Latin America is perhaps the one remembered as the ball "of the Famous 41," referring to the forty-one individuals whose party was raided by Mexican police in 1901, under dictator Porfirio Díaz. The attendees were severely punished, even though many of them came from elite families. Scholars who have studied the events surrounding the police raid have reached the following conclusion, which applies in general terms to Nicaragua:

> The irony is clear. As Foucault has argued so persuasively, the mechanisms of repression cannot function without inciting the discourse about that which they seek to repress, and this discourse is, in the end, productive. The discourse of repression incites the same desires and behaviors that it strives to repress.[138]

In the case of Nicaragua, Bishop Vílchez y Carrera was not able to defeat the human impulse to dance and definitely was not able to dampen his parishioners' sexual desires. Religious elites would not be deterred, however, in their attempts to curb Nicaraguan private and public sexual expressions and would more often than not be joined by secular elites in that project over the following centuries. The battle between the governor and the bishop stands out as anomalous in this respect.

CONCLUSION: "IMAGINARY CRIMES PUNISHED WITH ATROCIOUS SENTENCES"

The Spanish pretended "sodomy," which to them was a sin/crime, was rampant in the New World so as to justify the killing and enslavement of Indigenous peoples. As the Nicaraguan historian Tomas Ayón (1820–87) has stated, the Spanish created "imaginary crimes [which they then] punished with atrocious sentences."[139] But many Spaniards in the Americas engaged in "sodomy" themselves, so the Spanish religious and political elites punished them too, as they would have had they still been on the peninsula. Nonetheless, it appears that in western Nicaragua the Spanish did not persecute every Spaniard who was accused of sodomy, but rather those, like Andrés Caballero, whose deaths or imprisonment were politically or economically beneficial to members of the ruling class.

While no records have been found of Nicaraguan Indigenous men or women of any background being prosecuted for sodomy, there is evidence of "cross-dressing men" being eaten alive by Spanish attack dogs for this offense. This is significant, for it shows that a simple suspicion of sodomy could lead to someone's death sentence, without a trial or investigation. If the Spanish sources can be trusted, the equivalent of the "passive" Spanish sodomites among Nicaraos also were punished harshly for their same-sex sexual practices. But there were no Indigenous institutions that formally called for such punishment and no Indigenous gods that required it.

The "passive" Indigenous cuylon over time became the ever-so-Nicaraguan cochón of the twentieth century. There were other transformations as well. In this chapter, for instance, I make a case for a transgender Indigenous tradition in western Nicaragua that allowed transgender women to have an economic role in society. I note that Nicaragua has a somewhat unique precolonial association between femininity and local commerce, particularly in open-air markets still today known as tiangues. Working-class trans and cisgender women have played and continue to play a crucial role in western Nicaraguan markets, one that has allowed them to have their own income and survive as independent financial entities while often pooling resources with other family members, given the meager wages earned. While not the subject of this chapter, future research might build on the U.S. historian Elizabeth Dore's research and my own in order to document how postcolonial "patriarchal laws [that] required married women to secure their husband's consent to engage in trade" affected the role transgender women played in the markets after independence.[140] With so many unanswered questions, mine is truly only a first draft of Nicaragua's colonial LGBTQIA+ history.

2

"VERY DELICATE MEN" AND "QUEER" FILIBUSTERS

The Nineteenth Century

AFTER THREE hundred years of colonialism, Nicaragua gained its independence from Spain in 1821, along with Mexico and the rest of Central America. Independence, however, did not translate into an all-encompassing cultural or legal revolution. There were possibly as many cultural and legal continuities as there were ruptures. Additionally, independence did not bring about economic and political stability or peace at the national or local level. And independence affected subaltern groups in myriad, and often contradictory, ways.

There is relatively little in the archives to document the lives of nineteenth-century Nicaraguans who today would call themselves LGBTQIA+ or members of the community of sexual diversity. However, sources do reveal that national and local elites throughout the century worked hard to create and implement laws punishing "public scandal" and "immorality," terms that sometimes served as euphemisms for resistance to heteronormativity and binary gender roles, identity, and expression. All along, elites sought to promote what they considered to be proper heterosexual behavior under the rubric of morality and progress, so as to normalize their version of heterosexuality as they moved to consolidate the nation-state, privatize Indigenous communal lands, codify individual rights, and eventually secularize society—all processes that at the time were deeply "differentiated by gender."[1]

This chapter addresses the postindependence nineteenth century and the first years of the twentieth century in such a way as to highlight intersectionality in the lives of LGBTQIA+ Nicaraguans affected by some of the processes noted above. It is crucial to document the ways in which race and class intersected with gender (including gender identity and gender expression) and sexuality during this century to fully understand the complexities in the lives of LGBTQIA+ individuals during this period, for they inhabited raced and classed bodies as well as gendered and sexed ones. In fact, it is my contention that sexism and discrimination based on sexual orientation, gender identity, and gender expression *coexisting with* discrimination based on race and/or class is what often still makes life difficult for some LGBTQIA+ individuals. This point was alluded to in the last chapter by contemporary trans activist Ludwika Vega when she noted the ongoing discrimination against transgender Nicaraguans in the workplace. Lack of opportunity for economic self-sufficiency and upward mobility is a significant contemporary LGBTQIA+ problem, and its roots date back to the colonial period and the nineteenth century. Addressing the origins of discrimination might help us end it.

In addition to discussing the specific ways in which gender, race, and class intersected with LGBTQIA+ history during the nineteenth century and the first decade of the twentieth century, this chapter also addresses the policing of heterosexuality that led to the institutionalization of *a particular type* of heteronormativity. Moreover, I discuss the ways in which citizenship, adultery, and sex work were gendered during this period. Lastly, I address the invasion of Nicaragua by William Walker from a perspective that centers gender (including gender identity and gender expression) and sexuality.

NICARAGUA'S POSTINDEPENDENCE POLITICAL HISTORY

The following paragraphs constitute the standard narrative of roughly the first century of Nicaragua's political history after independence. In 1822 Nicaragua proclaimed its annexation to Mexico, and in 1823 Nicaragua became part of the United Provinces of Central America. A year later Nicaragua formed part of the Federal Republic of Central America or Central American Federation (República Federal de Centroamérica). It was not until 1838 that Nicaragua declared itself an independent nation, even though it joined with El Salvador and Honduras in the short-lived Central American Confederation from 1842 until 1845. The period between 1838 and 1853 is known as the Period of the Directorate. During that fifteen-year period, the ongoing conflict between the two rival cities of Granada and León, a conflict that dated to the colonial period, continued unabated.

In 1853 Fruto Chamorro became the supreme director of Nicaragua and then went on to become Nicaragua's first president in 1854. A civil war broke out that year, building on the long-standing power struggles between the Conservatives in Granada and the Liberals in León. The Liberal faction declined to recognize Chamorro and allied itself instead with the U.S. businessman Byron Cole, who brokered the arrival in Nicaragua of the now infamous Euroamerican William Walker.

Walker, a political chameleon and opportunist who was supported by pro-enslavement southerners as well as others who opposed enslavement, arrived with his own agenda, and it was not to help the Liberals defeat the Conservatives. Instead, Walker declared himself president of Nicaragua in 1856 and proceeded to proclaim the enslavement of peoples of African ancestry legal in Nicaragua even though it had already been abolished soon after independence. Once they realized the threat they were facing, Central American forces united and formed the Central American Allied Army (Ejército Aliado Centroaméricano) against Walker and his followers, which numbered over ten thousand men and women.[2] Walker was eventually captured and shot to death in Honduras in 1860.

After Walker's defeat, Nicaragua was ruled by Conservatives for the next thirty years, unlike other Mesoamerican countries which at the time had Liberal heads of state. The seeming political continuity, however, did not necessarily bring about peace. Armed conflict erupted in 1863 and 1869. Eventually, the Liberal general José Santos Zelaya became president in 1893, governing the nation for fifteen years and bringing about a series of Liberal political and economic reforms already in effect in other parts of Latin America, many of which had started to be implemented in Nicaragua even before his rule. The U.S. government and Zelaya initially had a very good working relationship, in part because both sides looked forward to a U.S. interoceanic canal being built in Nicaragua. However, after the U.S. Congress voted in 1902 to build the canal in Panama, the relationship between the United States and Zelaya soured.³ Zelaya sought out new economic partners in Europe and Asia, and the United States was not pleased. Looking out for its own economic and political interests in the region, the United States helped finance the armed opposition to Zelaya, leading to his ouster in 1909.

While this standard narrative is not incorrect, it is incomplete and might lead readers to believe that history was made only by those men who held political power at the national level and that patriarchal relations were absent from national politics and developed primarily in the home. The late U.S. historian Elizabeth Dore, however, one of the few scholars to extensively address gender relations in nineteenth-century Nicaragua, has stressed that national as well as local elites played an important role in creating a patriarchal society during this period. Dore argued that Nicaragua's economic and political development during the nineteenth century was highly gendered. She wrote that, indeed, the "public regulation of gender was an aspect of [Nicaraguan] state formation," the latter a process she defined as "the politics of legitimating rule."⁴ Additionally, Dore found that "in the interim between independence and the coffee revolutions [of the late nineteenth century] power was exercised mostly at the local level in Central America. This was an era of municipal government formation and the consolidation of regional ruling elites. Central to these processes was the public regulation of sexuality by municipal authorities."⁵ Moreover, Dore revealed that "municipal juntas took on the role of adjudicating gender norms and sexuality and in exercising that authority they fortified their political domination."⁶ Nonetheless, she clarified:

> I am not suggesting . . . that social control over women or regulation of gender norms (and the two are not the same thing) occurred mostly within the public sphere. My argument is that the patriarchal household was not the only, probably not even the primary, site of regulation and contestation of gender relations. The construction of gender is a social, as opposed to an individual, process.⁷

While gender and sexuality are usually left out of standard historical interpretations of Nicaragua's nineteenth-century history, race is sometimes addressed. The following section summarizes some of the racial dynamics on the Pacific and central regions of Nicaragua during the nineteenth century before addressing some of the ways in which racial discrimination intersected with LGBTQIA+ history during this period.

THE ENSLAVEMENT OF PEOPLES OF AFRICAN ANCESTRY, RACIAL CATEGORIZATION, AND INDIGENOUS COMMUNITIES AFTER INDEPENDENCE

One of the most important changes to take place after independence was the end of enslavement for peoples of African ancestry in 1824. Indeed, elites proclaimed, "Every man is free in the Republic. No one who follows the laws can be enslaved, nor can someone who traffics slaves be a citizen."[8] While enslavers were compensated for their economic "loss," however, enslaved peoples were never compensated, and reparations were not considered by those in power.[9] It is difficult to know with certainty how many thousands of enslaved Africans were brought by the Spanish to Nicaragua. We do know, however, that at the time of independence there were probably still hundreds of enslaved people of African ancestry. We also know that after three centuries of racial mixing, a large percentage of Nicaragua's free population had African ancestry, and, in some areas, they even constituted most of the population, a fact still unknown to many today. The groundbreaking Nicaraguan historian Germán Romero Vargas has documented that a few decades before independence, in 1790, people of African ancestry constituted approximately 70 percent of the population in Granada. Out of 12,400 individuals, 8,500 had some African ancestry.[10] The Nicaraguan scholar Jorge Eduardo Arellano has also written about this subject, noting that

> The "pringue de África," then, was central to strengthening the middle layers formed by zambos, mulatos, cuarterones—those who had a quarter of African ancestry—and other mixtures; so that in 1820—according to the writings of the Political Chief (Jefe Político) of León, Nicaragua, dated the 29th of November of that year—they constituted 84% of the population.[11]

What this means is that on the eve of independence, as in other Latin American countries, there were four broad "racial" groups in western and central Nicaragua: Indigenous peoples, Spaniards, people of exclusively (or mostly) African ancestry, and mixed-race people, many of the latter with substantial African heritage. Due to the dynamics described below, by the 1950s only two groups would be acknowledged: Indigenous peoples (usually referred to as Indios) and mestizos (those with a mixture of Indian and Spanish ancestry). Spanish Nicaraguans (a numerical minority) would come to be relabeled as mestizos, and Black Nicaraguans would be ignored, along with the African ancestry of mixed-race peoples.

Another crucial change to take place after independence, along with the end of enslavement, was the theoretical end of legal racial categorization. Under Spanish colonialism, individuals had a legal racial category that was applied to them, and, although there was some room for negotiation, individuals often had no say in how they were classified or how they were treated as a result. Racial classification was meant to aid the Spanish Crown in extracting tribute and labor from people of color and preventing those who did not exhibit so-called purity of blood or limpieza de sangre (including Jews) from holding political and economic power. In theory, there was no longer a need for racial labels after independence because there would no longer be state-sponsored (legal) racial discrimination. This sentiment was expressed by a Central American independence leader, the presumably criollo (of Spanish ancestry but born in Central America) Pedro Molina, who in 1821 stated, "Blessed be independence! There will no longer be distinctions among Americans beyond those granted by merit and virtue!"[12] However, most Latin American countries, including Nicaragua, would continue to ask questions about ethnic background, phenotype, or race in their censuses until the early to mid-1900s.[13] And, regardless of the law, and sometimes because of it, social discrimination against darker-skinned individuals would continue until the present.

By the mid-twentieth century a radical change had taken place regarding the way in which Nicaraguan elites sought to racialize the nation-state in their efforts to consolidate power. The U.S. historian Jeff Gould found that by 1950, the term *mestizo*, originally used during the colonial period to refer specifically to a person of mixed Spanish and Indigenous heritage, "had become a self-description for the whole of [Nicaraguan] society."[14] In other words, a country with a sizable Indigenous population and a significant African presence came to be labeled and/or self-label as all/only "mestizo." Through this process, western Nicaragua would witness the linguistic disappearance of its Indigenous and Black populations, even though these communities continue to exist until this day.

The idea that everyone in Nicaragua had both (and *only*) Spanish and Indigenous heritage and that therefore there were "no more Indians left" in the Pacific and central regions would prove to be a powerful one.[15] It would become a useful tool for Nicaraguan elites (some with no Indigenous or African ancestry at all) in their consolidation of economic and political power even though it contradicted the everyday reality that many knew firsthand. Non-Indigenous Nicaraguan elites (some of them mestizos and Afro-mestizos) embraced this view because they were eager to justify the theft (otherwise known as "privatization") of communal lands held by the Indigenous communities (Comunidades Indígenas) to which many Indigenous Nicaraguans still belonged. What better way to justify taking away land from Indigenous peoples than to suppress and deny Indigenous communal identity? Indigenous resistance, however, was often able to prevent and/or delay the takeover of communal lands. For instance, Gould documented eight cases of "thwarted . . . governmental attempts to abolish the long-standing Comunidades between 1877 and 1923."[16] In the end, many Comunidades were abolished in the twentieth century, but quite a few remain in the twenty-first century.[17]

TRANS WOMEN AND RESISTANCE

Ironically, even though elites pretended Indigenous peoples no longer existed, they still discriminated against them and anyone who "looked" or "acted" like one. Certain features, customs, and practices became (or continued to be) racialized as Indian and classed as poor, since race and class became conflated over time. It is my contention that because trans and non-trans (cisgender) women's economic participation in western Nicaraguan markets was an Indigenous tradition and was understood as such, discrimination against all women market sellers in western

Nicaragua has an anti-Indigenous component. Equally significant, I wish to put forth the argument that because western Nicaragua's community of transgender women has Indigenous historical origins, attitudes against trans women are deeply linked to the long-standing anti-Indigenous racism that developed in the colonial period and thrived in the nineteenth century. In other words, discrimination against trans women is not only based on sexism, homophobia, and transphobia, but also on racism/classism due to the association between trans women and Indigeneity. Additionally, one could argue that this group of women's *economic* participation is not only long-standing but is a symbol of Indigenous resistance to colonialism, *as is their continued existence as trans women.*

The presence of trans women is particularly visible in Nicaragua. A 2010 survey by ANIT, the Asociación Nicaragüense de Transgenero, showed that out of the 256 transgender individuals the organization surveyed that year, 245 were trans women.[18] Their 2016 survey showed an increase in trans men, but trans women still predominated. Almost 90 percent of the individuals surveyed in 2016 identified as transgender women.[19] This stands in contrast to the United States, where "out of 135,367 likely transgender people who changed their names with the Social Security Administration [since 1936], 65 percent were transgender men and 35 percent were transgender women."[20]

GENDER IDENTITY AND EXPRESSION, INDIGENEITY, TIANGUES, AND MESONES

As previously discussed, in the late 1400s and early 1500s, working in open-air markets did not stigmatize women vendors in western Nicaragua as "public women"—nor did it place them at the bottom of the social hierarchy. To the contrary, it seems that most women at the time engaged in market work and that their contribution to their community's economic well-being was expected and appreciated by their families and neighbors. During the colonial period, tiangues continued to attract Indigenous vendors, but tiangues were no longer women-only spaces. Moreover, the expectation was that only poor women would be found working there.

Throughout the colonial period, upper-class (mainly Spanish) women were not usually employed, although before and after independence, they were allowed to own property, and some did actively seek to increase their wealth. In general, wealthy women (a numerical minority) spent most of their time at home so as to preserve their sexual honor as well as their racial privilege and class status. Working-class and enslaved women, on the other hand, had to work outside the home, and that often made them sexually suspect, as they were out in public and thus could easily become "public women," a synonym for "prostitutes" in the public imaginary.

After independence from Spain in the 1820s, despite greater racial mixing and no official state-sponsored racial discrimination, tiangues were still associated with Indigenous women. This is evident in the writings of a politician from Granada, Pío Bolaños (1873–1961). He wrote fondly of the women at the tiangue in his hometown's main plaza during the late 1800s, before the market was moved in 1887.[21] The patronizing way Bolaños writes about the young women working there reveals the racialized way in which working-class market women were viewed by the elite. Moreover, the sexualized way in which Bolaños writes about them reveals the predatory nature of elite men who would have never dared to write in this way about each other's wives, sisters, mothers, or daughters:

> They arrived at the tiangue, well bathed, fresh, and with clean though humble clothes, with a low-cut white cotton shirt, and some embroidered by hand, exposing the throat, part of the chest, and arms. The petticoats were wide and had floating skirts, also made of cotton and of garish colours, starched and ironed.
>
> Almost all of them were barefoot, and their hands and bodies showed careful grooming. They were generally young, brown in color [*de color moreno*] with well-formed and healthy bodies, with abundant, black, and lustrous hair.
>
> Some were headdressed with two long braids and at the end of these they attached black or brightly colored silk ribbons, while others left their wavy hair loose, which, with the graceful and natural movement of the body, floated over their bare backs or their uncovered breasts. Their skin was smooth, and their arms robust and well-shaped. They were always in a good mood, trying to please their customers with their friendly smiles and their seductive movements. They were very quick to respond to whoever directed compliments at them, accompanying their answers with happy and sonorous smiles that showed their white and even "coconut teeth."

Their soft and swaying hips attracted the gaze of the male that passed near them like a magnet; but their humble outfits [*humildes trajes*] and their naive and natural coquetry, although provocative, did not produce that other fluid of sensual attraction of those who trade with their bodies.

On the contrary, these were fresh and healthy girls capable of giving themselves for love, choosing the man they liked. Married or with a lover, they knew how to be faithful and to receive, with resignation, the good or bad luck that came with their choice or to feel happy when love arrived with good fortune . . .

The plaza presented . . . a pleasant and friendly picture, with that group of vendors, happy with their luck . . . those voices of the women vendors, [who] tried to obtain with their small industry, a few cents to take to their humble home to satisfy their urgent [financial] needs . . .[22]

Throughout the nineteenth and twentieth centuries, working-class trans and non-trans women as well as "very delicate men" (who may or may not have identified as women) continued to work in open-air markets, and in *mesones* (buildings that lodged out-of-town vendors and were located next to the markets). Their working-class status as well as their gender identity and/or gender expression put them in a disadvantaged position when it came to sexual harassment and assault, as evidenced in the following report in *El Comercio* from February 27, 1906: "Juan Miguel Robleto was arrested for impertinences with the mesonero, a very delicate man, like all of those who hold that job."[23] An important fact about this report is that it is, to my knowledge, the only documented case of someone being detained by the police for sexual harassment of an LGBTQIA+ person in western Nicaragua during the early twentieth century.

Jobs at tiangues and mesones were available to many different people. But in addition to the possibility of sexual harassment and assault, a long list of rules and regulations made it difficult for heterosexual cisgender women and LGBTQIA+ individuals to work there. Throughout the nineteenth and early twentieth centuries, the government, at the national and the local level, was adamant about creating "modern" markets to replace the traditionally Indigenous ones. Apparently, modernity in these spaces was partially predicated on the disruption of long-established "unhygienic" practices that enabled mothers (whether biological or not) to work. Among other things, officials became obsessed with the presence of young children of breastfeeding age (approximately zero to five years of age) in the markets. Thus, new laws were passed to prohibit market workers from bringing young children to work. In 1906 the market police were to be held liable if these laws were broken:

> The Market police will be held responsible for the lack of compliance with the last provision, which strictly prohibits taking children who are breastfeeding to that establishment as well as their presence there. Interested people take note.[24]

That law failed to work, as *El Comercio* noted two weeks later:

> Until now the police order has not taken effect regarding the prohibition of not taking children of breastfeeding age to the central market, since one finds such creatures everywhere.[25]

Faced with absolute failure, the authorities five years later decided to not ban the actual children but rather their beds and their presence on the floor:

> Under no circumstances will the use of hammocks be allowed inside the markets, nor will children of breastfeeding age be allowed on the floor.[26]

Given that market women today still take their young children and grandchildren to work in Nicaragua's open-air markets, it is fair to say that the 1911 law was yet another failure. Moreover, it appears to be that the authorities gave up on this issue after 1911, for I have found no additional laws that attempted to ban the presence of young children in the markets. This did not mean, however, that all women could work unencumbered in the markets, or anywhere else for that matter, for there were other laws that regulated certain women's ability to work outside the home.

Documenting women's ability to work outside the home is crucial to writing a more accurate and inclusive women's history, one that includes trans women and lesbians. As groundbreaking U.S. historian Lillian Faderman has noted in her work on the history of lesbians in the United States during the twentieth century:

Before women [in the U.S.] could live as lesbians the society in which they lived had to evolve to accommodate, however grudgingly, the possibility of lesbianism—the conception needed to be formulated; urbanization and its relative anonymity and population abundance were important; it was necessary that institutions be established where they could meet women with similar interests; it was helpful that the country enjoyed sufficient population growth so that pressure to procreate was not overwhelming; it was also helpful that the issues of sexuality and sexual freedom became increasingly open; and *it was most crucial that women have the opportunity for economic self-sufficiency* [my emphasis] . . .[27]

While the history of Nicaragua is very different from that of the United States, women's ability to be financially independent is crucial to LGBTQIA+ history in both places. In the case of Nicaragua, where the vast majority of women had historically worked outside the home before the conquest *and* during the colonial period, "the opportunity for economic self-sufficiency" (albeit *minimal* self-sufficiency) was not a "modern" or recent achievement. Other "rights," particularly for single women over twenty-five, were also not new.

THE LAW, WOMEN, AND WORK

During the colonial period and the nineteenth century, Nicaraguan women, like most women throughout Latin America, had more legal rights than most people today imagine. Ironically, many assume that the very restrictive laws that governed married (white) women's lives in the United States were even more restrictive in places like Nicaragua. It was in the United States and England that nineteenth-century white married women could not write wills, could not inherit property, could not own property in their own names, and had little control over their own wages (obviously, the restrictions placed by white men *and white women* on enslaved women and other women of color were more severe than those endured by married white women).

Latin American women were governed by a different legal tradition.[28] The commonalities among women in so-called Spanish America make sense since the countries colonized by Spain shared the same laws during the colonial period. And even after independence many Latin American countries simply copied each other's legal codes when it came to women's legal rights.[29]

Although no Latin American woman could opt for the priesthood, vote, or hold office in the nineteenth century, non-enslaved single women over twenty-five in Nicaragua basically had all the legal rights that men of their same age, race, and class had. They could own, administer, and inherit property. They could write their own wills. They could also litigate and serve as witnesses without having to ask anyone for permission. Non-enslaved *married* women, on the other hand, had limited juridical capacity (as did all enslaved women *and* men).

The restrictions on free married Nicaraguan women after independence (all people in the Pacific and central regions were legally free after 1824) were largely a continuation of colonial policies and could be found in the civil code. Article 132 of Nicaragua's 1867 civil code, based on the Chilean civil code drafted by the legislator Andrés Bello (1781–1865), stated that "the husband owes the woman protection and the woman owes the husband obedience."[30] Out of 2,524 articles in the code, this was one of two that included the word *obedience*. The other, article 222, stated that legitimate children owed obedience to their father and mother but "will be especially subjected to their father."[31] These articles remained intact when the civil code was amended in 1871. The crux of the matter was that, although married women could own property and inherit it, and in fact owned half of the goods acquired in a marriage due to the existence of community property (*sociedad conyugal*), their husbands were legally tasked with administering their property, unless other arrangements, such as a prenuptial agreement, had been made.[32] Moreover, women needed their husbands' authorization for most legal activities, including participating as litigants and working outside the home. Article 139 of the 1867 civil code stated, "Without the written authorization of the husband, the married woman cannot appear at trial on her own or with an attorney, whether suing or defending herself."[33] Article 140 went on to specify that

> Without the authorization of the husband, woman cannot enter into any contracts, nor withdraw from a previous contract, nor remit a debt, nor accept or repudiate a donation, inheritance, or legacy, nor acquire an onerous or lucrative title, nor alienate, mortgage, or pawn.[34]

To add insult to injury, article 141 stated, "The husband's authorization must be granted in writing, or by expressly and directly intervening himself in the act. The authorization of the husband cannot be presumed, except in the cases that the law has provided."[35]

A separate section of the civil code dealt specifically with women who worked outside the home. Article 153 stated that

> If the married woman exercises a profession or regular industry, such as that of school director, school teacher, actress, midwife, innkeeper, wet nurse [*nodriza*]; the general authorization of the husband is presumed for all the acts and contracts related to her profession or industry, as long as there is no claim or protest from her husband that intervenes.[36]

Additionally, a totally separate article in the civil code dealt exclusively with married market vendors. Article 154 stated: "The married woman merchant is subject to the special rules dictated in the Commerce Code."[37] The 1869 commerce code added additional restrictions to married women who wished to engage in commerce. In article 3, it noted that women could be merchants [*comerciantes*] as long as they had "license from their husbands" and "had already turned twenty one."[38] And there were even more specifications in article 4, which stated that "the women who exercise commerce with license from their husbands bind their assets and those of the conjugal partnership of any kind in their contracts."[39]

By 1914, the commerce code placed no constraints on married women who wished to engage in commerce.[40] Even earlier, in 1904,[41] the civil code had eliminated previous restrictions on married women's rights, including the order that women obey their husbands in almost everything, a legal concept known as *potestad marital*. Moreover, while the word *obedience* disappeared from the 1904 civil code, this new code provided a definition of marriage that did not necessarily benefit women. Although by 1904 civil marriage was the only one recognized by the state,[42] article 94 of the 1904 civil code proclaimed that "marriage is a solemn contract by which a man and a woman are united for life, and its purpose is procreation and mutual aid."[43] The emphasis on procreation (based on Catholic doctrine that would eventually change with the reforms of Vatican II in the twentieth century) would solidify the heterosexual nature of marriage for years to come. And it underscored the fact that secular laws were not necessarily less patriarchal than Catholic ones.

While married women finally gained the right to administer and manage their own property in the 1904 civil code, other changes made in that same code put some women at an economic disadvantage.[44] As noted earlier, laws rarely affect all members of a group equally, even when they are expected to. This differentiation of outcome was particularly obvious in the aftermath of land privatization.

The takeover of Indigenous lands in the late 1800s had mixed results for Indigenous women, depending on their geographical location and the local circumstances. While it was disastrous for many Indigenous women elsewhere, in the Indigenous community of Diriomo the historian Elizabeth Dore found that some women ended up benefiting on a personal level from privatization. This was because the land that was owned by the Comunidades Indígenas (which were patriarchal colonial inventions) was governed by men. And privatization meant that some individual Indigenous women could get a title to a plot of land. Dore argues the following:

> One of the gendered contradictions of liberalism is that land privatization destroyed the very basis of the community's collective existence and created preconditions for the commodification of land. However, that same process partially freed women from dependence on men's command over property, and by extension from patriarchal control. Where women's land rights had rested on being a constituent part of a family unit, after the revolution in land, women were able to claim private property in their own name. Consequently, the liberal impulse and the politics of land privatization conferred on the women of Diriomo's comunidad indígena certain, albeit limited, individual rights.[45]

While it is beyond the scope of this book, Dore's work paves the way for much more research to be done on the ways in which some Indigenous women's ability to own land in the nineteenth century intersected with LGBTQIA+ history. Her work also suggests important links between women's marital status, women's ability to own land, and women's participation in the cash economy. My hope is that other scholars will build on Dore's work and write local economic histories that center LGBTQIA+ experiences.

ESTABLISHING THE INDEPENDENT NATION'S FIRST ANTI-SODOMY LAW AND THE ONGOING MONITORING OF HETEROSEXUALITY

This section of the chapter documents the ways in which local and national elites attempted to regulate all sexuality so as to impose their own version/s of heteronormativity on the brand-new nation. In 1826, when Nicaragua was no longer a Spanish colony but still part of the Federal Republic of Central America, a decree was passed to punish those who were found guilty of committing "sodomy," an undefined offense. Punishment was three years in jail for first-time offenders. Recidivism brought about a doubling of the sentence.[46] It is noted within the decree itself that the three-year sentence replaced the death sentence, which had been abolished with independence:

> Considering: that the federal Constitution abolished the death penalty [*la pena del último suplicio*], which was the punishment for the nefarious criminal: and wishing to substitute in its place the most adaptable of the benefactor institutions that govern us, it has seen fit to decree and decrees
>
> 1°. Every person regardless of their status ... will suffer a sentence of three years in prison.
>
> 2°. In the case of a first recivicism, the penalty will be doubled, in a second it will be tripled, and so on....[47]

Elites used carrots and sticks to encourage the mostly rural, mostly poor, mostly Indigenous and mixed-race inhabitants of the new nation to learn to act as sexually "civilized" and "decent" heterosexual people throughout the nineteenth century. The eradication and prevention of homosexuality were considered fundamental for the formation of the "moral" and modern nation-state before Nicaragua separated from the Central American Federation in 1838 and after. The postindependence state also depended on the legal, political, economic, and sexual subordination of women. The monitoring and surveillance of women's sexuality was key to the establishment of the modern heterostate, but so was the monitoring and surveillance of all expressions of men's sexuality, including heterosexuality. In this respect, what U.S. scholar Robert McKee Irwin writes about nineteenth-century Mexico is also true about Nicaragua during that same period:

> [Unchecked h]eterosexuality... was feared... Bonds of matrimony (heterosexuality's civilized form) ... do not last, not because of competing homosexual relations... but because of the inadequacy of heterosexual desire of maintaining its own institutions... The institutions that promote heterosexuality and attempt to civilize it are under constant threat from heterosexuality itself....[48]

I would add to Irwin's analysis that the imposition of heterosexuality was crucial to women's subordination and vice versa, although, ironically, sexism itself often got in the way of cementing patriarchal relations. For example, if women needed to be subordinate to their husbands, women needed to be married, usually for life. But what if the father of a woman's child did not want to marry her to begin with?

In Nicaragua, as was the case of Mexico documented by Irwin and others, homosocial relationships (social interactions solely between men or solely between women) predominated in the nineteenth century. Irwin has argued that in Mexico, "male homosocial bonding, with or without women as intermediaries," was "the major means of allegorizing national integration" in the nineteenth century.[49] Historian Justin Wolfe's research reveals that a similar situation took place in Nicaragua. Wolfe cites Supreme Director Jose Nuñez in 1834 wishing "that Nicaragua be a family of brothers."[50] Unlike Irwin's study, which focuses primarily on literature, my research on the nineteenth century relies more heavily on newspaper accounts and legal records such as constitutions, decrees, regulations, and codes to document elite national imaginaries. Surely future studies on Nicaragua will build on this one and attempt to address the historical development of Nicaraguan masculinities in light of Irwin's thought-provoking work. The next few sections of this chapter go on to address the ways in which women's and men's heterosexuality was curtailed and monitored in the nineteenth century so as to create the sexually ideal nation elites desired.

THE MUJER HONRADA AS A LEGAL CONCEPT IN THE NINETEENTH CENTURY

Initially, all government officials were men, and even though they had differing views on the political future of Nicaragua, they agreed on the important role women needed to play as wives and mothers. Even the male politicians who advocated on behalf of giving women limited political, legal, and social rights in the 1830s thought women's most important roles were in the home, which was heterosexual by definition.[51] The new laws passed during this period would reflect this priority by centering the figure of "the honest woman" (*la mujer honrada*),[52] a creature with an impeccable or close-to-impeccable heterosexual history.

The mujer honrada (present also during the colonial era) was codified in the new nation's legal apparatus in the mid-1800s. For instance, the mujer honrada makes an appearance in article 78 of the 1848 draft of the constitution.[53] Had this draft become law, the constitution would have only protected citizens, who by definition or implicitly were men, and "honest women," from the crime of breaking and entering. Presumably, women who were not "honest" and whose homes were violated would be at the mercy of home invasions:

> Anyone who, not being authorized by law enters violently into the home of a citizen or an honest woman, and the one who is authorized but enters violently without the . . . procedures prescribed by law, will be imprisoned for assault in a home.[54]

A few years later, the "Regulatory law for the tribunals and the courts of the Republic" stated that "honest women" had to give their declarations for any criminal or civil cases from home, just like the elderly and the sick would:

> The officials of the Supreme Powers, even when they are not in office, the Ministers of the office, the General Commander, the priests who obtain jurisdiction, or dignity, the sick, the elderly over 70 years of age, and the honest women, all must give testimony from home.[55]

The construct was even enshrined in the 1854 draft of the constitution, which stated in article 84 that the homes of honest women who were heads of household could be searched only under the circumstances allowed by law:

> The home of any inhabitant of the Republic is a sacred asylum. And they can only be searched, in the cases and with the formalities that the law determines, doing it in such a way that greater consideration be given to citizens, and to honest women, heads of family.[56]

One could argue that the specific inclusion of "honest" women heads of households (presumably women who through no fault of their own had been widowed or abandoned by their husbands and/or the fathers of their children) in the constitution was an important acknowledgment that there were indeed many households headed by women at that time in Nicaragua, a trend that is still evident today.[57] Notably, for our purposes, is that there appeared to be a consensus among the elite early on in the republic that a woman's honor could potentially remain intact if she had children yet lived without a man. In other words, being a single mother in and of itself did not make a woman "dishonest."

Of course, it is crucial to point out that there was no "honest woman" without her counterpart, the "public woman" or sexually suspect woman, who, according to the constitution, would have fewer legal rights than an "honest" one. Not surprisingly, the constitution was silent on who got to decide whether or not a woman was "honest." Women's identities in the nineteenth century were impacted by their sexual status, as they had been in colonial times,[58] and this in turn affected their legal and political rights.

LINKING MARRIAGE, FATHERHOOD, AND WEALTH TO CITIZENSHIP

As long as they were married to Nicaraguan men, and not foreigners, western Nicaraguan women's marital status during the nineteenth century did not affect their limited citizenship status. Their gender alone prevented them from being full citizens with voting rights.[59] In fact, the idea of women having political rights was so inconceivable to most male politicians that they did not even feel a need to specify in the early constitutions that only men could be citizens. The 1848 and 1854 constitutional *drafts* did state that men alone could be citizens. However, the 1858 constitution did not specifically state that only men had that right. Women would eventually be explicitly excluded from citizenship in the 1939 constitution. They then became passive citizens under the 1950 constitution and full citizens, with voting rights, in 1955.[60]

Very young wealthy men, however, could demonstrate they were able to handle the duties of citizenship by being ready for the duties of heterosexual marriage, effectively underscoring the importance of heterosexuality for citizenship. Thus, as early as 1824, article 14 of the constitution indicated that men under the age of eighteen who had "some useful profession or known means of subsistence" could be citizens if they were married.[61] Later on, the constitutional draft of 1848 would have allowed wealthy young men under twenty-one to become citizens if they were married.[62] In the end, article 8 of the 1858 constitution changed marriage to fatherhood as a prerequisite for citizenship for those wealthy young men of "good conduct" between the ages of eighteen and twenty-one: "Citizens are: the Nicaraguans . . . who are eighteen years old who . . . are parents . . ."[63]

Citizenship was a new concept after independence, not equivalent to reaching the age of majority, a colonial concept linked to *patria potestad* (a father's authority over his legitimate children),[64] which was already familiar to Nicaraguans. Given the new laws regarding citizenship, there was so much confusion over when men and women reached the age of majority after independence that Congress in 1881 felt a need to pass a decree "clarifying the law of . . . 1875, regarding the legal age [of adulthood]." The decree stated: "[male?] Nicaraguans who have turned twenty one years of age are of legal age. However, those who are younger than twenty five will not be able to hold the positions of Judge, Administrator of Public Treasuries, and property of minors as guardians, nor the offices of Notary or Advisor."[65] Ironically, this clarification raised more questions than it answered. When and under what circumstances men under twenty-five could achieve certain rights remained unclear during this period. Like their colonial predecessors, postcolonial elites had mixed feelings about granting power and rights to young people, in this case specifically to young men, since unmarried young women under twenty-five would not gain rights and privileges until much later.

A few decades later, article 20 of the 1893 constitution under the Liberal general Zelaya would expand male citizenship: "All Nicaraguans over the age of 18 are citizens, and those over 16 who are married or who know how to read and write."[66] Automatic citizenship at eighteen or even twenty-one was an improvement over the colonial era and most of the nineteenth century, when unmarried young men reached the age of majority at twenty-five. But patria potestad would continue to be the law of the land until 1982, when the Sandinista revolution abolished it in favor of one that gave both fathers and mothers custody over minors.[67]

Although mothers and fathers in the early twenty-first century have parity in legal guardianship, the age of majority in Nicaragua, which is stipulated in the 2015 family code (Código de la familia) as eighteen for both men and women, does not apply to everything. As is the case in many other countries, Nicaraguans become adults at eighteen, but there are certain privileges, rights, and responsibilities that are acquired at different ages. For instance, young people can get married without consent of their parents after the age of sixteen. And Nicaragua is one of the few countries in the world where sixteen-year-olds can vote. But parents in Nicaragua today are obligated to support their children (*manutención de alimentos*) until the age of twenty-four.[68] In other words, as in the nineteenth century, the age of majority continues to function independently of citizenship rights like voting. Nonetheless, the exclusionary practices that abounded in the 1800s, and were particularly obvious in the law, have disappeared.

In the nineteenth century, elites believed that citizenship and other rights were not meant for everyone, and they purposefully excluded those individuals who they believed were not "fit" enough, hence the emphases on gender, literacy, employment, age, reputation, marriage, fatherhood, and property ownership. Political independence did not automatically lead to inclusion. And those who *were* included were not included equally, a subject discussed in further depth below.

MEN'S BEHAVIOR, CITIZENSHIP, AND RIGHTS

Under colonialism, the Spanish had been very concerned with circumscribing women's and men's heterosexuality and preventing and punishing sexual relationships that today would be considered LGBTQIA+ ones. Indeed, the Spanish were concerned with eradicating sexual and gender behaviors that, in their minds, would make people dishonorable. But the obsession with propriety went beyond the gender and/or sexual desires of colonial subjects. The colonial world was so divided into the categories of "worthy" and "not worthy" that elites even classified occupations that had nothing to do with sex or gender as honorable and honest, or as dishonorable and dishonest. For example, it was not until 1783 that the Spanish Crown declared manual crafts to be "honest and honorable," thus allowing artisans to hold municipal office.[69] Postcolonial elites were also eager to ascribe moral labels to almost all aspects of daily lives. As has been noted about Latin America as a whole, during the early postcolonial period, "in their attempts to build strong and stable states, national elites ... continued the trend begun during the Enlightenment ... increasing the degree to which they regulated the lives of citizens."[70] Thus, in order to become citizens and obtain and retain certain rights, Nicaraguan men after independence had to accept a series of rules that bolstered specific heterosexual practices and put some limits on their overall sexual and financial freedoms.

Not surprisingly, a man's heterosexual promiscuity was not specifically mentioned as an impediment for legal rights in any of the constitutions or anywhere else, for that matter, which was a clear example of the gender-based double standard that was so pervasive at the time with regard to heterosexual activity. Nonetheless, this did not mean that men could do whatever they wanted within the confines of heterosexual/patriarchal relationships. Men were constantly being reminded that there were limits placed on their heterosexual behavior. These limits were imposed by the state and the Catholic Church but often implemented by local elites, which meant that men potentially had a great deal of leeway. Men often broke the rules and suffered no consequences or very few consequences, especially when compared to the potentially dire consequences women could suffer for similar behavior. However, if a man had enemies in high places, even something as commonplace as heterosexual adultery could get him into a great deal of trouble.

Efforts to mold heteromasculinities can be found in article 14 of the 1824 constitution, quoted earlier, which made citizenship available only to men "as long as they have known means of subsistence," presumably seeking to exclude thieves as well as sex brokers/procurers (pimps), gamblers, and vagrants, the latter a catchall category. This constitution also stated that a man's rights as citizen could be suspended "due to criminal proceedings in which an arrest warrant was issued for a crime that, according to the law, deserves more than a correctional penalty." I have found only one example of this. In 1881 Captain Simón Corea was found guilty of abuse of authority against Brigade Sargeant Francisco Javier Elizondo. As a result, Corea was imprisoned, and his patria potestad and marital authority (*autoridad marital*) were taken away from him. By

1882, however, all his rights had been restored to him, and he was able to hold office and exercise all his political and legal rights.[71]

The 1824 constitution also made it posible for a man to lose his citizenship "for conduct notoriously full of vices" or "for physical or moral incapacity qualified as such by the judiciary."[72] The 1826 and the 1838 constitutions were similar to the 1824 one. Clearly, these constitutional articles could be interpreted as restrictions on homosexual relationships, although I have yet to find evidence that they were ever used at all, which might simply indicate that the nation was so new and so poor that having their citizenship taken away from them was irrelevant to most men. Nonetheless, the fact that it was in writing was significant, for it conveyed to the population at large the values of their new rulers.

The 1848 draft of the constitution was similar to the previous constitutions but added that (male) citizens needed to have "notoriously honest conduct" and that an individual man needed a "profession that grants him the means to live honestly." Additionally, in the draft, a man could lose his citizenship "due to ungratefulness towards his parents . . . for abandoning his wife or his legitimate children, notoriously failing in his family obligations."[73] The 1858 constitution ended up including article 11, which made it possible for a man to lose his citizenship "due to ungratefulness towards his parens or *unjust* abandonment of his wife or legitimate children."[74] The difference between "abandoning his wife" and "*unjust* abandonment of his wife" in theory could have been significant, for it forced the woman in a marriage to prove that the abandonment was "unjust." However, I again have no evidence that any man ever lost his citizenship over this issue, even though I assume women did take their husbands to court over unjust abandonment.

The U.S. historian Bradford Burns argued that during this difficult and violent period of Nicaraguan history it was the family (understood as the heterosexual family) that elites looked to as a stabilizing force in society, and not the individual. He cited the Friends of Progress, who, in 1849, stated that "morality, property, and family" constituted the foundation of society. Burns also argued that elites believed that extirpating immorality would "strengthen the family and thus order and stability."[75] The focus on marriage was intrinsically connected to an interest in promoting and preserving the heterosexual family and thus the nation. Burns quoted the controversial Nicaraguan priest Agustín

Vijil (1801–67), who proclaimed that "only marriage can preserve society and guard morality."[76]

Nowhere was the importance of the family to the nation-state more obvious than in article 106 of the 1871 civil code, which linked the legal concepts of patria potestad and *autoridad* (also known as potestad marital, or a husband's authority over his wife) to the well-being of the family and the country. This article explicitly noted that men could not renounce the privileges they had been automatically awarded over their wives and their children, because the power they had been granted was for the benefit of societal *order* and not for their own benefit:

> Laws that are of interest to public order are those whose main purpose is the general interest of society. As they do not only concern the private interests of citizens, citizens cannot validly renounce them. Thus the husband cannot renounce marital power nor the father parental authority. The stipulations that these people made regarding such resignations would be null, because the marital and paternal authorities ["la potestad marital y paterna"] are institutions of public interest since without them there would be no order in families.[77]

In order to protect marriage and bolster women's subordination to men even more, and lacking the immense power of the colonial Inquisition to broadly prosecute those who were sexually suspect, postindependence elites enacted new laws to punish women who strayed from patriarchal norms. One of these laws penalized adulterous wives and was added as a new article in early 1865 to the existing penal code. It stated: "The woman who with full consent and without a superior force that compels her, commits adultery, will be punished with a sentence of one to eight months in prison."[78]

No such laws were ever passed after independence punishing men for "simple" adultery. The laws that punished a man for adultery did so only if he had sex with another man's wife or brought his mistress to live in the same house as his wife. For instance, the 1873 penal code stated the following in article 338:

> The husband who, offending his legitimate wife, maintains a concubine in the same house as his own wife, and without her consent: or forces her

due to bad treatment to leave his house because of the concubine . . . will suffer a fine of no less than three hundred and no more than six hundred pesos, will be jailed no less than three and no more than six months, and will lose his civil rights for a year.[79]

Here is evidence of men being threatened with punishment for something that they could have in theory been entitled to in a patriarchal society. This specific type of adultery was punished because it failed to meet the elite vision of proper heterosexuality. Nonetheless, I have not found evidence that any man was ever punished for adultery in this way. Moreover, it is important to point out that the law was not punishing adultery per se but rather what would amount to informal bigamy, a sexual crime associated in the Spanish, criollo, and mestizo minds with Indigenous practices.

SEX WORK IN THE NINETEENTH CENTURY

Postindependence male elites feared cheating wives and punished them harshly. Adulterous women were considered a threat to marriage, since the assumption was that no man would stay married to one, given the possibility of potentially leaving an inheritance to a nonbiological child, among other fears. But these same elites had mixed feelings about female prostitution. Over the course of the nineteenth and twentieth centuries, elites passed laws to suppress (criminalize) it, and other times they enacted laws to regulate (legalize) it. During most of the nineteenth century there appeared to be a pro-suppression/criminalization consensus in Nicaragua.

In 1852 the Nicaraguan director of state decreed that the newly created police judges and police governors (*jueces de policías* and *gobernadores de policías*) would have to, among their many tasks, "enforce the laws that prohibit games of luck and chance, as well as prostitution and public houses destined to such immoral objects."[80] Ten years later, the law was even more explicit. Under the heading of "Public decency and good customs," article 63 of the 1862 police regulation stated:

The police must exercise the most constant supervigilance so that there are no houses of prostitution, nor places destined to the reprehensible practices of debauchery and depravity ["del desenfreno y del libertinaje"]. When the existence of one of these houses is discovered, they must be suppressed immediately, promoting in accordance with the law the punishment of the people who guard and direct them.[81]

The 1880 police regulation had even greater detail in its description of the crime of prostitution and those who committed it. The regulation stated in chapter 12, article 127 that both *rufianes* (procurers/madams/pimps) and prostitutes "will be considered as vagrants and will be punished as such."[82] This was pretty consistent with laws throughout Latin America and elsewhere, where categorizing sex workers as vagrants had a purpose: "to make a link between perversion and poverty."[83] The U.S. historian Sandra Lauderdale Graham, for example, notes that in Brazil in the late 1880s, women suspected of being sex workers were charged as vagabonds and with provoking disorder.[84] This was also the case in Costa Rica, both before and after laws were passed to regulate prostitution.[85] Once regulation became the law in Costa Rica in the late 1800s and prostitution was considered "a trade" (*un oficio*), anti-vagrancy laws were used against clandestine sex workers who were "considered a threat against the health of the nation."[86]

One crucial point to make about the 1880 police regulation is the definition of a "prostitute." Article 126 stated the following:

> A woman prostitute is understood to be one who habitually traffics her honor, committing [*entregándose*] to the vice of sensuality.[87]

Why did the law seek to define who was a "woman prostitute"? Why the need to include the word *woman*? For those of us interested in LGBTQIA+ history, this raises a flag. Could it be that the police were aware of sex workers who were LGBTQIA+ even though there were no laws to prohibit their engagement in sex work? Was there confusion over whether men or trans women engaging in sex work would be prosecuted under "sodomy" or "prostitution," and this was a way of clarifying that it would fall under "sodomy"? While we do not fully know the answers to these questions, we do know that, in theory, prostitution was gendered in such a way as to only be a cis woman's crime. In practice, however, some men and trans women might have been prosecuted for prostitution.

This might have been the case in Managua on August 30, 1905, when *El Comercio* reported that "the police in this capital are actively prosecuting vagrancy, drunkenness, and prostitution. The day before yesterday more than 30 individuals, of both sexes, entered correction."[88] We might never know whether there were any LGBTQIA+ individuals among those in this group persecuted for sex work. We do know, however, that the emphasis was usually on preventing and punishing female sex work, and many women were punished for sex work.

It was common for newspapers to report the names of women arrested for sex work and to give brief details about them. For example, in 1905, right below an ad for pills to treat syphilis, the newspaper *El Comercio* reported the following: "María Ordeñana of flawed conduct [*de conducta viciada*] was taken to corrections: police officer Benito Ramírez captured her at eleven pm the night before last. Josefa Madríz de León, single and 38 years old, was captured for the same reason."[89] But sex workers did not necessarily accept their capture peacefully, and they sometimes fought back against police brutality.

In 1906 *El Comercio* reported that Isaura Pérez resisted arrest by the police:

> As a measure of morality the police tried to pick up those women who had no trade, and since the young Isaura Pérez was included among them, the police officer Mercedes Cinco proceeded to capture her, receiving bites and all kinds of insults from her. Not being able to carry out the capture, due to Pérez's opposition, the director of the Police gave his orders to the policeman Felicitos Mendoza so that using the authority he exercises, he would reduce the opponent to obedience in accordance with article 14 of the Pol., so that the action of the authority would not be mocked.[90]

This description of what happened was a summary provided by the police director to the "judge from the 2nd criminal district, responding to the discharge order that the judge requested for policeman Mendoza, who was accused of abuse of authority."[91]

The punishments for women accused of engaging in sex work varied a great deal. Paula Aguilar, for instance, was detained for thirty days in 1906: "she was given thirty days of arrest for vagrancy and engaging in bad activities [por vaga y mal entretenida]."[92] Other women appeared to have been fined. Still others, like María Zelaya, were made to work for the city: "she was sentenced to 30 days of public works for having vagrancy as a profession and living a bad life [por ser vaga de profesión y de mal vivir]."[93]

Even when sex work was eventually regulated (legalized), after 1918, on paper women were the only ones regulated as prostitutes. That said, there were plenty of other laws in addition to the anti-sodomy law that could be used to punish and prosecute male sex workers, men who wore "women's clothing" (even for religious celebrations or festivals), and men who had sex with other men—as well, of course, as women who had sexual relations with other women and women who wore "men's clothing." For instance, the following municipal ordinance was passed in 1875:

> Those who offend public morals with words or acts that are dishonest and repugnant—will be fined 4 reales.[94]

There were other laws too. For example, article 68 of the 1862 police regulation specifically targeted men who cross-dressed in public:

> Since in public festivals there are often those who appear masked, dressed as priests, as military men, or as members of other professions that are of a public nature: similarly men dressed as women or semi naked or making obscene gestures in public view, all the police employees must make sure that such corruption is destroyed, jailing every person dressed in such a manner.[95]

As was the case during the colonial period, after independence laws against immorality were being passed to target specific people, places, and practices. In addition to targeting public feasts, politicians continuously sought to target markets, which remained predominantly working-class spaces. The 1882 laws for the Central Managua market included the following article:

> Art. 7°—The following incur a penalty of a fifty cents fine:
>
> *Whoever utters swear words*
> *Whoever commits dishonest or immoral actions*

> *Whoever exhibits or sells figures or stamps that offend morality and good manners.*[96]

As noted earlier, markets were, from the perspective of elites, places with a high degree of potential for lewd behavior, especially sex work. This was in part because markets were working-class hubs where women (including trans women) and men interacted freely, and in part because markets were open at nighttime and early in the morning, all before the advent of electricity in Nicaragua. For instance, the Central Market was open from 4:00 a.m. to 9:00 p.m., which meant that it needed to be lit with lamps for about five hours a day. Since elites worried about what poor people might do when they gathered together in the dark, the law stressed that the market intendent had to enforce these rules:

> 2.°—Do not allow drunk people or those of notoriously bad conduct to enter the building.
> 3.°—Prevent immoral, impudent, and dishonest actions from being committed.
> 4.°—Do not allow words to be spoken if they injure modesty or honesty, or if they offend decorum in some way.[97]

The Central Market was considered so dangerous that the law stated that the intendent was also in charge of making sure children and servants did not become corrupt when they spent time shopping there:

> 11—Do not allow children or servants who come to make purchases to stay longer than is necessary.[98]

The laws regulating the Central Market also included one of Nicaragua's first anti-graffiti and anti-vandalism laws and what appears to be an early precursor of the bathroom bills debated in the United States in the late 2010s and 2020s. Those committing either of the following infractions were to be fined fifty cents:

> The person who uses a latrine [*excusado*] destined for a different sex. Whoever writes on, stains, deteriorates, or damages in any way the doors, windows, walls, or any part of the building . . .[99]

I do not know the initial reasoning behind creating a gendered latrine system or what provoked the fines against men and women using the same excusado in 1882. However, I do know that during this decade new laws were emphasizing the need to separate individuals in other contexts. Incarcerated women were to be housed separately from men. Youth under eighteen were being separated from adults in jails, and new laws explicitly allowed some prisoners to have better conditions in jail than others, at the discretion of judges.[100] The separation of individuals according to gender, age, and status was not something new, and it made a lot of sense to elites who wanted to prevent prostitution and other immoral behaviors like "fornication" (sex between people not married to each other) from taking place in latrines or jails while simultaneously modernizing their institutions by copying foreign models.

There is, of course, a small chance that latrines were gendered due to a concern over the sexual assault of women. This is unlikely, however, because elite men were not overly preoccupied with preventing or punishing sexual assault, especially not when it happened to working-class women who were by elite definition already considered sexually suspect. In fact, it seemed that, for elite men, sexual violence against women was as heinous a crime as *adultery* engaged in by women, given the sentencing for these crimes. For instance, the punishment for an adulterous woman was up to eight months in prison in 1865.[101] But the punishment for kidnapping by force for sexual purposes (*rapto por fuerza*)[102] or incest (with a direct line of consanguinity) was not much greater in 1851: imprisonment (*presidio*) of six to eighteen months and a fine of a hundred to three hundred pesos:

> Kidnapping by force [rapto por fuerza] and incest in a direct line of consanguinity will be punished with imprisonment [presidio] between 6 and 18 months and a fine of 100 to three hundred pesos: incest in the transversal line of consanguinity in the second degree will be [punished] as the others, the difference being that instead of presidio, they will be put in prison [*prisión*]. The other incests and kidnapping by seduction [*rapto por seducción*] will be [punished] by 6 to 12 months of prison [prisión] and a fine of 60 to 150 pesos.[103]

Additional evidence for making a case that politicians were not too concerned with preventing sexual violence against women is that none of the laws regarding prostitution sought to protect sex workers from potential violence enacted by their clients. In fact, the men who paid for sex were never mentioned at all in the law, and women sex workers (and sometimes their procurers) were made to bear the entire burden for their "crime." I have found only one mention of clients at all during this period. In 1883 the "Statutes for the Philarmonic Society of Granada" ("Estatutos de la sociedad filarmónica de Granada") were approved by the government. In those statutes, among the duties of the president was to "watch over the conduct of the partners, finding out if they get drunk, engage in prostitution [*entregan a la prostitución*] or if they play prohibited games." The statutes then proceeded to lay out potential punishments ("a fifty-cent fine for each offense") for members who engaged in excessive drinking, prohibited games, or concubinage (cohabitation without marriage), but *not* prostitution: "This fine will be double or triple in the first and second [instance of] recidivism; and if the person being fined does not reform, he will be expelled from the Society."[104]

There is yet another explanation for the separate latrines. It also could also be that elites then, like some elites now, in the United States and other places as well, wanted to prevent transgender women from using the women's latrine. This explanation seems plausible, given the presence of transgender women working in the markets.

PROSTITUTION: FROM CRIMINALIZATION TO LEGALIZATION

While Nicaragua was embracing the suppression of prostitution, or rather the criminalization and persecution of sex workers, other Latin American nations had moved on to regulating or legalizing it. Regulation in Latin America generally took place after the 1860s and had to do with a myriad of factors, among them religion, imperialism, and the much-sought-after goal of modernity. Initially, regulation tended to be favored by Catholic countries, according to U.S. historian Donna Guy and others who have studied the history of sex work in Latin America, since Catholics were more likely than Protestants to view prostitution as a "necessary evil," following the Augustinian and Thomist traditions.[105] However, self-interested imperialist nations as well as local modernizing elites often coincided in seeking regulation in the second half of the nineteenth century and during the early twentieth century in Latin America. The former sought to make it easier for their occupying military forces to have sexual relations with local women without fear of disease or retribution. The latter felt that involving the medical profession in the regulation of women's sexual lives was an important step in the path toward progress and greater control over the working classes.

The convergence of religion, imperialism, and modernity is perhaps best seen in Mexico, where sex work became regulated by the French after they invaded Mexico in 1865.[106] What happened in Mexico and other Latin American countries, as well as the U.S. Marines' presence in Nicaragua during the early twentieth century, would bring about a discussion in Nicaragua regarding a prophylaxis law in 1904 and eventually the regulation of sex work between 1918 and 1955.[107] Prophylaxis laws (understood as laws that regulated prostitution) were passed in 1918 and 1927; the 1927 law was eventually repealed and replaced in 1955.[108] Because the regulation of sex work in Nicaragua was meant in part to protect and indulge U.S. Marines in Nicaragua, Nicaraguans came to associate legalized sex work with U.S. imperialism.

Since the Somoza government (the right-wing regime backed for forty-three years by U.S. dollars) took over the administration of brothels after 1936, the figure of the sex worker and prostitution in general under the Somoza regime would become politicized. Prostitution, along with homosexuality, would become, in the public imaginary, clear examples of state-sponsored sexual deviancy and capitalist excess. This perception would eventually help make women sex workers targets of the new leftist Sandinista revolutionary regime in the post-1979 era.

The regulation of the bodies of women sex workers (perhaps including trans women?) from 1918 onward was extreme. When they were not being jailed for noncompliance, sex workers were being fined or forced to register and stand in line twice a week for regular medical checkups or forced into special clinics to treat sexually transmitted infections. Moreover, there were all sorts of restrictions on where they could live, what they could wear, what events they could attend, and whom they could interact with. For instance, they were not allowed to go anywhere with other sex workers except for the brothels they worked at. But they were also not allowed to interact with women of "good conduct," and they were not allowed to live near churches or schools. Even when they decided to leave sex work, women had a really hard time getting their names off the infamous "lists" of prostitutes that were created in each city, town, and village. At one point, they even needed someone to vouch for them and post bail for them to get off a list. Sex workers were, in effect, at the mercy not only of their brokers (madams and pimps) and their clients, but of doctors, local politicians, neighbors, and the local police officer in charge of supervising them, for the latter had almost complete control over their lives.[109]

Women in the nineteenth and twentieth centuries who were considered prostitutes were considered a threat to the nation's morals and its future, even when the men who railed against them sometimes paid for sex themselves, and many men and women saw prostitution as a "necessary evil." Some Nicaraguans did perceive prostitution in non-moralistic terms, noting the economic difficulties that made women turn to sex work as well as the exploitation and discrimination sex workers were subjected to by their procurers, clients, doctors, and the police. However, it was only in the late twentieth and early twenty-first century that sex workers themselves started organizing collectively to demand rights and gained a voice in public outlets, in large part as a result of feminist organizing.

WILLIAM WALKER

As noted earlier, William Walker was a racist Euroamerican who initially arrived in Nicaragua to aid members of the Nicaraguan Liberal Party in their ongoing civil war against the Conservative Party during the 1850s. Walker, however, had his own agenda, and instead of helping out the Liberals, he quickly proclaimed himself president of Nicaragua, instituted English as the official language, and brought back the enslavement of peoples of African ancestry. His actions soon united many Nicaraguans and other Central Americans against him, and William Walker was eventually defeated and shot to death. While short-lived, his time in Nicaragua had a long-lasting influence on the country's social, political, and sexual landscape, forever impacting Nicaraguan national identity.

Walker was born in 1824 in Nashville, Tennessee. He completed medical school at the University of Pennsylvania at the age of nineteen and then spent some time in Europe, where he learned German, Italian, and French. He eventually became an attorney in New Orleans but turned to journalism in the years preceding his incursion into filibustering. He was a writer and editor of newspapers in both New Orleans and San Francisco before leaving the United States to invade first Mexico, in 1853, and then Nicaragua in 1855. His press connections would prove particularly advantageous as he sought to gain popular support throughout the nation for his illegal mercenary adventures.[110]

Walker has been described as "the most dangerous international criminal of the nineteenth century" by the U.S. Pulitzer Prize–winning author T. J. Stiles.[111] Indeed, Walker caused tremendous destruction in Nicaragua and burned down the colonial city of Granada out of spite. But Walker was even more dangerous because of what he represented: a racist, arrogant, and expansionist version of the Euroamerican self. As U.S. historian Amy S. Greenberg notes, "[The ... U.S. American] critique of labor and manhood in Central America was hardly peripheral to the other claims for the naturalness of ... [a U.S.] presence in ... [Latin America] ... [N]othing was considered more natural than the ultimate triumph of white American manhood."[112]

Walker adamantly stated in one of the many public speeches he gave in the United States:

> I was not a mere soldier of fortune and adventure—risking the lives of my countrymen for selfish purposes—the actions of my hand prove a more noble purpose. If I have exerted myself for any thing and for any purpose, *it has been to extend American influence and Americanize Nicaragua* [emphasis in the original].[113]

Walker knew that even though not everyone in the United States agreed with his colonialist vision or his lawbreaking filibustering methods, his imperialist self-centered message still resonated in "middle America." The U.S. historian Robert E. May defines *filibusters* as "[U.S.]-American adventurers who raised or participated in private military forces that either invaded or planned to invade foreign countries with which the United States was formally at peace."[114] May went on to argue that the United States during the nineteenth century became a filibuster nation in the sense that "filibustering infiltrated American popular culture."[115]

This helps explain why, when Walker asked the twenty thousand people who came to hear him speak in New Orleans in 1857, "Who of you cannot feel proud of the spirit of manhood manifested by an American, one born within your midst?" the audience cheered in response.[116] Walker brought out the worst in his fellow Euroamericans, and that is how "he became one of the key cultural icons of the 1850s."[117] According to Greenberg he was particularly popular among white working-class men in the South and New York City.[118]

Walker was able to garner the support of white Americans, and white men in particular, by appealing to their racism. He called the war in Central America a "war of the races. The great battle of the mongrels and the white men."[119] Walker in fact saw the main "problem" in the Central American isthmus to be a racial one:

> Mongrelism was the secret of its waning fortune. What was to be done? It was left for us to Americanize Central America; on whom rests the right of regenerating the amalgamated race, and no other than the people of the United States, and especially of the Southern States, I call upon you to execute this mission.[120]

Walker's war in Nicaragua was a race war, and Walker fancied himself a race hero.[121] Not just any race hero. A manly race hero. And perhaps even a godly one. It turns out that Walker wanted white Americans to believe that Nicaraguan Indigenous peoples thought he was a God, "their rescuer and their messiah," effectively a "latter-day Quetzalcoatl."[122] Walker's newspaper in Nicaragua, *El Nicaragüense*, even made up an updated version of the Quetzalcoatl story, stating that there was an Indigenous tradition in Nicaragua that said they would be liberated from Spanish oppression by a "gray-eyed man."[123] The U.S. historian Camilla Townsend has debunked the myth that the Aztecs considered the Spanish conquistadors to be the god Quetzalcoatl, who supposedly was expected to come back to restore his kingdom. Her conclusions can be applied to the case of Nicaragua in the 1850s. Townsend argues that this narrative

> is essentially a pornographic vision of events, albeit in a political rather than a sexual sense . . . It perhaps comes as no surprise that the relatively powerful conquistadors and their cultural heirs should prefer to dwell

on the Indians' [supposed] adulation for them, rather than on their pain, rage, or attempted military defense.[124]

In addition to being racist and illegal, Walker's conquest of Nicaragua (and filibustering in general) was intrinsically linked to the very strong anti-Catholic sentiment which permeated U.S. society at the time. Several of Walker's supporters, for instance, wrote extensively on this topic, arguing that Nicaraguans needed to be liberated not just from themselves but from the Catholic Church. Anna Carroll was one of these supporters. She "pontificated . . . God wanted Walker to 'deliver' Nicaragua's 'misguided' people from the 'humiliating condition to which tyranny and priestcraft' reduced them."[125] If Walker could not be God, then at the very least he could be God's anti-Catholic messenger on earth.

Given the filibusters' prejudices against Catholics, it is ironic that Walker converted to Catholicism and actually received support from at least one priest in Nicaragua.[126] Much has been written in Nicaragua about Agustín Vijil, the priest who publicly supported Walker. José Dolores Gámez (1851–1918), one of Nicaragua's most prominent historians, strongly criticized Vijil and the entire priesthood in Nicaragua for their active and tacit support of the invader in his well-known book *Historia de Nicaragua*, published in 1889. Gámez wrote:

> The clergy, who could have been alarmed by the introduction of the Protestant element, were instead humble courtiers seen frequently in the waiting rooms of the autocrat, waiting as a favor for permission to enter to congratulate him for the good he was doing to Nicaragua. The jewels of the temples were given to him by the order of the Head of the Nicaraguan church, to be invested in the purchase of rifles and items of war: while the most notable people in the clergy, such as the Priest from Granada, don Agustín Vijil, who passed through the first sacred orator, exhausted the vocabulary of adulation, calling him from the tribune of the Holy Spirit "Tutelary Angel" and "North Star."[127]

Vijil's reasoning behind his support for Walker had to do in part with the way in which he thought the imperialists' presence in Nicaragua would impact the nation. In his most famous sermon, Vijil stated:

[Walker] would be the envoy of Providence to cure wounds and reconcile the Nicaraguan family that others had divided, because being the instrument of peace, achieving the end of such cruel hostilities, is to deserve the appreciation of this land afflicted by the worst of all misfortunes: civil War.[128]

As noted earlier in this chapter, Vijil believed the heterosexual family was the foundation of the nation, so it makes sense that he would act to preserve it. But there was no reason to believe that Walker's invasion would lead to the unification of Nicaraguan families torn apart by the ongoing conflicts between Liberals and Conservatives. This leads me to concur on this issue with the historian Michel Gobat's assessment that what Vijil valued, like many other Nicaraguans who initially welcomed Walker, was U.S.-style progress. Vijil felt Walker's presence would finally allow Nicaragua to "become part of the 'civilized world.'"[129] Initial support for Walker was so great in some sectors that some Nicaraguans even wrote songs in support of the invaders—before they quickly realized that he sought only his own aggrandizement. Gobat quotes the following song written and performed by Nicaraguans who welcomed Walker's forces:

O Patriots, sing
A thousand happy hymns
To the redeemer
Of our freedom.

The world amazed
Shall obey and respect
The intrepid son
Of the great Washington.

And Free Nicaragua
Shall forever proclaim,
Hail the conquering Walker!
Hail our Liberator![130]

The initial support that Walker received by some Nicaraguans has been strongly emphasized by Gobat. But it is clear to me, based on

Gobat's own vast research and my own, that most Nicaraguans (or most of Walker's non-Nicaraguan supporters, for that matter) could not have possibly understood Walker's intentions, given that Walker was more opportunistic, egotistical, and manipulative than anything else, changing his mind when it benefited him and telling people what he thought they wanted to hear.[131]

While Walker was not interested in healing the partisan wounds in Nicaraguan families, his expedition was as much about gender and sexuality as it was about religion and race. Amy Greenberg, for instance, argues that "Nicaragua became the perfect place" for white "men [from the United States] to reclaim their manhood" at a time when white manhood was in great flux.[132] Another historian, Robert E. May, has noted that "filibustering was a lopsidedly male activity, readily identified with the nation's footloose young men, especially southerners bent on expanding slavery and restless urbanites."[133] May cites Shelley Streeby's work on novels of the period, where "'empire-building in the Americas' provided 'possibly redemptive sites' for the rehabilitation of 'damaged urban masculinities.'"[134] Walker and his ilk believed they could do a better job at protecting "mongrel" women than "mongrel" men could. That is how inferior they believed "brown" men to be.[135] And they portrayed Latin American women as welcoming the "blue-eyed race" with open arms.[136] A chorus of Latin American men responded by labeling the Euroamerican filibusters "sexual predators," which they sometimes were.[137] May notes, quoting historians Lowell Gudmundson and Héctor Lindo-Fuentes, that "when Costa Rican president Juan Rafael Mora rallied troops going off to battle Walker, he urged them to expel the 'scum of all peoples' who intended, once they pacified Nicaragua, to 'invade Costa Rica to find in our wives and daughters . . . gratification for their ferocious passions.'" Mora wanted Costa Rican troops to "defend the homeland" as they would the Virgin Mary: "the sacred mother whom we all love."[138]

While some white men were making themselves feel better by fighting wars against people they deemed inferior, some white women were acting behind the scenes and sometimes in plain sight, to facilitate such ego-boosting escapades. Robert E. May and others have written extensively about the role white women played in enabling U.S. imperialism via filibustering during this era. White women raised money for the filibusters in Nicaragua, wrote poems to Walker, and sewed banners supporting his cause. Others lobbied their politicians or wrote editorials in support of the filibusters and their exploits. Moreover, dozens of white women traveled to Nicaragua with their husbands, hoping to claim the 350 acres of Nicaraguan land that Walker had promised to families from the United States emigrating to Nicaragua. (Single men hoping to farm could only claim 250 acres.) Once they were in Nicaragua, it turned out that aspiring U.S. male farmers had to first serve a year in Walker's army before they could receive their land allotment, land which Walker intended to confiscate from Nicaraguans who defied his rule. While their husbands fought with Walker, white women took on the role of nurses and sometimes even fought themselves. Other white women went to Nicaragua to accompany their husbands as they pursued random jobs and business ventures.[139]

In contrast to the women who supported Walker and even moved to Nicaragua, there were many white women who were opposed to filibustering and to U.S. imperialism, and some were quite vocal in their opposition.[140] But what is notable here, for our purposes, is the way in which filibustering, a term almost synonymous with manliness, was grounded in heterosexuality. The complementarity of the sexes, Protestant white men's worldwide God-given mission of protecting the "weaker sex," and "brown" men's supposed inability to protect their own women (from everyone, including white men) were part of the foundation upon which filibustering was built. Understood in this way, it is not surprising at all that white women played such a crucial role in sustaining filibustering, or that Walker encouraged married couples and their children to move to Nicaragua as "colonists." The example of filibustering clearly demonstrates the interconnectedness of racism, sexism, imperialism, and heteronormativity.

Many Nicaraguans came to quickly understand that Walker's expedition was predicated on their racial, religious, gender, and sexual inferiority. The more well-known and more common insults that Walker and his supporters used against Nicaraguans were racist, like "mongrels," "half-breeds," "half-civilized," "semi-barbarians," and "greasers," but some of them were also sexist, heterosexist, and sexual in nature.[141] *Afeminados* or "effeminates" was one of the most frequent insults the filibusters used against Nicaraguans.[142] The term was actually used against all Latin Americans, as noted by Amy S. Greenberg:

Americans understood their relation with Latin Americans in gendered terms. The United States was the dominant power because it was vigorous, and the states of Latin America should be submissive because they were not. The pro-slavery ideologue George Fitzhugh... declared that Mexico should be filibustered because, it was, in essence, effeminate. "Her mixed population has all the vices of civilization, with none of its virtues; all the ignorance of barbarism, with none of its hardihood, enterprise, and self-reliance. It is enervate, effeminate, treacherous, false and fickle."[143]

Nicaraguans responded to the filibusters' put-downs in kind, noting Walker's own "feminine demeanor" and reaching all sorts of conjectures regarding why he never married and had "problems" getting along with women. The Nicaraguan medical doctor-turned-historian Alejandro Bolaños Geyer's five-hundred-page biography of Walker, which took decades to research, cites a classmate of the young Billy Walker, who stated that Walker "was the smallest, most quiet, and most queer [*marica*] boy he had ever known; so much so that he was the target of bullying [*burla*] from his classmates, who called him 'my love' [*amorcito*], 'girly' [*nena*] and other equally offensive epithets."[144] Bolaños Geyer went on to argue for a psychological interpretation of Walker's actions in Nicaragua that centered not Walker's implied homosexuality but his supposed Oedipus complex, a perspective that has been criticized by other Central American scholars, including the Costa Rican historian Iván Molina Jiménez, who wrote:

> It was ... as options to consolidate a social position within the United States became exhausted or increasingly difficult for him, that Walker began to look abroad, first to Mexico and then to Central America. In light of the evidence provided by Bolaños Geyer himself, an alternative interpretation of the process that led Walker to Central America is possible, without resorting to a pathological explanation ... From this perspective, the filibuster episode ... [should be] presented not as the result of an individual pathology, but rather as a product of the strategy of social and political ascent of groups that, in the context of expansionism in the United States, tried to take advantage of this current for their own benefit.[145]

Molina's interpretation of Walker's motives is today a standard interpretation of events and should go undisputed. But those of us interested in LGBTQIA+ and gender history must still interrogate the fact that Walker made a great deal about other people's manliness or lack thereof while presumably aware of being perceived as feminine. In the book he wrote about his time in Nicaragua, titled appropriately *The War in Nicaragua*, Walker pointed out in other people whether they appeared and acted "manly" or not. At one point he described some Euroamerican women who had been rescued and were stepping onto a boat as "virago [mannish] in appearance."[146] He also had this to say about a few of his fellow soldiers:

> Some of the men capable of bearing arms, and even some officers, had disgraced themselves by deserting women and children, as well as the sick and wounded, at the first alarm. Two or three of these men, as they might by courtesy be called, escaped to the mainland.[147]

While Walker chided some men for not being brave enough to be called men, he at least on one occasion described a seemingly feminine man, Captain Crocker, in warm terms:

> ... the death of Crocker was a loss hardly to be repaired. A boy in appearance, with a slight figure, and a face almost feminine in its delicacy and beauty, he had the heart of a lion; and his eye, usually mild and gentle, though steady in its expression, was quick to perceive a false movement on the part of an adversary, and then its flash was like the gleam of a scimetar as it falls on the head of the foe. With little military experience and less military reading, he was a man to lead others where danger was to be met; and none who knew him feared he would get a command into any position from which his courage ... would be unable to extricate them. To Walker he was invaluable; for they had been together in many a trying hour, and the fellowship of difficulty and danger had established a sort of freemasonry between them.[148]

Ironically, the way in which Walker described Crocker is similar to the way in which Walker's contemporaries and chroniclers since then described *him*. The scholar Brady Harrison, after examining many U.S. literary works about Walker, has written:

One... "fact" about Walker continuously receives attention...: he was, like Napoleon, a physically small man. He stood barely five feet, five inches tall [others say barely over five feet tall], and weighed approximately one hundred and twenty pounds [others say one hundred pounds]. Nearly all of his chroniclers remark upon his size...[149]

... in an oft-cited letter, Jane H. Thomas, a friend of the [Walker] family, characterized the boy [Billy Walker] as "very intelligent and as refined in his feelings as a girl."[150]

Indeed, most everyone who ever wrote about Walker had something to say about his appearance, as well as his disinterest in pursuing relationship with women before and after the death of his only girlfriend, Ellen Martin, a deaf woman who died in 1849 of yellow fever. The U.S. author Noel B. Gerson describes Walker as follows in his 1976 book *Sad Swashbuckler*:

> In the autumn of 1839, more determined than ever to become a physician... he attended strictly to his studies, showed a tremendous capacity for work, and paid no attention to girls.
> By this time, he had reached his full height, and he was lost in a crowd. He had dark, straight hair, with a high forehead and narrow face, and his delicate frame was as slender and fragile as that of a young girl. Only his eyes were memorable: they were pale, sometimes described as gray and at other times called blue, and his gaze was so intense that people sometimes seemed hypnotized by his stare...[151]

Even the newspapers that supported Walker mentioned his appearance. For instance, *Harper's Weekly* ran a piece in 1857 that stated that Walker was "certainly one of the most remarkable men of the age" "but was effeminate in appearance."[152]

Walker's followers were certainly puzzled (and some were disappointed) by his feminine features and voice. Greenberg argues that the reason why Walker ended up being called "the Gray-eyed man of destiny" was because his eyes were the only thing that his supporters considered manly about him. They argued he had a penetrating gaze—reminiscent of Crocker's—that made up for his slight build and his short stature.[153] The

Canadian author Brady Harrison, meanwhile, goes further in his analysis of what others have written about Walker's appearance:

> An expert reader in some ways of Walker's adventures... [Darwin Teilhet, a U.S. writer of the 1955 romance *The Lion's Skin*] cannot seem to make up his mind about what, precisely, was *wrong* with Walker. Was he a woman disguised as a man? Was he an androgyne? Was he a homosexual? Was he a homosexual who attempted to conceal his homosexuality through a heterosexual affair with a Nicaraguan woman?... Teilhet cannot make sense of Walker's performance of gender. If he was the gray-eyed man of destiny, why did he look and sound like a woman? If he was a freebooting agent of empire, why did he not drink whiskey and chase women?[154]
>
> Some commentators (novelist Robert Houston, for example, and historian Laurence Greene) have suggested that Walker may have been, to use a term from our era, queer... A cross-dressing agent of empire? ... What image of American imperialism and ideal manhood would that be?[155]

Does it matter to the history of imperialism, the history of Nicaragua, or LGBTQIA+ history that Walker might have been a transgender man, intersex, gay, or queer? The short answer is yes, even though Harrison correctly reminds that "if Walker was queer by late-twentieth century standards, his compeers would not readily have had the language to describe him in like terms, and what later readers have taken as evidence of homosexuality would not necessarily have been" understood in that way at the time, even though most everyone who met Walker noticed and commented, usually unfavorably, upon his feminine demeanor.[156] While the term *queer* was not used as a derogatory term for LGBTQIA+ individuals until the late nineteenth century, an article on Walker in a 1915 issue of *Pearson's* magazine, however, did describe him as queer: "Walker had... a pair of eyes so remarkably the instrument of his spirits that they redeemed the queer little figure from any suspicion of insignificance and impressed all who met him with their almost hypnotic power."[157]

Harrison addresses Walker's "queerness" and the history of empire through an analysis of the 1955 novel *The Lion's Skin*. Harrison argues that, examined through the homophobic lens of the United States in the 1950s, a time when homosexuality was seen as a "potential menace to U.S. imperialism," it was clear that queerness in the mid-twentieth United States was also perceived as posing "a serious threat to the nation."[158] Harrison describes the concern that many in the United States appear to have had in the 1950s: "what if we [Euroamerican men] are not men enough to command an empire?"[159] As in the 1850s, white masculinity was in great flux during the 1950s. In the mid-twentieth century there was great uncertainty over who would win the Cold War. Importantly, for our discussion, Walker, and therefore the United States, ultimately did not succeed in Nicaragua, a point not lost in 1955. Harrison describes how that defeat was portrayed in Darwin Teilhet's novel:

> Teilhet offers his own spin on the tenor of the day: Walker, as an un-American deviant, threatened American power in the isthmus . . . Responsibility for American defeat, Teilhet suggests, rests with the American themselves. The freebooters' sexual and political duplicity contributes to the[ir] undoing . . . Like Roosevelt and McCarthy, Teilhet worries that [U.S.] Americans, through their own corruption and weakness, will defeat themselves . . . *The Lion's Skin* stands as a cautionary tale: we had better watch out . . . we had better be vigilant and ready to act with force, or our softness and potential for corruption for within will lead to defeat. If we lose, we will only have ourselves to blame.[160]

Harrison explains the hysteria of the anti-communist McCarthy era by noting that Senator McCarthy's homophobia led the senator and other homophobes at the time to argue "that homosexuals must be forced out of government not only for ethical reasons but also because their behavior exposed them to blackmail and manipulation of foreign powers."[161] Harrison goes on to cite a U.S. 1950s explicitly homophobic Senate report that "confidently asserted that . . . 'those who engage in overt acts of perversion [meaning homosexuality] lack the emotional stability of normal persons . . . One homosexual can pollute a Government office.'"[162]

Harrison and others present convincing evidence to back up the claim that anxieties about masculinity (often accompanied by anxieties about homosexuality) have been at the center of U.S. expansionism and imperialism. I note that anxieties about masculinity have also played a central role in the Nicaraguan anti-imperialist response to Walker's invasion. This was especially noticeable in Nicaragua's popular culture of the 1850s.

Anti-imperialist discourse in Nicaragua developed as a sexed and gendered discourse, as is revealed in one of the most well known songs about the Walker invasion, "Mama Ramona." The historical "Mama Ramona" appears to have been Ramona Barquero, from the town of Masaya. According to Ephraim George Squier, U.S. envoy to Nicaragua in 1849–50, Barquero, the owner of a boarding house, was "a fat and cheerful lady, who was so happy that her 'pobre casa' should be honored by the 'hijos de Washington,' the sons of Washington!"[163] If from Squier's self-serving perspective what Barquero demonstrated was enthusiasm for her job, from an anti-imperialist perspective that enthusiasm represented a pact with the devil. In ballad format, the story of "Mama Ramona" demonstrated the tension between the victimization of women and the processes that helped construct nationalist representations of feminine sexuality. The song oscillated between pity and condemnation in its portrayal of "Mama Ramona," but it did not take into account the possibility of women's agency:

A terrible thing happened
to poor mama Ramona

she got involved with the Yankees
and as a result the devil took her

Poor mama Ramona
fell in love with a Yankee

The trotters took her
and she didn't even get a chance to tell us the story

There come the Yankees
there come the cabrones
to take Nicaragua
the whopping thieves

A terrible thing happened
to poor mama Ramona

> *For acting up and disregarding her condition as a woman [por andar de chinvarona]*
> *the devil took her.*[164]

There were other versions of the song with additional stanzas:

> *The Yankees are coming from over there*
> *with colored jackets*
> *saying "Hooray Hooray!"*
> *"There is nothing left in Granada."*
>
> *For the Yankees we have*
> *a beautiful reception:*
> *the sharp edge of the machetes*
> *in addition to the cannon balls!*
>
> *On Guadalupe street*
> *we will build a bridge*
> *with the ribs of a Yankee*
> *and the blood of a brave.*[165]

It is important to note that the song does not mention "Mama Ramona's" employment. Instead it emphasizes Ramona Barquero's condition as a mother and the painful consequences of her masculine conduct (*chinvaronismo*)—in other words, her contestation of a conservative model of motherhood and womanhood.

The song ultimately reflects the patronizing attitudes of most Nicaraguan men at the time as well as the apprehension that many Nicaraguans felt regarding the racialized and racist sexual and sexist nature of U.S. imperialism. Nicaraguan women were often the sexual targets of U.S. imperialists, making the fear of sexual violence completely legitimate. On the other hand, the song also reflected the complicated nature of women's work, which made working women's sexuality automatically suspect. According to Squier, another Nicaraguan woman owner of a posada revealed to him that she "liked the Americans . . . [since] they had 'mucho dinero,' much money, and paid double what other folks did, without grumbling."[166] Because U.S. filibusters sometimes sought women for sex work, and because working women's sexuality was already suspect, statements like this one only sealed the connection between prostitution and U.S. imperialism, a connection that would come to dominate discussions on sex work in Nicaragua in the early twentieth century and beyond. Moreover, sex work would become linked with homosexuality in the mid-twentieth century Nicaraguan imaginary, leading some anti-imperialists to portray both sex work and homosexuality as the sexual "excesses" of urban capitalism.

There were at least three additional responses to Walker in Nicaraguan popular culture of the nineteenth and twentieth centuries, and those were varied. Over the years, some Nicaraguans engaged in what could be labeled a "moral reframing" of the filibustering logic, embracing—at least strategically if not in earnest—the discourse that the world was divided into barbarians and civilized peoples, and using it against the imperialists. For instance, knowing that the Euroamericans valued civilization over barbarism, the Nicaraguan historian José Dolores Gámez wrote the following in 1889 as a play on words:

> [Walker] [f]ounded ... on October 20, 1855, a bilingual newspaper, which he called *El Nicaragüense* written one fourth in barbarian Spanish and the rest in good English.[167]

Here Gámez applied the filibuster logic of conquest to the filibusters' own writing to make their efforts to learn a new language seem futile and their arguments seem ridiculous. The idea behind this strategy is that it is best to adopt your enemy's frame because "if you negate a frame, you strengthen a frame." The U.S. psychologist Steve Rathje discusses research on moral framing by the U.S. linguist George Lakoff and others that argues that "people tend to frame political arguments in terms of their own values, but ... it is much more effective to frame your argument in terms of your opponent's values."[168]

Ultimately, over the course of the last 160 years Nicaraguans were only partially successful at reframing Walker's imperialist views on Nicaraguan racial, gender, and sexual inferiority. For sure, today in Nicaragua William Walker is the most infamous nineteenth-century villain. Nonetheless, some of his supposed descendants seem adamant about wanting to portray Walker as having had romantic love affairs with their female ancestors. While it seems highly unlikely that romantic relationships took place between Walker and two separate Nicaraguan women, what is most relevant here is that once again the conversation on Walker turns to sexual matters.

In 2014 the Nicaraguan author Eduardo Pérez Valle Jr. reprinted on his online blog an article from 1977 written by the Nicaraguan Pedro Rafael Gutiérrez that appeared in *La Prensa* titled "William Walker and Ricarda Cerda, Traces of a Romance," telling the story of William Walker's supposed descendants. The story goes that Walker had a child with the Nicaraguan Ricarda Cerda. If this story is true, the child was most likely conceived in Rivas, in unknown circumstances. Walker and Cerda obviously did not marry, so the child for legal purposes was considered illegitimate and carried only his mother's last name. Pío Cerda was an only child and went on to have five children himself.[169]

There are other Nicaraguans who also claim to be Walker's descendants. A 2012 article in *La Prensa* profiled María Pasos and her daughter, who firmly believed that Walker had a child with one of their ancestors, a woman in Granada named Juana Bendaña. While still pregnant, Bendaña supposedly met and married a wealthy man, Emilio Medina, who promised to give his last name to Walker's son. That child was named Emilio Medina. According to the article's author, "María Pasos . . . is convinced of her ancestry. The one that in Nicaragua was also a love story, she says."[170]

Two of Walker's siblings (James and Norvell) went with him to Nicaragua, so it could be possible that "the descendants of Walker" discussed above are actually the descendants of his brothers. If so, the window of time for these relationships to have taken place would have been very brief. James died of cholera while he was still in Nicaragua,[171] and Norvell died at sea in 1857 while in route to the United States from Nicaragua.[172] Regardless of which filibuster these Nicaraguans are descendants of, if at all, the fact that they appear eager to romanticize relationships that may not have been consensual is reminiscent of the "fantasy heritage" found in other parts of the Americas. Chicana author Rosalinda Fregoso reminds us that

> Carey McWilliams first coined the term "fantasy heritage" during the 1940s in his trenchant deconstruction of the Mission myth. Most often attributed to Helen Hunt Jackson's *Ramona* (1884), the Mission myth entailed reinventing a romantic Spanish history for California—a fictionalized past . . . "Fantasy heritage" named the selective appropriation of

historical fact, the transformation of selected elements of history (e.g., the economic system of missions and haciendas) into a romantic, idyllic past that repressed the history of race and class relations in the region. "Any intimation of the brutality inherent in the forced labor system of the missions and haciendas, not to speak of the racial terrorism and lynching that made early Anglo-ruled Los Angeles the most violent town in the West during the 1860s and 1870s, was suppressed."[173]

The third response to the Walker takeover is an anti-imperialist Sandinista one that sought to address the lack of historical knowledge among Nicaraguans living under the U.S.-backed Somoza dictatorship in the 1970s. Francisco Cedeño (1959–), one of the members of the very famous revolutionary musical group Pancasán, composed a song titled "Notes about Uncle Sam" ("Apuntes del tío Sam") in 1978. The composer recalls:

> An informal recording in early 79 allowed it to be broadcast in the clandestine Radio Sandino. The song appears in the second record by the group Pancasán called "We are Making History," and it is one of the most representative themes in the repertoire of revolutionary songs born in the 70s. [174]

The song tells the story of Nicaraguans' military triumph against Walker's failed invasion, linking it up to the twentieth-century anti-imperialist resistance of Augusto C. Sandino and the ultimately successful armed Sandinista struggle of the 1960s and 1970s. The song is triumphant, reminiscent in some ways of the lyrics of the Mama Ramona song, except this time "the imperialist gringo ended up running away like the devil" ("corriendo como diablo salió el gringo imperialista") *without* a Nicaraguan woman at his side:

> *In 1856*
> *the enslavers of the south*
> *of the United States*
> *came to conquer*
> *in other words to steal*
> *sent by William Walker*
> *and then found their match*
> *in San Jacinto*

*and the imperialist gringo
ended up running away like the devil.*[175]

In some respects, William Walker's invasion sealed the connection between effeminacy in men, homosexuality, prostitution, and U.S. intervention. But today in Nicaragua many people are unaware that Walker during his lifetime was mocked for having what were understood by his contemporaries to be feminine characteristics. The lack of awareness could be because an acknowledgment that he was not as "manly" as people think he should have been would make him less of a foe in Nicaraguans' eyes, diminishing in some people's view the Central American victory over Walker and his men. The German scholar Andreas Beer, however, argues that what happened was that the filibusters exhibited two different types of masculinity and one eventually prevailed. According to Beer, Walker personally exhibited a "restrained" masculinity while his followers embraced a "martial" one. The latter, a more aggressive and destructive one, ultimately came to represent all filibusters.[176] Indeed, over 150 years after it happened, Walker's invasion is still a symbol of U.S. military imperialism, which is associated with unbridled white racist masculinity, the kind that Walker maybe aspired to and definitely promoted, but ultimately was not able to personally embody.

CONCLUSION

U.S. historian Justin Wolfe described Nicaragua's nineteenth century as one where "elites of all stripes advocated a liberal project of modernity that heralded an increasingly secular, interventionist state, a growing export economy, an ample labor supply, and expanded private landholding ... Throughout the nineteenth century Nicaragua was a fundamentally agrarian multi-ethnic society. A project of liberal modernity meant to upend such a world, and inevitably, land, labor, and ethnic identity became the flashpoints of struggle and negotiation."[177] My contention is that aspects of gender and sexuality also became flashpoints of struggle and negotiation during this period and beyond.

Wolfe appropriately asks the following question: "What is it that leads people to see a state as their State, to see themselves as their sovereign subjects?"[178] Wolfe addresses the question by stating that "the answer is found not so much in the coercive imposition of elite ideology as in the construction of a nation-state that made this ideology appear, if not commonsensical and natural, then at least legitimate."[179] Some elite ideologies never made sense to the vast majority of Nicaraguans, and ultimately the elites retreated, knowing they had been beat. This was the case, for example, of the prohibitions against babies and young children in the markets. Women's presence in the markets was perceived as "natural" by a population that was largely Indigenous, if not in name, then by their history and traditions, and so their children remained there too.

Independence brought about ongoing conversations and contestations over the nature of the Nicaraguan state. But independence did not bring peace. Moreover, there was a great deal of cultural and legal continuity from the colonial era to the national period as the leaders of the new nation-state sought to maintain many of the social control mechanisms implemented through the Inquisition and the Bourbon Reforms of the previous century. Not surprisingly, postindependence elites throughout the nineteenth century continued to bolster heteronormativity, women's subordination to men, and the legal persecution and prosecution of "sodomites."

Significantly, some of the legal changes enacted after independence actually made gender inequalities between heterosexual cis men and cis women worse. This was the case with adultery. In theory, before independence, when there was no separation between church and state, both men and women committed a punishable sin/crime when they had sexual relations with anyone but their spouse. But after independence the definition of adultery changed, blatantly privileging men as it became secularized. A man in the mid-1800s *only* committed adultery when he cheated with another man's wife or if he brought another woman to live in the same house as his wife, the latter a crime similar to bigamy, a practice associated in the elite imaginary with Indigeneity. A woman, however, committed adultery by having sexual relations with any man who was not her husband.[180]

The nineteenth century brought about the theoretical end of racial categorization in Nicaragua, but racism continued unabated. It is my contention that trans and cis women's economic participation in western Nicaragua's open-air markets was a precolonial tradition that remained associated with Indigenous Nicaraguans in the nineteenth century. This meant that attitudes toward women market vendors became intertwined with anti-Indigenous racism. Additionally, perceptions of trans women, vendors or not, also became intertwined with racism against Indigenous peoples. Moreover, because race and class became conflated in Nicaragua after the conquest, discrimination against trans women (as well as discrimination against all women market vendors) became linked to class discrimination. These links are important to understand, for they explain why contemporary Nicaraguan attitudes toward trans women are often classist and racist, in addition to being transphobic, but are not necessarily ones of absolute rejection. They also help explain the relatively high visibility of trans women as well as the historical occupational segregation patterns for trans women in Nicaragua and allow us to better understand why so many trans women today work not only in markets but also as street vendors.[181] Most importantly, I argue that the continued existence of trans women in Nicaragua is an example of Indigenous resistance, as is the continued existence of trans and cis women market vendors, and possibly even street vendors, given the association of outdoor sales with femininity and Indigeneity.

The fact that in the twenty-first century almost half of all vendors in Nicaragua's largest open-air market, El Oriental, are women,[182] and that so many trans women engage in the informal economy as street vendors, is not a coincidence. While working as vendors is not ideal because of low wages, job insecurity, lack of benefits, difficult working conditions, and the stigma attached to working in markets and on the streets, these jobs, like those that attract LGBTQIA+ workers elsewhere in the world, "provide a high level of task independence (i.e., freedom to perform one's tasks without substantially depending on others) or require a high level of social perceptiveness (i.e., accurate anticipation and reading of others' reactions), or both."[183] While it is beyond the scope of this book to address LGBTQIA+ occupational segregation in Nicaragua in depth, it is my hope that this topic will receive the attention it deserves elsewhere.

In addition to examining the ways in which race, class, and gender identity and gender expression have intersected in the lives of LGBTQIA+ Nicaraguans, my discussion of the nineteenth century inevitably required a "queering" of the imperialist invasion by William Walker. The contradictions in white U.S. masculinities as they played themselves out in the 1850s in Nicaragua wreaked havoc on the new nation. Indeed,

Nicaragua in the U.S. imagination would become everything the United States believed itself not to be and made sure Nicaragua became: weak, poor, and dependent (i.e., feminine/effeminate).

With regard to homosexuality, one could argue that there are greater archival silences for the nineteenth century than for the colonial period. However, that probably says more about the instability brought on by the ongoing wars during the nineteenth century in Nicaragua and the colonial obsession with recordkeeping than anything else. Nonetheless, by the early twentieth century, the written word was flourishing in Nicaragua, leaving behind plentiful records of the period. These records reveal that the 1910s, 1920s, and 1930s, discussed in the next chapter, exhibited heightened concerns over homosexuality (particularly lesbianism) and gender dissidence, linked in part to the rise of first-wave feminism as an ideology and a political movement. The blatant homophobia and transphobia of the period, however, continued to make it very difficult to find self-identified LGBTQIA+ individuals in the historical archive.

3

THE MODERN NATION-STATE, FEMINISM, AND THE MODERN WOMAN

The Early Twentieth Century

TWO INTERRELATED themes dominated the first few decades of twentieth-century Nicaragua: modernity and U.S. intervention. Those themes would continue to impact Nicaraguan history throughout the 1900s and into the present. They would also affect LGBTQIA+ history profoundly.

This chapter addresses three Nicaraguan figures who were intimately linked to modernity and/or U.S. intervention: the Liberal dictator José Santos Zelaya López (1853–1919), the world-renowned poet Rubén Darío (1867–1916), and the so-called modern woman. President Zelaya embodied many of the contradictory attitudes that elite Nicaraguans had toward the United States and foreign intervention in general. He also embodied a misogynistic version of heteromasculinity that would be replicated by future dictators. Concomitant to the rise of the "modern" Nicaraguan state under Zelaya, I document the life of the country's first philanthropist, José Zacarías Guerra, a man victimized by anti-LGBTQIA+ harassment even after death. Rubén Darío, considered the "father of Spanish language modernist poetry," was Zelaya's friend. In his writings, Darío explicitly referred to feminism and had some harsh admonishments for feminists. My discussion on Darío is part of a broader attempt to document elite discourse on homosexuality, gender expression, gender identity, and feminism during the early twentieth century. I contend that the homophobic and transphobic elite discourse of this period had concrete negative consequences for all LGBTQIA+ individuals, and I document some of those consequences in this chapter.

This chapter also discusses in depth the rise of "the modern woman" and first-wave feminism in Nicaragua. I argue, in fact, that it was in response to the bourgeoning feminist movement of the early twentieth century that elites became intently focused on chastising lesbians and "masculinized" women from the pulpit and in the press. It is also during this period that the police became actively involved in persecuting not only "sodomites" but also gender-nonconforming and gender-fluid individuals, lesbians, masculine women, and transgender men and women.

Moreover, in this chapter I document the participation of women in sports and argue that there was an additional unease among Nicaraguan elites (beyond the one that male elites elsewhere in the world had) regarding the supposed "masculinization" of women that physical activity would produce, specifically because of Nicaragua's transgender Indigenous tradition. In other words, elites felt particularly threatened by the participation of the mostly mestiza middle- and upper-class women in sports because, prior to these women's involvement in basketball, tennis, softball, etc., homosexuality, gender fluidity, and transgender experiences had been associated almost exclusively with working-class and Indigenous populations. In particular, the advent of women baseball players made elites worry about the prospect of middle-class lesbians and transgender men. Most worrisome to them was the possibility that these "masculinized" "modern women" would not only want full political and economic rights but also would upset gender dynamics in elite families and simultaneously contribute and be a product of a particular type of "Americanization" in Nicaragua, one that was anathema to the type of Americanization that some elites wished to pursue. Furthermore, I argue that it was during this period that elites themselves disrupted (but did not eliminate) the link in the Nicaraguan imaginary between Indigeneity, homosexuality, gender dissidence, and transgender identity and advanced a new link: one between LGBTQIA+ populations and U.S. intervention. What this means is that the early twentieth century brought about a new insult to be hurled at LGBTQIA+ Nicaraguan individuals: "Americanized." The associations made between feminism, LGBTQIA+ rights, modernization, and U.S. intervention in Nicaragua during this period help explain the late twentieth and early twenty-first centuries phenomenon of "pink-washing" as well as the backlash against women's rights and LGBTQIA+ rights in the late 1900s and early 2000s.[1]

MODERNITY AND MODERNIZATION

The debates over modernity, especially in the context of Latin America, are ongoing and unresolved. Political philosopher Steven B. Smith provides us with a standard definition of modernity:

> Modernity is a problem. It is a word that means many things to many people. It is a name of both a process (modernization) and a state of affairs... Modernity came to be associated with the sovereign individual as the unique locus of moral responsibility, the separation of state and civil society as distinct realms of authority, the secularization of society or at least the lessening of the public role of religion, the elevation of science and scientific forms of rationality as the standard for knowledge, and a political regime based on the recognition of rights as the sole basis of its legitimacy.[2]

Latin Americans are generally understood to be latecomers to modernity, but Latin American scholars, such as Enrique Dussel and Anibal Quijano, have contested this characterization. Quijano has noted that "the intellectual and political movement of the Enlightenment... was produced and practiced simultaneously in Europe and [Latin] America."[3] But then, Quijano argues, modernity was not allowed to continue its development in Latin America as it was in Europe. This curtailment is what Quijano has called an unfortunate "metamorphosis" in Latin American modernism, one fundamentally connected to colonial and neocolonial impositions.[4] Quijano explained this process as follows:

> The imposition of English hegemony, linked as it was to the spectacular expansion of British industrial capitalism, consolidated the hegemony of the tendencies in the movement of the Enlightenment that conceived of reason primarily in instrumental terms. The association between reason and liberation was occluded. Henceforth, modernity would be seen

almost exclusively through the crooked mirror of domination. The age of "modernization," instead of modernity, had begun: that is, the transformation of the world, of society, according to the requirements of domination and control, specifically, of the domination of capital, stripped of any purpose other than accumulation . . .

For Latin America, this inflection of the history of modernity was more than decisive—it was catastrophic. The victory of the instrumentalization of reason in the service of domination was also a profound defeat for Latin America, which, because of its colonial situation, had associated modern rationality more than anything else with liberation. Latin America would not again encounter modernity except under the guise of "modernization."[5]

Quijano goes on to describe what eventually happened:

The subsequent predominance of the United States in capitalist imperialism and the imposition of "Pax Americana" after World War II not only consolidated and globalized the hegemony of instrumental reason (the association of reason and domination) over "historical reason" (the association between reason and liberation); it also exacerbated its consequences immeasurably. For it has been under this empire that all instances of society and each of its elements have ended up subjugated to the demands of capital. And it has been precisely during the period of its rise that Latin America, in particular, came to be one of the victims of "modernization."[6]

Modernization came to be understood as a particular kind of "progress" centered on industrial capitalist economic development, one at which Nicaragua largely "failed." But we have gotten ahead of ourselves. During the period addressed by this chapter, some Nicaraguans, particularly the elites, wanted U.S.-style economic modernity and modernization (and the accompanying accoutrements such as civic and literary associations, social clubs, literary magazines, etc.), and they were intent on modernizing Nicaragua.[7] They sought, with limited success, to copy modernization as it had occurred in the United States. Ironically, those efforts were met with a new round of foreign intervention. Somehow, while imitation may be the sincerest form of flattery, modernization in

Nicaragua could not take place on Nicaraguan terms. The United States wanted more than flattery; it wanted submission. And the ongoing love-hate relationship that many Nicaraguan elites had with the United States helped facilitate foreign intervention in the twentieth century as it had in the nineteenth.

Nothing symbolized modernization in Nicaragua (and the symbiotic relationship between the U.S. and Nicaraguan elites) more than the transoceanic canal that was to be built by the United States through Nicaragua's southern border in the early 1900s. President Zelaya courted the United States on this issue, and the deal fell apart at the last minute when the United States decided to build the canal in Panama instead. Today, however, Zelaya is celebrated as a nationalist who stood up to the United States, and the issue of a possible canal is still one that can potentially help bring a dictator down.

ZELAYA AND MODERNIZATION

The Liberal general José Santos Zelaya had already been in power for seven years when Nicaraguans witnessed the arrival of the twentieth century. He would rule for another nine years before being toppled with the assistance of the U.S. government. Under his administration a series of important laws were passed, many of them a continuation of reforms initiated by Conservatives in the earlier period known as "the Conservative Republic" or "the first Conservative Republic," which lasted from 1858 to 1893.[8] Among those laws were ones that continued the ongoing secularization process in Nicaraguan society, resulting in the advent of civil marriage and divorce, the secularization of cemeteries, and the confiscation of some church properties.

It was also under Zelaya that the forced military "reincorporation of the Mosquito Coast" took place in 1894. The U.S. anthropologist Courtney Morris notes that

> The Reincorporation forcibly brought the Atlantic Coast into the jurisdiction of the Nicaraguan state and dismantled the Mosquito Reserve. Creoles, who still refer to the event as the "Overthrow," saw their political and economic power completely diminished by the Nicaraguan state,

which viewed their demands for self-governance and political power as inherently illegitimate.

Morris also addresses additional impacts of this takeover:

From the beginning, Nicaraguans were overtly hostile to Creoles, whom they saw as Black foreigners whose racial inferiority disqualified them from participating in the governance of the region or full participation in its economic activities . . . The Mosquito Reserve was renamed the Department of Zelaya and the government instituted a series of policies designed not only to integrate the Coast into the economic life of the nation but also to assimilate the region's diverse communities into the project of Nicaraguan Mestizo nationalism. These reforms included establishing Spanish as the official language of Nicaragua and closing down schools that provided instruction in other languages. The Reincorporation remains the definitive moment in the formation of the vexed contemporary relationship between the Atlantic Coast and the Pacific. This geographical relationship was profoundly racialized as Mestizos viewed the Atlantic Coast and its inhabitants as racially inferior, backward non-nationals whose only route to citizenship was to take on the dominant Mestizo culture. Indeed, as [the Nicaraguan Political theorist Juliet] Hooker, notes, the Reincorporation marked a critical moment in the construction of Nicaraguan national identity as the Coast was mobilized to serve as the racial Other against which Nicaraguan Mestizos could define themselves. The representation of the Coast as an abject, primitive space relied on hegemonic ideologies of white supremacy and Black inferiority that formed a central part of 19th century racial common sense in Nicaragua and justified the subordination of racial Others because of their presumed incapacity to wield political power or understand the rights and responsibilities connected to the exercise of full citizenship.[9]

How to best understand Zelaya is a contentious matter among academics, politicians, and even the general public in Nicaragua. Most scholars agree with Morris and Hooker that Zelaya played a key role in solidifying the mestizo nation at the expense of Indigenous and Creole populations. Nevertheless, overall, the subject is understudied. For instance, very little research has been done into how the othering of Blackness as foreign allowed Nicaraguans on the Pacific coast to ignore and/or deny their own African ancestry. The following newspaper article, from *El Comercio* in 1906, exemplifies the ways in which Blackness on the Pacific coast was commonly associated with the Caribbean Coast and/or other countries and how race intersected with modernity and gender:

THE NOVELTY FROM DAY BEFORE YESTERDAY

A young Black woman from Granada named Carmela, who has traveled a great deal on the Atlantic Coast, accompanied by Manuel Solis, went out on Sunday afternoon in the streets of the neighborhood of the Penitentiary to demonstrate her dexterity in riding a bicycle. Her quality as a working-class young woman [*su calidad de mengala*], her Jamaican appearance, and the newness of those exercises among the feminine awoke in that neighborhood the curiosity of some and the hilarity of others... Large crowds followed her in an open race shouting so loudly that it could almost leave one deaf, but she was undaunted, and continued as if she were listening to the rain fall. Meanwhile, one could hear the expression: "Long Live 'la negra' Carmela!"[10]

The story of "la negra Carmela" allows us to examine the intersection of Blackness, gender, and modernity on the Pacific coast. In 1906, the bicycle symbolized modernity. This modernity, however, appears to have not been meant for single young women. It was generally considered inappropriate for them to ride bicycles, given the potential spatial freedom that such an activity entailed, the issues related to sitting on the bike with a dress, concerns about women possibly being "overstimulated" in their pelvic region by biking, and the physical strength that riding a bike demanded.[11] The newspaper *El Comercio* carried an ad for bicycles on the same page of the paper that reported Carmela's biking prowess. The advertisement stated that "Isidro J. Olivares sells bicycles for gentlemen, married women [*señoras*], and boys [*niños*]."[12] The only group missing from the intended target of the advertising were unmarried women and girls. This is part of what made Carmela on a bike so newsworthy.

Carmela was noteworthy because she was a young woman on a bike at a time when that was rare and a disruption of *gender* norms. However, she was also noteworthy because she was a *Black* young woman on a bike at a time when that was rare and disruptive of *racial* norms. Just being Black on the Pacific coast was a disruption of racial norms, even though many if not most Nicaraguans had African ancestry. That the newspaper mentioned Carmela's African ancestry in the first place supports the point made earlier by scholars Juliet Hooker and Courtney Morris regarding the othering of Blackness on Nicaragua's Pacific coast. Hooker notes that "the association of the Atlantic Coast with blackness ... facilitated the depiction of other areas of the country as devoid of black ... people ... despite their presence in these regions."[13] In this case, Carmela's Blackness is very explicitly connected in the newspaper article to the Atlantic coast ("ha viajado mucho por la Costa Atlántica") and to Jamaica ("su apariencia jamaicana"). There was no need to mention that she had been to the Caribbean Coast, and mentioning that she looked "Jamaican" was arbitrary. Both these details were irrelevant if the story was simply that of a young woman on a bike until we realize that they were necessary to make it seem like Carmela was a foreigner. If Carmela was indeed *just a granadina*, a person from the colonial city of Granada in western Nicaragua, how to explain that she was Black? Not associating Carmela with the Caribbean Coast and/or Jamaica would have necessitated a different conception of Nicaragua as a multiracial society and not a mestiza one. Moreover, it would have demanded an acknowledgment that before 1824, Spanish colonizers and their mixed-raced Nicaraguan descendants enslaved African peoples and their descendants on the Pacific coast, resulting in a legacy of anti-Black racism.

There is a third theme in Carmela's story, and that is the portrayal of women's embrace of modernity as a foreign enterprise. Those who read *El Comercio* in 1906 and knew nothing about Nicaraguan history might have gotten the impression not only that Carmela was from Nicaragua's Caribbean Coast or Jamaica, but also that she learned to ride a bicycle somewhere else. While it is true that bicycles were not made in Nicaragua at the time and thus had to be imported, portraying women's physical dexterity and autonomy as being the result of foreign influences undermined Nicaraguan women's achievements and was an insult to their intelligence. In the end, the article's author, who was most likely a man, appears to have had mixed feelings as to how to depict the events that transpired. In this respect, he was representative of many other men (and women) of the time. They were not necessarily in agreement with women's increased freedom but were undeniably in awe of someone who, in the midst of a deafening and not always supportive crowd, could bike along "undaunted," "as if listening to the rain fall."

The final themes in Carmela's story have to do with the absence of a last name and Black women's suspect sexuality. In the article, *la negra* somehow reads as if it were this young woman's first name, turning *Carmela* into her last name. The lack of a real last name could have hypothetically been a protective measure. However, it is unlikely that Carmela's last name was omitted to prevent readers from knowing her identity, for how many other Black young women on bikes were there in what was at the time a rather small town? The lack of a last name could have been a throwback to the pre-emancipation years, when enslaved peoples of African ancestry were often referred to only by a first name. On the other hand, it could have been the racialized nickname that Carmela was known by, therefore making a last name unnecessary. Alternatively, it could have been the product of sexism, a reflection of the practice where women are referred to only by their first names, creating a false sense of familiarity, while men are referred to by their last names, thus fostering respect. The lack of a last name for Carmela becomes particularly obvious because a man is also mentioned in the article, and he has a first *and* a last name: Manuel Solis. The question remains: Why not include Carmela's last name? I argue that the answer to this question is probably quite complex.

Manuel Solis's name is clearly a Spanish name. Since we are not privy to Carmela's last name, we are left guessing if hers is a Creole last name or a Spanish one. A Creole one would presumably confirm her "foreign" status in the eyes of mestizos. A Spanish one would have made her a local. Not knowing leaves open the possibility that Carmela is indeed an interloper, although the article starts out with the phrase *una negrita granadina*, in effect claiming her as a native of Granada.

While the lack of a last name for Carmela is not completely unexpected, the presence of Manuel Solis's name with no further explanation regarding his identity or their relationship is unsettling. Who is he? Are readers expected to know who he is? Was he famous? Infamous? Did he travel with her to the Caribbean Coast? Or was he with her when she was biking in Granada? Are they related? And if so, why not say that? One of the possible readings of this article in the absence of any additional information would be to conclude that Carmela was a sex worker and that Manuel Solis was her pimp. The lack of a last name would support this conclusion since sex workers were rarely referred to by their first *and* last names. At the very least, Carmela, a presumably unmarried woman, was traveling alone with a man, making her (like most other working-class Black and Indigenous women) sexually suspect in the eyes of local elites. Insinuating that Carmela was a sexually loose young woman was part of a vicious racist/sexist circle that was difficult to escape from, no matter how far you biked.

Carmela's story is important in part because it allows us to see how big themes in history such as racism, sexism, and modernity play out in the lives of real individuals and the nuances at the local level. It also sheds light onto the everyday experiences that took place under the Zelaya administration, a topic we return to below.

In addition to the debates over the racist mestizo takeover of the Caribbean Coast and its implications, there are at least two other ongoing major debates regarding Zelaya. One has to do with whether Zelaya deserves the credit he often receives for "modernizing" the country and the other has to do with the extent to which economic growth under Zelaya was "capitalist." The first is discussed at length by the Nicaraguan historian and politician Arturo Cruz Jr., who has argued that

> in the pantheon of the nation's mythology Zelaya stands out as a leader of great accomplishments. He is routinely given attribution for the initiation of public works in the nineteenth century, the intellectual conception of a truly liberal constitution, the introduction of direct elections, and the country's active engagement in regional affairs, culminating in a disastrous but patriotic confrontation with the United States. Zelaya, in short, is seen as a valiant champion of national sovereignty. The Conservative Republic that preceded Zelaya's government, in contrast, has been relegated to obscurity—deservedly so, it has often been said, given the obscurantist leanings of its founders.

Cruz, however, disagreed with this assessment and argued instead that the difference between the Conservatives and Zelaya "was one of tempo. The Conservatives believed in what they defined as 'moderate progress'... rather than spontaneous eruptions."[14] Historian Michel Gobat also contends that "even if the [William] Walker episode discredited the Liberal Party, liberal ideals guided the construction of the post-Walker state."[15]

The second controversy regarding Zelaya is addressed by historian Jeff Gould, who wrote,

> Nicaraguan historiography portrays the regime of José Santos Zelaya... as one that modernized the country, effectively mobilizing resources for the agro-export sector. Scholars disagree about whether such economic growth was "capitalistic" or not, given the extensive use of extra-economic labor coercion. Clearly, however, the regime did foster the expropriation of land and the coercion of Indian labor, although in this regard Zelaya did little more than intensify the policies of his Conservative predecessors.[16]

The questions of who were the real "modernizers" in Nicaragua and what exactly "modernity" entailed in the Nicaraguan context have generally been addressed by historians in relation to economics and politics, particularly the advent of the agro-export economic model, the Conservative/Liberal political divide, and the long-lasting U.S. military intervention. However, modernization processes were ones that were also intimately linked to issues of race, sexuality, and gender, as can be seen in the earlier discussion on Carmela and her bike. Elizabeth Dore, Michel Gobat, and Juan Pablo Gómez are among a handful of historians who have addressed the issue of modernity in relation to gender during the early twentieth century in Nicaragua, but the relationship between modernity and LGBTQIA+ history has remained largely unexplored.

What did Zelaya's modernity mean in relation to nonheteronormative sexualities, gender identity, and gender expression? The fact that Zelaya has been so associated with Nicaragua's modernization is significant for the nation's LGBTQIA+ history in part because he represented a hyper heteromasculinity that most men could not achieve.

José Santos Zelaya was considered an "illegitimate" child, and he was raised by his father's wife and eventually sent to study in France.[17] He is described by the U.S. historian Michael Rice as a strongly built man just under six feet tall ... with the black, later grey handlebar moustaches of the Victorian era, he possessed "a military bearing" and looked "like a natural leader." Mervyn Palmer noted: "His grip when he shook hands was that of a man of iron."[18]

New York Times reporter George MacAdam before his interview with Zelaya noted: "Whatever else he [Zelaya] might be, you can be certain, the person who has succeeded in governing a Caribbean republic for sixteen years is ALL MAN."[19]

Little is known about Zelaya's first wife, Ana Bone Prado.[20] His second wife was the daughter of a Belgian immigrant to Nicaragua.[21] Two things characterized Zelaya's private life: his sexual promiscuity, which resulted in at least forty-five children (only eight of which were a product of this two marriages), and his love of cockfighting.[22] Zelaya was not only promiscuous but also a sexual predator who raped young and vulnerable women.[23]

Ironically, one of the people who wrote extensively about Zelaya's private life was President José María Moncada Tapia (1870–1945), himself infamous for his promiscuity (he reportedly had as many children as Zelaya) and his love of cockfighting.[24] This is what Moncada, president of Nicaragua from 1929 to 1932, had to say about Zelaya:

> His doctors flatter him prescribing for him the use of a woman, so he does not die of congestion and when he goes to the cities and towns of Nicaragua, his agents and ministers go before him to hire virgins. He has children all over.[25]
>
> As always happens, the habits, customs, and vices of those who govern are a real school for the people, in Nicaragua all the friends ... of Zelaya are cockfighters. Medical doctors, attorneys, members of the military and even teachers, as well as women, enter into the circus.[26]
>
> They all call Zelaya ... the rooster/cock [*el gallo*] ... The best gift that his supporters can give him is a good fighting cock or a virgin and they take pride in serving him in this way.[27]

Cockfighting, a European tradition introduced in Nicaragua during the Spanish conquest,[28] would become particularly important during this period, for it came to symbolize "older, 'barbaric' manly values" challenged by some elite Nicaraguans who preferred the "modern, 'civilized' notions of manliness" supposedly embodied in baseball, an increasingly popular sport linked in the minds of many to the U.S. Marines in Nicaragua.[29] The underlying argument was the same one made by William Walker and his supporters in the nineteenth century: Nicaraguan men were inferior and backward mongrels who deserved to be taken over militarily and culturally by the United States because white men were inherently superior beings.

Almost eighty years later, in 1990, then-president Daniel Ortega chose as his reelection campaign song one that celebrated him as a "fighter cock" (*gallo ennavajado*). The song has been criticized by some as ridiculously sexist and old-fashioned.[30] Ortega ended up famously losing that election to Violeta Barrios de Chamorro, a woman candidate dressed in white who proclaimed she could bring peace to Nicaragua. Given what we know about the historical debates over cockfighting, the gallo ennavajado was probably meant to highlight not only Ortega's virility but also his nationalism, since the United States government was backing the candidacy of Barrios de Chamorro. In the end, both cockfighting enthusiasts, Zelaya (in 1909) and Ortega (in 1990), were ousted by elites who had the financial assistance of the U.S. government, making their passion for the animal blood sport irrelevant.

THE LIFE AND DEATH OF JOSÉ ZACARÍAS GUERRA RIVAS, 1855–1914

José Zacarías Guerra may or may not have been the most famous Nicaraguan LGBTQIA+ man of the late nineteenth and early twentieth centuries. But he was certainly the early twentieth century's most famous philanthropist. His name is used daily today in Nicaragua's capital as a landmark, because the buildings of his philanthropic organization—initially a home for orphan children—continue to bear his name, over one hundred years after he died.

José Zacarías Guerra was considered an "illegitimate" child. His father was a Conservative politician. His mother died when he was very young, and he was raised by his maternal aunt. He had a difficult childhood but eventually became a member of the local Managua elite, even becoming a local councilman.[31] The fact that he never married, had no known girlfriends or mistresses, and had no children became defining characteristics. People mocked him for that, and homophobic graffiti was written on the walls of his house:

> Zacarías Guerra was an austere man, an inveterate bachelor, with a reputation for being stingy . . . Ladies would whisper to each other when they walked past him, criticizing his advanced bachelorhood. The men in the neighborhood El Triunfo would mock the pride Zacarías demonstrated with regards to his anchorite life.[32]
>
> He was shy and had few friends. Working-class people [*el bajo pueblo*] mocked him, writing satirical labels on the walls of his house. He never fought with anyone. He stoically heard the offenses or pretended not to hear them.[33]

Neighbors even played humiliating pranks on Zacarías Guerra. The scholar Jorge Eduardo Arellano cites an anecdote documented by the Nicaraguan historian Gratus Halftelmeyer Gómez (1887–1976):

> Once, in the rainy season, he got caught in a rainstorm while he was on Zamora Street, a street he had to go through to get home. On that same . . . [street] was La Gallera, the cockfighting ring, bar, and billiards that belonged to General Aurelio Estrada and a place frequented by those who were fond of pranks. One of these individuals noticed that Zacarías was on the street waiting for the rain to stop. He called Chico Chapín and told him what to do, offering him a good remuneration. Chico Chapín, once instructed, walked over to Zacarías offering him his services to carry him across the street, which he accepted since he urgently needed to get back home. When they were in the middle of the street, in the middle of the stream of water, Chico Chapín pretended to stumble and dropped his charge . . . Zacarías got an unexpected soaking. Chapín escaped from Zacaría's anger, and those at the Gallera laughed to no end. This prank and others were done to Zacarías, who caused harm to no one . . . even though they did so many mean things to him.[34]

In 2013 the novelist Francisco Javier Bautista Lara fictionalized the event with Chico Chapín and told the same story but from Guerra's point of view. Like Carmela on her bicycle, Guerra had the inner strength to keep going, this time as if there were no rain:

> With difficulty, José [Zacarías] got up and ... soaked and anguished, folded the damaged umbrella, walked the five blocks he had left to get home, walked proudly confronting the storm, without looking at anyone ... without avoiding the rain or the puddles, under the gale that didn't cease.[35]

Despite Guerra's apparently stoic attitude toward his aggressors, the bullying continued. Once, in 1904, someone even threw a rock at him: "Yesterday, while at the door of his home, Mr. Zacarías Guerra received a blow to his chest from a rock thrown by an insane person who lives in the neighborhood."[36] Indeed, "he was made to go through a mill of ridicule..."[37]

The only time the historical record documented Guerra's voice was when, after living with his paternal relatives for a short while he was young man, he left his father's house and reportedly shouted, "Long live liberty! Long live the Prince Contreras!"[38] Nobody knew what prince he was referring to, or what sort of liberty Guerra sought, but his paternal relatives in the novel speculated:

> What is this about "Contreras"? By being "against" everyone, and especially against us, he did not seek liberty but rather licentiousness, in our home he could not do whatever he wanted to, nor could he satiate his inclinations and disorders, he was wayward, a rebel, he did not fit in under any rules, only the ones he imposed on himself, he was incapable of having relationships with others due to his stubbornness, that is why he ended up alone, Who would have put up with him? He fled from obligations and was truly strange [raro]...[39]

Guerra died from complications related to diabetes on May 5, 1914, in his late fifties, and hardly anyone went to his funeral:

> "He is good dead," said the neighborhood, "because he never did evil things, but he also never did a good deed for people." And very few people went to the funeral.[40]

Nevertheless, when his will was read, everything changed. It turned out he had been able to amass quite a fortune, presumably from lending money.[41] In his will, Guerra left what today would be millions of dollars to the orphan children of Nicaragua:

> . . . four days later, when they read Guerra's will, opinions changed . . . Mr. Zacarías had willed his immense capital to the orphan children of Managua.
>
> There were parades . . . all the way to the cemetery and many flower arrangements . . . on his grave, as well as fiery speeches by the best speakers in the capital who exalted the virtues of the deceased, which came to light only after his death.[42]

Suddenly, Zacarías Guerra became a hero, particularly for the Catholic Church, which took it upon itself to manage the funds and build an orphanage. The Zacarías Guerra Home still exists in Managua in the twenty-first century in an expanded capacity, and it is still run by the Catholic Church. According to its Facebook page it is "a nonprofit that serves children, adolescents, and youth at risk."[43]

After his death, several people published brief essays where they attempted to make sense of Zacarías Guerra's life. For instance, Lisandro Zambrana H. wrote the following:

> How can we not dedicate words of admiration for someone who . . . was strange [raro]? For someone who was able to overcome with resignation the mockery of his peers, the folly of those who laugh, of all who do not understand? They, those who used . . . the vocabulary of ridicule against him, today are in awe of his noble conduct, with which he has conquered immortality; his name, a symbol of mockery, will live eternally haloed by the gratitude of those who are in life forgotten by everyone . . .[44]

Zacarías Guerra is part of the geographical landscape of Nicaragua's contemporary capital. However, Zacarías Guerra's home was already a landmark while he was still alive. A 1906 ad in *El Comercio* for attorney J. Carlos Serrano stated as the location of his office "across from Zacarías Guerra."[45] Clearly, Zacarías Guerra was well known before death. However, he became so famous after his death that he is one of the few Nicaraguans to have an entire historical novel devoted to his life.

In the 2013 novel written about Zacarías Guerra by Francisco J. Bautista Lara, a former Sandinista police commissioner, Guerra is portrayed not as someone who was LGBTQIA+ but rather as a lonely introvert.[46] Given the discrepancies in the portrayals of his life, what are we to make of Guerra's life and legacy? This question is particularly relevant because at the time, the words used to describe Guerra, words like *raro* (strange) and *solterón* (bachelor), were ones that alluded to homosexuality and/or "queerness" but did not directly address it.

The best way in which to understand Guerra's life is to contextualize it. We know very little about asexual men or men who engaged in same-sex relations in Nicaragua during the early twentieth century. Every so often, as in earlier periods, someone engaging in same-sex relations make an appearance in the historical record, often in court documents. For example, we know that in 1916 Félix P. Paniagua was sentenced to fifteen days of hard labor for sodomy.[47] We also know, however, that not everyone who defied gender and sexual norms was arrested. For instance, two years earlier, in 1914, the newspaper *El Comercio* reported the following:

> The night before last, one of the police inspectors, a Sherlock Holmes type, did not feel right about the look of a lady in a hat with a great black feather, a silk dress, white gloves, and shoes of the imperial kind. The police officer followed her at a normal distance. The figure entered, after several visits, into the Social Club, and when she left, the "detective"'s paw fell on her . . . the elegant lady was no more than a young man who wanted to play a prank on the neighborhood.[48]

For unknown reasons, Félix P. Paniagua was tried and sentenced for sodomy and his name made it into the paper, while the latter individual was able to remain anonymous and have his case be dismissed as a "prank." Could the difference have been their class background? Not just any young person (*jovencito*) could have afforded "a hat with a great black feather, a silk dress, white gloves, and shoes of the imperial kind."

The case of "the elegant lady" who was able to enter the Social Club also points to the possibility that there could have been a private gay world in Nicaragua that held private drag parties, as was the case elsewhere in Latin America during the early twentieth century. The most famous ball in the region, one that some people in Nicaragua might have been aware of, was the 1901 event held in Mexico City, remembered today as the Dance of the Forty-One. During the rule of the dictator Porfirio Díaz, Mexican police raided a private party made up of forty-one individuals who at birth were assigned the male gender, half of whom were wearing dresses. The scholars Robert McKee Irwin, Edward J. McCaughan, and Michelle Rocío Nasser argue that

> ... a raid would not normally gain national attention. However, Mexican cultural trends in literature, art, the sciences, and in journalism were inciting an atmosphere of sexual curiosity that was in search of the right turn of events to ignite a discursive explosion and focus interest on what was not a new phenomenon, but what was about to become a new concept: homosexuality.[49]

The comparison between Mexico and Nicaragua during this period, while useful, should not be taken too far. In the nineteenth and early twentieth centuries Nicaragua had very few of the features that characterized the larger Latin American nations. Unlike Mexico (which had 13 million inhabitants in 1900) and Argentina (which had 4.5 million inhabitants in 1900), for example, Nicaragua (which had only half a million inhabitants in 1900) had no widespread railway system, no important shipping routes, no expanding industrial economy, no mass immigration, no large urban centers that could grant anonymity, no emerging psychiatric tradition, and no functioning mental health system.[50] Moreover, unlike the situation in these larger countries, today there are few surviving police and penitentiary records in Nicaragua. If the differences between countries like Mexico and Argentina were significant, and they were, the differences between Nicaragua and those two countries were even greater.

Unlike the situation in Mexico, where there was a perceived "need for new mechanisms of social control to maintain order in an age of progress,"[51] the Argentinian historian Pablo Ben argues that in Buenos Aires, "sex between men was not an issue that concerned the state beyond the rhetoric of physicians, criminologists, and writers until the 1930s. In a country with a liberal sexual legislation, the actual persecution of male same-sex sexuality by the police was not significant."[52] Nicaragua probably was closer to Mexico than Argentina when it came to state interest in the regulation and persecution of sex between men during the first decade of the twentieth century.

In addition to briefly comparing Nicaragua to Mexico and Argentina during this period, it is insightful to address what was happening in the United States. The U.S. historian George Chauncey, in his groundbreaking work on gay New York between 1890 and the beginning of World War II, found a vibrant, "highly visible, remarkably complex, and continually changing gay male world ... [L]aws were enforced only irregularly and indifference or curiosity—rather than hostility or fear—characterized many New Yorkers' response to the gay world for much of the half century before the war."[53]

Chauncey writes about three enduring myths regarding gay life in New York before the rise of the gay rights movement: the myth of isolation, the myth of invisibility, and the myth of internalization:

> The myth of isolation holds that anti-gay hostility prevented the development of an extensive gay subculture and forced gay men to lead solitary lives ...
>
> The myth of invisibility holds that, even if a gay world existed, it was kept invisible ... but gay men were highly visible ... in part because so many gay men boldly announced their presence by wearing red ties, bleached hair, and the era's other insignia of homosexuality ...
>
> The myth of internalization holds that gay men uncritically internalized the dominant culture's view of them as sick, perverted, and immoral, and that their self-hatred led them to accept the policing of their lives rather than resist it ... But many gay men celebrated their difference from the norm, and some of them organized to resist anti-gay policing.[54]

Chauncey goes on to argue that

> we lost sight of that world in part because it was forced into hiding in the 1930s, '40s, and '50s ... A second reason ... is that ... nobody looked for it ... A third reason ... is that ... it took shape in such unexpected places and was so different from our own that we have often not even known where to look or what to look for ... the most visible gay world of the

early twentieth century was a working-class world... A final reason we have failed to see the gay subculture that existed before World War II is that it has been obscured by the dramatic growth of the gay subculture *after* the war.[55]

Chauncey also points out that during the first three decades of the twentieth century, "it was not a world in which men were divided into 'homosexuals' and 'heterosexuals'... many conventionally masculine men... [were able to engage in] extensive sexual activity with other men without risking stigmatization and the loss of their status as 'normal men.'"[56]

Chauncey's observations about New York are quite relevant to Nicaragua's LGBTQIA+ history. The existence of the "elegant lady" mentioned above hints at a whole world that has yet to be documented and that I hope later studies will shed light on. But instead of privileging World War II in Nicaragua's chronology, it is the U.S. Marines' occupation of Nicaragua in the 1910s, 1920s, and 1930s and the ensuing right-wing Somoza regime (1936–79) that would be the turning points in the timeline.

The myths Chauncey describes are also applicable to Nicaragua. I contend that the myths of isolation and internalization are ones that some contemporary scholars and writers have used as a lens through which to portray the life of Zacarías Guerra. However, his story is more complex than that.

Finally, as was the case in the United States at this time, Nicaragua during Guerra's lifetime was not divided into homosexuals and heterosexuals. Guerra was suspect because he lived alone and had no wife, no mistresses, and no children. He was mocked because there was no proof that he had sex with women, not because there was proof that he had sex with men. Moreover, there was no documented talk of him being effeminate. Additionally, it is important to point out that while he was mocked, he was not feared and appeared to have had no run-ins with the police.

In the end, we will probably never know if Zacarías Guerra had sexual relationships with men or not. Regardless, he paid a price. Rumors were enough for his neighbors to mock him, throw rocks at him, deface his property, throw him into a stream of rainwater, and make his life very difficult. His life and death point to the difficulties that men who were suspected of engaging in same-sex relations had at the time. On the other hand, Guerra figured out how to get back at his critics, and, in many respects, he had the last laugh: fame and a lasting philanthropic legacy that was not marred by the possibility that he might have practiced a nonheteronormative sexuality. That he placed a curse in his will on everyone who did not carry out his wishes might have helped him secure a spot in history and might have also helped stop the rumor mill about him. According to Bautista Lara, his will "closed with a curse that was famous in Managua and disturbed many neighbors who looked down on him as well as scared the relatives who thought it was directed at them... 'Any citizen who impedes the fulfillment of this will, MAY YOU BE DAMNED A THOUSAND TIMES.'"[57]

FIRST-WAVE FEMINISM AND THE WRITINGS OF FEMINIST JOSEFA TOLEDO DE AGUERRI (1866-1962)

One useful way in which to understand the history of feminism in the nineteenth and early twentieth century is to label the early organizing in favor of women's suffrage and increased social and political rights for women a "first wave" of feminism. For various reasons discussed extensively elsewhere, until fairly recently, many believed that Nicaragua did not experience a "first wave" of feminism, only a "second wave," and that the latter was a by-product of the 1979 Sandinista revolution.[58] The historical record shows, however, that a vibrant first wave of feminism did develop in Nicaragua in the nineteenth and early twentieth centuries. In fact, politically independent feminist organizations thrived until women's suffrage became co-opted by the Somoza government in the mid-twentieth century.[59] After women gained the right to vote in 1955, the Somoza regime was able to take all credit for women's increased political, social, and economic opportunities, successfully erasing the existence of first-wave feminists from the Nicaraguan imaginary.[60] This is how the narrative that the government "granted" rights to women became dominant, even though most of the gains that women have made in Nicaragua have been achieved through the grassroots struggle of women (and men) who believed women deserved equality.

I contend that the rise of first-wave feminism in Nicaragua made conservative elites nervous. As a result, feminists suffered a great deal of harsh criticism and persecution from the Catholic Church and other conservative elements of society. Although they were accused of being lesbians, or perhaps because of these accusations, first-wave feminists went out of their way to distance themselves from homosexuality. Feminists like Josefa Toledo de Aguerri (1865–1962), Nicaragua's most prolific first-wave feminist, wrote specifically against lesbianism. She also espoused many of the other bigoted beliefs prevalent at the time. This section of the chapter focuses extensively on the writings of Josefa Toledo de Aguerri, thus providing a better understanding of the complicated relationship between first-wave feminism and the pursuit of equality for all Nicaraguans.

In the January 18, 1920, issue of the *Revista Femenina Ilustrada*, the editor, Josefa Toledo de Aguerri, devoted an entire page to personally answering the question "What is feminism?":

> Feminism, like socialism, says an author, has not been defined in a precise manner because "more than a set of doctrines formed systematically, they constitute a state of spirit, a way of thinking and feeling." Nonetheless . . . Naudet defines it in the following manner: "Feminism is a doctrine through which woman's rights in the legal order can be obtained, certain rights that today are unknown to her, and in society, a legitimate position that has been denied by custom."
>
> Feminist aspirations manifest themselves in three orders of ideas: in the political, in the legal, and in the economic. The first is about the vote. The second refers to the legal order with respect to the inequality in which the Codes place the two sexes. The third mainly covers . . . work and woman's free access to careers, in equal conditions to man . . .[61]

Josefa Toledo de Aguerri was Nicaragua's most important feminist *and* woman intellectual in the second half of the nineteenth century and the first half of the twentieth century. Her importance to Nicaraguan history, and more specifically to Nicaraguan feminism, cannot be overstated. In part because of her longevity, she was involved—often successfully and usually in a leadership role—in almost every endeavor to expand women's rights in Nicaragua for almost a century. She was a "teacher of generations," inspiring many of her students to become feminists and pioneers in their fields. "Doña Chepita," as she was known, was brilliant and brave. Yet she was also a complicated and flawed individual.

For forty-seven years, Toledo de Aguerri held the highest possible administrative position in five different secular schools for young women in Nicaragua. She founded all but the first school, the one she herself attended as a teenager. It is truly no wonder she is currently acknowledged as the mother of Nicaragua's public/secular educational system.[62] However, what was most important about Toledo de Aguerri's schools was not necessarily that there were so many of them or that they lasted for so many years. The importance lies in the events that took place in these five institutions as well as in the students who attended the centers. First, it must be noted that the schools became the foci of cultural, intellectual, and sociopolitical events for the Pacific and central regions of the nation.[63] Second, we must acknowledge that, not coincidentally, Nicaragua's first female college graduates included many of Toledo de Aguerri's former students. Toledo de Aguerri's schools became magnets for female (and male) artists, thinkers, and politicians. Indeed, during the early twentieth century, most of Nicaragua's artists and politicians set foot in Toledo de Aguerri's colegios.

Although Toledo de Aguerri sought to promote women's rights in the broadest sense, she was very conscious of the economic differences and the rural/urban split that divided women in Nicaragua and throughout the world. A mestiza born to a middling family in an agricultural region (in Juigalpa, Chontales), and perhaps influenced by the pedagogical innovations of the Mexican revolution, one of Toledo de Aguerri's special projects was the training of rural schoolteachers. During her brief tenure as general director of public instruction ("directora general de instrucción publica") in 1924, she personally traveled to remote areas to evaluate the quality of rural education throughout the nation and to lecture on the need for its improvement.[64] Even earlier, Toledo de Aguerri had wanted to alleviate the specific educational problems faced by working-class urban women and had taken more concrete steps toward that goal. In 1919, she founded the Feminine School for Journalism (Escuela Femenina de Prensa). Set up as a night school, the *escuela* was funded by newspapers throughout western Nicaragua. Two hundred sixty female students enrolled during the first few months of the school's existence.[65]

In addition to advocating for women's suffrage and increased education for women, Toledo de Aguerri was engaged in promoting kindergarten, pay equity, and developing special education programs for children with disabilities. Moreover, Toledo de Aguerri was interested in fostering women's cultural expression, creating child care centers (called Sala Cunas) for working mothers, improving the situation of women in prisons, stopping U.S. intervention in Latin America, giving refuge to those fleeing from European fascism, promoting industrialization in Nicaragua, and furthering worldwide peace activism.[66] Additionally, during the 1930s Toledo de Aguerri, like many Latin American, U.S. American, and European intellectuals of her generation, embraced eugenics.

The eugenics movement was founded in England by Sir Francis Galton (1822–1911), a cousin of Charles Darwin (1809–82).[67] According to historian Vern Bullough, "the purpose of eugenics was . . . to increase from one generation to another the proportion of individuals with better-than-average intellectual endowment," a very subjective—and usually racist and classist—endeavor.[68] Some, but not all, followers of eugenics, agreed with eugenicist Karl Pearson's (1857–1936) view that the "higher races" needed to supplant the "lower" ones.[69] Bullough notes, for example, that "although the [U.S.] American eugenics movement, founded in 1905, initially adopted Pearson's view wholeheartedly," other eugenic groups like "the English Eugenics Society founded by Galton, eventually opposed Pearson's racist views."[70] Toledo de Aguerri did not subscribe to the more virulently racist expressions of eugenics nor to the language that differentiated between "higher" and "lower" races. She generally used the term *race* to mean the human species or to refer to Latin Americans as a group. Rarely, if ever, did she use the term to distinguish among Nicaraguans on the basis of skin color, ethnicity, race, or wealth.

Although she did not deal with "racial" differences (differences historians acknowledge to be socially constructed) among Nicaraguans in relation to eugenics, Toledo de Aguerri did address the issue in the educational policy context. Like many other Nicaraguan elites, most of whom were mestizos, Afro-mestizos, or mestizo-identified, she wanted to integrate the nation's highland Indigenous peoples as laborers into the rural economy, "training them for a civilized and useful life."[71] What perhaps differentiated Toledo de Aguerri from other elites, however, was that she wanted to make the transition a peaceful one, accomplished through education. In order to instill "habits of peace, order, cleanliness and work" among the Indigenous population, a Normal School for Indigenous peoples (Escuela Normal de Indígenas) was founded in Matagalpa in 1925 during her tenure as general director of public instruction.[72] There, teachers were to be specially trained to deal with Indigenous individuals' "false ideas, absurd preoccupations, sloth, superstition, and mistakes . . ." Toledo told the students at the Normal school that "great tact, perseverance . . . edifying example and sustained virtue . . . will be the weapons that will conduce you to victory."[73]

Toledo de Aguerri's racism (and the racism of her peers) was undoubtedly a contributing factor to the destruction of many Indigenous communities in northern Nicaragua, a thoroughly reprehensible act. Nonetheless, it seems unwise to dismiss her importance to Nicaraguan feminism or to the general history of Nicaragua because of this. Her racism might actually be another reason to further study her thought. Investigating the elite racist ideology of a nation that prides itself in its mestizo heritage[74] can help us to understand how race has been theorized in the past and how racist conceptions of difference have molded current Nicaraguan identities, including feminist ones.

It is important to reiterate the obvious: Nicaraguan elites have rarely spoken out on behalf of Indigenous Nicaraguans in antiracist terms. They instead have promoted and benefited from the takeover of Indigenous lands and the erasure of Indigenous culture. I am not singling out Josefa Toledo de Aguerri as a racist. Among mestizo-identified Nicaraguans, she was the rule, not the exception.

In addition to believing that Indigenous peoples were inferior to mestizos and mestizo-identified Nicaraguans, Toledo de Aguerri was a homophobe. Not surprisingly, perhaps, this did not mean that she did not interact with or befriend gay and lesbian individuals. Toledo de Aguerri had at least one close male friend who was assumed to be gay.[75]

In general, even when it came to feminism, Josefa Toledo de Aguerri tried to position herself as a moderate, perhaps in order to win more converts to her cause, perhaps to avoid some of the consequences that challenging the status quo entailed. In Josefa Toledo de Aguerri's opinion, there existed a very sharp differentiation between radical/theoretical/social and moderate/practical/conservative feminists. She identified with the latter, although she seemed to see a historical need for both groups.

Whether in her view, the former disappeared, as it evolved into the latter, however, remains unclear:

> There are two types of feminism: a social kind which is radical and sectarian, which proclaims woman to be equal to men in everything; and an opportunist feminism [which is] moderate, conservative, and practical. The first is the theoretical one, the second is the one which gets results ["el de las conquistas de hecho"].
>
> The masculinized [social] feminism has given way to the opportunist feminism, where woman, without leaving aside the prerogatives [already] conquered by the socialist campaign, acts today with the femininity which is inherent to her.[76]

In her published works and in her speeches, Toledo de Aguerri made great efforts to stress the importance femininity (those physical and behavioral characteristics she felt differentiated women from men) had for feminism and vice versa. She wanted Nicaraguan women's femininity to be "injected with feminism."[77] Ideally, there would be a "transition"[78] from femininity to feminism with a "blissful duality"[79] of both as its end result.

Toledo de Aguerri's definition of femininity dealt with two interrelated issues: women's morals and their behavior. She wished women would realize the importance of excelling in those activities which were "noble and worthy."[80] And she implored women to refrain from imitating "men's vices and liberties" (drinking and smoking) and dressing like them.[81] Most importantly, femininity for Toledo de Aguerri was about heterosexuality and the complementarity of the sexes.

In 1938 Toledo de Aguerri warned women about the dangers of lesbianism, "what in Germany they call the *third sex*."[82] She also assured her readers that "feminism is not contrary to [heterosexual] marriage. It is said that the stronger a woman's personality is, the more intense the love she feels for a man will be."[83]

Even though Toledo approved of heterosexuality, she advised couples to de-emphasize sexual attraction. She believed that "the foundation of the home is love, not desire."[84] Moreover, it was women's duty to make sure men combined "real love" with "physical love": "the educated woman will sublimate the marital ideals leading man to . . . a noble and disinterested affection."[85]

Although she did not approve of men's "vices," or of the way in which women were raised to act, Toledo de Aguerri did believe men and women could benefit from some of each other's characteristics. "The ideal" in her view was "the moral masculinization of woman and the moral feminization of men," a combination that would bring together the complementary and "opposite qualities" the sexes had.[86] Because she felt men and women were opposites, Toledo de Aguerri distanced herself from feminists who wanted to erase differences and "be like men."[87] On the other hand, because she felt they were each other's counterparts, Toledo de Aguerri strongly disapproved of those who proclaimed woman's superiority to man or supported a war between the sexes:

> . . . An active, crude, and rude feminist struggle between man and woman took place in the world. As a result, some fell to ridiculous levels and others to flawed ones. Now that the atmosphere is calm, one is able to notice that arguing over a supposed masculine or feminine superiority is unproductive. Given that the sexes are formed in different ways, their functions cannot be compared . . . Woman is not inferior or superior to man; she is simply his counterpart since the active qualities of man are complementary to the passive qualities of woman.[88]

Like many other intellectuals of the time, in Nicaragua and elsewhere, Toledo de Aguerri was highly influenced by the racist, classist, sexist, ableist, and heterosexist eugenics movement described earlier. But at no point in her available writings do her eugenic beliefs appear to have intersected explicitly with her homophobia. In 1938 she stated:

> . . . Eugenics is very important for strengthening the [human] race. [Nonetheless] in Central America . . . the word eugenics twitches the nerves of the ignorant [and] makes hypocrites holler . . . When these ideas [finally] flower in the mind, fervent campaigns will be waged in eugenic's favor throughout 'the media, the schools, the universities and the pulpit.' This will purify the current of social life, which today exhibits symptoms of decay . . .[89]

In the 1930s, before eugenics was discredited by the genocide committed in Nazi Germany, Toledo de Aguerri believed that eugenics could serve an admirable purpose. In what was quite a horrific dystopian vision, it would prevent children "who were a burden" from being born and "sick" adults from breeding, although it is unclear how exactly that would happen in her view:

> ... In order to have better selected descendants, among both vegetables and animals, vigorous types are chosen. Among mankind however, the biological laws are not applied, due to ignorance and hypocrisy. This allows man to procreate, even though sick or full of vices, weak ... crazy, epileptic, abnormal creatures ... who are a burden on the family and on society ... [90]

Although state-funded forced/involuntary sterilizations of people considered "inferior" took place throughout the twentieth century in the United States and elsewhere, there is no evidence that unwanted sterilizations of any kind took place in Nicaragua during the early twentieth century. In practical terms, by the 1940s eugenics in Nicaragua appears to have become synonymous with sex education.[91] Thus, increasing the population's awareness of the reproductive process was a central goal of its proponents.

Toledo de Aguerri wanted to institutionalize sex education in public schools. For her, sexual instruction was part of the modern, scientific education children needed to receive. It would help prevent unwanted pregnancies as well as sexually transmitted infections at a time when both were rampant. Toledo de Aguerri was widely criticized, however, specifically for her endorsement of sex education, particularly by the Catholic Church hierarchy. Nonetheless, she did not remain silent against her enemies. She responded to those who opposed sex education by arguing that, unlike her critics, who merely "pretended to be honest," she was actually doing something to prevent "the advance of secret [sexually transmitted] diseases."[92] Her foes, on the other hand, "remain[ed] passive ... and ... cruelly critique[d] those who attempt[ed] prophylaxis campaigns."[93] They were wrong, she believed, because "hiding certain knowledge ... [from the population could only] ... harm ... individuals and the [human] species."[94]

In relation to sexuality, Josefa Toledo de Aguerri wanted to deter homosexuality, curtail heterosexual desire/expression, promote the nuclear family, implement (hetero)sexual education, prevent unwanted pregnancies, and diminish the spread of sexually transmitted infections. It is important to note that the three issues she was concerned with the most—institutionalizing sex education, providing wider access to birth control, and preventing STIs—have still not been fully achieved in Nicaragua, or hardly anywhere else in the world, for that matter.

Despite her racism, her classism, her homophobia, and her embrace of eugenics, Toledo de Aguerri espoused some ideas about sex that even today would be considered quite liberal and progressive, even radical. Hers was the face of the sex education movement in Nicaragua, and she suffered greatly for that. In 1934, Josefa Toledo de Aguerri had the support of the minister of public education, Lorenzo Guerrero, to implement sex education in her schools. However, a group of elite Catholic women from the Conservative city of Granada were able to successfully lobby the president of the republic, and, as a result, the planned curriculum was canceled.[95]

Josefa Toledo de Aguerri did not always have the support of the Ministry of Public Education. In 1910, for example, she had to publicly defend the right of her teachers at the Normal School for Señoritas (Escuela Normal de Señoritas) to participate in public protests.[96] Four female teachers were being targeted for having "descended to a terrain that is prohibited to them due to their position and their sex."[97] The case was in the newspapers for days, and conservatives kept up the attacks:

> We are in complete agreement with the Minister of Public Instruction . . . with respect to the teachers who are perorating in the clubs and political gatherings.
> Women with these propensities must be kept away from schools.
> We shall never be convinced that a chatterbox high school graduate who is not afraid of being in bad company can be a good teacher for girls; and we think that only a crazy father, or at the very least one that is mentally unbalanced, would choose a Theroigne de Mirecourt or a Luisa Michel to direct the education of his daughters.[98]

Not surprisingly, anti-lesbian and transphobic insinuations were central to the criticism of the teachers:

D. Pedro Torres Ruiz, astronomer [astrologist] from Chinandega, spiritist, and thaumaturge recently found out—extraterrestrial revelations for sure—that Ms. Teresa J. Morales, "liberal thinker and speech giver," is Joan of Arc, the maid of Orleans . . .

Anyone who knows Ms. Morales and who has seen innumerable portraits of the maid of Orleans, assure us that they differ physically in their hair, color, size, etc. Teresita looks more like D. Pedro Torres than Joan of Arc.[99]

Even Toledo de Aguerri's seemingly less controversial policy proposals (like the creation of Sala Cunas where working women could leave their children while at work) were seen as "attacks against [society's] morals and good customs" because they were believed to foster women's sexual promiscuity.[100] In response to the Sala Cunas proposal, a priest singled out Toledo de Aguerri for criticism, and even her physical appearance was used against her in his Sunday sermon. Father Moreira insinuated that Toledo de Aguerri's prematurely gray hair and decorous manner masked her true (deviant) nature. As part of a sermon, he once noted that Toledo de Aguerri had "white hair but a green stem, like an onion."[101]

Accusations and insinuations focusing on Toledo de Aguerri's integrity were made throughout her life and even after her death. When Conservatives fired her from her post as director of the Normal School for Señoritas in Managua in 1910, Toledo de Aguerri was accused of stealing a piano, an allegation she always denied.[102] After her death, a particularly offensive rumor gained strength. Her detractors claimed that during the early twentieth century, Toledo de Aguerri had saved her prettiest students for Liberal president José Santos Zelaya, a known predator. In interviews I conducted over the course of twenty years, I learned that additional misogynist rumors continue to circulate today. It is said that she also offered her students to Anastasio Somoza García and that she dated a married man for many years before getting married. Moreover, she is accused of having been an intellectual fraud. According to this last rumor, Toledo de Aguerri did not personally write the many books and articles she signed; they were all ghostwritten by her protégés. Clearly, Toledo de Aguerri put her sexual and professional integrity on the line by advocating for the institutionalization of sex education, even though her own sexual (particularly her marital) life was by most accounts fairly impeccable and traditional. Her example demonstrates the hazards feminists (even today) encounter when they attempt to talk about sex in public.

What to make, then, of Josefa Toledo de Aguerri, her writings, and first-wave feminism? One key characteristic of first-wave feminism was that, despite the radical nature of some of Toledo de Aguerri's activism and writing, it did not seek to drastically alter the overall social order. Moreover, except for Toledo de Aguerri, first-wave feminists in Nicaragua did not publish extensively. This means that we do not know where other feminists of her generation stood on the controversial issues "Doña Chepita" cared so deeply about. Additionally, while we know that Toledo de Aguerri was not the only Nicaraguan intellectual to embrace eugenics (her friend, Edelberto Torres Espinoza, another giant in education, was also a supporter), the history of eugenics in Nicaragua has yet to be written and is beyond the scope of this book.[103] That said, evidence shows that, like Toledo de Aguerri, Torres Espinoza was targeted specifically for supporting and implementing sexual education in public schools. In 1941, the same conservative forces that had defeated Josefa Toledo de Aguerri's efforts to implement sex education in 1934 came after Edelberto Torres Espinoza. He was forced to leave the Technical Council for Education (Consejo Técnico de Educación) for supporting the introduction of sexual education in sixth grade.[104]

Specifically with regard to homosexuality, there is no way to know how Toledo de Aguerri's views changed over time or how she treated lesbian students and fellow lesbian feminists, who presumably existed. On the other hand, she and other feminists were often vilified by anti-lesbian rhetoric.

One of the individuals who strongly criticized women's rights (including women's right to work for pay outside the home) as well as homosexuality was the conservative intellectual Francisco Palma Martínez (1892–1950?). In his 1949 book titled *El siglo de los topos*, he stated:

> I combat the ills of this century, which are: women's painting [makeup], sports fanaticism, the proletarianization [working outside the home for a wage] of women, music ... jazz, sexual debauchery ... and children whistling in the street ... .[105]

> Women's painting is bad because with that they provoke passions, corrupting men; exaggerated sports ... turns people into brutes ... the

proletarianization of women is grave, because her economic independence brings with it physiological independence... birth control in marriage, through artificial systems is unnatural, anti-religious, unpatriotic, unhealthy and immoral; whistling is detrimental, because it increases infantilism among adults. Infantilism means that a grownup has the mental capacity of a 5- or 6-years old child. Most women suffer from this. You have my word that this is true....[106] Woman was, has been, is and will be the eternal corruptor of men...[107]

Homosexuality in women is immoral... it is a constant source of cancer transmission, which originated in the womb of those who abort...[108] I firmly believe that if the Holy Inquisition had continued, we would be in better shape... The inquisition tried to eliminate criminal abortion, homosexuality, and masturbation.[109]

Palma Martínez continued:

The dyke [*marimacho*] ... has the brain of a man and the body of a woman. She is male in all her actions, because instinctively she thinks like a man; believes she is a man...[110] [The] dyke [*marimacho*]... smokes and drinks with men and greets them by hitting them on the back, like pals: she is good-natured [*campechana*]. She does not get married because marriage between women does not exist, but she falls in love with the pretty young women; she likes to kiss them on the mouth, but kisses the ugly and the old ones on the cheek. She wears pants, men's shoes, rides astride. Children, no way [she would have any]. In New York I met one of these mistakes of Nature...[111]

Honestly, I cannot understand why women are not ashamed of some of the things they do. They are just like the effeminate man who does not realize that others see him with disdain and laugh at the way in which he walks, the style in which they talk and the ways in which they are different from a man. A masculine woman is also detestable...[112]

In the 1930s the Catholic Church in Nicaragua also tackled the issue of women's homosexuality directly. Managua's first archbishop, José Antonio Lezcano y Ortega (1866–1952), was particularly vocal in his condemnation of women's rights and women's sexual freedom. Lezcano's highly conservative views earned him worldwide recognition from other conservatives. In the mid-twentieth century, the Spanish dictator Francisco Franco awarded him the Orden de Alfonso el Sabio (Order of Alfonso X the Wise).[113]

In a 1939 homily Lezcano managed to link homosexuality and women's suffrage in a long diatribe against women's insubordination:

> In these times of rebellions and misunderstood liberty, society is in disorder and almost complete ruin . . .
>
> . . . the Catholic clergy wants woman to be angel and queen in the home, not head of electoral gangs in the streets, for our father Adam when he received his wife Eve, created from his side, called her Hembra [female], that is, delicate and most noble part of his being, and not Hombruna or Marimacho, independent being who rivals man . . .
>
> [N]ot too long ago it was said in a very public place that "if women were given the vote in the elections for civil authorities, it would be giving [the vote] to the clergy, who . . . dominate completely the feminine sex." [He is presumably referring to Anastasio Somoza García's son-in-law, Guillermo Sevilla Sacasa, the anticlerical liberal delegate to the Constitutional Assembly who made such a statement in 1939.] God wishes that were true for the good of the indicated sex . . . ! For the clergy could make sure everything conformed to the doctrine of Christian morals. But unfortunately it is not so, as is proven by the well-known feminine rebellions in relation to: the impudence of her fashion, her attendance at the corrupting movie theaters, new-fangled dating, profane outings during Holy Week, and the disastrous divorces; all situations in which the clergy has suffered an almost complete defeat.
>
> If the feminine sex listened to our preaching, our society would be very ordered . . . she reminds us, not of a docile little donkey, but of an indomitable little mule, who . . . resist[s] the halter that guides her to where she should go obediently and submissively.[114]

Also in 1939, according to journalist Ignacio Briones, during the congressional debates over women's suffrage, "groups 'of fanatics that were in charge of ridiculing and even insulting the women suffragists . . . arrived at the sidewalk in front of the Escuela Normal de Señoritas . . . [the school Toledo de Aguerri administered] with posters asking the young women if they would rather have been born men. And they branded them "dykes" [*marimachas*].'"[115]

No one was publicly defending LGBTQIA+ Nicaraguans in the early twentieth century. Not even feminists. Nonetheless, feminists (some of whom might have been lesbians) were not hurling public insults either (the only exception was Toledo de Aguerri's reference to "the third sex"). It was mostly male intellectuals, male poets, male politicians, and priests who insulted and sometimes even called for severe measures against LGBTQIA+ individuals. Moreover, all feminists were subjected to lesbophobia and transphobia, in part because so many people believed that equal rights would give women the freedom to do whatever they wanted with their bodies.

THE MODERN WOMAN

Public elite fear and hatred of lesbians, transgender, gender-fluid, and gender-nonconforming individuals was a reaction, in the early twentieth century, to the advent of first-wave feminism and "the modern woman" associated with feminism. Once women started organizing politically to demand educational, legal, and political rights, the Catholic Church and many men (along with some women) of different political persuasions expanded their public concerns over subaltern Nicaraguan sexuality to include the possible threat of lesbianism and what today might be called gender fluidity, gender dissidence, and nonbinary and transgender identities. They loudly denounced feminists and other "modern women" as marimachas and *marivarones*.

The advent of women's "modernity" (and lesbianism) in Nicaragua was often blamed on the influence exercised by U.S. Protestant missionaries and/or U.S. Marines. Historian Michel Gobat has written extensively about Catholic male elite members of the Conservative Party and their concern over the modern woman. That concern was evident in Pedro Joaquín Chamorro Zelaya's 1927 novel *Entre dos filos: Novela nicaragüense*. Chamorro (1891–1925), a Catholic activist from the Conservative city of Granada, was the grandson of a president, a prominent politician, and the editor of the influential newspaper *La Prensa*. His novel is considered "'foundational fiction' for a new national project . . . [that] helped crystallize the anti-American . . . spirit then emerging among elite Conservatives."[116] Gobat noted that one of the main women characters, Angelita, "embodies cosmopolitanism." "Educated in the United States, this English-speaking, car-driving 'amazona' displays all the manly qualities supposedly characteristic of the U.S.-based 'modern woman.'" An older female character in the novel sees Angelita, the daughter of an anticlerical and Freemason man, riding a horse "like a man" and exclaims: "It's fine that *Yancas* [women Yankees] and *marimachas* do it; but not girls educated in the Christian way. God save us from seeing you riding like a man."[117]

Panic over the Yankeeized woman was prevalent among different sectors of society. Conservative Catholics like Chamorro Zelaya and Francisco Palma Martínez shared a fear of this modern woman. Palma Martínez argued that

> More than industrialization; more than women's economic independence, more than the last two world wars, what is at fault for feminine moral corruption in these times is something that appears innocent and harmless: lipstick . . .
>
> We saw how makeup started in the American world. The Marines brought it with the occupation in 1926, to subject the young women of the working class who up until then had resisted using it. The middle-class ones had learned this new fashion at the movies, and the wealthy ones who had been to the United States, it was there that they learned the diabolical art of seducing men. Now we see the moral corruption of the modern woman and where all her arrogance and abandon has led her to . . .
>
> Now that she is wearing makeup, the most natural thing is for her to go someplace: to the movies, dancing, to bars, to the meetings for union women, everywhere where there are men . . . That is where the flood begins . . . she thinks of herself as a "free woman" who "wants to live her life" . . .
>
> Now she looks for work and finds it, and she becomes economically independent. She infringes upon the laws of nature: woman was not made for work, woman was made for the home, and for motherhood . . . She runs the gamut of all excesses, all prostitutions, all the debauchery and thinks she has arrived at the apotheosis of her happiness.
>
> Now comes the descent . . . She went through the chromatic scale of pleasures, personal abuse, aberrations, masturbation, homosexuality . . . Maybe she has syphilis, tuberculosis . . .

My purpose in saying this is to contain the moral decay that modernism brings with it, at least in my country . . . in others the collapse has advanced too far and it is not possible to suppress it . . .[118]

Opposition to U.S. imperialism (and the cultural changes associated with U.S. boots on the ground and U.S. cultural imperialism more generally) united what at first glance might seem to be unlikely allies. Michel Gobat has argued that elite Conservatives and Augusto C. Sandino, the nationalist leader who battled against U.S. Marines and was assassinated by Anastasio Somoza García in 1934, "converged mainly in their insistence that the end of the military occupation had not terminated Nicaragua's struggle against U.S. imperialism."[119] According to Gobat, "Sandino and his Conservative supporters" were united in "their crusade against the Americanization of Nicaraguan culture."[120] While Sandino focused on the influence of Wall Street bankers and the Americanized National Guard, Conservative elites rallied against what they saw as "the principal cause of Americanization," which was the "valorization of U.S. culture. In particular, they targeted the 'modern woman,' whose Americanized lifestyle the *Caballeros Católicos* had been attacking since the 1920s."[121] However, Sandino and the Conservatives "shared more than just simple anti-Americanism."[122]

It was during the 1920s and 1930s that a link was made between supposed urban sexual excesses and homosexuality, to be contrasted with the simplicity of heterosexuality in rural areas. In this, too, Sandino and his Conservative supporters seemed to coincide. According to Gobat, both entities "advanced corporatist ideals. Both also extolled an agrarian-based and highly moralistic . . . vision of the nation that emphasized class harmony. They thus contrasted what they considered to be the autochthonous and healthier ways of the [Nicaraguan] country folk with the Americanized, cosmopolitan hedonism of urban Nicaraguans. Homosexuality, for example, was an 'urban degeneration' that the *guerrillero* claimed did not exist in the countryside."[123] Sandino is quoted as saying, "There hasn't been a single case of homosexuality registered during the war. Those urban degenerations are taboo here."[124] And because women were readily available, rape was supposedly also nonexistent:

Here my soldiers have the freedom to woo anyone they want, zambas or others and to get them the nice way [*por las buenas*], since it is a strict law that in the army anyone who rapes a woman ["al que viola o estupra una mujer"] is shot [*se le fusila*] without contemplation and since here there is an abundance of Indigenous and peasant women, there aren't any problems.[125]

Despite the agreement between Sandino and some Conservatives on some aspects of anti-Americanism, Gobat is quick to point out that a "main difference was that Sandino championed the egalitarian futuristic peasant cooperative as the nation's building block, while Conservatives valorized the hierarchical cattle-based hacienda of colonial origin as the backbone of society."[126] Although "Sandino's nationalist project . . . was obviously much more inclusive" than that of the Conservatives,[127] the U.S. scholar Erin Finzer correctly pointed out that "the affirmative appraisal of male Sandinistas' sexual conquests of women points to the cultural importance in [the] 1920s . . . of emphasizing vigorous heterosexual masculinity as an essential trait in leaders."[128]

Male leaders at the time appear to have been obsessed with the supposed relationship between modernity and women's sexual insubordination. In 1929 Nicaragua's Liberal president under U.S. military occupation, José María Moncada (1871–1945), wrote a book replete with advice for one of his daughters, Elsa Moncada de Inestroza. In it, he commented extensively on the perils of modernity for women:

Modern literature! How it has perverted us! It stirs in one's conscience a sea of doubts and things one did not know. It incites, excites . . .

When I read certain books . . . I too feel their inducement and understand how dangerous they are for women's virtue.

Reject also that poetry called modernist . . . it should be considered illicit commerce, prohibited like alcoholism.[129]

Moncada then went on to state his opinion on feminism:

. . . I appreciate . . . modern feminism. I want woman to be educated, to think, to reflect and write. This writing profession is good also for the brain of a woman, the same as many other liberal professions that do not require strength or shrewdness. I do not wish to see her become an attorney, but an artist, yes.

I would not like to ever see her in politics or doing hard labor ... for it would be necessary to bid farewell forever to beauty and morality.

It is necessary to make woman beautiful, no matter how indirectly modern feminism wishes the opposite, asking for the rights and professions of men.

... Would mothers want to see their daughters ... guide and drive in the fields the plow and the oxen or take an ax to cut down a cedar ... ?

Or [see a daughter] political, crazy, feverish ... in the streets and plazas, seducing and carrying votes to the electoral urns, with a mouth full of improprieties and a soul full of passions?

Feminism gravitates also towards the ugliness of the soul. It wants to enter into the labyrinth of politics ... fight in the club and in the parks, go to parliament and shout against the government or the opposition ...

Make sure then, prudent mother, that your daughter helps you at home and looks into the great ideal of education instead, which is greater than rights, than liberties, and the republic, greater, in short, than civilization ...[130]

Ironically, Moncada was considered a "friend" by suffragists, who had high hopes for the vote at the time, given Moncada's support for women's suffrage.[131]

RUBÉN DARÍO, FEMINISTS, AND LESBIANS

In the early twentieth century, Rubén Darío (1867–1916), Nicaragua's most famous poet, joined the antifeminist and anti-lesbian male intellectual chorus of his time. Even before explicitly insulting feminists, he was largely unoriginal in his literary treatment of women. Like other male writers, he often portrayed women in his poems as simple, sometimes evil, characters. For instance, in one of his early poems, "Ecce Homo," written at age eighteen, he wrote:

Oh beautiful creatures which are not anything other than a herd of lucifers!

As the scholar Jorge Luis Camacho notes, "here woman is compared simultaneously to the anti-Christ and to a herd of animals."[132] Camacho goes on to explain that

> in many modernist texts ... woman appears as the eternal rival of man, someone to fear, and from whom he should protect himself so as not to succumb to her claws or desires. The modernist poets, according to Robert Glickman, self-described as "slaves" and described women as "queens" when in reality they ... relegated the opposite sex to a subaltern and dependent position.[133]

Specifically with regard to feminists, "in at least two articles, Darío was harsh against feminists, resorting to stereotypes of them that many in his time [also] resorted to."[134] In 1912, Darío complained that French feminists were old (*viejas*), ugly (*feas*), and fat (*jamonas*),[135] "and criticized the 'scandalous behavior, sometimes rude, sometimes comical, of the British suffragists.'"[136] Darío spoke out in particular against "the loud mannish women of militant feminism."[137] Camacho reminds us that "his main criticism focused on those who sought to take on political posts, in city halls, congress or the senate."[138] Indeed, in his 1912 brief essay "¡Estas mujeres!" (These Women!) Darío infamously wrote

> Following the unruly British [feminists], turns out that here in France women also want to vote, want to go to Congress . . .
> That women persist in wanting to do many things that men do and that there are some that surpass masculine competence: perfect . . . A few [*una que otra*] mannish woman has distinguished herself in explorations and incursions into savage lands or inaccessible places. You cannot argue against them . . . But these dykes [*marivarones*]—let's soften the word— that find themselves ready for the farsical roles in which men distinguish themselves and that . . . rush to take a role in the electoral farce, they deserve punishment.[139]

Camacho has correctly pointed out that Darío, just a year before his death, might have had a change of heart regarding feminism, as evidenced in an interview he granted to a woman reporter at the *New York Tribune* during a trip to the United States in 1915. Camacho explicitly asks: "Is it possible that Darío might have changed his mind on this topic?"[140]

In his 1915 interview, Darío admired the advances that women in the United States had made and spoke of U.S. feminists and women pioneers as prodigies, although he seemed to be particularly in awe of what he perceived to be the moderate nature of U.S. feminism as compared to that in England:

> The women here are all so capable, so efficient. And there are no fanatics, like we read about in England. I admire them very much and I must confess my amazement is as great as my admiration.[141]

The interview, titled "Latin Poet Suggests an International Thought Exchange to Help Spanish Women Free Themselves," promoted racist and sexist stereotypes about Latin Americans and non-Europeans, and made Spanish women sound frightfully "backward." While the article stated that according to Darío in Nicaragua "there was a broader life for women" than in Spain, it was clear from the interview that Darío was unaware of the full extent of feminist organizing in Nicaragua.[142] Darío probably would have approved of the "moderate" stance taken by someone like Josefa Toledo de Aguerri in the 1920s and beyond. Not surprisingly, Darío knew Josefa Toledo de Aguerri, and an event in his honor was held at one of her schools in 1908.[143] Moreover, "she was the one chosen . . . to welcome Rubén Darío when he returned [to Nicaragua]."[144] Unfortunately, Darío died too soon to see first-wave feminism blossom fully in Nicaragua.

THE CONSEQUENCES OF ANTIFEMINIST, HOMOPHOBIC, AND TRANSPHOBIC DIATRIBES

Sometimes antifeminist, homophobic, and transphobic rants were made by well-known individuals in print or in public places. On other occasions, however, there were articles signed only with initials, like the following one, published in 1905:

> There are ladies, known to all, that have abandoned completely their domestic duties, to go do politics. They don't care that the house is a

mess [*ande manga por hombro*] that the children don't change clothes, that the maid doesn't sweep the floor and that the cook makes culinary mistakes that attempt against [the family's] health . . .

I feel sorry for these marimachos.

They don't understand how much they lose in the eyes of sensible and prudent people, forgetting their duties by entering into matters prohibited to the fairer sex.[145]

Politicians and businessmen who were not necessarily well known at the national level also felt the need to reveal their anxieties over women's rights, homosexuality, gender fluidity, and gender nonconformity on paper. And newspapers like *La Tribuna* obliged. J. D. Mondragón wrote a long piece in 1921 under the title "Woman's Rebellion":

. . . [in] all places, in almost all countries, a crusade is starting by that being, that, while the most beautiful on earth, wants to tear away from man his natural supremacy.

. . . and there they are, trying to end the natural inequality from years ago . . . as a demand for *modern progress* . . . [emphasis in the original].

Many women today want to exercise men's occupations and to exercise like they do, the same political rights: to be *citizens*, to vote in elections . . . to be *members of congress and senators* and . . . *ministers* and *subsecretaries* . . . Not to mention *doctors* of medicine and jurisprudence or *engineers* [emphasis in the original].

They also want to have a pistol in their belt and a saddle to ride a horse, because if it comes to that, the military institution is also not something that is prohibited for them. Are they not already wearing pants? What more do they need?

. . . we have in our homes the bacillus of feminism led by the beautiful priestesses of the new idea. The government, ahead of this revolutionary movement, has started to open the doors to some public offices . . .

. . . to convert woman into man . . . and to convert man into woman . . . will at the very least obstruct and never improve the progressive development of societies . . .

Feminism, as we see it, takes woman away from marriage, because, to be honest, very few will be the foolish [men] who will want to marry a professional who works outside the home, leaving them with the domestic chores, with the cook's apron, taking care of the children and the darning of clothes. It is true that in the world there are some effeminate [men] who like to take on these womanly jobs and flirt and talk like females; but, let's understand, that in the purpose of *modern progress*, there is no room for increasing these deviations of sex.[146]

Animosity against feminists often manifested itself as homophobia and transphobia, and vice versa. Unfortunately, the publication of antifeminist, homophobic, and transphobic tirades was not a victimless exercise. It had quite dire effects on real individuals. It helped justify the persecution and prosecution of LGBTQIA+ Nicaraguans and helped foster a homophobic and transphobic antifeminist panic of sorts in the broader society.

Unlike the situation in the colonial period, where the state and the church teamed up to publicly burn sodomites at the stake, in the early twentieth century lawmakers and other elites focused (whether consciously or not I cannot say) on four strategies that curtailed the rights of LGBTQIA+ individuals. The first was to fire, or attempt to fire, middle-class individuals from their jobs, after insinuating that they were morally corrupt, as was noted earlier in the case of Josefa Toledo de Aguerri, the teachers at her school, and Edelberto Torres Espinoza. Although Toledo de Aguerri and Torres Espinoza were not LGBTQIA+, insinuations served to teach those who were LGBTQIA+ a lesson. In some ways, this was the twentieth-century equivalent of forcing the townsfolk to witness the public burnings of those who had been found guilty by the Inquisition.

Another strategy was to attempt to take jobs away from working-class women, preventing them from being financially independent, even though everyone knew that a high percentage of low-income homes depended on women's incomes. When the city of Managua laid off women street sweepers in 1931, an article in *La Prensa* noted that

> This measure leaves without work almost a hundred women heads of household [*mujeres madres de familia*] whose children will lack bread to live on. . . . [T]his means a new grade of misery and hunger for the women of Managua. If they are suppressed with the objective of putting those jobs in the hands of men, we don't think that is an opportune mea-

sure, because men can find some sort of work in the countryside, where women wouldn't be able to go to make a living.[147]

A third strategy was to attempt to pass laws that would discourage women from being "old maids" (*solteronas*). This was precisely what the representatives (*diputados*) Carlos Alberto Guadamuz and J. Filadelfo Robleto attempted to do in 1926 with the support of the senator Luciano García. They wrote a bill "against people who live bad lives and old maids."[148] This was a failed strategy from the beginning since there was no legal precedent for such a law. Moreover, culturally there was a great deal of acceptance for "old maids" (women who did not marry, did not have male partners, and did not have children) as well as for heterosexual couples who lived together without ever getting married and for never-married women who financially supported their children and did not live with their child/ren's father/s.

The fourth and possibly the most successful strategy was to increase police surveillance of gender nonbinary, gender-fluid, and gender-dissident or gender-nonconforming behavior and step up the apprehension and punishment of individuals who were not heteronormative. From the early 1900s onward, police sought to be hypervigilant in their effort to win the war against the vices they associated with modernity:

> The Director of Police, Colonel Vega T., has given very strict orders with the plausible objective that the vice of vagrancy in all its manifestations be persecuted with tenacity.
>
> He has arranged for the urban police to display greater activity visiting daily the public establishments such as taverns, billiards, bars, hotels, etc., in short, every place where there are games . . . liquor, prostitutes, madams and people who live bad lives . . .
>
> He has also warned that . . . after 9 pm., minors under 18 years of age not be allowed on the streets . . .
>
> The goal is to prevent young people . . . from surrendering to degrading vices that are and will be a terrible gangrene to modern nationalities.[149]

Police officers were actually quite successful in capturing and punishing LGBTQIA+ Nicaraguans during this period, and newspapers were quick to capitalize on their persecution. Ironically, given the destruction of police records in Nicaragua's many wars and environmental disasters, these accounts in the press are some of the only glimpses we now have into LGBTQIA+ life during this period, making each report worthy of being examined in depth.

THE LIVES OF LGBTQIA+ INDIVIDUALS AS REPORTED BY THE PRESS

Under the heading "Nocturnal Disguises," *El Comercio* reported the following in 1904:

> It was around 7:30 night before last when a man with short stature and a strange walk went past the Central Police Station, and a little while later a minor arrived saying that a man with braids was on Camelia street. An instant later the Assistant Director sent a police officer to follow him and in fact [the policeman] caught up with him in front of the water processing plant. There he became a prisoner and was taken to jail, but because it is a precaution to search everyone who is going to go in, when the prisoner was going to have this operation done he was profusely opposed [to it] until finally confessing to being a woman.
>
> Then the Assistant Director himself took her to the home for women's confinement ["casa de reclusión de mujeres"] from where she sent for her clothes from home that she had left over her foldout cot [*tijera*].
>
> She left the bedroom she occupies in the alley of Aurora [street] with a costume on, which means she went across the most central part of town going through the park.
>
> When she was interrogated as to the motive for her costume, she answered that she was simply trying to scare a female friend [*amiga*].[150]

Several issues stand out in this account. First, although the article made sure to reveal that this person was low income, by noting that they only had "a bedroom" (not a house) in an "alley" (not a main street) and that they slept not on a bed but on a "tijera," the reporter did not publish their name. Additionally, the reporter was willing to let the reason given for wearing men's clothes stand. The clothes were labeled a disguise/costume, and the reporter did not speculate beyond "scaring a female friend." On the other hand, the way in which this individual was treated by the police for simply being "a man with braids" was appalling. Ultimately, the police pursued him, interrogated him, and forced him to wear women's clothes, although it seems that they did not fine him or formally punish him with a jail sentence.

In 1919, *El Comercio* reported another arrest of someone under the heading "Disguised as a Man":

> The night before last the Police found Dolores Castellón, known as "Chicha," disguised as a man, and since that is not permitted according to the respective Regulation, she was condemned to 30 days of reclusion in el Buen Pastor.[151]

Here we are told that the law, at least in 1919, prohibited women from wearing men's clothing, even if it was a costume, and that at the time thirty days in jail seemed like a reasonable punishment for that "crime." In this story, we learn not only the name of the individual, but also their nickname, leading us to believe that the newspaper wanted to make sure readers could identify Dolores.

Beyond class considerations, there appear to be no obvious patterns in terms of the naming of arrested individuals in newspaper reports. Sometimes the papers published their names, and sometimes they did not. However, the newspapers were clearly trying to sensationalize these arrests, sometimes even acknowledging in writing that they were doing so.

On other occasions, reporters took the liberty of waxing poetically about individuals arrested by the police, as was the case in the following 1906 article titled "Clipped Wings" ("Alas cortadas") from *El Comercio*.

> Mercedes Moreira and Concepción Flores, two dark-skinned women who wear their hair up, were out very late last Saturday, enjoying the placid rays of the moon, who jealous of their flirting, guided a police officer towards them and he took them to get a rest from their prolonged outing; not only for abusing of their liberty, but for having offered the officer good remuneration in return for allowing them to continue enjoying their expansion.[152]

In this account, the writer appears to be insinuating that Moreira and Flores were lovers and that their only "crime" was abusing their liberty and attempting to bribe a police officer. Another interpretation could be that they were sex workers looking for work. However, I find the former to be more plausible since newspaper reports of sex worker arrests tended to use a very different type of language.

We must keep in mind that the language used in newspaper articles reporting "crime" had two objectives: to sell newspapers and transmit the values of the newspaper's owner/s. At the time, there were very few newspapers in Nicaragua, most of them were partisan, and no women, to my knowledge, were reporters. *El Comercio*, headquartered in Managua, was one of the most successful newspapers in the early twentieth century. It had a large circulation and lasted several decades.

Not surprisingly, given my arguments in earlier chapters regarding the importance of Nicaragua's long-standing tradition of transgender women, all the additional newspaper reports found on LGBTQIA+ and gender-nonconforming individuals during this period dealt with individuals who today might have identified as transgender women. Moreover, as in the following 1906 article from *El Comercio*, not all the cases involved capture by the police:

> The night before last around midnight, two young men, Ignacio Peralta and Benito González, walked past the corner of Mr. Alcibíades Fuentes at the same time as two women were walking on Mr. Juan Aguirre's sidewalk. The young men stopped to watch the women go by, but they did not achieve their objective because the women had covered their faces with shawls [*rebozos*]. The strollers stood to watch the women until the women arrived at the market, where, with amazement, they watched the feigned women take off their hair and blouses while hurling sarcastic laughs and directing mocking words to González y Peralta . . .[153]

This is a story of sexual harassment that did not happen the way in which it was intended. Two young men stopped to harass and/or hire or even possibly assault two women they most likely assumed to be sex workers, given the fact that it was midnight. However, they were foiled in their attempts because the two women fought back and made fools of Ignacio and Benito. In addition to entertaining their readers, the moral of the story, according to the author, appears to be that men like Ignacio and Benito were unfortunately prevented from going about business as usual.

I found four additional cases that did involve arrests by the police in the years between 1906 and 1920. The first one, from 1906, was from *El Comercio* under the heading "At the Police":

> Mr. Francisco López went before the . . . local crime Judge for thinking of himself as a woman and for putting on a pair of gold earrings that he stole from Mrs. Ramona González.[154]

A second case, from 1919 and also from *El Comercio*, under the heading "Disguised as a Woman," was unique because the police appeared to have paraded an individual in the streets, a very uncommon punishment:

> We have been told that in Chinandega the police walked an individual through the streets who was disguised as a woman and who additionally displayed a voluminous and false belly.[155]

A third case, from 1920, was reported in *La Tribuna*:

> The following were taken to jail: . . . Celso Martínez, for going around suspiciously dressed as a woman; when he was booked, he angrily stated that they call him a man but that they are wrong because he belongs to the weaker sex.[156]

This third case is unusual in that the newspaper acknowledged Martínez was adamant about being a woman. Not surprisingly, however, the reporter referred to Martínez as angry and to women as the "weaker sex" in order to ridicule Martínez.

The final case uncovered, from 1917, stands out because of the level of detail found regarding the life and arrest of Elia Martínez in two separate newspapers, *La Tribuna* and *La Noticia*. In *La Tribuna*, the article on Elia Martínez was titled "A Man Disguised as a Woman":

> Elia Martínez was captured in a drunken state Saturday night by a police agent in this city. Once taken to the central office, the official on call, Manuel Argeñal, had some suspicions, due to certain details, that the person detained was not a woman, but rather a man.

Sunday morning the Police Director, who knew nothing about this, was speaking to the detainee thinking she was a woman, since her appearance and dress did not show the contrary. When the secretary Cajina read him the information so that he could dictate a sentence, it caught his attention that he referred to Martínez . . . as a man. To gain complete certainty, the secretary Cajina interrogated her and from her answers deduced she was a man; but in spite of everything, he commissioned Jesús María López Niño to do an expert examination through which all their suspicions were confirmed.

The Police Director condemned the detainee to 30 days in jail and to wear the clothes proper of his sex.

When he was asked about his origins, etc., he said he was from Granada, where he had also been discovered by the authorities of that city; that his mother, from an early age, called him Elia, and that she had gotten him so used to wearing women's clothing that it would be impossible for him to obey the Director's order. He is 28 years old, does not have facial hair, wears falsies [*postizos*] to look more like the fairer sex and the timbre of his voice was that of a woman's. The hair on his head is recently cut and he wears rags to . . . cover up. His aspect is that of an Indigenous woman who is of pure race. He has served in various hotels and in some of the most important homes in Granada and Managua and a thousand conjectures are made on this topic.

An audience filled up the room where the Police Director has his office.

It would not be a bad idea to photograph this man and to distribute his photo profusely so that he can be known throughout the world. A man of this type is dangerous for all homes, since thinking he is a woman, nobody takes precautions.[157]

In *La Noticia* Elia's story was told under the headline "The Man-Woman in Managua":

The curious . . . public from the capital day before yesterday had an appetizing delicacy.

—A man dressed as a woman has been captured.

In fact, Sunday at dawn, in the vehicle of Dr. Ocón . . . Francisco Martínez was captured, the same one that was discovered about a month ago by the police in Granada.

Francisco, dressed as a woman, is a woman: the high voice, the feminine manners, tall, of Indigenous appearance.

When they took him before the Director of Police Mr. Ibarra, the latter asked: "How can I help you, Ma'am?"

"I am not a ma'am. I am a man!"

"How's that?" [*Y eso?*]

"Yes sir. I am a man, but since childhood I was raised as a girl; I do not know how to do heavy jobs, I barely can chop wood, but I know how to cook, iron, all very well, as Mr. Francisco Reñazco, in whose house I served, can attest. In Granada, the police cut my beautiful hair . . . But now I am going to dress as a man, for now I bought a hat, which is what I needed. What got me lost is that last night I had a few drinks and they noticed that I was a man."

The Police Director condemned this degenerate to 30 days of public works and they sent him to sweep the streets.[158]

Elia Martínez's story exemplifies what life was like for working-class LGBTQIA+ Nicaraguans in the early twentieth century. Looking like "an Indigenous woman who is of pure race" (*una india de raza pura*), her job prospects were limited to serving the rich, as long as she was accepted as a woman. She thus depended on the goodwill of her wealthy employers.

Francisco Reñazco, Martínez's previous employer, was a "coffee grower . . . owner of the hacienda San José del Cardón, located in the mountains of Managua." He was a Conservative politician who "became Minister of Public Instruction."[159] In an ironic twist of fate, Reñazco was also vice president of the board of the Zacarías Guerra Home for orphan children. The president of that board was Monseñor Lezcano.[160]

Further research into Elia Martínez's life led to a death record that appears to be hers. An unmarried woman by the name of Elia Martínez (also called Elisa Martínez in the same document) died in Managua in 1946 of cirrhosis of the liver. She is listed as having worked in the home (*ama de casa*). She was considered an illegitimate daughter, and her mother had already passed away. She was being treated by a doctor when she died, and the person who reported her death (José Dolores Martínez) shared her last name. These last two facts lead me to believe that she was most likely living with family members at the time of her death, although, given how common the last name Martínez was, it is possible that José Dolores was her partner. She was fifty-five years old when she died.[161]

In the end, despite the abuse, the persecution, and the ridicule, Elia Martínez continued to live her life as a woman for almost thirty years after she was arrested in 1917. Cutting her hair and forcing her to do "public works" for thirty days was not enough to prevent her from living her life on her own terms. While she might have succumbed to alcohol, she fought bravely against the heteronormative pressures of her time.

GENDER, GENDER EXPRESSION, SEXUALITY, AND SPORTS IN THE EARLY TWENTIETH CENTURY

Sports have always been about more than the game. Bodies are on display, exposed to extreme scrutiny. Moreover, games are performances: of skill, gender, race, sexuality, nationality, etc. Sports also intersect with the broader world. Which sports are played by whom and where are decisions that are not made only at the individual or family level. Because so many people feel that sports can represent the "heart and soul" of a nation, nation-states take great interest in monitoring teams, athletes, and the rules of a sport. Elites, among them local politicians and church representatives, frequently take on the task of policing the uniforms, the symbols, and the overall perimeters of sports. However, players often rebel, fashioning complex and sometimes contradictory experiences of their own bodies in motion while representing and ascribing meaning to those experiences in their own way and for their own purposes.

This section of the chapter documents the history of sports in Nicaragua in the early twentieth century from an intersectional perspective, one that highlights the intersections between gender, sexuality, race, and class, in order to contextualize the lives of LGBTQIA+ Nicaraguans, particularly lesbian athletes, whose lives were curtailed by both homophobia and sexism. Sports during this period served as an arena in which women could push the boundaries of what it meant to be a woman at a time when, much to the chagrin of some very vocal men and some less vocal women, political and social rights for all women were expanding. The ongoing crisis in heteromasculinities, fueled in part by the success of feminism and the reality of U.S. intervention, also played itself out in sports.

WOMEN IN SPORTS

Young Nicaraguan women from the early twentieth century onward gravitated toward sports, particularly toward basketball, tennis, softball, volleyball, and baseball. Other sports, like golf, were exclusively male enterprises, and disproportionally played by the U.S. Marines who were occupying Nicaragua at the time.[162] According to historian Michel Gobat, one of the few scholars outside Central America to study Nicaraguan women and sports during this period, "female athleticism boomed in Nicaragua during the 1920s, with basketball quickly emerging as the most popular women's sport and tennis a distant second."[163] The Central American historian Chester Urbina Gaitán, a sports historian who, like Gobat, also focuses on this period, has found evidence of women playing sports even earlier:

> On Tuesday October 1, 1917, two groups of young women from the capital's elite started to practice cricket in the field of Momotombo street. They did this with the goal of training and be able to play in public games to benefit the Managua hospital. It was thought that afterwards they would execute tennis, basketball, and other sports. These young ladies had mentioned that on Tuesdays and Saturdays they would gather together in the afternoons to practice.[164]

A 1923 newspaper noted that a women's basketball team called Las Brumas had been formed in Jinotega, a city in north-central Nicaragua.[165] The team had a board, and all three positions were held by women: Berta Von Berswordt Wallrabe was president, Florentina de Noguera was the treasurer, and Amanda López was secretary.[166] Two other women's basketball clubs already in existence elsewhere in 1923 were El Alpino y El Deportivo.[167] In Jinotepe, a women's basketball club called Iris was formed that same year.[168] In 1924 the club Argentino was formed in Managua with the following members: Sofía Bárcenas, Manuela Vélez, María Haydé P., Dominga Zelaya Bolaños (a cousin of President Zelaya), Muriel Burns, Anita

Mejía, and Haydee Zúniga. They were set to play a friendly game against El Deportivo, whose members included Haydee Portocarrero, Rosa Cousin (niece of President Zelaya's wife), Argentina Pertz (possibly the daughter of the German immigrant Alfredo Pertz), Margarita Belli (related to President Emiliano Chamorro), Emelina Castillo, Lolita Torres de Sola, and Clementina Tellería.[169] Almost every large city had some kind of women's sports team in the 1920s, 1930s, 1940s, and beyond.

By 1940 there were at least two women's basketball teams and one volleyball team in Granada alone.[170] Gobat has noted: "Women of all social classes watched sports [in the 1920s], but most female athletes [during these years] came from the upper classes and were usually in their late teens or early twenties."[171] The class background of women athletes would certainly expand over time, although rural women and Indigenous people would largely be excluded from organized sports during much of the twentieth century.

THE CRITICS

Michel Gobat has argued that in the 1920s "for many Nicaraguans, the clashes between 'modern' and 'reactionary' ideals of femininity were most noticeable in the conflict triggered by women's growing participation in sports."[172] Gobat documented the opposition of the Catholic Gentlemen (Caballeros Católicos) to women in sports during this period. The group, as the name suggests, was made up of Catholic "gentlemen" from the Conservative city of Granada. In the context of the U.S. military occupation of Nicaragua, the Caballeros Católicos led a moral crusade against "the new female consumption and leisure habits that appeared in the postwar era and were most strongly embraced by elite women."[173] The Caballeros embraced a "religiously based anti-Americanism"[174] to prevent what they felt was the ongoing deterioration of their patriarchal power in society due to the influence of Protestantism and U.S. cultural values. They felt threatened by Nicaraguan feminists demanding political and legal rights, and they also were simultaneously opposed to what they perceived to be the masculinization of women through sports and (simultaneously) their over-heterosexualization via skimpy uniforms that revealed too much of their female bodies. In particular, they worried about lesbianism, heterosexual women's sexual independence, gender nonconformance, and gender fluidity. "'The day nears,' a prominent Caballero Católico polemicized, 'when all of us will need to carry a sign on our back, saying: I am a man, I am a woman.'"[175]

Many priests agreed with the Caballeros and made it a point to lash out against women athletes in their sermons. In the 1940s, clergy were still railing against women's participation in sports. A sermon given by Father Matamoros in November 1940 was paraphrased as follows in *La Prensa*, one of Nicaragua's most important newspapers:

> Father Matamoros, closely following the Sacred Scripture, said more or less: "The enemy of man spoils virtue and drags souls to eternal perdition. In the modern sport of basketball, so fashionable among the fairer sex, they want to sow discord suppressing decency in woman, corrupting the soul of society, ending the Christian morals of society." From this one cannot deduce that the Church is an enemy of sports, they actually encourage it as an indispensable means for the body's and the soul's health. What the Church disapproves of is the immorality, the indecency, the provocative and dishonest uniforms on the ladies who are ornaments of the home, of society and of our motherland.[176]

There were others who spoke out against women in sports. The conservative misogynist Francisco Palma Martínez from León was of course one of them. In his book *El siglo de los topos* (1949) he railed extensively against women athletes. He did so for several reasons. He thought that "physical work turns people into brutes,"[177] and then extended that logic to argue that "sports and exercise . . . taken to excess, also turn people into brutes . . ."[178] Palma Martínez was particularly opposed to women playing baseball, a sport he linked to lesbianism: "the dyke [marimacho] . . . plays baseball."[179]

In Palma Martínez's opinion, men needed to be masculine, and women needed to be feminine. He believed certain activities were masculine/masculinizing and others feminine/feminizing:

> The baritone is generally effeminate . . . the violinist [Palma was a violinist] is always masculine . . . Why are the vast majority of pianists effeminate? . . . Composers of songs and ballads have always been effeminate . . . The composers of more serious works have always been masculine . . .

The classical dancers are effeminate . . . Writers are virile, even women writers . . . The woman who does a man's job becomes masculine and that is why it is detrimental for them to lead orchestras, play wind instruments, and play baseball.[180]

Another reason Palma Martínez was so opposed to women playing baseball was because he associated the game with a type of U.S. cultural imperialism that he found to be degrading to Nicaraguans. He firmly believed Nicaraguans were not ready for such "luxuries" as baseball, nail polish, and lipstick. He noted:

Nail polish is an American luxury . . .

Lipstick is an American luxury. Those women have money in excess, food, a good bed in which to sleep, but our poor young women who sleep on the floor . . . who do not have a clean sheet nor a pillow, it is ridiculous for them to use makeup . . . Those American luxuries for working-class Nicaraguan women are pure nonsense.

Baseball is an American luxury. Not long ago all of León went to Managua to watch a ball game and many were left in debt. Wouldn't they have gotten more out of staying at home to read a book?[181]

Overall, the opposition to baseball sometimes had an anti-U.S. tone, sometimes a classist/racist one, sometimes a sexist one, sometimes a homophobic one, and sometimes it had all four. On other occasions, it seemed like personal reasons were behind the opposition to Nicaraguans playing the game. For example, in the early 1890s a fistfight broke out among baseball fans in Granada, leading the political chief (*jefe político*) there to ban the sport. Around the same time, Juan de Dios Matus, the editor of the Managua newspaper *El Duende*, was so opposed to kids playing baseball on the streets and disrupting pedestrians that he successfully lobbied for its prohibition.[182] These two examples might seem like overzealous individual efforts to curtail baseball's popularity because of isolated incidents and nothing more. However, a second glance reveals possible partisan motives behind the opposition to the sport. Juan de Dios Matus was a member of the Conservative Party, and his newspaper often attacked Liberal politicians. This leads me to postulate that in the minds of some Nicaraguans, baseball might have been considered a sport promoted by Liberals. Corroborating this argument is the fact that baseball would see a resurgence after 1893, under the incoming president, the Liberal general Zelaya. According to the U.S. author Dan Gordon, "city officials in Managua and Granada prohibited street baseball... But when José Santos Zelaya took over the country... one of his first moves to win over the public was to lift the ban."[183] In one of the few histories of Nicaraguan baseball written in English for a non-Nicaraguan audience, Gordon concludes that "the tentacles of *Pinolero* [Nicaraguan] politics and sports are wrapped so tightly around one another that it's challenging at times to distinguish one from the other."[184]

In the end, male baseball would reign in Nicaragua for the entire twentieth century. However, in the mid-twentieth century it did seem like women baseball players would become commonplace. An article titled "Enthusiasm for the Feminine Baseball Series That Will Be Inaugurated This Sunday at the Stadium" was published in *La Prensa* in 1949. It seems reasonable to believe that those reading this piece might have reached the conclusion that Nicaragua and the world were ready for women baseball players:

> Unusual enthusiasm has been observed in all the sports sectors regarding the inauguration of the Feminine Baseball Series which will be inaugurated next Sunday. The enthusiasm for Baseball has not only spread among fans, but also among groups of young women who are ready to play this sport, which for the first time will be presented in Nicaragua. In three sectors of the capital there are groups of females ready to play baseball: in the neighborhood of San Sebastian, in Candelaria, and in San Pedro. In the first one of these, [a group] with the name "General Trujillo" has already signed up with the National Baseball Advisory.[185]

While the article stressed women's baseball teams on the Pacific, women had been playing baseball on the Caribbean Coast as early as 1937. There were at least two teams on the Caribbean Coast: "The Acorn of Bluefields and the Yellow Rose in Pearl Lagoon."[186] Not only were these two teams made up of women, but they were also scheduled to play against all-male teams in 1938. Jorge Eduardo Arellano quotes an article that appeared on November 11, 1938, in *La Noticia*: "This is hard to believe. Two feminine baseball groups in Bluefields are ready to fight against the masculine ones in the interior."[187] Like Arellano, I do not know if the games took place or who won. We also do not know when women in Nicaragua stopped playing baseball, if they ever truly stopped, when they picked it back up, and when they started to pursue softball. What we do know is that on the Pacific coast in the early 1940s young women were playing softball, but "they would throw the ball above their arm" ("tiraban la pelota por arriba del brazo").[188] Like the men's baseball teams, women's softball teams on the Pacific coast also included Afro-Nicaraguans along with mestizas early on. Some of the most famous women softball players from Bluefields were Anita Hodgson, Erika Omier, and Emely Wilson.[189]

WHAT WOMEN ATHLETES WERE UP AGAINST

The interrelated nature of sexism and homophobia is clear in the writings of one of Nicaragua's most famous and recurring Catholic priests in this story, Monseñor Lezcano, whose name is familiar today to many in Nicaragua because of the large working-class Managua neighborhood named after him. In his exhortations to the Daughters of Mary (Las Hijas de María), a women's Catholic group, gathered together in one volume and published in 1938, Monseñor Lezcano gave them a great deal of misogynistic and heteronormative advice:

> The Holy Virgin was in the most intimate part of her home and her bedroom and not outside the home, when she received the ambassador from heaven.
> Since the Holy Father wishes so much that women attend efficiently to their domestic lives, that he has ordered that we pray for that, the Daughters of Mary should be the first ones to satisfy those wishes which are the ones of Jesus our Lord and those of the most Holy Virgin. A very pious and intelligent young woman once said: "I never had a reason to regret being shut in my house; and many times I have regretted going out on the street."[190]
> It is a great social good for women to love the enclosure of their homes, and a great evil for them to dedicate themselves to life on the streets.[191]
> This has been understood even by peoples which are not Christian, like the Turks and the Chinese; Muslim Turks force their women to leave the house completely veiled so they cannot be seen; and we know that

the Chinese press the feet of girls from a tender age onwards with shoes that are too narrow so that they can have very small feet and thus cannot walk too much, nor go too far from home . . .

Jewels must be kept locked and only the things that have no value are left just anywhere.[192]

In addition to urging women to stay home to attend to domestic matters and remain pure for their husbands, Lezcano pointed out that there were two types of scandals: one—which presumably included homosexuality, among other practices—was direct, and the other indirect. "In the direct one there is a type called diabolic scandal because harm is done like the devil . . . As far as the indirect scandal . . . the use of indecent fashions" led potentially to "excite imaginations and impure desires." Moreover, young women "who engaged with too much familiarity with men" were to blame when "they were not respected, and men had the nerve to say things to them that offended modesty."[193]

Men like Palma Martínez, Father Matamoros, and Monseñor Lezcano had to walk a thin line between presenting heterosexuality as the only available option and scaring women enough to not "give in" too much to heterosexual desire. In other words, their critique of heterosexuality had to convince women that there was a heavenly (if not a worldly) reward for their subordination to men and for their sexual restraint in the face of unbridled heteromasculine desire. Otherwise, these early twentieth-century social "influencers" might have inadvertently legitimized the pursuit of lesbian relationships.

When Palma Martínez, Matamoros, and Lezcano could not come up with enough carrots, they resorted to sticks. Linking homosexuality and heterosexual "excess" (i.e., nonmarital sexual activity) to the devil was one of the long-standing tactics to which they resorted. Another tactic was reminding women of the unintended consequences of heterosexual sex outside marriage: pregnancy resulting in illegitimate children, social discrimination, and hell. A third tactic was to remind women that they would be blamed for whatever men did to them if they (1) were not "pure" enough, (2) spent any time outside their homes, and/or (3) wore indecent clothes. Women's involvement in sports necessitated defying at least two of Monseñor Lezcano's rules for modest living: going outside and wearing team uniforms that, by his definition, were indecent. It is perhaps because they were under such intense scrutiny that so many young women players played on teams with their siblings, were often mentored and coached by older male relatives, sometimes married early, and were willing to leave the country to live in the United States.

WOMEN ATHLETES

Ada Moncada (1924–1986), the (perhaps illegitimate) daughter of President José María Moncada, was a star athlete in the 1940s. She played softball and basketball along with Sary and Gloria Miranda, the Casco sisters (Castalia, Lila, and Tere), Anita Saballos, "Coco" Basset, "Payita" Tellería, Xinda Medal, and the Patiño sisters.[194] Ada was one of four of Moncada's daughters known as *las micas*. The four were originally from Granada. After her basketball career ended, Ada Moncada went on to work in Managua, selling cheese for a living and lending money on the side.[195] In 1962 she was the victim of a robbery that made national headlines in the anti-Somoza press because the individuals linked to the robbery of her safe had ties to the dictatorship and because, according to rumors that could not have possibly been true, the theft was of 45 million córdobas (approximately 6.3 million U.S. dollars at the time).[196]

It was after the 1962 press coverage of the theft that reporters and commentators first hinted that Moncada was lesbian, an issue that had not made the news in the 1940s. Moncada, like Zacarías Guerra decades earlier, was described as being unmarried: "she was a lady who appeared to have no husband" ("era una señora a la que no se le conoció marido").[197] Another writer alluded to her sexuality by noting her physical strength: "She had the necessary strength to do well in sports and she could have easily thrown a hammer, lifted weights, practiced ice hockey or wrestling [*lucha libre*]."[198] She is now remembered as a lesbian athlete, the only one of the period that I have been able to locate: "Her personal tastes with regards to sexual diversity (that is what they are called today) leaned towards preferring people of her same sex; in one word, she was a lesbian."[199]

Unlike Ada's situation, many of the young women athletes were coached by their older brothers or male relatives. Often entire families played sports. Moreover, some of the players ended up spending extended periods of time in, or moving to, the United States. Aura Lila

Casco (1930–?), for example, one of Ada's teammates, played on the same basketball team as her sisters. She had started working in her family's beauty salon at age sixteen. After her mother died, she took care of "her younger brothers, a nephew and two nieces."[200] Eventually Aura Lila ran a hair salon out of the home she and her husband Juan rented on a busy street near Managua's commercial district. She moved to the United States in 1963, and her sisters also ended up moving to the United States.[201] Another teammate, Sary Miranda Whitford (1923–?), who was a Nicaraguan Sports Hall of Fame inductee, was sent by Anastasio Somoza García to study in the United States and train with the Pasadena Ramblers, a softball team, for several years. She was expected to return to Nicaragua to train other young women and eventually did return, although I do not know when or for how long.[202]

Unlike her teammates who moved to the United States, Moncada stayed in Nicaragua. According to a reporter, "around the 1980s, doña Ada Moncada died peacefully in her home [*quinta*] on the Northern Freeway [*Carretera Norte*] and a few years ago the National Guard officer who was the main suspect in the case [the robbery of the safe] died in the United States, where he had sought refuge after retiring from the army."[203] Unfortunately, not much more is known about Moncada. Nor is much known about the lives of other lesbian athletes of that period. What is known, however, is that sometimes there was admiration on the part of spectators for "masculine" qualities demonstrated by women athletes. For instance, in 1904 the newspaper *El Comercio* reported on a woman bull rider:

> The Festivities Committee this year ... presented to the public the most sui generis bullfighting show: a woman who rides a bull.
> ... a large audience attended the ... [event] in order to watch this singular spectacle.
> The woman, Juliana Rivas, appeared ... with an ... admirable resolution; she rode as if she were used to it, and even when the bull was released, she resisted the jumps like an accomplished rider.
> She won, from the Committee, 25 pesos, and a bit more that was collected among the public.
> The event has been talked about a lot, and the name of the heroine is spoken by many ("es llevado de boca en boca").[204]

While Juliana Rivas was lauded on this occasion, future decades would witness great opposition to women's involvement in sports considered to be excessively masculine, like boxing. Article headings in 1971 read "Regulation Prohibits Boxing by Women" and "Unpleasant, Antifeminine, Very Repulsive."[205]

TEACHING GIRLS BASKETBALL

It appears that all the coaches for women's teams were men. However, there was an effort in the early twentieth century to send Nicaraguan women abroad to obtain an education and then have them return to Nicaragua to teach sports and other subjects. According to Don Odle, that is how basketball was introduced to Nicaraguan women:

> In 1922 Ms. Zoraida M. Matus (1903–1984) returned from Columbia University [briefly] and was asked by the president of Nicaragua to teach at a local girls' school. It was here that basketball was introduced to the country . . .[206]

The Conservative leader Emiliano Chamorro had been the one to send Matus abroad:

> I think that of the eight young women I sent to study [abroad] with a good monthly allowance so that they wouldn't experience economic difficulties, I think that none came back to the country, staying instead in the United States where some of them are now teachers at the service of the American government, others have died, and our compatriot, Zoraida Matus, married to Colonel [George W.] Lewis [1878–1963], is now President of the Unión de Mujeres Americanas (Union of American Women). She currently lives in New York.[207]

Zoraida Matus married Colonel George Lewis in 1930 at the age of twenty-seven. Lewis was fifty-two. U.S. historian Brian Shellum notes that at the time, Matus's father was Nicaragua's minister of war, but there is no evidence to corroborate that claim.[208] It appears that the couple never had any children. Lewis was described in a newspaper as a "well-known soldier of fortune, writer of verse and policeman."[209] According to Shellum, Lewis "had served as volunteer soldier in the Philippine war, and as a paid military contractor in the Panama Canal Zone, Puerto Rico, Dominican Republic, and Haiti."[210] When Lewis married Matus, he was stationed in Liberia.[211] They were married at the Church of the Sacred Heart in Monrovia.[212] By then, Matus was already a U.S. citizen, although she had been born in Puntarenas, Costa Rica.[213]

We do not know what motivated Matus to teach girls basketball, but we do know that she was a friend of Josefa Toledo de Aguerri and other feminists, and she was a lifelong advocate for women's rights. Moreover, we know that there was an ongoing national debate over whether or not teaching physical education in schools was necessary for young women. In 1926 an opinion article in the Conservative newspaper *La Prensa* stated:

> According to some people, sports for women are a source of dissolution and bad habits. Sportswomen acquire in a short period of time a sense of freedom and they no longer want to submit to the masculine yoke.
>
> This is preferable to having them continue being enslaved by small men, those who cannot find another way to win a woman's love than by using the chains that tie her, in other words, her physical weakness.
>
> Physical education for women will bring with it an intensification of the physical education for men, and when women are strong in body, mind, and spirit, on that day they will refuse to join in matrimony with those "almost men" who swarm God's streets and for whom the concept of manhood resides in having three or four of the most refined vices. The social importance of feminine education will serve as a basis for women's future redemption.[214]

The idea that women were morally superior to men (and more specifically that middle-class women were superior to working-class men) and could redeem Nicaraguan society was a popular one among certain Conservatives. This belief sometimes provided justification for implementing physical education in schools for girls, as in this case, but it could also provide justification for the opposite, as can be seen in the writings of Francisco Palma Martínez, Father Matamoros, and Monseñor Lezcano.

The belief in women's moral superiority would also fuel Conservative support for woman suffrage during this same period. However, Conservatives would become disillusioned when the vote for women allowed Liberal women to help maintain the Somoza dictators in power.[215]

In the end, the debate over the teaching of physical education in primary and secondary schools was a moot one. Calisthenics was taught at the Colegio de Señoritas de Managua as early as 1920.[216] And the Ministry of Public Education would embrace physical education throughout the century as part of a modern education for both boys and girls. Poverty and war, not prejudice, would prevent girls and boys from taking physical education classes in public schools throughout the twentieth century.

RACE AND BASEBALL

While feminist and "modern" educators were largely embracing the idea of physical education in schools, the debates over women and sports raged on. Moreover, the specific objections to women playing *baseball* did not take place only in Nicaragua. People in the United States were conflicted over women baseball players as well. The U.S. political scientist Jennifer Ring cites a former U.S. baseball player, who wrote in 1927 that "when women 'intruded into the game there was usually trouble.'"[217] Baseball in the United States today is mostly a male sport, but it was not always that way. Ring addresses the existence of women baseball players as early as the nineteenth century and documents how baseball became a white male sport when it became professionalized.[218]

As is the case of the United States and elsewhere, the LGBTQIA+ history of Nicaragua is the history of racialized individuals. And precisely because race is central to assumptions about physical abilities, it is crucial to center race in our discussion of sports in Nicaragua. This is especially the case in relation to baseball, which is symbolically tied to white supremacy and U.S. domination in both U.S. and Nicaraguan imaginaries.

When it came to race during the early twentieth century, baseball in the United States was legally more complicated than baseball in Nicaragua because of the ways in which anti-Black racism manifested itself in the United States through de facto and de jure segregation. Nicaragua had a different legal racial history, and perhaps because of that Afro-Nicaraguans played along mestizo and mestizo-identified baseball players (although not necessarily Indigenous players) on the same men's teams early on, on both coasts. But Nicaragua was unusual even when compared to some other Latin American countries, like Cuba, for example. Jorge Eduardo Arellano notes that in 1939 there were six Afro-Nicaraguan players on Nicaragua's national team. That year Cuba only had two players of African ancestry on a team of eighteen.[219] Some of Nicaragua's greatest baseball players have in fact been Afro-Nicaraguan. Oliver Stanley Livingstone Cayasso Guerrero, known simply as Stanley Cayasso (1906–86), for instance, one of Nicaragua's most famous baseball players, was originally from Bluefields, on the Caribbean Coast, but moved to the Pacific in 1932, where he played for multiple teams until his retirement over two decades later.[220]

The presence of Afro-Nicaraguans on baseball teams located on the Pacific coast, however, did not mean there was no racism against them. Racial stereotypes appeared to have been common. The journalist José Francisco "Chepe Chico" Borgen, for instance, stated in 1932 that "the behavior of [the men] from the [Caribbean] coast showed that the clubs on the Pacific were lacking a true sporting spirit, that of professionals, as those Black men [*negritos*] from the [Caribbean team known as] Navy truly have."[221] The idea that Creoles had a "true sporting spirit" (*verdadero espíritu deportivo*) was probably meant as a compliment. However, it underscored a commonly held belief among mestizos and others regarding the physical superiority of people of African descent. While at first glance some might argue that ascribing physical superiority to a marginalized group is not detrimental to their well-being, it is important to point out that this belief had racist origins, given that it was used to justify the shipments of enslaved African individuals to the Americas when Indigenous communities were decimated after the Spanish conquest. There is no evidence, however, that "Chepe Chico" himself thought the Creole players had innate characteristics. He once stated:

> We must understand that the Navy is not invincible nor superior to those teams on the Pacific ... The advantages of "los negritos" are circumstantial. They do not drink, they are disciplined, they sleep until [*sic*] 9 at night, they practice day and night. Why not imitate them? ... Our

players on the Pacific still have to learn, at least when it comes to the type of regimen that the true athlete must have.²²²

While mestizo and mestizo-identified athletes and observers on the Pacific coast might have seen the example of the Creole players as one to be followed to become more competitive, Creole players appear to have sought greater inclusion in the nation-state through their athletic excellence. Frank Hodgson made a case for rapprochement in 1932, after receiving an important trophy on behalf of his teammates on the winning Navy team:

> Hodgson mentioned that for a second time—the first time had been in 1916—"a delegation from the Coast" had arrived "seeking the longed for closeness between the Atlantic Coast and the country's interior" and that the objective of the Navy was fraternal; it came, "not to defeat the sports players from the interior, but to let them get to know us, so that we are counted in the national reserves, whenever necessary"²²³

Baseball teams in Nicaragua did not have to deal with legal racial segregation, but baseball had strong racial underpinnings in part because of its symbolic ties to the United States and the U.S. military occupation. In fact, baseball in Nicaragua during the early twentieth century is symbolized by a famous photo of white Marines playing baseball in Nicaragua in 1915. Moreover, Nicaraguan baseball teams would mirror the racist U.S. practice of naming teams after Indigenous peoples and having team mascots that promoted stereotypes about Native peoples. Additionally, Nicaraguan teams sometimes promoted anti-Black racist stereotypes among fans. According to Rory Costello and Alberto "Tito" Rondón, "Navy was highly successful on the Pacific side. [Because of their success] [t]hey were ... accused of witchcraft and had a 'black bat' burned, sprayed with holy water and buried—[but] they still won."²²⁴

Associating witchcraft with peoples of African (and Miskitu, Mayagna, and Rama) descent was a common racist practice among mestizos and others on the Pacific coast and central regions of Nicaragua. In the 1980s, it was still having an impact on baseball as exemplified by the story of the team Los Dantos and their bat carrier (*cargabates*) Keith Taylor. Taylor was born in Corn Island in 1951. He eventually moved to the Pacific coast and in the 1980s worked as a bat carrier and animator (*animador*) for Los Dantos. At the time, many teams had *animadores*. These were individual cheerleaders hired by the teams to foster team spirit among the fans during games, often by getting fans to laugh at their self-deprecating skits. "Chavelo," the cheerleader for the rival team El Boer was a little person, as was Freddy Siles, the cheerleader for the team called Los Productores de la UNAG. The other cheerleader for El Boer was nicknamed "Clodomiro el ñajo," after the famous Carlos Mejía Godoy song that has at its main protagonist a man with a speech disorder. A reporter described Taylor's job during this time as follows:

> Taylor had a little box that looked like a small casket. Inside it he had a doll that had the hands towards the back and after each batting, whether by the Dantos or the other team, he would go to Homeplate or first base and he would throw the doll on the floor. Then he would start to dance around it and immediately the bat carrier from the other team would come out or a player from another team and they would walk towards where the "witch" was. Taylor would immediately take the doll, put it inside the box again and flee towards the Danto's dugout. People would shout. Taylor also danced and the fans became excited. The fans of the other team would boo him. This caused a great deal of joy for the fans.[225]

In that same article the journalist interviewed Taylor, who contextualized his performance:

> "I made up [tricks] and those inventions worked because Los Dantos won. I pretended to be a witch and people thought it was true. The truth is I don't like to cause anyone harm. I danced just to give the team good luck[,]" explained Taylor.[226]

The history of anti-Black racism in Nicaraguan baseball is a longstanding one. Taylor's performance worked because many on the opposing teams and among the opposing fan base actually believed that Afro-Nicaraguans practiced witchcraft or could potentially do so. Nonetheless, Taylor was able to use their racism to his advantage, leading him to win a competition among cheerleaders (animadores) and instilling real fear in his team's enemies.[227]

The history of baseball in Nicaragua is intrinsically linked to the history of U.S. imperialism and anti-Black racism. However, despite the common perception that the U.S. Marines brought baseball to Nicaragua, there is a consensus among historians that baseball was brought to Nicaragua's Pacific coast by Nicaraguans studying in the United States: "baseball had captured the imagination of urban Nicaraguans well before the arrival of U.S. troops. By the early 1910s Granada boasted ten baseball teams but only one soccer club."[228]

Moreover, baseball had even earlier origins on the Caribbean Coast:

> The first time baseball was played in the country it was in Bluefields in 1889. Adolf Adlesberg—a German immigrant with more than twenty years living in the region—introduced it a year earlier, after getting bored watching the cricket teams Caledonia and Peace Club. And after he taught the rules to Creole youth of both teams, they started playing it with great enthusiasm ... immediately it was introduced in Managua and Granada by sons of the nation, specifically nine who had just graduated from a college in New York (seven from Granada and two from Managua), plus one, also from Managua, who had graduated from a college in Pennsylvania. Regardless, its elitist origin on the Pacific region led it to become a secular ritual—different from the religious ceremonies and the traditional national holidays—capable of bringing together different classes. And so, at the beginning of the twentieth century, it was played primarily by popular elements.[229]

WHY CARE ABOUT SPORTS?

> Sport in our culture is viewed by many as a "masculinizing project," a cultural practice in which boys learn to be men and male solidarity is forged ... when women actively participate in the symbols, practices and institutions of sport, what they do there is often not considered "real" sport nor in some cases, are they viewed as real women.[230]

The history of sports is important to the LGBTQIA+ history of Nicaragua in part because sports is fundamentally about gender and sexuality, and gender and sexuality are in turn inseparable from class, race, state formation, and nationhood. During the early twentieth century, elites fiercely attempted to uphold the existing gender binary in sports. It is my contention that elite men became centrally involved in monitoring and restricting women's involvement in sports precisely because so many elite women wanted to become involved in team sports. Gender dissidence had previously been associated mainly with working-class and Indigenous peoples. However, team sports changed that. Middle-class and upper-class women's participation in basketball, baseball, and even softball was a potential threat to the status quo. Elite men did their best to prevent women as a group from using their physical strength in creative and enjoyable ways. The record shows they failed.

Initially, participating in sports like basketball and baseball was an expression of class privilege for young, elite, unmarried women. However, it was also a challenge to the gender, racial, and religious norms of the time. For instance, although these young women were usually described as *señoritas*, some were actually married. Playing sports as married women at a time when marriage was expected to greatly curtail elite women's physical freedom was quite novel.

Like men's teams, women's teams needed to have ties to politicians and/or to the government itself to secure funding (for uniforms, travel, practice space, etc.) and to achieve legitimacy. Politics continues to permeate sports in Nicaragua today, as is the case elsewhere. Nonetheless, the drastic increase in women's university enrollment in the mid-twentieth century would significantly change the nature of sports for young women in Nicaragua. In the 1960s and beyond, many young women gained the opportunity to play on university teams that were not funded or supervised directly by individual politicians, which granted them increased freedom.

The mid-twentieth century brought other changes. In the 1920s and 1930s the young women players were described as "beautiful" and as "distinguished young women of our society." By the 1960s and 1970s, descriptions in newspapers focused more on the quality of the playing and less on the class background or "beauty" of the players. One can assume that an emphasis on skill instead of wealth and traditional standards of femininity opened more spaces for lesbian players in the mid- to late 1900s. Unfortunately, a detailed history of women in sports throughout the twentieth century, while important, is beyond the scope of this book.

HOMOSOCIALITY AND THE POLICING OF MEN'S SEXUALITY

Monsignors, priests, and social commentators attempted to police women's physical activities in very public ways. However, this did not mean that men were free to do whatever they wanted with their bodies. Male athletes had to continuously prove their heteromasculinity. Failure to perform hegemonic masculinities could result in long-lasting negative consequences.

Women's sports teams were semi-homosocial spaces, since team players interacted with male coaches and male financial supporters. Male teams, however, were entirely homosocial spaces where interactions were all among men. Given the historical association of some male homosocial spaces (for example, prisons and ships) with homosexuality, it is not surprising to note that, for male athletes in particular, teams functioned as yet another arena in which men's sexuality was heavily policed. Additionally, it is important to point out that male baseball and basketball sports teams were in competition with other male homosocial recreational spaces that were considered more "manly," such as cockfighting and bullfighting. The lack of blood and physical violence in sports like basketball and baseball made them suspect.

Although almost impossible to document, homophobic bullying was probably common among Nicaraguan players in the early twentieth century. One of the few cases we have been able to document is the teasing of Stanley Cayasso, one of Nicaragua's most famous early baseball players. According to Tito Rondón, Cayasso "did not smoke or drink and was very disciplined." These characteristics made him an excellent player but also led some of his teammates to make fun of him for what they considered ladylike behavior. In fact, some teammates gave Cayasso the nickname "La Cayassa," a feminized version of his last name.[231]

Rondón and Costello have contextualized Cayasso's nickname, noting that other early baseball players were also given feminized nicknames for seemingly "unmanly" behavior. U.S. baseball player Charles Baldwin (1859–1937), for instance, came to be known as "Lady Baldwin."[232] One commentator stated the following about "Lady Baldwin":

> The nickname? The mystery is not how he acquired it, but how he managed to survive in baseball as long as he did while bearing such a han-

dle. He earned the name not because he was effeminate, but because he behaved the way ladies were supposed to behave: he did not smoke, swear, or imbibe. In an interview he gave in 1934 when he was 74, he said he had yet to taste alcohol or tobacco.[233]

Today in Nicaragua a male athlete's choice to refrain from alcohol, tobacco, and drugs might not seem very unusual, given the greater understanding of the impact of these substances on an athlete's performance, the laws against doping, and the conversion of many Nicaraguans to evangelical Christianity. However, it is important to remember that during Cayasso's youth, Nicaragua was a predominantly Catholic country, and Catholicism did not and does not prohibit the consumption of alcohol or tobacco products.

Cayasso's self-discipline may or may not have been influenced by a religious affiliation. But it did earn him a "ladylike" reputation. Moreover, as noted earlier, it led to a debate among mestizos and others over whether or not that was the reason players from the Caribbean played so well. Ironically, while mestizos (and mestizo-identified members of the public) engaged in racist conversations over the relationship between race and athletic performance, and Cayasso put up with his teammates' homophobic mockery, many Creole players understood that they had to be twice as good as the other players if they wanted to simply be taken into account on the Pacific coast "to let them get to know us, so that we are counted in the national reserves, whenever necessary."[234]

CONCLUSION

The first three decades of the twentieth century were devastating for Nicaragua. In addition to dealing with fifteen different presidents (including acting presidents), U.S military intervention, and a worldwide depression, Nicaraguans were plagued by natural disasters (a severe earthquake struck Managua in 1931) and what seemed to be never-ending wars on Nicaraguan soil. Against this backdrop, it is not surprising that many in Nicaragua and abroad would be inspired by the anti-imperialist leadership of Augusto C. Sandino, the nationalist who fought against the U.S. Marine presence in Nicaragua, or that so many Nicaraguan women would turn to feminism as a way to achieve greater social justice. These were terribly difficult decades but also hopeful ones. To the chagrin of many socially and politically conservative elites, Sandinismo and feminism would go on to become two of the strongest and longest-lasting political ideologies in Nicaraguan history.

Women's same-sex relations are largely absent from the historical record prior to the early 1900s. There was a great deal of concern with policing women's sexuality before then, but the emphasis had been primarily on preventing women's adultery and their engagement in premarital heterosexual relations. This chapter examined elite fear and hatred of lesbianism and trans individuals that developed as a reaction, in the early twentieth century, to the advent of first-wave feminism and "the modern woman." The "modern woman," lesbianism, and gender dissidence were often blamed on U.S. Protestant missionaries and/or the U.S. Marine occupation during this time. Additionally, it was during this period that a link was made between urban sexual excesses and homosexuality, to be contrasted with the supposed simplicity of rural heterosexuality. Although they were accused of being marimachas, or perhaps because of the accusations, first-wave feminists sought to distance themselves from homosexuality. Once that generation of feminists was displaced in popular memory by the nonfeminist pro-Somoza women's movement of the 1950s and 1960s, lesbianism was hardly mentioned until fears over "free love" arose in the 1970s.

4

POETRY AND PERSECUTION

The Somoza Dictatorship, 1936–1979

IN 1929 the world spun into an economic depression, taking Nicaragua with it, and soon afterward, in 1931, an earthquake destroyed the city of Managua, killing thousands, leaving two-thirds of the city homeless, and causing 35 million dollars in material damage:

> Hundreds were crushed or trapped, many burned to death, it is said that the marines of the occupying troops, unable to rescue some who were trapped in the rubble, shot them to shorten their agonies...[1]

We do not know whether U.S. Marines actually shot Nicaraguans dead in the streets of Managua. But we do know that by 1932 there were still 1,500 U.S. troops stationed in Nicaragua. The Marines had failed to defeat the forces of Augusto C. Sandino (1895–1934), but they did succeed at preventing Nicaraguan women from voting in the elections they were there to supervise, telling suffragists to try again at another time, one more convenient for the imperialists.[2] It was not until the United States shifted toward the so-called Good Neighbor Policy that the Marines finally left Nicaragua in 1933, but women in Nicaragua were not able to vote until 1955.

The 1930s were indeed difficult years for Nicaragua. Sandino was assassinated in 1934 by the Liberal general who headed the National Guard, Anastasio Somoza García (1896–1956). Political stability remained elusive even after Somoza García ousted President Juan Bautista Sacasa (1874–1946) in 1936 and officially took power in January 1937 for a four-year term. Moreover, the economic depression that affected most of the world had a profound effect on Nicaragua: "the price of the main export product, coffee, fell sharply from 86 U.S. cents a kilo in 1929 to 52 cents in 1930; it continued to decline until reaching 32 cents."[3]

Emilio Álvarez Montalbán (1919–2014), "the prominent ophtalmologist, conservative politician and essayist," remembered the impact of the depression as follows: "Nicaragua at that time lived from the export of coffee; then, with the reduction in international prices, came the drop in the salaries of the Government, which was the best employer. The commercial houses, seeing their sales reduced, fired half of the employees. It was very hard." Álvarez Montalbán lived in Granada at the time, and there "people . . . emigrated to the farms. They went in search of milk, eggs, cheese, chickens, vegetables, deer, and beef. Those who stayed in the city had to sell whatever to earn a living . . . Many people had taken out loans at 2% per month and [more] . . . mortgaging their houses and farms, and they had to . . . pay that interest in dollars. Unfortunately, they had to hand over their properties."[4]

The advent of World War II gave Somoza García the opportunity to demonstrate his support for the United States, consolidate political power, and increase his personal wealth. Somoza García declared war on Japan, Germany, and Italy, and "during the War his administration built a U.S. military base and an air base in Corinto." Somoza García used the war as a pretext to declare a state of siege (*estado de sitio*) and suspend all constitutional guarantees.[5]

Somoza García was able to change the political constitution so that he could rule until 1947. In spite of the nondemocratic nature of the regime, Somoza "from the beginning tried to attend to social issues, education, and the creation of jobs. He talked about building houses for workers, promulgating the Labor Code, promoting agrarian reform, and a social security program."[6] Somoza's Liberal Party also embraced women's suffrage and periodic elections, which were fraudulent but important at the symbolic and the practical level for Somoza's supporters. Somocistas embraced the presidential elections held in 1957, 1963, 1967, and 1974. In 1957 Somocistas elected Luis Somoza Debayle (1922–67), Anastasio Somoza García's son, to the presidency after the assassination of Somoza García in 1956. Luis chose not to run for reelection in 1963 and instead allowed someone loyal to the Somozas to become president. Luis died of a heart attack in 1967, and Somocistas elected his younger brother, Anastasio "Tachito" Somoza Debayle (1925–80) to the presidency of Nicaragua in 1967 and 1974.

During the post-WWII years Nicaragua's agricultural export economy expanded again, and the Somoza years—particularly the 1960s—ushered in Nicaragua's economic modernization, bringing about an increase in the middle class and the incorporation of large numbers of urban women into the workforce.[7] While it is true that the 1960s could be considered Nicaragua's economic golden age, given the growth in the export sector and the expansion of social services that took place in that decade, that "golden age" was short-lived. Moreover, it benefited the wealthy at the expense of the poor, and state violence was ever present. The aftermath of the 1972 earthquake that destroyed Managua and caused "over a billion dollars [más de mil millones de dólares] in [material] loses"[8] brought yet another economic downward turn, the increased militarization of Nicaraguan society, and a rise in the persecution of anti-Somocistas by the Somozas' National Guard.

Although all three Somozas embraced anti-communism, it would be the last Somoza who would face mounting opposition from the leftist Sandinista guerrillas in the 1960s and 1970s. A series of events, among them the unraveling of the coalition that supported him, a downturn in the economy, a growing support for liberation theology among the population, and a decrease in U.S. support, all contributed to the last Somoza's violent overthrow on July 19, 1979.

The Somozas presided over a right-wing dictatorship. They used repression and co-optation, sometimes simultaneously, and during the early and middle years of their rule they experimented with populism. The Somozas opposed class struggle and favored hierarchical survival strategies such as patron-clientelism. Moreover, they were generally opposed to the imposition of economic equality by the state.[9] Most important, perhaps, to Nicaragua's LGBTQIA+ history is the fact that their rule was always more opportunistic than moralistic.

This chapter does not provide a comprehensive account of LGBTQIA+ life in Nicaragua from 1936 to 1979. Instead, the chapter discusses some important individuals, places, and events from that era and provides a framework to understand LGBTQIA+ life under the dictatorship. Inevitably, since the chapter relies in part on oral interviews and recollections of that period, I also briefly address the issue of memory and how it is that Nicaraguans in the late twentieth and early twenty-first centuries remembered LGBTQIA+ life during the dictatorship. Memories of the past are always mediated by the lens of the present, making it important to address the biases of those lenses.

In this chapter I discuss Rigoberto López Pérez (1929–56) and his legacy for Nicaragua's LGBTQIA+ history. Unlike other martyrs of the Nicaraguan revolution, Rigoberto López Pérez chose the precise moment of his death. And indeed, as he predicted, his decision to assassinate Anastasio Somoza García was "the beginning of the end" of the Somoza dictatorship. López Pérez would go on to become one of the main heroes and martyrs of the Sandinista revolution.

This chapter describes the life of Rigoberto López Pérez, including the magnicide, the assassination of López Pérez, and the massive persecution carried out by the National Guard in the aftermath of the 1956 action. This chapter also analyzes in detail the conversations that took place in Nicaraguan media in 2013 regarding Rigoberto López Pérez's homosexuality. In addition to addressing debates over López Pérez's sexuality, I also cover the debates that took place over the poet Rubén Darío's sexuality in 2009 and 2012, also in the Nicaraguan press, since the two debates are intertwined.

This chapter also documents the life of Carmelo Aguirre (1930–71), a Somocista business owner who, in the 1960s, led his life as a self-made man. Known as La Caimana, which I have translated as "the Alligator woman," Carmelo's story sheds light not only on the dynamics of the Somoza dictatorship but also on theoretical questions dealing with identity, sex, gender, and politics.

Through oral interviews, archival research, and cultural analyses, I examine LGBTQIA+ life under the Somoza dictatorship and the ways in which it is remembered. Specifically, I argue that Carmelo Aguirre's life story is intimately tied to urban remembrances of Somocismo. Carmelo's story is also one enmeshed in Nicaraguans' complicated relationship to modernity and progress.

In this chapter I also address the iconic Charco de los Patos (The Puddle of the Ducks), a famous bar/club in the 1960s and 1970s with a mixed heterosexual and LGBTQIA+ clientele and the life stories of La Reina de los Tártaros (the Queen of the Tartars), who worked at the Charco de los Patos as a waitress, and La Sebastiana[10] (1941–2016), a famous Managua food vendor and performer in the Torovenado and religious festivals of the 1960s and 1970s. La Sebastiana was raised as a boy and identified from the age of six as a girl.[11] La Reina and La Sebastiana's lives demonstrates the vulnerabilities of working-class LGBTQIA+ Nicaraguans under the dictatorship. I also examine the efforts made by anti-Somocistas to link homosexuality to the moral decay of the dictatorship. Finally, I discuss a surge in anti-LGBTQIA+ persecution during the late 1960s and early 1970s (a surge identified and described by the scholar David Rocha) and what that moral panic meant for LGBTQIA+ Nicaraguans.

RIGOBERTO LÓPEZ PÉREZ

Some poets have changed the course of history. Rigoberto López Pérez was one of those poets. In fact, he is so well known in Nicaragua that many refer to him simply as Rigoberto or by his initials, RLP.

He was born in 1929 and was considered an illegitimate child. As such, he was placed in a Catholic home for orphan boys by his godfather, the Reverend Agustín Hernández.[12] It was at the Hospicio San Juan de Dios that Rigoberto completed elementary school and learned a trade.[13] His skills as a tailor enabled Rigoberto to pay for his studies in stenography and help his working-class mother, Soledad López, whom he adored.[14] Rigoberto was the oldest of his mother's four children and one of thirty-two children on his father's side. There is no evidence that Rigoberto ever met his father, a well-known medical doctor, or that his father ever recognized him as his son.[15]

Rigoberto was an avid reader, a violinist, a composer, and a writer. In the late 1940s, he played in a musical group called Buenos Aires, and their songs could be heard on Radio Colonial. He was also a contributor to *El Cronista* and *El Centroamericano* before being fired in 1950. After that, he left for El Salvador but made many trips back to Nicaragua to visit his family and perhaps Amparo Zelaya Castro, sister of his friend, the journalist Armando Zelaya, who gave him a fateful ride in 1956.[16]

At 9:00 p.m. on September 21, 1956, at the age of twenty-seven, Rigoberto shot the U.S.-backed right-wing dictator, Anastasio Somoza García, at a dinner-dance taking place in the colonial city of León, Rigoberto's hometown. Somoza García had just finished dancing when he was shot. He would survive for another eight days. Rigoberto, however, knew that once *he* walked into the Workers' Hall where the event was taking place, he would not make it out alive. In the letter he wrote to his mother before his death, asking her to not mourn for him ("no sadness") he called the assassination "a duty, not a sacrifice."[17]

Rigoberto went on to become a hero, a martyr, and an inspiration for many of those who opposed the Somoza dictatorship. The leftist Sandinista guerrilla movement that developed in the mid-twentieth century to fight against the ongoing Somoza dictatorship named one of its guerrilla columns after him, and in 1974, Carlos Fonseca Amador, one of the founders of the FSLN, wrote an essay in which he analyzed the letter Rigoberto wrote to his mother.[18] Once the Sandinistas came to power in 1979, the revolutionary government named Managua's main stadium after Rigoberto López Pérez.[19] And a special school that had originally been created in 1960 to educate the children of Somocista army members was also renamed Rigoberto López Pérez.[20] In 1981 he was officially named a National Hero (*Héroe Nacional*) by the new Sandinista government.[21] Stamps were also created in Rigoberto's honor, and the 1985 one hundred córdoba bill carried his image. Today most Nicaraguans in the capital are familiar with Rigoberto because there is a roundabout in Managua named after him, and it has a gigantic statue of Rigoberto at its center.

From 2013 to 2015, a handful of Nicaraguan intellectuals, all men, engaged in a series of public conversations in the nation's major newspapers, *La Prensa* and *El Nuevo Diario*, about whether or not Rigoberto was "homosexual" and what that meant for Nicaraguan history. Seven of those articles written by five different male scholars can be found on a website hosted by Eduardo Pérez Valle Jr., one of the authors of one of those articles.[22]

Just as revealing as the articles were the dozens of anonymous comments made by readers responding in the online version of the newspaper articles. Unfortunately, the online comments are not part of Pérez

Valle's collection and are no longer available. Moreover, one of the newspapers, *El Nuevo Diario*, ceased publication in 2019.

The online commentators, some of whom might be considered right-wing or left-wing "trolls," were most likely Nicaraguans. While it is impossible to know who they were or whether they lived in Nicaragua or outside the country at the time, access to the internet at an inexpensive "cyber cafe" was relatively widespread in urban Nicaragua during the 2010s. This means that these comments most likely reflected the sentiments of a segment of the country's urban population. The online world was then and continues to be now replete with videos, still images, and written pieces about Rigoberto López Pérez.

The debate that took place in the first half of the 2010s over Rigoberto can only be understood in the context of what was then Nicaragua's thriving LGBTQIA+ rights movement and the politically polarizing nature of Daniel Ortega's rule. This makes sense since debates about the present are often about the past and debates about the past are often also about the present.

That Rigoberto might have had sex with men was first discussed at length in the Nicaraguan media in the twenty-first century, but it was not a secret in the 1950s. A confidential telegram sent on October 4, 1956, by Thomas C. Mann, the U.S. ambassador to El Salvador, to the secretary of state in Washington, stated the following:

> Nicaraguan Ambassador [unclear if it is U.S. Ambassador to Nicaragua or Nicaraguan Ambassador to the U.S. or to El Salvador or Salvadoran Ambassador to Nicaragua] called on me at his request last evening and summarized evidence available to him re Rigoberto López Pérez as follows:
>
> 1. Lopez was homosexual and subject [to] fits of epilepsy. He was introvert who often went to movies and baseball games and wrote bad poetry...
>
> 2. Lopez salary was only $80.00 a month yet he spent considerably more...[23]

An earlier document, sent on October 3, 1956, as an unclassified notification from the U.S. embassy in Managua to the Department of State in Washington, translated the statement made by the director in chief of the National Guard on September 29, 1956:

> ... Col Anastasio (Tachito) SOMOZA D., Director in Chief of the Guardia National, issued a statement which is translated below:
>
> The Command of the National Guard issues a communique to the effect that the Army of Nicaragua has supported unanimously the designation by the National Congress of Deputy Luis SOMOZA D. as legal and constitutional successor to the expired President of Nicaragua ... and adds:
>
> ... that the hopes which the cowards and rabble which used a communist psychopath, degenerate and homosexual to assassinate President Somoza have been frustrated in that they speculated that with the death of the Nicaraguan Chief of State there would have been confusion and anarchy...
>
> The above communique was published on October 1 ... in ... *Novedades*.[24]

Clearly, the Somoza family as well as the U.S. embassies in El Salvador and Nicaragua felt that Rigoberto's sexuality was worth noting. Additionally, Ambassador Mann and the command of the National Guard tried to discredit Rigoberto by fostering the image of a physically and mentally ill loner who could not succeed in mainstream society. Moreover, given that Nicaragua is known as a nation of poets, it makes sense that Ambassador Mann bothered to report that Rigoberto fancied himself one but failed at that too.[25]

In the 1950s, despite what the Somozas, the National Guard, and the U.S. ambassador said about Rigoberto, there was no public national conversation on whether or not Rigoberto had sex with men or whether that mattered. That conversation did not take place until 2013. But the issue was very much present in 1956 and will be addressed later in the chapter. First, however, it is important to document a conversation that took place in Nicaragua over the sexuality of another poet: Rubén Darío. In other words, to understand the 2013 debate over Rigoberto López Pérez's sexuality, it must be noted that there were in fact a series of earlier debates over Rubén Darío's homoerotic writings and practices. Those two conversations, one on Darío, one on Rigoberto, are intertwined.

PROSA PROFANA

Up until very recently, the sexual orientation of male poets and writers like Rubén Darío, Nicaragua's most famous poet, and Rigoberto López Pérez, a less impressive writer, had remained unexamined in the public eye. That changed in the twenty-first century, when their sexuality was addressed and sometimes heatedly debated by academics, politicians, and the broader public. In 2002 Blas Matamoro, the Argentinian scholar and attorney working on behalf of the gay movement in Uruguay, wrote a biography and an article on Rubén.[26] Some of Matamoro's arguments were broad ones about modernism in general, as when he noted that "the modernist sensibility was 'manflorita' and 'maricona', regardless of the sexual customs of each writer."[27] Other arguments were more specific to Rubén Darío. For instance, Matamoro wrote of "homophile aspects [*tintes homófilos*]" between Darío and other famous authors, among them Pedro Balmaceda Toro.[28]

Matamoro was certainly not the only scholar to discuss Darío's relationships or the way in which sexuality was addressed in Darío's writings. Seven years later, in 2009, the Peruvian scholar Lorenzo Helguero noted in his PhD dissertation that in Darío's writings "one can discover references to types of sexual conduct that sexologists of the epoch defined as illness, such as homosexuality or fetishism. But what abounds definitively is an interest in making sex speak. Here sexual pleasure appears separated from its procreative function, thus its transgressive nature."[29]

Matamoro's writings in particular, however, caused consternation among some Nicaraguans. The scholar Nicasio Urbina, for instance, wrote the following:

> Matamoro's biography is inspired by a derogatory treatment of Darío, written with some malice and lacking in real contributions to the understanding of Darío's life and work. This biography has very little documentary value and is riddled with unsubstantiated claims. The biogra-

pher seems to have no admiration for the subject of his study, relying on isolated verses and individual phrases from Darío's correspondence, to make controversial and sensitive statements regarding Darío's sexuality and literary knowledge. With a beginner's knowledge of psychology and very elementary rudiments of psychoanalytic criticism, Matamoro intends to elucidate Darío's relationships with women, his father's absence, his mother's abandonment, his bohemian lifestyle, and his alcoholism, in a book that without adding anything to the previous biographies, presents a series of conjectures that are impossible to prove and lacking in hermeneutical value.[30]

The topic of Darío's sexuality was deemed so important that a conference was held on July 9, 2002, at the Library of the Central Bank in Managua titled precisely "¿Rubén Darío Homosexual?" According to the Nicaraguan poet Héctor Avellán, "in front of a small group made up mostly of elderly people, the main speakers on this panel were psychiatrist and film critic Ramiro Argüello Hurtado . . . Paulo Kraudy, and Doctor Jorge Eduardo Arellano."[31] The controversy over Matamoro's work died down rather quickly, possibly because the biography he wrote was not widely available in Nicaragua or online.[32] However, another much bigger controversy arose in Nicaragua in 2012 in response to an academic article written by the Spanish scholar Alberto Acereda, a former professor at Arizona State University (ASU). Acereda's article, titled "'Our Most Profound and Sublime Secret': The Transgressive Loves Between Rubén Darío y Amado Nervo," was published in 2012 in the *Bulletin of Spanish Studies*[33] based on letters supposedly written by Darío to the Mexican poet Amado Nervo.[34] While Lorenzo Helguero's 2009 findings reveal that Darío *wrote* about transgressive nonheteronormative sexualities, Acereda argued that Darío and Nervo had "a secret love" that helped explain, among other things, the "existential tragedy" that these authors shared, making their histories, and that of modernism in general, more complex. Many Darío specialists and fans, especially Nicaraguan fans, were troubled by this allegation and overwhelmingly refused to believe Acereda. This response had to do with more than blatant homophobia, although homophobia definitely played a role.

One of the most homophobic and transphobic responses was published in Spanish in a Nicaraguan academic journal but was written by a non-Nicaraguan scholar, Gunther Schmigalle, in 2012:

To date, Rubén Darío's sexual profile seemed well defined. It is true that he was not a "super macho." His public image cannot be compared to that of a Hemingway. He never went to Africa to hunt lions, boxing disgusted him, he ran away from duels, he couldn't stand bullfights, and he was very afraid of the Apaches. Hemingway volunteered in three wars; Darío, when the 1914 war broke out, went on a peace tour. Biographers and critics have extensively described his shyness, his parsimony, his nightmares, his anguish, and anxieties. But rarely had they come to doubt his masculine identity. It is known that no one like him has sung the celestial flesh of woman. His wife was from his land, his mistress from Paris. In the course of his life he had two wives and a partner. He had about fifteen mistresses . . . in various countries. He had children. He was also friends with many men, mostly Latin American or Spanish poets and writers. Some of those friendships were intimate, intense. But there is no document or testimony to indicate that sexual impulses had an influence on those friendships. Rather, Darío was horrified by the "communications / between lesbians and *gitones*," which for him formed part of an apocalyptic scenarios, along with the "palace of the Antichrist." However, gender studies advance relentlessly. Gender mainstreaming is widely funded on many levels. It is not enough that men and women have the same rights; their differences, it is argued, are a social construct and have to be eliminated; men and women have to be the same. Heteronormative sexuality, attacked from all sides, is losing ground; transgressive love is on the offensive and they don't even let the dead rest. In North American universities and those in other countries, the imperative to "publish or perish" pushes academics. Morbid fascination also helps.[35]

It appears that Acereda did not engage with Nicaraguan intellectuals or with the Nicaraguan public on the issue of Darío's relationship with Nervo prior to the publication of his article, most likely because that is not something academics tend to do. Some Nicaraguan scholars and writers were upset for two additional reasons. First, Nicaraguans claim Darío as their own even though Darío spent most of his adult life outside Nicaragua. Having a Spaniard (based in the United States no less!) claim to have inside knowledge on Darío was adding insult to injury. Moreover, some Nicaraguan scholars, among them the revered novelist and former vice president Sergio Ramírez Mercado, argued that the documents

Acereda used, documents recently purchased by ASU, were *forged*. That ASU did not immediately or explicitly address how they obtained the documents served to fuel the belief of some Nicaraguans that Rubén Darío, the "prince of Castilian letters," was being maligned.[36]

In 2012 ASU announced that it had "acquired a privately held collection of manuscripts created by Nicaraguan poet Rubén Darío."[37] ASU quoted "David W. Foster, Regents' Professor of Spanish and Women and Gender Studies at ASU," who stated:

> the acquisition of such a collection, which has the possibility of suggesting a major revision in our understanding of Rubén Darío's sexuality, is only possible through the efforts of outstanding senior faculty like Acereda, who have the advanced (and often anonymous) contacts necessary for such material to become part of ASU's superb research collections.[38]

At a time when museums and libraries all over the world are being called upon to decolonize their collections, the action taken by ASU seemed particularly egregious. It does not appear that ASU worked or consulted with Nicaraguan institutions to co-own the collection, nor did it grant Nicaraguans special access to the collection through special scholarships. (While the documents have since then been digitized and made public, being able to see documents in person still holds value, particularly when there is a possibility that they might be forged.) ASU apparently believed that purchasing documents that helped tell the story of a "third world" nation's past would go uncontested. ASU also appeared to believe that the secret processes and negotiations through which U.S. institutions obtain these collections would be accepted by all as legitimate and ethical. That was definitely not the case.

In 2019 I contacted the Arizona State University library via email, stating that I was "interested in knowing how the Darío collection was acquired" and asking, "Is it possible to know who purchased it and from whom? Also, why are some documents [in the archives] only available as photocopies?"[39] I received the following email response from a person associated with the collection at ASU: "We acquired the papers from a vendor that we have worked with for many years. I am not sure why some of the documents are photocopies."[40] Presumably there was a fear that the controversy created by the documents could lead to their destruction by visitors to the archives. Hence, the ASU Special Collections website read in March 2020: "Correspondence between Rubén Darío and Amado Nervo and Darío's English 'Sonatina' have been removed to Series IV: Restricted Documents for security reasons. Photocopies of these items have been placed in the collection for research use."[41] By January 18, 2023, however, the wording had changed to the following: "Series VI: Restricted Materials consists of a single box of manuscripts restricted for security reasons. Photocopies of these items have been placed in the collection for research use."[42] Presumably the originals of the letters between Darío and Nervo are now available to the public. However, if that is the case, then what exactly is in the box of restricted manuscripts?

Although ASU did not explicitly engage in a conversation over the acquisition of the collection, Professor Acereda did explain in his 2012 article that

> This unusual collection of manuscripts that we have consulted in detail was assembled during Darío's lifetime by his own personal secretary: Alejandro Bermúdez Núñez, an important figure in the last years of the poet's life . . . Kept by the Bermúdez family, in 1936 it passed to his son, Raúl Bermúdez Baca, a lawyer and historian who was also Nicaraguan and who decided to take care of the manuscripts for sixty years, until his death in 1995. In the 1960s, and in line with the centenary of Darío's birth in 1967, Bermúdez donated six of those letters to the National Library of Nicaragua as an exploration to donate his entire collection. However, the 1972 Managua earthquake and subsequent events in Nicaraguan history in the 1980s led to the loss of those donated documents, prompting the rest of the collection to be taken out of the country for fear of further loss. The collection ended up being stored in a private home in California for years until today.[43]

In 2013 Acereda published another article dedicated exclusively to making a case for the importance of the collection. Acereda addressed the forgery accusations in detail, explained inconsistencies in the collection, and engaged with the work of Nicaraguan Darío scholars, among them Jorge Eduardo Arellano, José Jirón Terán, and Eddy Kühl. Acereda's explanations are very convincing. Moreover, he indirectly addressed the question of why these documents could not be housed in Nicaragua by noting that

> the issue of Darío's manuscripts . . . is always the subject of controversy and disquisitions, such as the one that Nicaragua experiences in 2007 when President Daniel Ortega gave his colleague and host Hugo Chávez two supposed autographs of Darío.[44]

Even if one agrees that the documents housed at ASU are from Darío's time, one of the possibilities that still exists is that at least some of the documents could have been forged over one hundred years ago, either by his personal secretary or by someone else. If that were the case, it may or may not change how we understand the relationship between Darío and Nervo. What is undeniable is that Darío and Nervo were very close friends and at one time shared an apartment.[45] When Darío died, he held in his hands the crucifix that Nervo had given him.[46] And Nervo wrote the following poem at the news of Darío's death:

Rubén Darío is dead
The one of the precious stones!
So many intense years we lived next to the Seine
Setting in the gold of a common ideal
The youthful verses that we sometimes saw sprout
As two roses sprout at one time in one rose bush![47]

Back in Nicaragua during 2012, however, when Sergio Ramírez engaged in the debate over the ASU documents, he titled his opinion piece, published on November 22, 2012, "The Simple Art of Allowing Oneself to Be Fooled."[48] As far as many Nicaraguans were concerned, there was really nothing left to say. It is not surprising therefore, that eighteen months after this very public debate over Darío and Nervo took place, an exhibit of postcards "testifying to the passion" between Rubén Darío and his longtime partner, a Spanish woman named Francisca Sánchez del Pozo, was sponsored by a prominent Nicaraguan university in conjunction with the Spanish embassy in Managua.[49]

QUEERING DARÍO

While some Nicaraguans could not fathom the idea of a sexual relationship between Rubén Darío and Amado Nervo, for others the possibility of queering Darío was quite meaningful. The writer and translator Francisco Aragón (1968–) wrote the following:

> During the years I lived in Spain, my literary friends had given me the skinny on the closeted Amado Nervo, so no surprise there. But Rubén Darío?! His name had never been a part of that conversation. Lorca? Yes. His contemporary, Vicente Aleixandre? Yes. Luis Cernuda, another member of the noted *"generación del '27,"* who died in exile in Mexico? Yes again. But *not* Rubén Darío.
>
> The plot took an interesting, if disappointing, turn when Sergio Ramírez, the noted Nicaraguan novelist, penned a piece alleging that the Darío-Nervo letters were fake. This prompted me to imagine a response in the voice of Rubén Darío—from the grave: an epistolary poem addressed to Sergio Ramírez, one which pushed back, underscoring, in essence: the letters to, and my love for, Amado Nervo were real. I titled my letter-in-verse, "January 21, 2013," in reference to the day Richard Blanco became the first Latinx, and the first openly gay poet, to read an inaugural poem to begin Barack Obama's second term...
>
> [Aceredo's articles] forced me to re-examine and re-consider some of my earlier English versions [rough translations] of Rubén Darío.

In conclusion, Aragón noted that when imagining translation as a form of activism, his activism was queering Rubén Darío: "These things are part of my work at resisting and combating efforts by others to erase (or silence) our GLBTQ histories, our LGBTQ lives; it has become part of my literary DNA."[50]

Sergio Ramírez, meanwhile, when pressed further on the issue of whether or not Rubén may have had sexual relations with men, responded by saying that he was not concerned with Darío's sexuality:

> When questioned about the possibly homophobic perspective that would prevent accepting a homosexual relationship between Darío and

Nervo, Sergio Ramírez categorically clarified that, when making his . . . analysis, he was not bringing up for debate anyone's sexual tendencies. "That to me is legitimate. There are great poets that I respect who have been homosexual, such is the case of Oscar Wilde or that of Federico García Lorca, who left a collection of poems that is one of the largest in the Spanish language . . . dedicated to his male lover," he said.

His point, Ramírez states, is that Professor Alberto Acereda, from the Arizona State University, cannot posit a possible relationship as he has detailed in his essay in the *Bulletin of Spanish Studies* . . . if the documents on which he bases his allegation are false, since the poem he cites was written much earlier, was not dedicated to Nervo, and also does not contemplate Darío's handwriting.[51]

The Argentinian scholar Daniel Link had yet another perspective on the possibility of a queer Darío. In 2016 Link wrote:

In what sense could we affirm a queer Darío today? Precisely in the sense of suspending any decision regarding a gay Darío or a non-gay Darío . . . There is not, there could not be, a gay Darío due to historical impossibility but, also, because Darío raised, against fin-de-siecle normalization systems, "lo raro" (the queer).

In *Epistemology of the Closet*, Eve Kosofsky Sedgwick stressed that what was new, at the end of the last century, was the articulation of a universal cartography according to which, in the same way as before it had been considered necessary to assign each person a masculine gender or a feminine one, now it was equally necessary to assign them a homosexual or heterosexual sexuality, that is, a binarized identity that was full of implications, albeit confusing ones, and that affected even the ostensibly less sexual aspects of personal existence . . .

A queer Darío, a pure enigma, because [according to Darío himself] "every form is a gesture, a number, an enigma; in each atom there is an unknown stigma; each leaf of each tree sings its own song."[52]

Ironically, what is probably the most controversial aspect of Link's article is one that is not inherently related to Darío's sexuality but very much related to the way in which he is to be remembered. Link argued that Darío belongs to the world because he is "cosmopolitan . . . Maybe, but in the sense of a cosmopolitanism of the poor, that of someone who has nothing and eats the leftovers of others, and with them prepares an exquisite banquet to which we are invited."[53] To back his point, Link quotes what Darío said about José Martí (1853–95), the Cuban poet and hero: "Cuba admirable and rich and a hundred times blessed by my tongue . . . Martí's blood did not belong to you; he belonged to a whole race, to a whole continent; he belonged to a spirited youth who lost in him perhaps its first teacher; he belonged to the future!"[54] Link urges the reader: "Let no one try, then, to appropriate Rubén Darío. Darío's homeland is the poem, the story, the chronicle, the figure and the rhythm. Its properties are music and color . . ."[55]

In an ideal world, Darío could belong to the world. But Nicaraguans have yet to live in that ideal world. Nicaraguans continue to insist that Darío is theirs and that the poet who wrote that "if one's homeland is small, it is big in one's dreams" understood their plight like no other.[56]

On a practical note, Héctor Avellán, a gay Nicaraguan poet and author of the 2001 book *Los huérfanos de Rubén*, has offered some advice moving forward: "What we have to do as Nicaraguans is to demand that any study on his life and work be well-founded, and that obviously these investigations reach our country and be accessible to the entire public."[57]

RIGOBERTO LÓPEZ PÉREZ: "MIS GAY ETERNO DE NICARAGUA"

On August 10, 2013, about six months after the debate over whether or not Darío had ever sent love letters to Amado Nervo died out in the press, an article written by the Nicaraguan attorney Iván de Jesús Pereira was published in the newspaper *La Prensa*. The article noted that the old Workers' Hall where Anastasio Somoza García had been assassinated was being renovated, after being practically abandoned for years. The article never mentioned Rigoberto's sexual practices and described him in glowing terms as someone who, "in addition to being an idealist and a poet he had in his personality [the trait of] being a true believer . . . in [the Virgin] Mary."[58] The article ended with the following exhortation:

> Hence, the restoration of that house is very important for León, for the history of Nicaragua and for its future generations. A mural should be

made that describes all these events. A great painting that synthesizes the love these men had for Nicaragua, the lesson they leave us and that the old house become a true altar to sacrifice that reminds us all of what it has cost us to aspire to have a true democracy.[59]

Six weeks later, on September 21, 2013, the medical doctor Ulises Huete Maltés, published a response to Pereira's piece, also in *La Prensa*. In the piece Huete questioned the need to restore the old Workers' Hall and asked "for what? To turn the building into a cult of death?" He added: "the . . . murderer was a psychopath, with sexual identity disorders, which turned him into a human bomb, no different from a fundamentalist Islamist."[60] Huete continued:

> Known were his links to Rafael Corrales Rojas, a protege of the Debayle Sacasa family, in-laws of the dictator. Corrales, an effeminate bachelor, had a newspaper . . . where he allowed Rigoberto López Pérez to write some little poems, which became dust, with Corrales himself, who was the one who allowed him to enter the Worker's Hall, falling Rafaelito into disgrace.[61]

On September 22, 2013, novelist and historian Jesus Miguel "Chuno" Blandón published a piece, also in *La Prensa*, recounting the assassination that had taken place fifty-seven years earlier. Blandón did not mention Rigoberto's sexuality. However, that topic was definitely addressed in the online comment section. Rigoberto's assassination of Somoza and his homosexuality were then discussed in depth in other newspaper articles, at least two of them written by Jorge Eduardo Arellano, one of Nicaragua's most prolific intellectuals and a world-renowned expert on Rubén Darío.

The ways in which Rigoberto's identity and actions were described and understood by the dozens of people who got involved in the conversation were varied. Some writers and commentators agreed with Ulises Huete Maltés and focused primarily on Rigoberto's homosexuality, linking it to mental illness and violence. A commentator named Rafael thus noted the following: "Many of these murderers are psychopaths, for example, Lee Harvey Oswald, John Wilkes Booth, both with homosexual tendencies."[62] A second perspective, alluded to by Ulises Huete, was that Rigoberto was easily manipulated by others, among them Corrales, the "effeminate bachelor" who directed the Somocista newspaper in which Rigoberto published some of his poems. A corollary to this last perspective was the insinuation that because Rigoberto's poems were so poorly written, he was only able to publish them in exchange for sexual favors. These points of view were ones that appeared in the comment sections and in the debate that would explode in the press. But other points were also made.

Some commentators questioned the nature of heroism and asked: Could an assassin be a hero? Should heroes be nonviolent? Others argued that what Rigoberto did to the first Somoza dictator needed to be done to Daniel Ortega. The latter position was obviously one that was found only in the anonymous comments, not one expressed by any of the academics and intellectuals engaged in the public media debate.

Yet another viewpoint was to question whether an assassin could also be a true Christian. Jorge Eduardo Arellano, for instance, categorically proclaimed that "Christians do not glorify assasination."[63] Joaquín Absalón Pastora's response was to argue that this was about justice, not about murder.[64] Still others noted that no matter what anyone said about Rigoberto, you had to be a very brave man to kill a dictator. Arellano, in fact, argued in one of his articles that in the immediate aftermath of the assassination, Rigoberto's name became synonymous with manhood and bravery. He claimed that eggs, the slang term used in Spanish for testicles, came to be called *Rigobertos* in León, at least for a short time. And Arellano tells the following anecdote:

> In fact, just after the assassination, the people who frequented the "Popular René" or "Cucaracha," in order to eat the famous bean soups of those eateries in León, expressed their admiration for the courage by calling chicken eggs, which are associated with testicles, "rigobertos":
>
> "How many rigobertos should I put in your soup?" they would ask the customer.
> "Two. He wasn't missing one, was he?"[65]

Admiration was one of the more common responses to Rigoberto's actions. Davíd, for example, wrote in the comment section of an article by Jorge Eduardo Arellano that Rigoberto should be appreciated even more if he was homosexual. He wrote: "If Rigoberto was cochón, his heroism is increased, not diminished; homosexuals of his time were . . . isolated, politically and socio-economically discriminated against. Then we could know . . . that Rigoberto not only brought justice to the tyrant, but also infiltrated [a] social, political, and military world that was not his own."[66]

An additional perspective was the one expressed by Douglas, who stated: "what they say about him being homosexual, in my way of thinking, they say to defame him."[67] Douglas also argued that Rigoberto was a hero because he acted alone and did not feel a need to involve peasants in his war like Sandino, the Sandinistas, and the Contras had done.[68]

Still others felt that Rigoberto's personal life was irrelevant to his actions. A person in the comment section who used the name Adriana expressed dismay at reading that Rigoberto had sexual relations with men: "if I wanted to read about the private lives of personalities and gossip about them, I would read . . . the gossip magazines."[69] Another commentator pointed to the hypocrisy of those who refused to accept that Rigoberto was not heterosexual: "they are shameful homophobes who would prefer a Rigoberto who beats women."[70] Other commentators took a predictable route, which was to suggest that the authors who wrote about Rigoberto being homosexual were probably homosexual themselves.

Orlando Morales Navarrete, one of the authors engaged in the conversation over Rigoberto, was so distressed by what he considered to be false accusations against the poet that he launched a campaign against those who said Rigoberto had sex with men. His main target was Jorge Eduardo Arellano. Morales Navarrete alluded to the long-standing rivalry between the city of León (Rigoberto's hometown) and Granada (Arellano's hometown) when he wrote: "I propose to the mayor [of León] . . . that he retract the naming of the Granada native Jorge Eduardo Arellano a 'beloved son of León' for such defamation of the memory of someone from León."[71]

Another commentator, who wrote under the name Ramiro, made a rather unusual request. He wrote the following: "the gay community of Nicaragua demands that the Chamu [Rosario Murillo] and Daniel [Ortega] government put on the back of the statue in the roundabout a large cape that flies throught the skies, with the diverse colors that represent our homosexual community. And that he is granted in the National Assembly the postmortem title of Miss Eternal Gay of Nicaragua."[72] This might have been said tongue in cheek, but given the efforts of the Ortega administration to co-opt LGBTQIA+ activists and retell Nicaragua's history in its favor, as well as the administration's passion for big public monuments, it did not sound like an unrealistic proposal at all. It is also not surprising that Jorge Eduardo Arellano wrote in one of his articles that Rigoberto "with his action . . . implied a defeat for the homophobic machismo of Nicaragua and a victory for the gay community who would have a national hero among their people."[73]

With regard to this very public debate over Rigoberto, it is important to discuss a crucial point made by one of the authors involved, Rafael Casanova Fuertes. Casanova Fuertes wanted his readers to know that in the 1950s "whoever did macho favors to a homosexual was considered lazy, naughty, or other terms . . . the 'naughty' or 'lazy' youngsters of the time did not necessarily carry the weight of sodomites, nor did the relationship with them affect them in the least with female partners."[74] Casanova noted that "it is not until very recent times that both science . . . [and public opinion] have agreed to define as an active homosexual the person who, within the couple, acts as male."[75] This characterization adds to U.S. anthropologist Roger Lancaster's findings on cochones and "hombres-hombres" in the late 1980s.[76] Unfortunately, however, an in-depth discussion on the subject is beyond the scope of this book.

While Casanova insisted that in his research he found no evidence of Rigoberto fitting the category of "passive" homosexual or "naughty" (*travieso*) or "lazy" (*vago*), he noted that everyone agreed that the pro-Somoza Rafael Corrales Rojas was considered homosexual.[77] Pastora also confirmed that Corrales was "a sodomite."[78] And according to Arellano, Corrales was "the most notorious sodomite of León," echoing what had been said centuries earlier about Andrés Caballero.[79] Arellano also argued that "the relationship Corrales Rojas-López Pérez, obviously, was of a homosexual nature and that is how it has traditionally been known. There are even historians who identify other 'friends,' still alive, of Rigoberto."[80] Pastora further stated that at least one witness in the 1950s noted that "the concordance [between Rigoberto and Corrales Rojas] became closer and closer to the point of seeing [Rigoberto] enter and leave the office of the homosexual [Corrales Rojas] with suspicious frequency."[81]

Although in 2013 Arellano and others noted that Rigoberto's homosexuality was "obvious," the scholar David Rocha accurately pointed out in 2019 that "in the official historiography . . . [Rigoberto López Pérez is not assumed to be] a homosexual [but] it is an open secret that the poet from León had a relationship [*mantuvo relaciones amorosas*] with Rafael Corrales."[82]

After Rigoberto's death, the Somoza's National Guard captured and tortured many whom they thought had aided Rigoberto and/or opposed the dictatorship. His mother was jailed, tortured, and threatened with rape. His younger brother and sister were tortured, even though they were still teenagers and had no knowledge of Rigoberto's plan.[83]

After the assassination, Rafael Corrales bore a great deal of the brunt. His newspaper was dismantled, and he was immediately jailed. He was raped and tortured so viciously that he died soon after both Somoza and Rigoberto were killed.[84]

How are we to understand the sexualized murder of Corrales by a regime that had accepted him as a political insider up until his supposed betrayal? As Pastora has noted, "having been a Somocista his whole life did not serve as a credential to be exempt from jail."[85] Many people were jailed and tortured (possibly even castrated) in the aftermath of Somoza's assassination, but the sources thus far available reveal that only Corrales was raped to death. The pattern of relative sexual tolerance of an LGBTQIA+ political insider followed by an always sexualized and usually violent reprisal against them for supposedly betraying a regime is a familiar and ongoing one in Nicaragua (and elsewhere in the world). State reprisal such as this one is often informed by the homophobic and unproven belief that LGBTQIA+ individuals are potential security risks. The message the reprisals send to the population at large is that political insider status for LGBTQIA+ individuals is available but always tenuous and that any real or perceived betrayal will be punished in such a way that emphasizes and draws attention to an LGBTQIA+ person's sexual orientation and/or gender identity and expression. I find that a term I coined, *sexualized political correctives*, is a useful one to refer to these reprisals, which are often violent and always demeaning. It is also important to emphasize that these *correctives* are sometimes justified, at the time or in retrospect, as "following the law" or "informing the public," when the reality is that the violence (whether real or symbolic), defamation, and/or infringement of rights that takes place against the LGBTQIA+ individual is done primarily, if not solely, for political expediency.

Seconds after shooting Somoza García, Rigoberto López Pérez "received four hits with a weapon on his face and at least 54 bullets throughout his body."[86] Rigoberto was killed instantly, and minutes later the National Guard began their search for potential accomplices. "Among all the captured . . . 21 people were judged by a council of war . . . and 14 people were sentenced . . . Among all the sentenced . . . only 11 were able to leave jail . . . supposedly the [other] three had tried to flee and two guards riddled them with bullets."[87]

Rafael Corrales Rojas was one among more than three thousand suspects who were jailed in the aftermath of the magnicide (out of a population of slightly over one million Nicaraguans). According to the journalist Eduardo Cruz,

> Rafael Rojas' sin was to have recognized Rigoberto's pierced body . . . "Yes, it is the poet Pérez," Corrales said during what was almost López Pérez' last instance of life.
>
> It was because of Corrales that the guards knew who the gunman was and where his family lived. And it was because of him that they were able to show up before that day of September 21 had ended, to his mother's house.
>
> That recognition of the body . . . cost Corrales a great deal . . .[88]

Another version (albeit an unproven one) of Corrales Rojas's involvement in the assassination was the one Ulises Huete Maltés proposed earlier, that Corrales was the one who had allowed Rigoberto to enter the Worker's Hall.[89]

Yet another version of the role Corrales Rojas played that night at the Worker's Hall is the following:

> Doctor Corrales Rojas was showing . . . the copy of his newspaper in which he approved of [sic] and enthusiastically encouraged the proclamation of General Somoza García, who was holding a copy of the newspaper in his hands, when the first shots were heard that the journalist Rojas said he thought were fireworks at first.
>
> The Director of *El Cronista*, despite being an unconditional friend of the ruling family, was immediately imprisoned and his newspaper was dismantled. Its machinery was taken to the warehouses of the National

Bank of Nicaragua, to the León branch, which had granted him a loan with the machinery as collateral.

The case of Dr. Rafael Corrales Rojas is well known throughout the country, since he notified the authorities and Somoza García himself that the poet López Pérez harbored ill-will against the Chief of the Executive. But no one paid attention to him until the tragedy struck and he was subjected to severe torture that caused his death, shortly after he was released after a long detention... In this way, *El Cronista*, which Dr. Corrales Rojas maintained as a spokesman for Somocismo, ceased to exist.[90]

While no one denied that Corrales Rojas had sexual relationships with men, some scholars continue to deny the possibility that Rigoberto was close to Corrales Rojas. Rafael Casanova Fuertes, for instance, has argued that "the apparatus of Somocismo in general played to distort the image of the direct participants [in the assassination of Somoza García], to question their manhood in a society as conservative as that of León... That was the main reason for linking in any way Rigoberto to Corrales, [the latter] someone servile to the system and effeminate."[91]

It seems highly unlikely that in the aftermath of Somoza's assassination, the National Guard tortured Corrales Rojas to death to discredit Rigoberto. While it is possible that Corrales Rojas was targeted simply for being a gay man after another gay man killed the president, that is also improbable. What is most likely is that in the 1950s, as in earlier times dating as far back as the 1520s, some men in León were able to create nonheteronormative spaces for themselves and both Corrales Rojas and Rigoberto participated in those spaces. Like Andrés Caballero over four hundred years earlier, Rafael Corrales Rojas had been a middling member of the local León elite with ties to the highest authorities in the land. Their lives ended when those authorities turned on them, demonstrating the limits to LGBTQIA+ rights in heteronormative and undemocratic regimes.

SEXUAL AND GENDER DIVERSITY IN NICARAGUANS' MEMORIES OF THE SOMOZA DICTATORSHIP

How did turn-of-the-century LGBTQIA+ urban Nicaraguans of different political orientations remember LGBTQIA+ life during the 1950s,

1960s, and 1970s? Here I specifically address the intersection between memory, sexuality/gender, and politics in the life stories of three individuals: Erika, Alejandro, and Carlos. Erika identified as lesbian, a mother, and a disillusioned Sandinista. At the time of the interview in the late twentieth century, she worked for a lesbian and gay AIDS prevention nongovernmental organization (NGO) in an urban center outside Managua. She was eighteen years old in 1979 and had a daughter at seventeen. Alejandro was a Somocista from Managua with a vast knowledge of gay life for Somocistas under the Somozas. He was thirty-one in 1979. Carlos could be considered a "passive Somocista" under the Somozas. He then became a Sandinista sympathizer and worked for the Sandinistas during the revolution. After 1990 he worked for the Liberals in an urban center outside Managua. He always identified as homosexual and was forty-four years old in 1979.

When asked about sexual diversity and/or homosexuality before the Sandinista revolution, many in Nicaragua tend to focus their narratives on LGBTQIA+ public figures, specifically Bernabé Somoza, a member of the Somoza family rumored to be bisexual; La Caimana, a strong Somoza supporter who was the LGBTQIA+ owner of a Managua firecracker factory; and La Sebastiana, a famous food vendor in pre-earthquake Managua. LGBTQIA+ Nicaraguans themselves, however, have a great deal more than that to share.

The Somozas lacked a comprehensive policy of repression against LGBTQIA+ individuals. Theirs was a populist clientelistic dictatorship that rested upon nineteenth-century liberalism. Unlike the Sandinistas, the Somozas did not preside over a regime that pretended to hold a higher moral ground. As was the case for the Sandinistas, however, loyalty was paramount for the Somozas. But in the pre–identity politics era of the 1950s and 1960s, a sexual preference that was kept private did not interfere with the "don't ask, don't tell" attitude of the dictators. Moreover, unlike the Sandinistas, the Somozas never had to deal with an emergent gay and lesbian political movement that demanded rights.

Not surprisingly, sexual silence permeated Nicaraguan society under the Somozas. Carlos, a high school graduate who avoided socializing with other gay men, gives us a glimpse into how he managed his homosexuality in this context:

[Back then] they looked at you like a strange animal. For my part, I never had any problems at work, perhaps because I was the best student [in school]. Yes, there was marginalization but I did not suffer it, especially in private industry. They pretended not to notice. I worked for the Nicaraguan beer company. At that time I was the only high school graduate among all 300 employees . . . I haven't drawn too much attention to myself. In Somoza's time, gay people didn't draw too much attention to themselves ["No me he dado demasiado color . . . en la época de Somoza las personas gay no se daban mucho color"]. Everyone acted like they were Somocistas even if they weren't.[92]

Carlos's story was quite different from that of Erika, a Sandinista party member, in part because her memories of the Somocista period are filtered through the persecution she experienced as lesbian during the revolution. She stated: "[Before 1979 it was a repressive era,] repressive against the Sandinistas, yes, but for me personally the [Somoza] Guardia never bothered me and I remember that I would walk holding hands with a girl [*muchacha*] and they never said anything to me . . . I was always boyish [*varonil*] . . . [but] the dictatorship never fucked up my life."[93]

Under the Sandinistas Erika felt like she was under constant surveillance:

Everywhere I looked a member of the State Security would show up, once they found out about my sexual option. [The Sandinistas] twice [tried to catch me in the act], in 1984 and 1985. Once it was the police and once it was State Security. I asked for my discharge [within the police as a result of this]. They asked me [if I was lesbian]. I told them no, I had a daughter. A woman from State Security summoned me to her room and in the room she had a camera. She begged and begged me and she hugged me and everything. The next day a [male] friend from [State] Security called me to tell me "they were going to [discover you]."[94]

One of the women involved in harassing her has since apologized.

After sharing the persecution she suffered at the hands of the FSLN, Erika requested that I call her Erika because that was the pseudonym she used when she joined the Sandinistas as a teenager in the 1970s.

Alejandro's narrative was quite different from both Erika's and Carlos's stories. During the interview Alejandro volunteered: "Here there was a great liberal, with lineage and a pistol, La Caimana. If you told La

Caimana that she wasn't a Somocista, she would kick your ass, like a man would, and she was a woman, 'Don Carmelo' among friends. That was her nom de guerre, 'Don Carmelo.' [Hilda Scott,] that is the woman, the heiress of La Caimana's assets, she was the famous wife of La Caimana, the one they say had a baby boy with her."95

At that point, Alejandro asked a rhetorical question: "Do you know the secret at La Caimana's funeral?" He went on: "There were two boxes [coffins] and after that there was hers. Because there [in the additional coffins] supposedly there were plastic penises . . . and all the things she used to make love."96

When I asked Alejandro why he thought the Somozas accepted La Caimana as a friend and a supporter, he said: "I'm going to tell you something, the Somozas had a great quality, if you were with them, [they would support you] until death . . . but you couldn't betray them . . . La Caimana was a Somocista from the heart. She loved Somoza."97

Alejandro had a lot more to say about LGBTQIA+ life for Somocistas during the dictatorship:

> The thing is that there was a place here called el Charco de los Patos . . . It was a small house with a dirt floor where they served you the most exquisite baho [a dish with beef, yucca, tomatoes, and plantains steamed in banana leaves] at two a.m. It was a private bar. Anyone could show up . . . but for the Miss Nicaragua elections that the cochones had, it was only people who were very upper class. Because here homosexuality has existed in all stages. When they had the elections for Miss Nicaragua, the one the cochones had, a Sacasa would show up, a Somoza . . .
>
> Bernabé [Somoza] went there a lot, to the Charco de los Patos . . . Bernabé Somoza, my friend, my soul brother . . . he was bisexual, because he also liked women . . . The thing is Bernabé . . . was a vulgar son of a bitch . . . He did not use his gifts as the president's son, he was naturally simple [un campechano nato]. He was the legitimate son of Doña Hope [sic]. Bernabé was the son of the General [sic] . . . Tacho would say that that son of a bitch was not his son, because he [Tacho] had big balls [era huevón]. [Bernabé was actually Tacho's nephew and not his son.] But Bernabé had balls as big as his dad's. Don't think that because they said he was homosexual . . . To me he was bisexual. He was good at fighting . . . And no kicking . . . Clean hits, really good at breaking bottles. That guy wasn't grossed out by anything.

[From the Charco de los Patos] we would go out in a procession to talk to the gods and read poetry. The lesbians were a Méndez girl and a Solorzano girl. These two have already died. The advantage of hanging out with this type of people is that pretty women were always around, some to get something and others because they liked partying. Some of us were there to take advantage and others because . . . the man [Bernabé Somoza] would call . . . and say, "I'll be there such and such a day." [Bernabé] hated for the Guardia [the National Guard] to be looking after him. He would come to you and say, "watch my back . . ." We would go to the cemetery . . . who wouldn't open the doors to Bernabé Somoza, the son of the president? They had huge parties. Then we would go to their haciendas . . .

[Or] you would go drink at Las Brisas del Xolotlán, it was a bar . . . you would pass by the Manchester, you would go by the shore of the lake and there were all kinds of vegetables . . . you would arrive at the bar . . . it was practically falling down . . . The waves would hit there from Lake Managua . . . They sold moonshine [*guaro lija*] or [Santa] Cecilia. But the exquisite appetizer there was rabbit. Because rabbits were plentiful there. So they would roast you a rabbit . . . It was a wholesome Managua in spite of them being corrupt back then ["Era una Managua sana a pesar de ser corruptos en ese entonces"].

How do we piece together the history of LGBTQIA+ life under the Somoza dictatorship in a way that takes into account the wide variety of experiences with regard to gender, gender expression, age, political affiliation, class background, and region? In the next section of this chapter I address La Caimana's story in depth, for it gives us additional clues into the freedoms and limits faced by prominent LGBTQIA+ individuals during the dictatorship. Just as importantly, La Caimana's life story can help us understand why some Nicaraguans remember Managua under the Somozas as "wholesome in spite of them being corrupt back then."

THE ALLIGATOR WOMAN'S TALE: THE STORY OF NICARAGUA'S "FIRST SELF-ACKNOWLEDGED LESBIAN"

In mid-August 1971, police closed down entire streets in Managua as thirty thousand people gathered together in very hot weather for what could have been a rather somber event. Instead, however, the occasion boasted spectacular fireworks, lots of liquor, a live mariachi band, other musicians (*chicheros*), and even marimba music. A very important person had died at a relatively young age, and people from all walks of life, from naked hippies to the president of the Central Bank, had come together to say their final good-byes. At age forty, Carmelo Aguirre was dead.[98]

Raised as a girl, Carmelo led his life as a man. He was known to all as La Caimana, but La Caimana was actually the name of Carmelo's fireworks factory, which continued to be in operation until the early twentieth century, under the ownership of his widow. The Caimana nickname was derivative. Carmelo's father, Lolo, was nicknamed "el Caimán" "because he lied so much" ("porque era bien tapudo").[99] La Caimana inherited the feminized version of the name.

Carmelo's life story has been fictionalized by Sergio Ramírez Mercado, Nicaragua's former vice president, in the 1998 novel *Margarita, está linda la mar*, and "in the novel no other history regarding the life of a character is reconstructed as exhaustively as that of *la Caimana*."[100] Carmelo's story also came up regularly in the many oral interviews I conducted as I sought to record Nicaragua's mid-twentieth-century LGBTQIA+ history.

La Caimana's support for the Somoza dictatorship and his embrace of an "alpha" masculinity made him famous.[101] Today, those urban Nicaraguans who lived through the last years of the Somoza regime as adults and young adults have understandings of sex, gender, and dictatorship that are mediated through their memories of this powerful historical figure.

I contend that sexual and gender transgressors like La Caimana did not pose a significant threat to the established heterosocial Somocista order, given the absence of a broader critique of patriarchy and authoritarianism. In other words, La Caimana's story illustrates the limits of homonormativity, understood in this case as the tolerance and relative acceptance granted by an undemocratic regime to an LGBTQIA+ individual who did not publicly question heteronormative roles within a right-wing hegemonic system of domination.[102] La Caimana's tale is thus an example of how undemocratic governments, on the left or on the right, can incorporate LGBTQIA+ individuals into their ranks as long as these individuals support the established political regime and the male privilege encrusted in the dominant gender binary. Moreover,

La Caimana's life story leads us to continue questioning monolithic and essentialized notions of identity, which fail to account for the complexities of most people's lives, including his.

There are additional ways in which to understand La Caimana. Scholar-activists such as the U.S. historians Elizabeth Lapovsky Kennedy and Madeline D. Davis, in their groundbreaking study on working-class lesbians in pre-1970 New York, wrote extensively on the importance of butch–femme roles within lesbian communities in the years before second-wave feminism. Kennedy and Davis focused on the "internal logic and multidimensional meanings" of these roles to argue that even though "butch-femme culture drew on elements of the patriarchal gender system . . . it also transformed them."[103] Consequently, these authors concluded that butch–femme roles were prepolitical ways of resisting heterosexual dominance, allowing lesbians to carve out public lives on their own. While this book does not focus explicitly on butch–femme roles, it is true that La Caimana was able to successfully counter discrimination and gain individual power and prestige through his embrace of what some might have labeled a "butch role." That he was allowed to do this in such a bold fashion in the context of a right-wing dictatorship points to his courage as well as to the co-optive, pragmatist nature of Somocismo and the dictatorship's active pursuit of working women's support.

The title of this section of the chapter is meant to highlight the limits and complexities of both language and identity. La Caimana is remembered by some as "Nicaragua's first self-declared lesbian," but as an adult Carmelo identified as a man. Meanwhile, his wife self-identified as lesbian and called Carmelo by his birth name, Carmen. Carmelo's children called Hilda "Mama Hilda," and they called Carmelo "Mama Carmen."[104] One of his sons has stated about La Caimana, "I remember her as my mom. The best mom in the world."[105] Labeling Carmelo a transgender man is perhaps most appropriate as long as we remember that the term *transgender*, unlike the terms *lesbian* and *marimacha* (butch/dyke), has only recently become incorporated into the Nicaraguan vocabulary, making its use anachronistic. What is most important, however, is to avoid making La Caimana's identity seem seamless, coherent, uncontested, and knowable. The juxtaposition of Carmelo/La Caimana throughout the book and the use of the word *lesbian* in the subheading are meant to remind us of that La Caimana's sexual and gender identities were fluid, complicated, and often performative, and that, indeed, "ambiguity lives at the core of identity."[106]

While La Caimana was a household name in urban Nicaragua from the 1970s on, he gained international notoriety in 1998, when Ramírez Mercado's novel won the Alfaguara Prize, one of the world's most prestigious prizes for literature in Spanish. In *Margarita*, La Caimana is portrayed as an ambiguous character rewarded for his almost complete loyalty to Somoza but ultimately betrayed by the Somoza family when it came to his gender identity. In the narratives of many other Nicaraguans, La Caimana also becomes an avenue through which to address intersections between sex, gender, and partisan politics. Additionally, discussions on La Caimana reveal long-standing collective anxieties about women and work, women in politics, and proper gender roles in a "modern" society, anxieties discussed at length in chapter 3. Preoccupations over women in public and "modern" women's sexual promiscuity have permeated the Nicaraguan collective imaginary throughout the twentieth and early twenty-first centuries, making it important to understand how these concerns, along with those over "progress," relate to contemporary understandings of what LGBTQIA+ life was like before the 1979 Sandinista revolution toppled the U.S.-backed dictatorship.

REMEMBERING LA CAIMANA

Slightly over a year after La Caimana died, all of Managua was in mourning, destroyed by the 1972 earthquake that left two-thirds of the city's half-million inhabitants displaced and over five thousand dead.[107] In the political and economic turmoil that would subsume Nicaragua for almost half a century after the earthquake, Carmelo Aguirre would figure prominently in heteroperformances of nostalgia over the so-called old (pre-earthquake) Managua among urban Nicaraguans. His story is often told as an example of the simpler life that disappeared in the turbulent 1970s. In fact, Carmelo was esteemed by many common folks, who found him to be a benevolent patron in the clientelistic system that enveloped Nicaraguan life under the dictatorship. Carmelo was particularly admired for his entrepreneurial skills and for his engagement with the broader community. He owned the biggest and most successful fireworks factory in Nicaraguan history and every year offered his financial support to dance groups so that they could perform in exquisite costumes during the carnival-like celebration of Managua's patron saint, Domingo de Guzman. He would also sometimes join in the celebration and dance with the crowd. Moreover, he held extravagant celebrations on the eve of the feast of the Immaculate Conception of the Virgin Mary, one of the country's most important Catholic holidays (at a time when most Nicaraguans were Catholic). La Caimana was considered a working-class philanthropist. Proof of this is that, at his funeral, mourners stressed his support for his workers' families when they were injured on the job. In the absence of a safety net, Carmelo did not hesitate to give his injured employees food and housing.[108]

Carmelo's rags-to-riches story inspired awe, but so did his apparent espousal of hegemonic masculinity. Carmelo led what at first glance seems a very traditional family life. At the time of his death, he and his partner of ten years, Hilda Scott, had legally adopted half a dozen children and were raising even more informally. Although she helped run their factory, Hilda was a housewife who appeared to have taken on a submissive role in the relationship. Carmelo, meanwhile, was the breadwinner, an alcoholic, and a womanizer. He would disappear for days at a time during a drinking binge and would not hesitate to use violence against anyone who crossed him.

More than half a century after his death, Carmelo's nonexistent firecracker factory continued to be a landmark in Managua, a city where streets often have no names. This means that younger generations who do not remember Carmelo himself, or even the factory, are nonetheless familiar with La Caimana as a marker in what one scholar has called "the sophisticated, often bitingly ironic, popular geography that [*Managuas*] use to navigate the city."[109] While La Caimana factory has become a "ghost address"[110] that haunts the ways in which Nicaraguans maneuver their chaotic capital, La Caimana himself haunts more than urban Nicaraguans' sense of geography. La Caimana haunts older urban Nicaraguans', particularly Managuas', most basic understandings of who they were, who they are, and who they will become.

In the context of neoliberal and free-trade economic practices that dominated the post-1990 period and promoted the country's saturation by products made elsewhere, including cheap foreign fireworks, there is strong nostalgia for *lo nuestro*, and an overwhelming grief for the end of local industrial productivity. La Caimana factory's closure in the early twenty-first century represented not only the loss of local jobs but the end of an era that, in the minds of many, reflected one of Nicaragua's best economic periods.[111]

That so many people remember La Caimana at all has to do, in part, with the fact that so many attended his funeral, one of the largest Nicaragua has ever seen. Moreover, the funeral became a media spectacle with a message that associated homosexuality with the nascent hippie, "free love," and drug cultures of urban Nicaragua. However, as noted by the U.S. scholar Douglas Kellner, the "politics of the spectacle is unpredictable and ... spectacles do not always succeed and manipulate the public, and may backfire."[112]

The press undoubtedly contributed to the longevity of La Caimana in Nicaraguans' historical memory. But La Caimana today is not associated with hippies or drug use or "free love." While some Nicaraguan hippies like Roberto Rappaciolli, the owner of the famous disco and nocturnal center La Tortuga Morada, were openly gay, there is no evidence that La Caimana had any connection to the counterculture movement of the late 1960s and the early 1970s. We do not know, for example, if he ever attended La Tortuga Morada, which shut down due to police pressure and economic reasons in 1970.[113] However, the counterculture hippie movement in Nicaragua (*el jipismo criollo*) was relatively short-lived. Police pressure and raids, the 1972 earthquake, and the increased militarization and political polarization of society eventually led many urban youth away from full-blown public hippie lifestyles and toward armed insurrection. Police censure and the earthquake so disrupted the public spaces for these subcultures that many young Nicaraguans in the 2020s do not know there were ever hippies there, even though many older Nicaraguans alive today, including Sandinista and former Sandinista leaders, experimented in their youth with marijuana, "hard" drugs, and so-called alternative lifestyles.

There is no evidence that La Caimana himself engaged in drug use beyond cigarettes and alcohol. The presence of young "potheads," "drug addicts," and hippies at his funeral most likely had to do with two factors: the carnivalesque nature of the funeral, which at the time was compared to Managua's saint's day celebrations, and the draw that La Caimana might have had for those who indeed identified as LGBTQIA+ or were open to the possibility of homosexuality as part of their "free love" ideology. It is important to note, however, that whatever the reason for the counterculture presence at the funeral, what was most obvious was the generational and cultural gap between the hippie youth and La Caimana. This contrast can best be observed in their musical tastes and their appearance. La Caimana idolized and emulated the Mexican crooner and movie star Pedro Infante (1917–57), the quintessential ladies' man, and a hero to many working-class people throughout Latin America. La Caimana even dressed like his hero. Carmelo had "a little moustache something between [what] Pedro Infante and Cantinflas [would wear],"[114] and for special occasions Carmelo would wear a charro (Mexican cowboy) suit, carry a pistol, and even ride a horse. Nicaraguan hippies, on the other hand, were looking mainly to the United States and Britain for musical inspiration. The Beatles, the Rolling Stones, and Santana were all big hits in Nicaragua. And hippies could be easily recognized by their bell-bottoms, Afros, or long hair.

LA CAIMANA IN LITERATURE

Carmelo Aguirre, born in 1931, was only eleven years older than the former Sandinista Sergio Ramírez Mercado, born in 1942, but in his novel *Margarita*, Ramírez Mercado chose to make La Caimana a contemporary of a different character in Nicaraguan history: the dictator Anastasio Somoza García, born in 1896. By changing Carmelo's birth date in the novel to 1900, La Caimana was able to interact with Somoza García in his youth. Moreover, in the novel La Caimana's life intersects with that of Nicaragua's most famous medical doctor, Luis H. Debayle (1865–1938), the father of Salvadora Debayle (1895–1987), wife of Anastasio Somoza García. Those interactions are crucial to the novel as is the one between the fictional Caimana and an equally fictional Rigoberto López Pérez.

In the novel, La Caimana gains the first Somoza's trust after both are involved in a money-falsifying scheme in 1917, long before Somoza became president or head of the National Guard. La Caimana is arrested and fails to implicate Somoza. Somoza, in a gesture of thanks, asks Luis

H. Debayle, his future father-in-law, if he will conduct gender-affirming surgery (a "sex change") for La Caimana. Debayle—a medical genius and pioneer—who was previously unwilling to allow Somoza the opportunity to date his daughter, relents at the rare opportunity to conduct such a risky and controversial operation. In this way, Somoza is able to pay La Caimana back for his loyalty, while simultaneously pleasing his future father-in-law. According to the novel, Somoza might not have been able to marry Salvadora Debayle in 1918 had it not been for La Caimana's interest in this surgery and Debayle's eagerness to engage in medical history. The surgery was, in the end, unsuccessful, but that did not minimize La Caimana's loyalty and gratefulness to Somoza.

La Caimana is, undoubtedly, one of the main characters in Ramírez Mercado's novel, his life intersecting continuously with that of the Somoza family members. In the novel, he is, in fact, a political leader who mobilizes thousands of people on behalf of the dictatorship. He is also a spy for the Somoza government and the owner of a brothel called Baby Dolls. By choosing to give the brothel a historical name, Ramírez Mercado once again demonstrates his obsessive attention to historical detail and his vast knowledge of Nicaragua's past.

The character in the novel combines characteristics of two real historical figures: La Caimana and Nicolasa Sevilla. Sevilla was the alleged sex worker and sex broker ("madam") who, from the 1940s through 1979, led violent gangs of working-class Somocista men against the anti-Somocista civilian population.[115] In the novel, La Caimana headed these gangs, known as Somocista Popular Fronts. Ramírez Mercado describes La Caimana as dressed in red, the color of Somoza's liberal party, and always wearing dark sunglasses. These characteristics also correspond to Nicolasa Sevilla, a woman who was a generation older than La Caimana and someone who lived through the Sandinista revolution, dying in exile during the 1990s, almost twenty-five years after La Caimana died. Sevilla was feared by many Nicaraguans, and she came to symbolize the manipulation of the working class by the Somoza dictatorship, although she is best understood as an important member of the Somozas' clientelistic networks. Today, the term *Nicolasa* is used as an insult to degrade men and women alike who lead violent political groups of working-class peoples. It is also used as an insult against anyone in the political world who uses vulgar language or violence in a public space.[116]

One of the most detailed aspects of La Caimana's life, as told by Ramírez Mercado, is the story of how he came to live his life as a man. In Ramírez Mercado's version, La Caimana lost his mother at birth during a fire. Consumed by poverty, his father eventually decided to leave the seven-year-old in an orphanage for boys. The boys gang-raped the child, and La Caimana subsequently fled the orphanage. La Caimana then ended up seeking solace and employment at a brothel called Las Animas Benditas. It was at this brothel that the U.S. Marines showed up one night, in 1912, after closing, in search of sex workers. In an episode quite similar to the one recorded in the nation's newspapers in 1929, Ramírez Mercado describes how the Marines kidnapped several underage sex workers—among them La Caimana—and proceeded to get them drunk before they raped them in a nearby cemetery, amid a great deal of commotion and destruction. At the Guadalupe Cemetery La Caimana was rescued by Quirón, a twelve-year-old gifted boy who was born in an outhouse, as his mother tried to hide the product of her affair with a priest. In the novel, it was as a result of the rapes and the other events that transpired in childhood that La Caimana decided to become a man.

In *Margarita*, La Caimana proceeded to live life as a man, despite the failed operation, which took place when he was seventeen, five years after his arrival at the Animas brothel. After the operation, La Caimana took on Minerva Sarraceno as his lover and together they managed the Baby Dolls brothel, as well as the famous fireworks factory, which Sarraceno inherited with La Caimana's death in 1971.

In the novel, despite his friendship with Somoza, and his position as a Somocista leader and spy, La Caimana and his lover Sarraceno were arrested, along with Rafael Parrales (a character based on Rafael Corrales Rojas), on suspicion of having collaborated in the 1956 assassination of Somoza García carried out by Rigoberto López Pérez. There is no evidence that the historical Caimana was ever arrested. In the novel, however, La Caimana is minimally involved in the murder by holding the pistol Rigoberto eventually used in the murder, something La Caimana did as a favor to the poet.

In the novel Rafael Parrales died in jail. But both La Caimana and Sarraceno were ultimately released and exonerated, and La Caimana returned to work as an informant for the dictatorship. Nonetheless, during his captivity, and in response to a question by the first lady about

La Caimana's gender, "after much thought." La Caimana was declared a woman by Van Wynckle, the U.S. consultant in charge of assisting Somoza García in security matters:

> Is he a man, or is he a woman? The First Lady still asks, turning to Van Wynckle, who, taken by surprise, shrugs ... Once he is in Managua he will type up a report with the results of the investigation. And now that ... Captain Prío can read that report, that never made it to the acts of the Council of War, he smiles. After much thought, Van Wynckle ended up declaring her a woman.[117]

In the fictional version of his life, La Caimana's story was one that exemplified the ins and outs of political loyalty. Ramírez Mercado depicted political loyalty, like sexuality and gender, as fluctuating but only to an extent. La Caimana in the novel was not completely loyal to the Somozas, but his sexuality and gender, in the end, was defined in rigid terms. After being humiliated by his captors, he was officially declared to be a woman, by the U.S. representative, no less.

With regard to La Caimana, the novel focuses a great deal on two questions: Was La Caimana a man or a woman? And did s/he or did s/he not have a penis? The fictional Rigoberto asked the question: "The operation that the sage conducted on *la Caimana*, did it work or not?"[118] Whether La Caimana had gender-affirming surgery, had a penis all along, or used dildos has been the subject of debate in Nicaragua, as can be seen in the interview with Alejandro quoted earlier in the chapter. Alejandro favored the version in which La Caimana used dildos, so many in fact that he needed two extra coffins to bury them in. Another version held that there was one small extra coffin at the funeral. It was that of an impoverished child whose death had coincided with the death of La Caimana. Hilda had graciously agreed to provide the casket and bury the child along with Carmelo.[119] Different versions of this story have become urban legends.

In the novel, when Rigoberto told another character, Sergeant Paniagua, that "the sage Debayle ... was the one who operated on *la Caimana* to turn her into a man," Paniagua responded, "that is nonsense. What is more likely is that *la Caimana* had a penis and everything else from the moment of birth" ("traía su pichita y todo lo demás desde que nació").[120] The idea that lesbians have penises appears to have some appeal in the population at large. According to a study conducted in rural and urban Nicaragua during the late 1990s by CISAS, a nongovernmental health promotion organization, some of the men who participated in focus groups sponsored by the organization believed "with unshakeable confidence that lesbians have penises (albeit somewhat smaller ones than men: 'two to three inches')."[121]

In *La Prensa Literaria*, the weekly literary supplement of *La Prensa*, Nicaragua's conservative anti-Somocista (and later on anti-Sandinista) newspaper, a 2001 poem titled "La Caimana," by an unknown author, stressed La Caimana's promiscuity and his sexual transformation through surgery, this time emphasizing his breasts, not his penis:

Heavy gunpowder illuminated the sleep
of many concubines
she made her breasts disappear out of spite
leaving to cows that mammal privilege.[122]

It is important to point out that while in the novel La Caimana was ultimately a failure, a hoax as a man, in real life La Caimana was accepted by many as a man. La Caimana appeared as Carmelo (or as Pedro del Carmen Aguirre Ocampo) on his marriage certificate.[123] And Carmelo was buried in a suit and tie, with his moustache, a source of pride for him, visible.[124] Although Carmelo's political loyalty was questioned in the novel, this was not the case in real life. Carmelo was a bona fide Somocista, often seen dressed in military garb and armed in the company of Somoza family members. When he died, "over the coffin, among the wreaths sent by a long list of officials, those of President Anastasio Somoza Debayle and his brother José R. Somoza stood out. La Caimana used to serenade [José] with gunpowder during every feast of St. Joseph."[125] Although we do not know for sure what came first, La Caimana's incorporation into the Somozas' clientelistic networks or his support for the Somozas, in 2004 Carmelo's widow suggested that Somoza García himself was the one who helped Carmelo start the factory by lending him three córdobas (the equivalent to fifty U.S. cents), at the height of Carmelo's despair, soon after he fled from his family's abuse and ended up homeless as a teenager.[126] There are discrepancies in this story, for in 1971 Hilda had noted that the man who had given La Caimana those three córdobas was his uncle Rodolfo.[127]

While it is almost impossible to identify with La Caimana as he is portrayed in the novel, in real life most Nicaraguans did not and do not express hatred of La Caimana. Instead, the more common responses were and continue to be awe, curiosity, and admiration. The situation is different, however, for the figure of Nicolasa Sevilla, probably one of the most hated women in the nation's history. Descriptions of Sevilla such as this one were common: "the blue eyes of Nicolasa Sevilla resembled two burning embers of hatred and evil while her mouth, always painted prostitute red, seemed to spit tongues of fire and incandescent lava."[128]

What Nicolasa Sevilla and La Caimana had in common was their loyalty to the Somozas, their political and/or business acumen, and their reputation of being willing and able to physically fight with anybody who crossed them. Their non-elite status and their "questionable" sexuality marked them both as outsiders within some Somocista circles, although they both were established patrons in the well-oiled Somocista patron-client system. One huge difference, however, became greater than their similarities. La Caimana died before the war between the Sandinista guerrillas and the Somozas' National Guard escalated in the 1970s. Thus, La Caimana never had to prove his loyalty in the 1978 insurrection or in the 1979 final offensive. Meanwhile, Nicolasa Sevilla was loyal to Somoza until the very end. Unlike many of Somoza's wealthier supporters, Sevilla did not flee Nicaragua before July 19, 1979. After she was jailed by the Sandinistas, she shouted her never-ending support for the Somozas from her cell, until finally, after fifteen months, the Sandinista government released her due to her advanced age. She sought refuge first in Venezuela and later in the United States, where she died.[129]

IDENTITY MATTERS

While literature has focused extensively on *La Caimana*'s sexuality, that is not the only way in which he has been remembered in Nicaragua. In 2001 the First Congress of Female Business Owners took place at the exclusive beach resort Hotel Montelimar. One of the goals of the Congress was to pay tribute to pioneer female business owners and, ironically, given that La Caimana lived his adult life as a man, La Caimana was one of the first people mentioned. La Caimana was referred to as Carmen Aguirre, his birth name: "she was the first woman to dedicate herself to the business of fireworks, when she was only 13 years old and she decided to become independent of her father..."[130] This part was also ironic, given that La Caimana was forced to leave home because he was not accepted by his family as LGBTQIA+.

La Caimana was also remembered as "Nicaragua's first self-acknowledged lesbian" in a widely read 2004 magazine article, leading me to stress the fluid nature of identity.[131] Carmelo married a lesbian and lived life as a man. La Caimana was also a businessperson, a philanthropist, a Catholic, and a Somocista. It is clear that narrow or essentialized understandings of lesbian identities (especially ones that ignore female masculinities), trans identities, or Somocista identities cannot address the complexities of La Caimana's life. La Caimana was complex in every way. The gifted and poetic journalist Amalia del Cid describes La Caimana as follows: "she believed in horoscopes as much as in the Psalms and using the knowledge acquired in herbalist books, cured the children brought to her from rural areas. She was good with her fists and in business and danced almost as well as she drank ... She was tough and she was sweet. A serious person and a jokester. She was feared and she was loved. She was a partier and she was noble. She was Carmen and Carmelo. She was, according to her son José Dolores, 'a lion and velvet.'"[132] La Caimana, moreover, was resilient: "suffer[ing] catastrophic fires six times and [rising] from the ashes six times."[133]

Given La Caimana's complex identity, one has to wonder to what extent the public version of Carmelo's masculinity (i.e., his hypermasculinity) was performative. It is unlikely that he could have lived such a public life and received such public acclaim if he had only been understood as lesbian. He surely would not have been welcomed in the Somocista women's organizations of the 1950s and 1960s, for those women went to great lengths to avoid being labeled lesbians.[134] Moreover, homosexuality during this period was criminalized. Carmelo truly had few options available. He made a difficult choice: to attempt to outdo men at masculinity. That he was able to pull it off so well was a colossal feat. In the face of myriad obstacles, La Caimana, by achieving national recognition and status, became a true pioneer and rightly deserves that title in business and in the LGBTQIA+ arena.

Undoubtedly, the most nuanced portrayal of La Caimana is the one given by his widow, Hilda Rosa Scott Hernández, who has always referred to him as Carmen. Hilda was originally from Diriamba and was the daughter of Carlos Eduardo Scott and María Magdalena Hernández. According to the journalist Edgar Barberena, Hilda's grandfather was a British engineer who built Nicaragua's first artesian well.[135]

In her interview with Amalia del Cid, Hilda remembered her first encounter with La Caimana. It was Friday, September 2, 1960, and she remembered it because La Caimana would later give her a ring with the date on it.[136] Hilda was twenty-two at the time, seven years younger than La Caimana, and very petite. She had a young daughter, worked as a nurse at El Hospital Bautista, and had had female partners before meeting La Caimana. Hilda remembered that when they first met, La Caimana "wore skirts below the knee." Hilda told del Cid, "I put pants on her" ("yo le puse el pantalón").[137]

Since 1971, Hilda Scott has probably been interviewed dozens of times about Carmelo Aguirre. In 2004 she told the press that La Caimana was the daughter of José Dolores Aguirre, the owner of Tata Lolo, a very famous bar in pre-earthquake Managua. Hilda recounted that La Caimana, like her, loved women and knew this from an early age. Carmelo encountered great difficulties because of this. In fact, when Carmelo's mother found out his sexual orientation, she married Carmelo off at the age of thirteen to an older man. That is why Carmelo left his home. His mother then put Carmelo in jail to keep Carmelo away from a woman lover. After his escape, Carmelo was homeless, but he never gave in.[138] This story is somewhat different from the one Hilda told the press in 1971, but certain things are constant. Over fifty years ago Hilda also emphasized the ill treatment Carmelo received at the hands of his family because of his masculine demeanor, noting that as a child he was forced to sleep on the sidewalk, he was deprived of food, and he never had a real toy.[139]

Everyone agrees that Carmelo proceeded to make some very good financial decisions early on in life. Then, Carmelo achieved national attention when the newspaper *La Prensa* published a photo of him wearing a suit and tie.[140] The newspapers featured several articles on La Caimana before his death, and many more after. They noted in their reporting that Hilda was his longtime partner but also made sure to include at least one photo of him with another young, very feminine, and very beautiful, woman, perhaps to emphasize his promiscuity in order to buttress the hypermasculine public persona that the media itself had helped construct. La Caimana so embraced this hypermasculine persona that some of the children he brought home to raise with Hilda were the unwanted children of his female lovers.[141]

According to Hilda, they were married in 1962.[142] Hilda and Carmelo's marriage was a rocky one. Hilda recalls: "one day she hit a man with a glass pitcher . . . Almost nobody dared say things to her because she responded in her own way. If someone disrespected her, she responded violently and she would fight with anybody."[143]

Amalia del Cid confirmed that Carmelo

> Could fight with blows like any man. It is known that on one occasion, swinging a glass pitcher "s/he broke open the head" of an individual who tried to touch her to find out "if s/he was a man or a woman." And that one night s/he knocked down a smart-aleck. The anecdote was captured by the journalist Francisco Gurdián Guerrero on August 1, 1987 in *El Nuevo Amanecer Cultural*:

> "One night while at the gardens of the Brewing Company, I saw *la Caimana* at a table with a pretty little woman drinking beer. She looked the way she usually did, dressed as a man, and was wearing a hat kept on the table. When the orchestra played, a male friend of Carmelo's asked for permission to dance with his/her lady, to which she happily agreed. Since the music they were playing was a romantic bolero, the fellow squeezed the pretty lady more and more. *La Caimana*, who was observing them, there reached a moment when [s/he] couldn't take it anymore and [s/he] got up in search of the couple, grabbing the unfortunate dancer by the neck and letting go a tremendous blow that knocked him out. Carmen's [*la Caimana*'s] only comment was 'He was being abusive.'"[144]

Hilda objected to Carmelo's behavior. In 2004 she recalled: "at first, I would complain to her, then I got tired of it. Since I loved her, I stopped fighting and dedicated myself to my work. Although Carmen misbehaved, she always respected me . . . since I did everything at home, I didn't have any problems. I obeyed her."[145] In 2018 Scott told her interviewer that

Carmelo "was the love of my life" and that she remained single because she wanted to (*por decisión propia*) after Carmelo died.[146] Carmelo died of complications related to diabetes and a gallbladder operation.[147] However, there was speculation in the media that he had died from complications related to gender affirming surgery for which he had paid 35,000 Nicaraguan córdobas, approximately 5,000 U.S. dollars.[148] The journalist del Cid confirmed that La Caimana had surgery to remove his breasts, but that had happened months earlier: "It is true that *la Caimana* had breast surgery at the El Retiro Hospital, because they caused back pain and that after that s/he loved wearing men's camisoles; but that was not the cause of his/her premature death."[149]

After Carmelo's death, Hilda raised their five sons and two daughters. One of them became an evangelical pastor, and another worked as a chauffeur. One of them, who had greatly resented Carmelo because of the beatings he received as a child, committed suicide years later after a romantic breakup.[150] Another one died in a vehicular accident.[151] In 2004 Hilda told a reporter that none of them had ever criticized her for being lesbian,[152] but when I spoke to her eight years later, she told me her daughter had convinced her to become a Jehovah's Witness and forget her past. Hilda, however, had short hair and was wearing pants when I spoke to her, and was presumably the owner of the bar named La Caimana, the place where we met. At the bar there were beer ads of scantily clad women alongside an enlarged photograph of Augusto C. Sandino, Nicaragua's nationalist hero, standing next to a poster of Anastasio Somoza García, the dictator who ordered Sandino's assassination. With these reminders of the past all around her, it must have been impossible to forget. In fact, I had the feeling that if her daughter had not been standing next to her, Hilda would have granted me a formal interview, for she quickly brought out newspaper clippings that told the story of La Caimana when her daughter stepped inside for a few minutes.

Ironically, La Caimana, by being simultaneously remembered as "Nicaragua's first declared lesbian" *and* one of Nicaragua's most successful business owners, is a misogynist's nightmare come true. As addressed extensively in chapter 3, in the late 1940s Francisco Palma Martínez, one of many "moralists" who spewed hatred against lesbians, predicted that modernity would lead to Nicaragua being populated with financially independent women who, believing themselves to be "free," would descend into all sorts of pleasures, including homosexuality.[153]

Over half a century after Palma Martínez made his predictions, there continues to be fear, nostalgia, ridicule, and a yearning for modernity in Nicaragua. The tension is between the past and the present, between inequality and the rights that modernity (and possibly consumer capitalism?) would presumably bring for LGBTQIA+ Nicaraguans, all of this taking place in what so many consider to be already a postmodern world, one that has left behind the promises and pitfalls of modernity many years ago.

The story of La Caimana reveals that, in certain contexts, particularly in the absence of a viable feminist movement, sexual outlaws and gender transgressors can help uphold stringent gender dichotomies. Indeed, Carmelo and Hilda appeared to the outside world to have adopted very conservative gender roles, ones that did not seek to alter traditional relations between men and women. In that respect, they were not a threat to established sexual mores, and Carmelo was able to openly live his life as a man, with many of the rights and privileges that that entailed.

La Caimana's life story sheds light on the dynamics of gender and sexuality under the Somoza dictatorship. It also sheds light on the dynamics of the dictatorship itself. Moreover, it can also be useful to contemporary debates in Nicaragua and elsewhere over homonormativity and the contradictions created by lobbying for specific lesbian, gay, bisexual, and transgender rights (like marriage or adoption) without advocating for a radical transformation of patriarchy, or a democratic society. Meanwhile, until La Caimana's story is told in full, new generations of Nicaraguans on the political left, right, and center will continue to remember La Caimana only as a placemark that helps them navigate their tangled urban metropolis and not as one that can help guide their travels through their complicated past.

EL CHARCO DE LOS PATOS AND LA SEBASTIANA

El Charco de los Patos (The Puddle of the Ducks), also sometimes referred to as El Lago de los Cisnes (Swan Lake), was located in the working-class neighborhood of Cristo del Rosario in northwest Managua.[154] Some

Nicaraguans believe that this bar/club, with its mixed heterosexual and LGBTQIA+ clientele, was owned (or co-owned) by Bernabé Somoza Urcuyo (1948–), a son of President Luis Somoza Debayle (1922–67).

The name Charco de los Patos could be construed as derogatory, since *patos* is a derogatory term for gay men, although some gay men have embraced the term and given it new meaning. The name Swan Lake also has multiple meanings. It is a reference not only to the Russian ballet that premiered in 1877 but also to Rubén Darío's poetry. The swan figures prominently in Darío's poems. According to the U.S. scholar Dan A. van Meter, the image of the swan in Darío's poems "can be viewed as a type of androgynous figure, with the masculinity of its phallus-like neck balanced by the femininity of its soft and full body."[155] In one of Darío's most well-known poems, aptly titled "El Cisne," the swan from Richard Wagner's opera *Lohengrin* occupies a central place. While in the opera, however, the swan eventually dies, in "El Cisne" the swan sings to live.[156]

In Alejandro's description of LGBTQIA+ life during the dictatorship quoted earlier, El Charco de los Patos figured prominently. Alejandro went to El Charco de los Patos in order to spend time with Bernabé Somoza, who he mistakenly remembers as the son, and not the nephew, of the last Somoza dictator. In fact, Alejandro called Bernabé "mi hermano del alma," his soul brother, and had very fond memories of their time together.

The upper-class patrons at the bar and their luxury vehicles, according to the journalist Anuar Hassan, provoked "admiration and scorn" among the bar's poor neighbors.[157] Alejandro corroborated the elite nature of the bar/club, although, according to him, the bar was open to the public most of the time, with one important exception:

> Anyone could show up . . . but during the elections for Miss Nicaragua held by the cochones only people who had close ties [to the dictators would come], only those who were of the upper classes [could attend] . . . When the elections for Miss Nicaragua took place, the one held by the cochones, a Sacasa[158] would come, a Somoza . . .

The tradition of conducting Miss Gay Nicaragua pageants is still alive in Nicaragua—after a hiatus during the Sandinista revolution—and it raises some important questions. According to the U.S. anthropologist

Cymene Howe, the pre-2006 pageants sponsored by Xochiquetzal, a lesbian feminist AIDS prevention NGO, sought "to create solidarity for homosexuals in Nicaragua."[159] The Xochiquetzal pageants also sought to "bring together gay men and women, to emphasize solidarity, or similarity, amongst Nicaragua's sexual minorities."[160] The meaning of more recent pageants has changed perhaps, given that they are often financed and sponsored by the Sandinista party and/or corporations. But what about the pageants that took place at El Charco de los Patos? According to Alejandro, the audience of the Miss Nicaragua Charco pageants was the domain of the Somocista elites. In all likelihood, they sought to foster solidarity among Somocista LGBTQIA+ Nicaraguans while simultaneously allowing Somocista elites to exercise their class privileges. The location of the bar seems significant in order for them to have met both of these objectives. Perhaps middle- and upper-class LGBTQIA+ Somocistas could only carve a space for such sexual and gender transgression (in a manner that did not affect their class position) in the outer limits of the city, among the poor and disenfranchised.

Gay and bisexual men of the Somocista elite who frequented El Charco de los Patos might have been able to shield themselves from some of the homophobia that permeated society at large by gathering in a place far removed from the centers of power. Working-class bisexual men, gay men, and transgender women at that same bar, however, had fewer options and were sometimes subjected to the ridicule of the heterosexual patrons. According to writer Anuar Hassan, "the heterosexual people who . . . visited [El Charco de los Patos] amused themselves with the antics of one of the waiters, self-baptized as '*La Reina de los Tártaros*' . . . such as dancing scandalously or flirting with the other clients before the gaze not without envy of her peers."[161] Hassan wrote, "*La Reina de los Tártaros* really had a Mongolian type, with slanted eyes and thick lips" ("tenía realmente un tipo mongólico, con ojos rasgados y labios gruesos").[162] With this description Hassan converted La Reina into a racialized other, a non-mestizo Nicaraguan. Hassan, in fact, goes a step further by suggesting that La Reina and LGBTQIA+ patrons were of a different "species": "what the modest clients of her own species could not do due to their inhibited nature, *la Reina de los Tártaros* did with complete ease" ("lo que los recatados clientes de su misma especie no podían hacer por su natural inhibido, *la Reina de los Tártaros* lo hacía con total desenfado").[163]

Although Hassan mocked La Reina for her name, she might have chosen her name to honor the 1960 Italian movie of that name. In this adventure film "an orphan, raised by a foreign tribe, becomes a warrior queen."[164]

It appears that the drag performances and "feminine" behavior of working-class nonheterosexual men under the Somozas could be empowering and/or disempowering, depending on the context. The "admiration and scorn" that Hassan recalls working-class heterosexuals felt for the LGBTQIA+ Somocista elite customers at El Charco de los Patos are also present in Hassan's description of La Reina's transgressive performances. Admiration and scorn were less common but were sometimes present in the media coverage of La Caimana's death in 1971, as can be seen in headlines that stated "Managua Observes the Strangest Wake," "Incredible Quantity of People in Strange Funeral," and "Music, Drugs, and Gunpowder."[165] This tension often permeated late twentieth century and early twenty-first century heterosexual Nicaraguan recollections of homosexuality before 1979.

Howe has written that "the way in which travesti pageantry is played-out [in the Xochiquetzal competition of the late twentieth century], in the context of 'pride' celebrations, suggests that these performances are political; these shows are a symbolic tool to create a sense of collective identity."[166] The performance of specific types of femininity at the center of the Somocista Miss Gay Nicaragua contests of the mid-twentieth century probably fostered a sense of collective sexual identity among LGBTQIA+ Nicaraguans that cut across class differences. The closed nature of some of the events, however, most likely reinforced class differences within the group. The legacy of the Miss Nicaragua pageants in this context is contradictory and ambiguous. What it does prove, however, is Alejandro's assertion that "here homosexuality has existed in all [political] stages."

The scholar David Rocha has added a great deal of nuance to our understanding of LGBTQIA+ life in Managua during the late 1960s and early 1970s. Rocha conducted an interview with an older woman who recalled that at El Charco de los Patos "homosexuals . . . did very nice shows.'" Rocha notes that

> these . . . were cross-dressing performances [*performances de travestismo*] that included everything from beauty contests to erotic dances.

Doña M . . . was very close to *la Reina de los Tártaros*, a homosexual who became very famous for having won one of the beauty contests at *El Charco*. In the interview, doña M . . . remembers a particular event that combines . . . the memory of *la Reina* and *El Charco*:

> So he was famous and he even got married and the wedding party left from "*El Charco de los Patos*" to come here. The wedding dress had a long train, beautiful; he married a boy who was of high class, from the high society ["de la alta alcurnia, ¡de la sociedad!"]! That is what we used to call those who had money. That is who *la Reina* married. Her name was Reinaldo but she was the famous Reina de los Tártaros. . . .

Rocha went on to state that "Doña M . . . finished up the anecdote affirming that the entire neighborhood went to the party." Moreover, her story reminded Rocha of what Rubén, another person interviewed by Rocha, had told him: "I had my quinceañera there."[167]

Rocha interviewed someone else who knew La Reina and remembered her as "a very good person. Very helpful, in the neighborhood they loved him very much. He worked as a maid."[168]

La Reina de los Tártaros was well known by everyone who attended El Charco de los Patos, as was La Sebastiana. In another interview conducted by Rocha, his collaborator/interviewee stated:

> The show that *la Reina* gave, uf! She wasn't playing! You know how homosexuals are when it comes to dressing, their nails, everything. I have always admired them, as well as la Sebastiana. La Sebastiana did such a beautiful job with her makeup, she had green eyes . . .[169] He made a living selling here at the Mercado Oriental . . .
>
> . . . everyone knew *la Reina* here, because they gave him a place to stay. I gave him a place to stay and he lived here. But he got, like disappointment, his family lived in las Brisas [a middle-class neighborhood in Managua], he is from a good family, because when he died we went to look for his family and that is when we found out that he was from a good family. I held the wake here . . . people were crying, because everyone here knew him and he was well-loved . . . he was a good cook . . . and he was very loved here. After the earthquake they all disappeared. Each

one went their own way. Only *la Reina* stayed here, the famous *Reina de los Tártaros* ...

La Reina has been dead about 12 years ... his family came from Las Brisas, but he was disappointed in that family. You know that there are families who discriminate against you because you are like that.[170]

In yet another interview conducted by Rocha, his collaborator/interviewee expanded on La Reina and corroborated the earlier account:

There was *la Reina de los Tártaros*, who worked like a woman, she married a young man, you see ... she got married and they lasted a few years, like ten years she lasted with that young man but he died and she outlived him.[171]

La Sebastiana's life is a bit harder to document than that of La Reina de los Tártaros. La Sebastiana was born in Masatepe and grew up with her mother, but her mother did not accept her and forced Sebastiana out of their home as a teenager. She finished fourth grade and started working at age twelve. Her life was highly impacted by her looks: "since I was as beautiful as the sun in Maracaibo, I was very coveted."[172] For a time, she sold "grapes and apples on the sidewalk [in front of the very famous store of] Carlos Cardenal," but she left that job due to police harassment.[173] After that, she stated, "I devoted myself to entertainment, bars, in short, the patron saint festivities."[174] La Sebastiana became famous in part because of her participation in the Masaya celebrations of El Torovenado and other cultural events and for her presence at El Charco de los Patos:

Can you believe that once I dressed up as Eve, Adam's wife, naked, I went to a flower shop and told them to make me two fig leaves, one in front and one in the back, I had a long wig, that went down to my boobs and ... I quickly got lots attention, the queen of Spring, the queen of the Americas and that is how I gained more and more fame ... [E]veryone would say ... if la Sebastiana isn't there, the Torovenado [festival] is no good, la Sebastiana draws a crowd, floats come and all kinds of shit, anything to see the artistic skill the fucker has ("el arte que tiene el jodido").[175]

David Rocha wrote the following about La Sebastiana after he interviewed her:

> Upon meeting her ... this visible and important cochón for homosexual urban culture is dying of loneliness and alcoholism. The loca that all Managuas remember tells me: "Governments have come and gone and I remained as history 'why?' ... they would tell me: Sebastián is the oldest cochón in Managua."[176]

La Sebastiana's poverty, gender expression, and gender identity greatly impacted her life. I agree with Rocha's assessment that it is useful to contrast Bernabé Somoza's life story with that of La Sebastiana. Rocha argues that "Bernabé represents discrete masculinities, that is, the masculine homosexual, while La Sebastiana will represent the figure of the cochón, that is, the feminized homosexual. Both figures will be intersected by social class and race."[177] Indeed, their class status, appearance, gender expression, and gender identity determined their fate. After the entire Somoza family fled Nicaragua in the aftermath of the Sandinista revolution, Bernabé was able to make a living as an art dealer in Houston, Texas, for many years, despite an eventual cancer diagnosis.[178] La Sebastiana, meanwhile, died alone in 2016, living in squalid conditions for most of her later years.

CREATING A NATIONAL NARRATIVE THAT LINKS SOMOCISMO TO HOMOSEXUALITY

In my earlier work I have documented the portrayal of the Somoza period as one of sexual disorder. Before the emergence of the Sandinista National Liberation Front during the 1960s, the nation-building agenda pursued by the Nationalist Liberal Party under the Somozas was the most extensive ever seen in Nicaragua. However, it presented numerous paradoxes for women. While it integrated women into the country's economic framework, their roles were primarily confined to low-wage positions. Similarly, their participation in the political system was primarily as loyal voters organized within pro-government organizations. This Liberal legacy, which stood out in contrast to the Conservative one, led to the development of a populist Somocista Liberalism that was not necessarily grounded in moralistic or maternalistic ideals but rather on the display of exaggerated heterosexuality.

During the Somozas' tenure, certain misogynistic sexual practices—such as husbands' public extramarital affairs, male promiscuity, and the exploitation and assault of women through prostitution and rape—were writ large on the national canvas. Male members of the Somoza family came to personally epitomize promiscuity by openly engaging in numerous extramarital affairs. Prostitution became institutionalized under their rule, along with state-sanctioned sexual violence against female anti-Somocista detainees. The era of the Somozas is etched in memory as a period marked by various forms of sexual excess. However, moral and sexual degradation came to be symbolized by the figure of a woman, often a sex worker or someone accused of being one, rather than a Somoza male.[179]

Along with other anti-Somocistas, Anuar Hassan has been adamant about portraying the Somoza period as one of sexual disorder. In the early 2000s, Hassan focused specifically on linking homosexuality, which he saw as deviancy, to the National Guard and the Somocista upper classes. In articles in the Nicaraguan press and in his 2001 book *Grandes crímenes del siglo XX en Nicaragua*, Hassan focused on several high-profile murders that involved men who presumably had sex with men either as the victims or the perpetrators. Hassan recounted the unresolved 1975 murder of Gerardo Gómez Martínez, a twenty-year-old man whose wife was seven months pregnant. Gómez Martínez was found tortured and raped, with a bullet hole in his head, lying naked on a rural road near Managua. In the investigation, a captain and a lieutenant in Somoza's National Guard, Gómez Martínez's alleged lovers, became implicated, as well as other Somocista members of the so-called "'high society' of those years," in Hassan's view, "all afflicted with the same common aversion to women."[180]

In order to stress what he perceived to be the homosexual corruption of the Somoza National Guard and Police, Hassan recounts "something curious" that happened during the investigation.[181] Without any evidence to back his claim, Hassan stated that the working-class police detectives in charge of the case, although highly homophobic, were deferential to the "high society" suspects, possibly because the working-class police officers too, had sex with men:

... those "detectives," coming from the lowest strata of society, many of them illiterate and all imbued with a visceral extremism, to whom the mere presence of a maricón stirred their bile, had an inexplicable deference towards them.

Probably, deep down, they sympathized with those kinds of people, and one cannot discard the possibility that many of them had had intimate relations with some of the suspects.[182]

Hassan suggested that the murder might have been done in retaliation by one of Gómez Martínez's male lovers, upset due to Gómez Martínez's marriage to a woman. In fact, Hassan noted, Gomez Martinez's male friends "could not conceive such betrayal."[183] Hassan argued that rumor had it that Gómez Martínez had previously married one of his male lovers, in a private ceremony, insinuating that his second marriage, to a woman, could have been reason enough to kill him. Ironically, while Hassan was adamant about linking homosexuality to the Somozas, he felt it necessary to refer to the suspects in the Gomez Martínez case by their initials only, in order to protect their identity because they were still alive at the time his articles and book were published.

The late historian Francisco J. Barbosa noted that in the political struggles against the Somoza dictatorship, questioning National Guardsmen's heterosexuality was not uncommon. Barbosa described the violence that broke out in León during a confrontation between middle-class students and working-class members of the National Guard in the aftermath of the massacre of four students by the Guardia on July 23, 1959. In the confrontation, male students called the guardsmen "cowards and even '*cochones*,' a derogatory term for homosexuals ... A hegemonic middle-class masculinity ... underlay these insults, and despite the participation of women in the protest, the confrontations that afternoon played out as contests between men over the ability to claim masculine identity and privilege."[184]

The association between those on the right of the political spectrum and homosexuality was strongly promoted by some leftists in Nicaragua and elsewhere during the twentieth century.[185] Sometimes leftists did not proclaim that there was a link between homosexuality and right-wing politics but rather that homosexuality made it impossible for someone to be a good leftist revolutionary. The most infamous declaration might be that of the

Cuban leader Fidel Castro, who stated in 1965, "We would never come to believe that a homosexual could embody the conditions and requirements of conduct that would enable us to consider him a true Revolutionary, a true Communist militant. A deviation of that nature clashes with the concept we have of what a militant Communist must be."[186]

In many contemporary Nicaraguan imaginaries, homosexuality has been the domain of the urban middle and upper classes and/or the domain of the U.S.-supported Somozas, especially the Somocista elite (even though the association between sexual/gender dissidence and Indigeneity remains in the national imaginary). Linking homosexuality to Somocismo, especially to the Somocista elites and/or to the much-hated National Guard, helped foster anti-LGBTQIA+ feelings among Sandinistas, anti-Somocistas, and non-Somocistas, with detrimental results for LGBTQIA+ Nicaraguans in the post-1979 period. The FSLN mounted campaigns against sex workers (including LGBTQIA+ sex workers) in the early years of the revolution, and some Sandinista party members, like Erika quoted earlier in the chapter, were persecuted and harassed by the FSLN.

Nonetheless, the situation in Nicaragua was never as dire as the situation in Cuba was at one point, since the FSLN did not have an official anti-LGBTQIA+ position. Indeed, sometimes the Sandinista revolution opened spaces in which LGBTQIA+ Nicaraguans thrived. Moreover, even if they had wanted to, and there is no evidence they did, the FSLN leadership could not have pursued the inhumane anti-LGBTQIA+ policies that the Cuban government did. By 1979 the Cuban labor camps had closed, and the world had changed. The Nicaraguan revolution gained worldwide solidarity in part because it was more inclusive than the Cuban one.

Ironically, Somocistas as a group did not want to be associated with homosexuality, despite the claims made by anti-Somocistas. In the next section of the chapter I discuss the campaign the Somoza government mounted against LGBTQIA+ Nicaraguans in the late 1960s and early 1970s.

THE ANTI-LGBTQIA+ CAMPAIGNS OF THE LATE 1960S AND EARLY 1970S

David Rocha is one of the few scholars who has documented LGBTQIA+ life in Nicaragua during the 1960s and 1970s. He does so in his 2016 master's thesis, in his 2019 book *Crónicas de la Ciudad*, and in his 2022 book *Cartografías de espacios en fuga: Managua, 1968–1975*. One of his findings is that the late 1960s and early 1970s saw a wave of criminalization and persecution against LGBTQIA+ Nicaraguans, particularly against those who were considered cochones or *locas*:

> During the decades of 1960 and 1970 the Somocista dictatorship created a discourse that criminalized homosexuality. Many locas ... were locked up in jails and exhibited in the newspaper *Novedades* as dishonorable criminals.[187]
>
> The Somoza dictatorship repressed and persecuted homosexuals in the city of Managua between 1968 and 1972. As a policy of control and social sanitation, the feminized male body was rejected in public spheres by the Nicaraguan state.[188]
>
> The body of the cochón subject appears criminalized because it subverts the performativity of gender.[189]

Rocha explains that the May 1969 "case of [twenty-three-year-old] Alejandro Díaz Figueroa is vital to understand this [subversion],"[190] and he carefully examined the pro-Somoza newspaper report detailing Alejandro's arrest:

> COSTUME PARTY—On Tuesday night, when he was going to a costume party, 23-year-old Alejandro Díaz Figueroa was captured by a Managua Police patrol near the Mercado Oriental. The young man dressed as a woman caught the attention of the enlisted G.N. [National Guard members], who immediately proceeded to arrest him. Once at the Hormiguero [prison] his head was shaved as punishment. Díaz Figueroa said that it did not matter since he always wears a wig.[191]

Rocha's analysis is as follows:

> In the note, the street, the night, and the transvestite body appear as significant elements that connect. Alejandro is being arrested for being a cross-dresser on the street. He is imprisoned because his body subverts the idea of gender performance expected by a male body. However, I am intrigued by the curiosity of the enlisted G.N. [members of the National

Guard]. Perhaps at night, while trying to seek female sexual companionship, the officers approached the feminized body and upon realizing that the person was not a woman, their "surprise"/anger led to the capture.[192]

In interviews with La Sebastiana, she also talked about being harassed and persecuted by the police and having her hair cut off: "the police messed with me so much ... they would cut off my hair, they would ruin my nails."[193] La Sebastiana also spoke of police raids in an interview with David Rocha: "That night they took everyone prisoner, except me (cries) but I was saved because I hid behind a door ..."[194] When Rocha asked, "Why would the police take you?" La Sebastiana answered: "because they would do a raid, understand me, wherever we were from, wherever we are from, it's the raid. And where do we end up? In jail ... That is where we would end up, to sweep, to clean."[195]

The harassment, the persecution, the arrests, and the punishments that La Sebastiana and Díaz Figueroa experienced are reminiscent of the police behavior against LGBTQIA+ Nicaraguans in the early twentieth century that are documented in chapter 3. There was indeed a moral panic that took hold among Nicaragua's elites in the late 1960s and early 1970s, as it had in the early 1900s.

Historian Richard Ward has summarized historian Peter King's criteria for a moral panic as follows: "he identifies a six-stage pattern common to all, that might be briefly summarised as follows: firstly, an initial act (or acts) provokes media attention on a particular theme; secondly, the media then exaggerate the threat posed by the type of offence under attention; thirdly, this leads to an increase in crime reported to the authorities; fourthly, the extent of crime is overestimated by the media and the authorities; fifthly, new and heavier control and punishment measures are introduced; and finally, after a couple of months or so, the panic dies away."[196] The last stage is that "the new methods for controlling and punishing become the new norm."[197] King has defined a moral panic as "a discrete event or cycle of events with a beginning and an end, which follows a process and has a product."[198] In this case, there was definitely an end to the moral panic (albeit not an end to discrimination against LGBTQIA+ Nicaraguans or their arrests), and that was caused in part by the earthquake in December 1972. We know less about the origins of the panic, although both David Rocha and the journalist Bosco León Báez have investigated a series of punitive measures taken by police from 1968 through 1970.

Several "sanitation" campaigns were carried out in working-class neighborhoods during the late 1960s.[199] Authorities stated that they were worried about prostitution, drugs, homosexuality, and hippies. The restrictions, however, were not universally accepted, and León Báez has documented a rebellion conducted by madams against the new rules that the Somoza administration attempted to impose on bars and brothels in early 1970. According to León Báez, the president, Anastasio Somoza Debayle, was being pressured by his mother, Salvadora Debayle, to clean things up:

> Mrs. Hortensia Bermúdez ... took the lead in the singular protest that the majority of the owners of brothels and gambling houses would carry out, against the measures announced by the Police and the Ministry of Health against these dens ...
>
> At noon on March 16, 1970, doña Hortensia's house was full of these human flesh merchants, who were determined to do anything against whoever ...
>
> ... the owners of the brothels in the capital, agreed to summon the media to a press conference to show documents where the Police and Health granted them permits to "work."
>
> The next day, some 20 journalists ... arrived ... to see the angry owners who explained ... that the Police and Health were playing dumb, because they received money weekly depending on the quality of the business ...
>
> One by one, the owners of these businesses actively participated in the conference, all of them carrying, in addition to receipts, their "magnífica" (the voting card that the Nationalist Liberal Party, PLN, gave to those who voted for that party in elections) which operated as a kind of proof that they were active members or sympathizers of the government party.
>
> At the end of the assembly, they formed a three-member commission [to] go and talk with the Police Commander ...
>
> A week later, the meeting was held between the Commander of the Managua Police, Colonel Rodríguez Somoza, and the Minister of Health, Francisco Urcuyo Maliaños, and the commission of business people who managed brothels ...

... at the meeting they agreed to try ... to keep things calm in each venue ...

The journalists located the Commander of the Managua Police ... and when they asked him about the agreements ... the soldier responded curtly that everything had been resolved ...

But Colonel Rodríguez Somoza issued an unusual warning against the famous bar "*El Charco de los Patos*", a place visited only by homosexuals, which he ordered to close permanently. "Does this mean," a journalist asked him, "that it will never open again?" Comandante Rodríguez Somoza firmly replied:

"What I close is not opened again by anyone."

The Comandante's words were carried away by the wind, because the order issued in the first days of April 1970 did not take long to be annulled. At the end of May, of that same year, *the Charco de los Patos* closed the premises with that name, and reopened, from the Church of Santo Domingo one block towards the lake, half a block down. They opened "*El Lago de los Cisnes*" [The Lake of the Swans] with great fanfare.

This venue was opened legally and with the signature of Comandante Rodríguez Somoza, with the difference that the owner of this venue was Bernabé Somoza, son of the former president Luis Somoza Debayle.

The figurehead of the venue was the same owner of the deceased *Charco de los Patos*, due to his knowledge of managing this type of business, specializing in homosexuals.

Another difference is that the *Lago de los Cisnes* had the reputation of having more class and people of lineage than el ... *Charco de los Patos*.[200]

According to León Báez, the earthquake did not change the order given by Somoza Debayle to close the brothels, but the police were unable to close any: "Three months after Colonel Rodríguez Somoza promised to close the brothels in Managua, the earthquake hit ... the National Guard and the Health authorities were unable to close a single brothel during that time, instead hundreds were born on the outskirts of what was Managua before the earthquake."[201]

David Rocha has argued that the order to close El Charco de los Patos can be found in *Novedades*, the Somocista paper, on April 9, 1969 (not in 1970), and is critical to understanding the wave of repression. Rocha wrote, "the note orders the immediate closure of *El Charco* due to a public scandal caused by the newspaper *La Prensa* . . . [when they reported that] police forces [were] involved in a sodomite party."[202] Rocha cites the original text that appeared in the April 8 edition of the newspaper *La Prensa*, the anti-Somocista paper. The reference to "the holy days" is there because it seems that the party at El Charco took place during the Catholic Holy Week:

LA PRENSA, APRIL 8, 1969
"VIGILANCE FOR IMMORALITY"

While the Christian society devoid of all police security celebrated the holy days, somewhere in Managua, a group of sexual inverts engaged in grand sodomy ["se entregaba en gran sodomía"] under the watch of two law enforcement officers, to carry out one of the most repulsive parties known in Nicaragua . . . If it is already an attack against morality that such parties, symbol of the other crisis in Nicaragua: a moral one, take place precisely on the days that the Christian society of the world has consecrated to meditate under the light of the Redeemer, the more nefarious it is, that these parties enjoy police protection, when what is healthy, correct, logical and normal within a society that tries to preserve its essences, is that law enforcement officers act to protect that society. The event shows that Managua was morally and materially exposed. [203]

The answer from the police was immediate. Rocha cited an article dated April 9, 1969, and published in *Novedades* that denied police were protecting the gathering that took place on Sunday, March 30: "if any police officer attended the aforementioned meeting, which he doubts, they did so in their personal capacity . . . Police Officer Alfonso Macías Genie . . . informed the reporters that the so-called '*Charco de los Patos*' would be closed immediately."[204]

Rocha's analysis of the situation was the following: "Although *La Prensa* does not name Bernabé [Somoza], it leaves out on the public stage what was only known by the residents of the neighborhood . . . The scandal that 'makes *El Charco* famous' is related to the homosexual practices that have a public figure in Bernabé. Three months after this event, in July 1969, *Novedades* announce[d] the happy wedding of a member of the Somoza family."[205] Bernabé was only twenty-one years old.

Orlando Ortega, another Nicaraguan author, has suggested that Bernabé's visits to the Charco perhaps led to the presence of the National Guard there, due to his violent tendencies:

> On a certain occasion . . . the entire gay community came to show off their ingenuity, including a prominent member of the family clinging to power (at that time). La Sebastiana dressed up as Miss Universe, La Carola as a nun . . . and so on. It turns out that Bernie, the influential boy, had a serious disagreement with a peer and an altercation ensued, which in that milieu becomes violent, in such a way that the princess [*infanta*] left the premises shouting obscenities and in less time than a rooster crows a G.N [National Guard] patrol arrived, not to compete but to carry out a raid. La Sebastiana and some of her colleagues fled the place and did not stop running until they reached the San Luis neighborhood, where they fell asleep under the cover of a mango tree.[206]

The earthquake alone might not have signaled the end of the moral panic that enveloped Nicaragua during this period. Perhaps Bernabé's wedding and subsequent honeymoon abroad contributed to it. After analyzing the evidence presented by Rocha, León Báez, and Ortega, it makes some sense to argue that a dynastic grandma's fears for her fatherless grandson helped create the moral panic. According to the journalist Amalia del Cid, Lillian Somoza Debayle, Salvadora Debayle's daughter and Bernabé's aunt, felt that her mother "had a marked preference for her two sons, Luis and Anastasio, and reading between the lines [in the interview del Cid conducted with Lillian] one can deduce that [Doña Salvadora] was quick-tempered, impulsive, and willful . . . her temperament was made of steel."[207] Luis Somoza, her oldest son and Bernabé's father, had recently and unexpectedly died in 1967, and Bernabé was Luis's oldest child. This might have made Doña Salvadora worry about the negative attention her grandson was generating. It seems, however, that once the grandmother's fears were assuaged by a fancy wedding and an even fancier honeymoon (if one can trust the photos in the pro-Somoza newspaper *Novedades*), the moral panic was allowed to die a natural death after the earthquake destroyed Managua in December 1972.

Yet another event to keep in mind in terms of the escalation of repression against working-class LGBTQIA+ Nicaraguans during the late

1960s is the so-called Zelaya case, which received a great deal of attention in the press during 1969. The private secretary of the president, the attorney and university professor José María Zelaya Úbeda (1929–2018), was accused by the university student Anastacio Real Espinales (1944–?) of rape, although the charges were later reduced to "dishonest abuses" (*abusos deshonestos*).

According to the accusation, the alleged rape occurred one night after a group went out to eat and drink. Both Zelaya and Real Espinales then went to Zelaya's office to work on a document related to the Federation of Liberal Students (the Federación de Estudiantes Liberales, known as FEL), a group of Somocista students who were being mentored by the professor.[208] When the accusation became public, Zelaya Úbeda resigned from his post, after consulting with members of the government who, according to *La Prensa*, were all in agreement that "it was necessary to try to separate the government from this scandal."[209]

Since Zelaya had a government post, in theory he should have been tried by Congress. Instead, his case was taken to court like any other criminal case.[210] During the trial Real Espinales's medical records were made public, revealing that the young man had a history of depression and suicide attempts.[211] In the end, Zelaya Úbeda was declared innocent and the Somoza government blamed the Social Christian Party, an opposition party, for fabricating what the government called a "political conspiracy."[212]

The anti-Somocista newspaper *La Prensa* gave extensive coverage to the accusations against Zelaya, undoubtedly to try to create a link between homosexuality, moral decay, and Somocismo:

> The most general opinion is that, in his position as a functionary, on Sunday June 15, Professor Zelaya represented the government, and his resignation does not mean that the government can disassociate itself from that event.
>
> The results of the investigation that will take place—it is commented—will indicate the degree of morality not only of the accused but that of the government itself. [The government] is also seated in court as a defendant ["también está sentado en el banquillo de los acusados"].[213]

La Prensa also reported that Zelaya Úbeda "wishes to go to a place where he can 'find peace' after the trial."[214] Zelaya Úbeda then moved with his wife and children to New York, where he took on the position of ambassador extraordinary and alternate plenipotentiary permanent representative before the United Nations.[215] Anastacio Real Espinales, meanwhile, disappeared from the historical record.

In a declassified telegram, the U.S. embassy summarized the Zelaya case in the following manner for the Department of State:

> The Somoza administration has suffered a bit because of the Zelaya incident. Whether the accusation is true or false and even though the court exonerated Zelaya, the opposition, including the newspaper ... *La Prensa* ... every so often will point to this case as an example of "moral decadence" that has taken place during the Somozas' administration. Among the members of his own party, the incident has created doubts regarding the ability and good judgement of the President to choose qualified employees to serve in key positions of his administration.[216]

One additional matter to keep in mind with regard to the escalation in anti-LGBTQIA+ measures by the police and the health authorities during this period is that the Chamber of Deputies at the time was reassessing the penal code and specifically the article on sodomy. Extensive debates took place in the chamber on Thursday, February 15, 1968. At the end of the session the first part of article 203 was drafted as follows: "Sodomy and any other form of homosexual corruption will constitute crimes and will be penalized with inprisonment from one to three years."[217]

On Friday, March 22, 1968, the chamber met again to discuss the same article in the penal code. The minutes from the debates stated the following:

> Deputy Trejos Somarriba expresses that sodomy is classified by doctors as a disease and the crime appears when it is done publicly and offending modesty, why is why he is in favor of the reconsideration of the act and makes a motion so that the Article under discussion be drafted as follows: "Those who practice sodomy in a scandalous manner or offending modesty or public morality will suffer a prison sentence of one to three years; but if one of those who practice it, even in private, have disciplinary or command power over the other, as ascendant [*ascendiente*], guardian [*guardador*], teacher, boss, guardian [*guardián*], or in any other

way that implies influence of authority or moral direction, the prison for him will be of two to four years, the same as when it is practiced with a minor under fifteen years old or if force or intimidation are used."

Diputados Arroyo Buitrago and Argüello Hurtado withdrew their motion and adhered to the one presented by Diputado Trejos Somarriba. Diputado Montenegro Medrano expresses his agreement with the Trejos Somarriba motion, but given that there is no definition, in the motion, of what sodomy is, he motions for the drafting of the Article to begin as follows: "Sex [*concúbito*] between persons of the same sex or against nature constitutes sodomy and those who . . ."[218]

The debates showed that the laws were being discussed exclusively by male lawmakers even though there were a handful of women *diputadas*, and one of them, the attorney Olga Núñez de Saballos, was present. Moreover, some of the diputados were concerned that the law did not specifically target lesbians but should. Additionally, some lawmakers were concerned with issues of power and consent, although in the end the term *sodomy* remained a catchall word that could refer to consensual sex between adults as well as rape (including statutory rape). Surprisingly, perhaps, the anti-Somocista liberal attorney Arroyo Buitrago (1916–?)[219] at one point was willing to defend the complete decriminalization of homosexuality, and he had the support of at least one colleague, Diputado Quintanilla. Quintanilla's claim that the Nicaraguan penal tradition had been cautious with regard to sodomy was surprising, however, given that anti-sodomy laws had existed since the colonial period. In the end, the law's criminalization of those who practiced "sodomy in a scandalous way or offending modesty or public morality" ("sodomía en forma escandalosa o ultrajando el pudor o la moralidad pública") was a compromise. But it was one that disadvantaged the most vulnerable: sex workers, transgender Nicaraguans, and anyone who transgressed in public. Phrased in the language of scandal and public morality, the law would continue to be used as a weapon against all LGBTQIA+ Nicaraguans but particularly against working-class individuals labeled cochones at the time, those who like La Sebastiana and La Reina de los Tártaros lived in the liminal spaces of society carved out for them hundreds of years earlier by the Nahuat-speaking people of western Nicaragua.

CONCLUSION

Somocistas sought to portray the U.S.-supported dictatorship as a period of sexual order. However, the Somozas' enemies, Conservatives and Sandinistas alike, succeeded in portraying it as a period of sexual disorder. Indeed, the Somozas were not particularly intent on imposing a religious or moral agenda on the population. But there were important exceptions. One was the period between the late 1960s and the early 1970s. During those years a moral panic took place in Nicaragua, due in part to the worries the former first lady, Salvadora Debayle, had over the "public" bisexuality of her grandson and the press coverage it received. Working-class LGBTQIA+ Nicaraguans, particularly those labeled cochones who worked in open-air markets, brothels, and bars like El Charco de los Patos, bore the brunt of the heightened persecution. Discrimination against this group, of course, was ever present and built on the long-standing racism and classism against trans women market and food vendors discussed in earlier chapters. Nonetheless, I agree with David Rocha's assessment in a summary he gave regarding the events that took place in 1969. Rocha explained that even the wealthy and elite members of the LGBTQIA+ community suffered the effects of homophobia in that period: "Bernabé was a homosexual with money, and he enjoyed immunity, they never jailed him and his homosexuality was an open secret. There was a scandal at *El Charco de los Patos* published by the newspaper *La Prensa*. A month later Bernabé is married. Similar to persecution, this was a form of violence that targeted Bernabé's body."[220]

The Somozas' National Guard had instituted a system in which guardsmen's meager salaries were augmented by the fines and bribes that bar and brothel owners paid them. The system almost came to an end in 1969 and 1970, but the owners of the bars and brothels rebelled because they felt they had been playing by the rules and had done nothing "wrong" to elicit such treatment. The system survived in large part because it worked for the National Guard, for the government, and for the owners of the bars and brothels. The individuals who had the least amount of power in the system were the sex workers themselves (LGBTQIA+ and heterosexual), many of whom also worked as maids, cooks, food vendors, and waitresses to try to eke out a living. It is in part because of this quid pro quo that existed between the National Guard and brothel owners that the Somoza dictatorship was deemed morally corrupt by its enemies. The Sandinistas, in fact, prioritized the destruction of this system that profited literally from the flesh of the weakest in society. However, the FSLN's efforts to end prostitution in the early 1980s were unsuccessful, not because they lacked hubris but because they failed to understand sex work as anything but a by-product of capitalism.

Given the many contradictions within Somocismo, Nicaraguans are deeply divided over how to make sense of this long-lasting clientelistic and often brutal dictatorship, one of the most abhorred and adored in Latin America. Even La Sebastiana, who suffered terribly at the hands of the Somozas' National Guard and was built a small house by the FSLN in the twenty-first century, stated in an interview, "With Somoza we were free, we worked, we had money, now we don't . . . now everything is more expensive, before with five pesos you ate all day."[221]

My contention is that Nicaraguans' memories of the Somoza dictatorship are sometimes whitewashed by difficult situations they are experiencing at the time they are interviewed. Such is the nature of political memory. In La Sebastiana's case, however, the nostalgia was not only economic or even political. She longed for a time when she was more than an "intangible heritage of the community" ("patrimonio intangible de la comunidad"), as she was considered in her later years.[222] Instead, she yearned to be recognized as the beloved Queen of the Torovenado Carnival, a role she is still remembered for.

CONCLUSION

THE STORIES told about Nicaragua outside Nicaragua often fall into the category of trauma porn (*pobrecitos*) or revolutionary porn ("so brave and inspiring"), stories to be consumed by the readers/viewers for their benefit or that of the author, provoking guilt, or pleasure, or both. Other narratives vacillate between pity and derision and make offers that privilege the author's own best interest as the solution to the plight of Nicaraguans. The most infamous example of the latter are the writings of the white U.S. American filibuster William Walker, who invaded Nicaragua in 1855 to aid local Liberals in their ongoing war against the Conservatives. Walker declared himself president of Nicaragua and, among other proclamations, reinstated the enslavement of peoples of African ancestry, which had already been outlawed decades earlier. Alarmed by Walker's actions, Central Americans united and defeated Walker in 1860.

The Walker episode is particularly important because of its enormous impact on the course of Nicaraguan history. Not surprisingly, it has been addressed by scholars all over the world. Most recently, the U.S.-based historian Michel Gobat argued in his extensively researched and award-winning 2018 book that "Walker's global infamy cannot be understood unless we address a paradox that long marked U.S. liberal imperialism: the extraordinary threat *and* promise it represented to peoples outside the

United States."[1] Unfortunately, Gobat's book, titled *Empire by Invitation: William Walker and Manifest Destiny in Central America*, takes what he calls "Nicaraguans' infatuation" with white foreigners at face value.[2] I frame this so-called infatuation with liberal imperialism and whiteness differently when addressing the significance of foreign intervention on the last five centuries of LGBTQIA+ history in western Nicaragua.

I argue that with regard to the supposed promise of U.S. liberal imperialism confronted by Nicaragua soon after obtaining its independence from Spain in 1821, the emphasis should rightly be on the fact that it *was always also a threat*, a racist one no less. The carrot of political stability and economic growth that U.S. liberal imperialism offered (whether wrapped in white settler colonialism or a canal), along with the illusion of greater social equality, was predicated on the assumption that Nicaragua would forever be indebted to the United States and that Nicaraguans as a whole would forever be inferior in every way to U.S. Americans, particularly to Euroamericans. Since this inferiority needed to be incessantly performed (through speeches, songs, poetry, opinion pieces, etc.), regardless of whether it had been internalized by Nicaraguans themselves, it is impossible to know to what extent it was a reflection of people's actual beliefs. But the performativity of inferiority inevitably included elements of resistance. Indeed, it was often a way in which to "refuse the favor" of Euroamerican imperialism.

It is important to point out the obvious: unlike the "imperialism" component, the "liberal" component of "the promise of liberal imperialism" did not fully materialize for Nicaraguans in the nineteenth or twentieth centuries. And yet Nicaraguans have borne the burden of being considered inferior (and simultaneously being expected to perform that inferiority) collectively *and also* individually ever since their first interactions with Europeans and Euroamericans, even before the Walker invasion. Moreover, these have been uneven burdens: some Nicaraguans have carried a heavier burden than others. This book documents the burdens placed on LGBTQIA+ individuals and others in western Nicaragua as well as the spaces that they have carved out for themselves in/through resistance and contestation over the course of almost five hundred years. In doing so, the book sheds light on contemporary Nicaragua.

While twentieth-century anti-sodomy legislation—one version of which was in effect as late as 2008—was presented by its proponents as rooted in Nicaraguan tradition, such legislation was actually deeply rooted in the politics of a foreign (Spanish) tradition imposed through the Spanish conquest. Such homophobic legislation, then, was not traditional but rather *colonial*. In other words, contemporary efforts to eliminate or prevent the criminalization of homosexuality and gender dissidence should not be considered anti-traditional but rather anti- or decolonial. At the same time as these efforts might be considered examples of LGBTQIA+ Nicaraguans claiming the right to a "modern" identity and the right to have rights, they may also be understood as efforts to recuperate older traditions and transform them.

This book also sheds light on the historical role of individuals who today might identify as trans women. The very visible presence of trans women in modern-day western Nicaragua is not a new occurrence. As documented in chapter 1, colonial-era records suggest that, in precolonial times, the Indigenous people on the Pacific coast who sold food and other products in the open-air markets called tiangues were those who were perceived as feminine. To this day, selling food is a largely feminine activity, a job that is available to working-class cisgender and trans women who may have few other options. But selling food in a market, or on the street, is more than just available. Indeed, it is a job that is widely seen as *appropriate* for cis and trans women. So, while they would not have called themselves trans women in earlier centuries, there is evidence of a trans tradition among some Indigenous peoples in western Nicaragua that dates to precolonial times, one that appears to have spread throughout western Nicaragua (perhaps even before the conquest) and informs contemporary politics. Whether this was initially a Nicarao tradition that spread among the Chorotega, or vice versa, we might never know. But what we do know is that this historical continuity is an example of Indigenous survivance: survival and resistance to cultural, sexual, gendered, and economic domination by elites and the state. In short, those in power do not always win.

The ongoing link made between Indigeneity, local commerce, and femininity (cis and trans) in western Nicaraguan imaginaries is one that helps explain the relative tolerance among the general population toward trans market women. It also helps us understand why contemporary discrimination against trans women in Nicaragua, which certainly does exist, is not only transphobic and homophobic but also sexist, classist, and racist. Indeed, western Nicaragua's LGBTQIA+ history is a profoundly Indigenous history, although other traditions—such as those of Afro-Nicaraguans in the region—remain to be documented.

NOTES

Introduction

1. Jaime Incer Barquero, *Descubrimiento, conquista y exploraciones de Nicaragua*, Crónicas de fuentes originales seleccionadas y comentadas por Jaime Incer Barquero, Serie Cronistas, no. 6 (Managua: Colección Cultural de Centroamérica, 2002), 438.
2. Jorge Eduardo Arellano, "Nicaragua: 500 Años de Historia," *Temas Nicaragüenses*, no. 35 (March 2011): 56.
3. For more on this period, see Michel Gobat, *Empire by Invitation: William Walker and Manifest Destiny in Central America* (Cambridge, Mass.: Harvard University Press, 2018).
4. I have borrowed the term from Chicana historian Deena González, who countered the narrative of New Mexican women's complicity with U.S. colonialism in her book *Refusing the Favor: The Spanish-Mexican Women of Santa Fe, 1820–1880* (Oxford: Oxford University Press, 1999).
5. Gerald Vizenor, *Native Liberty: Natural Reason and Cultural Survivance* (Lincoln: University of Nebraska Press, 2009), 24.
6. I discuss this in more detail in my book chapter "Writing Western Nicaragua's LGBTQIA+ History: *Tiangues*, Indigeneity, and Survivance," in *Feminisms in Movement: Theories and Practices from the Americas*, ed. Livia De Souza Lima, Edith Otero Quezada, and Julia Roth (Bielefield, Germany: Transcript, 2024).
7. Vizenor, *Native Liberty*, 138.
8. For more on this history, see Alejandro Bendaña, *Buenas al pleito: Mujeres en la rebelión de Sandino* (Managua: Anamá Editores, 2019).
9. For more on LGBTQIA+ activism from the 1960s to the present, see Karen Kampwirth, *LGBTQ Politics in Nicaragua: Revolution, Dictatorship and Social Movements* (Tucson: University of Arizona Press, 2022).

10. For more on Nicaragua's Caribbean Coast, see Jennifer Goett, *Black Autonomy, Race, Gender, and Afro-Nicaraguan Activism* (Redwood City, Calif.: Stanford University Press, 2017); Edmund T. Gordon, *Disparate Diaspora: Identity and Politics in an African Nicaraguan Community* (Austin: University of Texas Press, 1998); Charles R. Hale, *Resistance and Contradiction: Miskitu Indians and the Nicaraguan State, 1894–1987* (Redwood City, Calif.: Stanford University Press, 1994); Juliet Hooker, "'Beloved Enemies': Race and Official Mestizo Nationalism in Nicaragua," *Latin American Research Review* 40, no. 3 (October 2005): 14–39; Juliet Hooker, "Race and the Space of Citizenship: The Mosquito Coast and the Place of Blackness and Indigeneity in Nicaragua," in *Blacks and Blackness in Central America: Between Race and Place*, ed. Lowell Gudmundson and Justin Wolfe (Durham, N.C.: Duke University Press, 2010), 246–77; Daniel Mendiola, "The Founding and Fracturing of the Mosquito Confederation: Zambos, Tawiras, and New Archival Evidence, 1711–1791," *Hispanic American Historical Review* 99, no. 4 (November 2019): 619–47; Courtney Desiree Morris, *To Defend This Sunrise: Black Women's Activism and the Authoritarian Turn in Nicaragua* (New Brunswick, N.J.: Rutgers University Press, 2023); and Baron L. Pineda, *Shipwrecked Identities: Navigating Race on Nicaragua's Mosquito Coast* (New Brunswick, N.J.: Rutgers University Press, 2006).

11. John Beverly in Erick Blandón, *Barroco descalzo: Colonialidad, sexualidad, género y raza en la construcción de la hegemonía cultural en Nicaragua* (Managua: URACCAN, 2003), 14. All translations are mine unless otherwise noted.

12. Blandón, *Barroco descalzo*, 30.

13. Rocha has a second book, titled *Cartografías de espacios en fuga: Managua 1968–1975* (Managua: Anamá ediciones, 2022), that builds on his 2016 master's thesis titled "Cartografías de homosocialización, espacios en fuga: Managua 1968–1975" (Universidad Centroamericana).

14. David Rocha, *Crónicas de la ciudad* (Managua: Soma Editores, 2019), 111.

15. Rocha, *Crónicas de la ciudad*, 86.

16. Gobat, *Empire by Invitation*, 2.

17. Richard Harding Davis, *Real Soldiers of Fortune* (New York: Charles Scribner's Sons, 1911), 147.

18. Jasbir K. Puar, "Feminists and Queers in the Service of Empire," in *Feminism and War: Confronting U.S. Imperialism*, ed. Robin Riley, Chandra Talpade Mohanty, and Minnie Bruce Pratt (New York: Zed Books, 2013), 48.

19. Jasbir K. Puar, *Terrorist Assemblages: Homonationalism in Queer Times* (Durham, N.C.: Duke University Press, 2017), 32.

20. Puar, *Terrorist Assemblages*, 9.

21. Miguel León-Portilla, *Religión de los Nicaraos: Análisis y comparación de tradiciones culturales nahuas* (Mexico City: Universidad Nacional Autónoma de México, Instituto de Investigaciones Históricas, 1972), 104.

22. Incer Barquero, *Descubrimiento, conquista y exploraciones*, 410.

23. G. F. Von Tempsky, *Mitla: A Narrative of Incidents and Personal Adventures on a Journey in Mexico, Guatemala, and Salvador in the Years 1853 to*

1855—Observations on the Modes of Life in Those Countries (London: Longman, Brown, Green, Longmans, and Roberts, 1858), 267, 268.

24. Frederick Starr, *In Indian Mexico: A Narrative of Travel and Labor* (Chicago: Forbes and Company, 1908), 170.
25. Frederick Starr, *Notes upon the Ethnography of Southern Mexico*, Part 1 (P. Putnam Memorial Publication Fund, 1900), 50.
26. León-Portilla, *Religión de los Nicaraos*, 91. Some of the oldest forms of gender and sexual transgression, such as that which happens at festivals and feast days, date back centuries, as seen in this example. The subject is discussed only briefly in this book due to lack of space, but other scholars, such as Erick Blandón, Katherine Borland, and Les Field have done extensive studies on public celebrations and plays in Nicaragua, particularly those that have taken place in Masaya, Nicaragua's fourth-largest city and one that prides itself in being the repository of western Nicaragua's "folklore." See Blandón, *Barroco descalzo*; Katherine Borland, *Unmasking Class, Gender, and Sexuality in Nicaraguan Festival* (Tucson: University of Arizona Press, 2006); and Les W. Field, *The Grimace of Macho Ratón: Artisans, Identity, and Nation in Late-Twentieth-Century Western Nicaragua* (Durham, N.C.: Duke University Press, 1999).
27. Pablo Antonio Cuadra, *El nicaragüense* (San José, C.R.: Asociación Libro Libre, 1987), 97.
28. Manuel Moncada Fonseca, "Las tribus que habitaban Nicaraguas según diversos autores," *Libre Pensamiento*, March 3, 2012.
29. Starr, *In Indian Mexico*, 162.
30. Chris Gonzalez, "Frida Kahlo and Appropriation of Indigenous Cultures," *OPB*, March 7, 2022.
31. Analisa Taylor, *Indigeneity in the Mexican Cultural Imagination: Thresholds of Belonging* (Tucson: University of Arizona Press, 2009), 2.
32. Field, *Grimace of Macho Ratón*.
33. Juan de Cordova, *Vocabulario en lengua zapoteca* (Mexico, 1578), 290 and 334.
34. For more on Muxe communities, see Alfredo Mirandé, *Behind the Mask: Gender Hybridity in a Zapotec Community* (Tucson: University of Arizona Press, 2019); and *Muxes: Auténticas, intrépidas y buscadoras de peligro*, directed by Alejandra Islas (Mexico: Instituto Mexicano de Cinematografía, 2005).
35. Analisa Taylor, "Malinche and Matriarchal Utopia: Gendered Visions of Indigeneity in Mexico," *Signs* 31, no. 3 (2005): 815–40.
36. Lynn Stephen, "Sexualities and Genders in Zapotec Oaxaca," *Latin American Perspectives* 29, no. 2 (2002): 41.
37. Miranda K. Stockett, "On the Importance of Difference: Re-envisioning Sex and Gender in Ancient Mesoamerica," *World Archaeology* 37, no. 4 (2005): 566–78.
38. "A hacer el nombre de Dios va la india al mercado. Sobre su rebozo, convertido en blando rollo, carga la canasta donde lleva frutas y flores . . . Ella madruga . . . para sentarse ancestralmente . . . en el Tiangue." Mario Cajina Vega, "Masaya: Un departamento con sus alforjas al hombro," *Revista Conservadora*, no. 28 (1962).

39. Field, *Grimace of Macho Ratón*, 182.
40. I expand on this argument in "Writing Western Nicaragua's LGBTQIA+ History: Tiangues, Indigeneity, and Survivance," 2024.

Chapter 1

1. The Nicaraguan historian José Dolores Gámez (1851–1923) described the encomiendas in the following manner: "since they could do nothing with the lands alone, those men [the Spanish] who were incapable of working the land, invented the encomiendas in which, under the pretext of religious instruction, every soldier became the owner of a considerable number of Indians, whose work they took advantage of." José Dolores Gámez, *Historia de Nicaragua: Desde los tiempos prehistóricos hasta 1860, en sus relaciones con España, México, y Centroamérica* (Managua: Tipografía del País, 1889), 130.
2. Jaime Incer Barquero, *Nicaragua: Viajes, rutas y Encuentros, 1502–1838* (San José, C.R.: Libro Libre, 1989), 68, 111–12.
3. Historically, the term *public woman* has refered to a sex worker. The dictionary for the Real Academia Española still defined a "public woman" as a "prostitute" in 2024. See Real Academia Española , "mujer pública," https://dle.rae.es/mujer #EYPrl9B. "To earn publicly" has the same connotations.
4. Pascual de Andagoya, "Relación de los sucesos de Pedrarias Dávila en las Provincias de Tierra Firme o Castilla del Oro, y de lo ocurrido en el descubrimiento de la mar del Sur y costa del Perú y Nicaragua," *Revista de Temas Nicaragüenses*, no. 38 (July 2011): 195. Reprint from *Colección de los viages y descubrimientos que hicieron por mar los españoles desde fines del siglo XV*, no. 7, 3rd sec.: Establecimientos o Primeras Poblaciones de los españoles en el Darién, vol. 3, ed. Martín Fernández de Navarrete (Madrid: Imprenta Real, 1829), 393–456.
5. Kathleen Ann Myers, *Fernández de Oviedo's Chronicle of America: A New History for a New World* (Austin: University of Texas Press, 2007), 49.
6. ". . . quieren más las corrompidas que no las vírgenes." Incer Barquero, *Descubrimiento, conquista y exploraciones*, 402.
7. Incer Barquero, *Descubrimiento, conquista y exploraciones*, 358.
8. Holly Wardlow, "Anger, Economy, and Female Agency: Problematizing 'Prostitution' and 'Sex Work' Among the Huli of Papua New Guinea," *Signs* 29, no. 4 (Summer 2004): 1032.
9. "Consentíanlas [a las mujeres casadas] tratar [tener relaciones sexuales] con otros hombres [que no eran sus esposos] en ciertas fiestas del año . . ." Incer Barquero, *Descubrimiento, conquista y exploraciones*, 490.
10. Pete Sigal, *From Moon Goddesses to Virgins: The Colonization of Yucatecan Maya Sexual Desire* (Austin: University of Texas Press, 2000), 53–59.
11. Louise Burkhart, *The Slippery Earth: Nahua-Christian Moral Dialogue in Sixteenth-Century Mexico* (Tucson: University of Arizona Press, 1989), 28.
12. Incer Barquero, *Descubrimiento, conquista y exploraciones*, 393; Terry A. Barnhart, *Ephraim George Squier and the Development of American*

Anthropology (Omaha: University of Nebraska Press, 2005), 177–78; James Lockhart, *The Nahuas After the Conquest: A Social and Cultural History of the Indians of Central Mexico, Sixteenth Through Eighteenth Centuries* (Redwood City, Calif.: Stanford University Press, 1992), 1; Paul F. Healy, *Archeology of the Rivas Region: Nicaragua* (Waterloo, Ont.: Wilfrid Laurier University Press, 1980), 22–30.

13. Incer Barquero, *Descubrimiento, conquista y exploraciones*, 387–88.
14. Incer Barquero, *Descubrimiento, conquista y exploraciones*, 388.
15. Incer Barquero, *Descubrimiento, conquista y exploraciones*, 389.
16. Incer Barquero, *Descubrimiento, conquista y exploraciones*, 359.
17. Pete Sigal, *The Flower and the Scorpion: Sexuality and Ritual in Early Nahua Culture* (Durham, N.C.: Duke University Press, 2011), back cover.
18. Sigal, *From Moon Goddesses to Virgins*, 246.
19. Josefina Ruiz y Torres, *A puerta cerrada: Inquisición y lectura en el siglo xvi novohispano* (Mexico City: Ediciones Clandestino, 2014).
20. Arellano, "Nicaragua: 500 Años," 56.
21. Quoted in Arellano, "Nicaragua: 500 Años," 56.
22. "Información iniciada en León contra Hernando Bachicao, denunciado de blasfemia, por cuyo delito fue condenado el 12 de marzo de 1530."
23. "Proceso ante el gobernador Contreras, contra Alonso de León, acusado de pronunciar palabras difamatorias contra el honor de las señoras de León. León, el 22 de febrero de 1541."
24. Klor de Alva, "Colonizing Souls: The Failure of the Indian Inquisition and the Rise of Penitential Discipline," in *Cultural Encounters: The Impact of the Inquisition in Spain and the New World*, ed. Mary Elizabeth Perry and Anne J. Cruz (Berkeley: University of California Press, 1991), 4.
25. de Alva, *Impact of the Inquisition*, 1991.
26. Incer Barquero, *Nicaragua: Viajes, rutas*, 136.
27. Tomás Ayón, "Viajes de Cristóbal Colón y descubrimiento de Nicaragua por el lado del Atlántico," chap. 1 of book 2 of *Historia de Nicaragua* (Managua: Colección Cultural Banco de América, 1977), 158.
28. Ayón, *Historia de Nicaragua*, 158.
29. Incer Barquero, *Nicaragua: Viajes, rutas*, 136.
30. Patrick S. Werner, *Época temprana de León Viejo: Una historia de la primera capital de Nicaragua* (Managua: Fondo Editorial Instituto Nicaragüense de Cultura-ASDI, 2000), 100.
31. For more on the Spanish debates over the origins of the "Great Flood," see Marta V. Vicente, *Debating Sex and Gender in Eighteenth Century Spain* (Cambridge: Cambridge University Press, 2017), 4, 5.
32. Incer Barquero, *Descubrimiento, conquista y exploraciones*, 383.
33. Peter Silver, "Unreliable Sources," *Harvard Review*, no. 37 (2009): 104–16; Camilla Townsend, "Burying the White Gods: New Perspectives on the Conquest of Mexico," *The American Historical Review* 108, no. 3 (2003): 659–87.

34. Arellano, cited in Blandón, *Barroco descalzo*, 148.
35. Luis Nicolau d'Olwer, *Cronistas de las culturas precolombinas* (Mexico City: Fondo de Cultura Económica, 2010 [1963]), 76.
36. Werner, *Época temprana*, 32.
37. José Argüello Gómez, "Plano esquemático de León Viejo," *Revista de Temas Nicaragüenses*, no. 14 (July 2009): 56.
38. José Mejía Lacayo, "La conquista, 1522–1572," *Revista de Temas Nicaragüenses*, no. 40 (August 2011): 113.
39. "Testimonio de las diligencias iniciado en León, el 31 de diciembre de 1530, para elegir alcaldes y regidores de su ayuntamiento mediante el voto de los respectivos funcionarios. Figura expediente en que se explica la conducta observada por el gobernador Pedrarias Dávila." Archivo General de Indias, Sevilla, Patronato, Legajo 185, Ramo 3. José Argüello Gómez argues that Caballero took on this post in 1527. See Argüello Gómez, "Plano esquemático," 56.
40. Arellano, "Nicaragua: 500 Años," 56.
41. Dan Stanislawski, *The Transformation of Nicaragua, 1519–1548*, vol. 54 of *Ibero-Americana* (Berkeley: University of California Press, 1983), 127–28. According to José Argüello Gómez, Castañeda left on March 18, 1535. Argüello Gómez, "Plano esquemático," 55.
42. Linda Newson, *Indian Survival in Colonial Nicaragua* (Norman: University of Oklahoma Press, 1987), 104.
43. David R. Radell, "The Indian Slave Trade and Population of Nicaragua During the Sixteenth Century," in *The Native Population of the Americas in 1492*, ed. William M. Deneven, 2nd ed. (Madison: University of Wisconsin Press, 1992), 72.
44. Incer Barquero, *Nicaragua: Viajes, rutas*, 89.
45. Stanislawski, *Transformation of Nicaragua*, 120; Clemente Guido Martínez, *Valdivieso: El obispo que murió por los chorotegas* (Managua: Alcaldía de Managua, 2010), 59.
46. Francisco Rodríguez, "La Valoración Histórica como corriente formadora de género en la narrativa centroamericana," in *Actas del simposio hacia la comprensión del 98: Representaciones finiseculares en España e Hispanoamérica*, ed. Jorge Chen Sham, 1st ed. (San José, C.R.: Editorial Universidad de Costa Rica, 2001), 225.
47. Ricardo Pasos Marciaq, *El burdel de las Pedrarias*, 4th ed. (Managua: Hispamer, 1997), 65.
48. Rodríguez, "La Valoración Histórica," 225.
49. "Petición de Diego Núñez de Mercado al Consejo de las Indias el 16 de noviembre de 1541, Acompaña diligencias del Teniente Gobernador de la conducta de Francisco de Castañeda."
50. "Constancia de irregularidades en juicios por no aparecer pagadas las multas que se imponían en diferentes juicios y casos. León, el 9 de mayo [1536?]."
51. "Petición de Diego Núñez . . . 1541."

52. "...dicho licenciado Castañeda muchas veces...habiendo favorecido a un Andrés Caballero que tuvo preso por sometido [*sometico*?] desde a pocos días, como el delito fue notorio y no se pudo disimular, fue preso segunda vez, y estando preso para quemar el dicho Andrés Caballero este testigo oyó decir al dicho licenciado Castañeda si Andrés Caballero hubiera muerto un hombre yo le librara porque es mi amigo y le quiero bien." "Declaración de Benito de Prado."
53. "Certificación librada por el Secretario de Gobernación y Residencia de las demandas en residencia que opuso el Tesorero Pedro de los Ríos. León, 12 de febrero de 1536."
54. "Declaración del Escribano Diego Sánchez."
55. "Petición de Diego Núñez ... 1541."
56. "Petición de Diego Núñez ... 1541."
57. "Declaración del Escribano Diego Sánchez."
58. "Petición de Diego Núñez ... 1541."
59. José Mejía Lacayo, "Cleto Ordóñez y la Guerra Civil de 1824," *Revista de Temas Nicaragüense*, no. 43 (November 2011): 113.
60. "Carta de la Audiencia de Santo Domingo al Rey transmitiendo la información dada por el licenciado Francisco Castañeda. Ciudad de Santo Domingo, 28 de mayo de 1537."
61. "Petición de Diego Núñez ... 1541."
62. Mejía Lacayo, "Cleto Ordóñez," 111.
63. Eduardo Pérez Valle, "¿Martín Estete y el Gobernador Castañeda eran Homosexuales?," 1971, https://eduardoperezvalle.blogspot.com/2014/01/puntos-oscuros-en-la-historia-de.html.
64. Jorge Eduardo Arellano, *Historia básica de Nicaragua*, vol. 1 (Managua: Fondo Editorial CIRA, 1993), 230–31.
65. "Declaración del Escribano Diego Sánchez."
66. Federico Garza Carvajal, *Butterflies Will Burn: Prosecuting Sodomites in Early Modern Spain and Mexico* (Austin: University of Texas Press, 2003), 8.
67. Pérez Valle, "¿Martín Estete?"
68. Pérez Valle, "¿Martín Estete?"
69. "Carta del licenciado Francisco de Castañeda, informando de la situación de la provincia, del estado de vejez de Pedrarias y de sus disensiones con éste. Pide, no se dé crédito a lo que llega a informar el veedor Alonso Pérez de Valer. León, 5 de octubre de 1529," Archivo General de Indias, Sevilla, Patronato, Legajo 26, Ramo 5.
70. Pérez Valle, "¿Martín Estete?"; "Información seguida en León ante el alcalde de aquella ciudad, Alvaro de Peñalver, a solicitud del alcalde mayor Francisco de Castañeda, con el objeto de establecer los motivos de su enemistad con el gobernador Pedrarias Dávila, el tesorero Diego de la Tobilla y el veedor Alonso Pérez de Valer. Se inició el 17 de septiembre de 1529," Archivo General de Indias, Sevilla, Justicia, Legajo 1.030, Ramo 2.
71. Pérez Valle, "¿Martín Estete?"; "Información seguida ... 1529."

72. "Información seguida ... 1529"; Eduardo Pérez Valle, *Centroamérica en los cronistas de indias: Oviedo*, Serie Cronistas, no. 5 (Managua: Banco de América, 1977,) xiv.
73. Garza Carvajal, *Butterflies Will Burn*, 33.
74. Garza Carvajal, *Butterflies Will Burn*, 31.
75. Garza Carvajal, *Butterflies Will Burn*, 31.
76. Incer Barquero, *Descubrimiento, conquista y exploraciones*, 438.
77. Garza Carvajal, *Butterflies Will Burn*, 40–41.
78. Garza Carvajal, *Butterflies Will Burn*, 42–43.
79. Las Casas, cited in Incer Barquero, *Descubrimiento, conquista y exploraciones*, 438.
80. Theodore de Bry, "Valboa throws some Indians, who had committed the terrible sin of sodomy, to the dogs to be torn apart," 1594, copper engraving, University of Houston Libraries Special Collection, Rare Books and Maps Collection.
81. "¿Que pena dan al que es puto, al cual vosotros llamáis cuylon, si es el paciente?" and "Los muchachos lo apedrean y le hacen mal y le llaman bellaco, y algunas veces mueren del mal que les hacen." Oviedo quoting Bobadilla in Incer Barquero, *Descubrimiento, conquista y exploraciones*, 404.
82. Oviedo in Incer Barquero, *Descubrimiento, conquista y exploraciones*, 363.
83. Blandón, *Barroco descalzo*, 149.
84. "Cuanto vieres a un fraile de la Merced, arrima tu culo a la pared." Blandón, *Barroco descalzo*, 149.
85. "... hasta sesenta personas, hombres todos, y entre ellos ciertos hechos mujeres, pintados todos y con muchos y hermosos penachos." Oviedo, cited in Incer Barquero, *Descubrimiento, conquista y exploraciones*, 348.
86. "Pues bien pudo ser que aquellos no sirviesen de aquello, sino por no ser para mujeres, fuese costumbre usada entre aquellas gentes que tomasen vestidos femineos, para dar noticia de su defecto, pues se habían de ocupar en hacer las haciendas y ejercicios de mujeres, como algunas naciones hicieron." Las Casas, quoted in Incer Barquero, *Descubrimiento, conquista y exploraciones*, 428.
87. Pete Sigal, "The *Cuiloni*, the *Patlache*, and the Abominable Sin: Homosexualities in Early Colonial Nahua Society," *Hispanic American Historical Review* 85, no. 4 (2005): 560–51.
88. Blandón, *Barroco descalzo*, 149.
89. See Roger Lancaster, "Sexual Positions: Caveats and Second Thoughts on 'Categories,'" *The Americas* 54, no. 1 (1997): 1–16; and his book *Life Is Hard: Machismo, Danger, and the Intimacy of Power in Nicaragua* (Berkeley: University of California Press, 1992).
90. Jorge Eduardo Arellano, "Acepciones y etimología de la palabra cochón," *La Prensa*, March 14, 2004.
91. Blandón, *Barroco descalzo*, 227.
92. Arellano, "Acepciones y etimología"; Carlos Mántica, *El habla nicaragüense y otros ensayos* (San José, C.R.: Libro Libre, 1989), 149.

93. Mántica, *El habla nicaragüense*, 149.
94. Arellano, "Acepciones y etimología."
95. Jeff Gould, *To Die in This Way: Nicaraguan Indians and the Myth of Mestizaje, 1880–1965* (Durham, N.C.: Duke University Press, 1998), 145, 170.
96. Gould, *To Die*, 143, 145.
97. Vicky Unruh, *Latin American Vanguards: The Art of Contentious Encounters* (Berkeley: University of California Press, 1994), 55.
98. Eladio Cortés and Mirta Barrea-Marlys, eds., *Encyclopedia of Latin American Theater* (Westport, Conn.: Greenwood Press, 2003), 332.
99. "Bailo la perinola / al son cochón de mi violón / o al son violento de mi instrumento de viento. / Pero amo sobre todo mi pianola, / mi pianola Manola." José Coronel Urtecho, *Oda a Rubén Darío: Poemas selectos* (Caracas: Biblioteca Ayacucho, 2005), 93.
100. "Aquí viene el almibar de frutas . . . / para las putas! / Traigo el manjar de leche . . . Para los cocheches! / Aquí estan las cajetas de marañones . . . / Para los cabrones!" "Poetas y locos invaden Managua," *La Prensa*, Memoria de ocho décadas, Parte dos de diez.
101. "El Loco Desiderio de la Quadra," *Revista Conservadora del Pensamiento Centroamericano* 26, no. 129 (1971): 41.
102. Mejía Lacayo, "Cleto Ordóñez," 158.
103. Arellano, "Acepciones y etimología."
104. Francisco J. Barbosa, "July 23, 1959: Student Protest and State Violence as Myth and Memory in León, Nicaragua," *Hispanic American Historical Review* 85, no. 2 (2005): 187–222.
105. Alejandra Palafox Menegazzi, "Sodomía y masculinidad en la ciudad de México (1821–1870)," *Anuario de Estudios Americanos* 72, no. 1 (January–June 2015): 294.
106. Gregorio García, *Origen de los Indios de el Nuevo Mundo e Indias Occidentales* (Valencia, Esp.: Casa de Pedro Patricio Mey, 1607), 269.
107. Stephanie Kirk, "Illicit Passions: 'Mala Amistad' in the Eighteenth Century Mexican Convent," *Latin American Literary Review* 33, no. 66 (July–December 2005): 5–30.
108. Garza Carvajal, *Butterflies Will Burn*.
109. Mary Elizabeth Perry, cited in Kirk, "Illicit Passions," 24.
110. For other cases of colonial investigations, see Martha Few, "'That Monster of Nature': Gender, Sexuality, and the Medicalization of a 'Hermaphrodite' in Late Colonial Guatemala," *Ethnohistory* 54, no. 1 (2007): 159–76. See also María Elena Martínez, "Archives, Bodies, and Imagination: The Case of Juana Aguilar and Queer Approaches to History, Sexuality, and Politics," *Radical History Review* 120 (2014): 159–82; and María Elena Martínez, "Sex and the Colonial Archive: The Case of 'Mariano' Aguilera," *Hispanic American Historical Review* 96, no. 3 (2016): 421–43.
111. Stephanie Kirk, *Sor Juana Inés de la Cruz and the Gender Politics of Knowledge in Colonial Mexico* (New York: Routledge, 2016).

112. Originally only Spanish women were allowed to enter into convents as nuns in colonial Mexico. As time went by, some elite Indigenous Mexican women demanded and received their own convents. Meanwhile, Indigenous women in Peru were able to obtain their own convents much earlier. Indigenous women had convents of their own only in places with large Indigenous populations that were also highly stratified (see Mónica Díaz, *Indigenous Writings from the Convent: Negotiating Ethnic Autonomy in Colonial Mexico* [Tucson: University of Arizona Press, 2013], 20). Convents often functioned as businesses, allowing nuns to earn their own living independently from their families. *Beaterios*, houses for cloistered religious laywomen known as *beatas*, also existed throughout colonial Latin America, but there do not seem to have been any in Nicaragua.
113. Nemesio de la Concepción Zapata, "Vida del guerrero bárbaro Nicaroguan," *Revista de Temas Nicaragüenses*, no. 64 (August 2013): 194.
114. Antonio Calvo Maturana, *Impostores: Sombras en la España de las luces* (Madrid: Cátedra, 2015); de la Concepción Zapata, "Vida del guerrero bárbaro," 186.
115. Incer Barquero, *Descubrimiento, conquista y exploraciones*, 347.
116. My emphasis.
117. Oviedo, cited in Incer Barquero, *Descubrimiento, conquista y exploraciones*, 410.
118. Cuadra, *El nicaragüense*, 116.
119. Enrique Bolaños Geyer, "Discurso en homenaje al Doctor Eduardo Montealegre Callejas," Masaya, December 17, 1976.
120. Manuel Fernández Vílches, "Lo femenino indio en la cultura nicaragüense, crítica de *El nicaragüense* de Pablo Antonio Cuadra," *Revista de Temas Nicaragüenses*, no. 64 (2013): 21.
121. ANIT (Asociación Nicaragüense de Transgénero), *Informe de sondeo de percepción de personas transgéneros sobre discriminación en el departamento de Managua*, August 5, 2016, 38.
122. Uriel Velásquez, "Nicas son más tolerantes a la diversidad sexual," *El Nuevo Diario*, July 27, 2017.
123. Velásquez, "Nicas son más."
124. Dawn Ennis, "Study: 55% of Americans O.K. with Gay, Lesbian, and Trans Coworkers," June 6, 2018, http://www.newnownext.com/study-55-of-americans-ok-with-gay-lesbian-and-trans-coworkers/06/2018/.
125. INN, "Agapito Díaz y la melcocha a peso," YouTube, 2016, https://www.youtube.com/watch?v=6zmjEhGjv1A.
126. INN, "Agapito Díaz."
127. ANIT, *Informe de sondeo*, 41.
128. INN, "Agapito Díaz."
129. John Petrus, "International News Network: Un análisis de transgresiones de género en la producción audio-visual nicaragüense," *Revista de Historia*, no. 29 (September–December 2013): 113.

130. Petrus, "International News Network," 122.
131. Petrus, "International News Network," 126.
132. William B. Taylor, *Magistrates of the Sacred: Priests and Parishioners in Eighteenth-Century Mexico* (Redwood City, Calif.: Stanford University Press, 1996).
133. Cory L. Schott, "Frontiers and Fandangos: Reforming Colonial Nicaragua, 1759–1814" (PhD diss., University of Arizona, 2014), 7–8.
134. Schott, "Frontiers and Fandangos," 59.
135. Schott, "Frontiers and Fandangos," 60.
136. ". . . los pecados públicos, y escandalosos que ejecutan en los bailes, y fandangos . . . a el que se convocan . . . mujeres, y hombres casados, y solteros . . . en que . . . acciones deshonestas, y provocativas, como son tomarse las manos, los hombres, y las mujeres con ademanes impuros abrazándose, y besándose, los rostros con tanta libertad, que hasta la gente vulgar se escandaliza . . . mezclándose mujeres, y hombres bebiendo aguardiente, y manteniéndose toda una noche en este desorden . . ." Schott, "Frontiers and Fandangos," 61. My translation.
137. Kampwirth, *LGBTQ Politics in Nicaragua*.
138. Robert McKee Irvin, Edward J. McCaughan, and Michelle Rocio Nasser, eds., *The Famous 41: Sexuality and Social Control in Mexico, 1901* (New York: Palgrave MacMillan, 2003), 5.
139. Tomás Ayón, *Historia de Nicaragua: Desde los tiempos más remotos hasta el año de 1852*, vol. 1 (Granada: Tipografía de "El Centro Americano," 1882), 339.
140. Elizabeth Dore, *Myths of Modernity: Peonage and Patriarchy in Nicaragua* (Durham, N.C.: Duke University Press, 2006), 106.

Chapter 2

1. Elizabeth Dore, "Property, Households, and the Public Regulation of Domestic Life: Diriomo, Nicaragua, 1840–1900," *Journal of Latin American Studies* 29, no. 3 (October 1997): 601.
2. Michel Gobat, *Confronting the American Dream: Nicaragua Under U.S. Imperial Rule* (Durham, N.C.: Duke University Press, 2005), 2. See also Gobat, *Empire by Invitation*.
3. Gobat, *Confronting the American Dream*, 68. See also Gobat, *Empire by Invitation*.
4. Dore, "Property, Households," 1997, 593–94.
5. Dore, "Property, Households," 1997, 600.
6. Dore, *Myths of Modernity*, 63. The power of local elites to define gender and sexual norms was a continuation of colonial practices. The U.S. historian Ann Twinam has found that throughout colonial Latin America, in the last few decades of the eighteenth century, "the ultimate negotiators of honor were local elites, for they had the last word. Only they could decide on a day-to-day basis whether to accept public constructions that differed from public reality—for

that was the arena in which the vast majority of honor negotiations took place." See Ann Twinam, *Public Lives, Private Secrets: Gender, Honor, Sexuality and Illegitimacy in Colonial Spanish America* (Redwood City, Calif.: Stanford University Press, 1999), 339.

7. Elizabeth Dore, "Property, Households, and the Public Regulation of Domestic Life: Diriomo, Nicaragua, 1840–1900," in *Hidden Histories of Gender and the State in Latin America*, ed. Elizabeth Dore and Maxine Molyneaux (Durham, N.C.: Duke University Press, 2000), 155.
8. "La esclavitud colonial en la Nicaragua del pacífico," *El Nuevo Diario*, May 29, 2010.
9. Rina Cáceres Gómez, "Indígenas y africanos en las redes de la esclavitud en Centroamérica," in *Rutas de la esclavitud en África y América Latina*, ed. Rina Cáceres Gómez (San José, C.R.: Editorial de la Universidad de Costa Rica, 2001), 100.
10. Germán Romero Vargas, "La Presencia Africana en el Pacífico y el Centro de Nicaragua," *Revista WANI* no. 13 (1992): 24.
11. Severo Martínez Peláez, *La patria del criollo: Ensayo de interpretación de la realidad colonial guatemalteca* (Guatemala: Editorial Universitaria, 1971), 727, quoted in Arellano, "Nicaragua: 500 Años," 61.
12. Cited in Frances Kinloch Tijerino, *Identidad y cultura política, 1821–1858* (Managua: Banco Central de Nicaragua, 1999), 34.
13. Mara Loveman, *National Colors: Racial Classification and the State in Latin America* (New York: Oxford University Press, 2014).
14. Gould, *To Die*, 18.
15. There are no book-length studies documenting Afro-Nicaraguan history in western Nicaragua after independence.
16. Gould, *To Die*, 18, 24.
17. Dora María Téllez, *Muera la gobierna!: Colonización en Matagalpa y Jinotega (1820–1890)* (Managua: URACCAN, 1999), 302.
18. ANIT, *Informe de sondeo*, 39.
19. ANIT, *Informe de sondeo*, 39.
20. Claire Cain Miller, "The Search for the Best Estimate of the Transgender Population," *The New York Times*, June 8, 2015.
21. Pío Bolaños, cited in *Obras de Don Pío Bolaños*, ed. Franco Cerutti (Managua: Banco de América, 1976), 254, 331.
22. Bolaños, cited in Cerutti, *Obras de Don Pío*, 261, 262, 263.
23. "Juan Miguel Robleto estuvo detenido por impertenencias con el mesonero, hombre muy delicado, como todos los de su oficio," *El Comercio*, February 27, 1906.
24. "Al policial del Mercado se le hará responsable . . . ," *El Comercio*, March 2, 1906.
25. "Hasta el presente no ha tenido efecto la disposición de la policía . . . ," *El Comercio*, March 15, 1906.
26. "Ley de higiene y saneamiento de los mercados de Managua," June 19, 1911.

27. Lillian Faderman, *Odd Girls and Twilight Lovers: A History of Lesbian Life in Twentieth-Century America* (New York: Penguin, 1991), 8, 9.
28. Carmen Diana Deere and Magdalena de León, "Liberalism and Married Women's Property Rights in 19th Century Latin America," *Hispanic American Historical Review* 85, no. 4 (2005).
29. Deere and León, "Liberalism and Married Women's," 2005.
30. Código Civil de la República de Nicaragua 1867, p. 24.
31. Código Civil de la República de Nicaragua 1867, p. 33.
32. Deere and León, "Liberalism and Married Women's."
33. "Sin autorización escrita del marido, no puede la mujer casada parecer en juicio, por sí, ni por procurador, sea demandando o defendiéndose." Código Civil de la República de Nicaragua 1867, p. 24.
34. Código Civil de la República de Nicaragua 1867, p. 24.
35. Código Civil de la República de Nicaragua 1867, p. 24.
36. Código Civil de la República de Nicaragua 1867, p. 26.
37. Código Civil de la República de Nicaragua 1867, p. 26.
38. Código de Comercio de la República de Nicaragua 1869.
39. "Las mujeres que ejercen el comercio con licencia de su marido obligan en sus contratos sus bienes y los de la sociedad conyugal de cualquiera especie que sean." Código de Comercio de la República de Nicaragua 1869.
40. Código de Comercio de la República de Nicaragua 1914.
41. The 1904 civil code is sometimes referred to as the 1903 civil code. This is because the code was approved in November 1903 but did not go into effect until 1904 (Código Civil de la República de Nicaragua 1904).
42. The situation was different in other Central American countries. In Costa Rica, for instance, according to the Costa Rican historian Carolina Mora Chinchilla, "Catholic marriage or marriage through the Church continued to have legal value in the civil codification of 1888." See Mora Chinchilla, "El nacimiento del Registro Civil como parte de un proyecto estatal (1888) y su aporte a la vida política democrática costarricense," *Revista Derecho Electoral*, no. 16 (July–December 2013): 181.
43. Código Civil de la República de Nicaragua 1904, p. 17.
44. Dore, "Property, Households," 1997; Dore, *Myths of Modernity*; Deere and León, "Liberalism and Married Women's."
45. Dore, *Myths of Modernity*, 101–2.
46. "Decreto estableciendo la pena de tres años de presidio para los que cometan los delitos de bestialidad o sodomía. 27 de enero de 1826."
47. "Decreto estableciendo."
48. Robert McKee Irwin, *Mexican Masculinities* (Minneapolis: University of Minnesota Press, 2003), 5–6.
49. Irwin, *Mexican Masculinities*, 5.
50. Justin Wolfe, *The Everyday Nation-State: Community and Ethnicity in Nineteenth-Century Nicaragua* (Lincoln: University of Nebraska Press, 2007), 29.

51. Victoria González-Rivera, *Before the Revolution: Women's Rights and Right-Wing Politics in Nicaragua, 1821–1979* (University Park: Pennsylvania State University Press, 2011), 25.
52. I have chosen to translate *mujer honrada* as *honest woman* because these are both coined phrases (idioms) that stress a woman's sexual reputation.
53. Constitución Política de Nicaragua 1848 Non Nata.
54. Constitución Política de Nicaragua 1848 Non Nata.
55. Ley reglamentaria para los tribunales y juzgados de la República.
56. "Proyecto Constitución Política Nicaragua 1854."
57. Álvaro José Altamirano Montoya and Karla María Damiano Texteira, "Multidimensional Poverty in Nicaragua: Are Female-Headed Households Better Off?," *Social Indicators Research* 132, no. 3 (2017): 1037–63.
58. Garza Carvajal, *Butterflies Will Burn*, 48.
59. Nicaraguan women who married foreigners lost their Nicaraguan citizenship. "Ley de extranjería," 1894.
60. González-Rivera, *Before the Revolution*, 49.
61. Constitución de la República Federal de Centroamérica 1824.
62. Constitución Política de Nicaragua 1848 Non Nata.
63. Constitución Política de Nicaragua 1858.
64. A father could have patria potestad over his illegitimate child under certain circumstances. For example, if "the parents were not impeded from marriage at the time of conception by canonical barrier" and if the father recognized the child as his. See Bianca Premo, *Children of the Father King: Youth, Authority, and Legal Minority in Colonial Lima* (Chapel Hill: University of North Carolina Press, 2005), 24.
65. "Decreto de 20 de febrero, aclarando la ley de 20 de febrero de 1875, sobre mayoría de edad."
66. Constitución Política de Nicaragua 1893.
67. This happened with the approval of decree 1065 in the "Ley de regulación de las relaciones madre, padre, e hijos." The new law was passed in June 1982 and published in the *Gaceta Diario Oficial* in July 1982. The term *patria potestad* was replaced by the term *relaciones madres, padre, e hijos*. See María José Arauz Henríquez, "De la patria potestad a la autoridad parental de tránsito hacia la humanización de los derechos de la niñez y la adolescencia" (master's thesis, Universidad Centroamericana, April 13, 2017), 11.
68. Carranza, "Código de la Familia en vigor en 180 días," *El Nuevo Diario*, October 16, 2014.
69. Sueann Caulfield, Sarah C. Chambers, and Lara Putnam, eds., *Honor, Status and Law in Modern Latin America* (Durham, N.C.: Duke University Press, 2005), 5.
70. Caulfield, Chambers, and Putnam, *Honor, Status and Law*, 6.
71. "Decreto indultando a Don Simón Corea. 1ero de marzo de 1882."
72. Constitución de la República Federal de Centroamérica 1824.
73. Constitución Política de Nicaragua 1848 Non Nata.

74. Constitución Política de Nicaragua 1858. My emphasis.
75. Bradford Burns, *Patriarch and Folk: The Emergence of Nicaragua, 1798–1858* (Cambridge, Mass.: Harvard University Press, 1991), 76.
76. Burns, *Patriarch and Folk*, 77.
77. Buenaventura Selva, *Instituciones de derecho civil nicaragüense* (Managua: Tipografía de Managua, 1883), 27.
78. "Decreto de 29 de marzo reformando varios artículos del código penal," 1865.
79. "Código Penal de la República decretado por la legislatura de 27 de abril de 1837 [should read 1873]."
80. "Decreto de 1ero de marzo de 1852 creando los Gobernadores de Policía"; "Decreto ejecutivo de 28 de abril de 1852 estableciendo Jueces de policía en el departamento Meridional y en los distritos de Granada y San Fernando."
81. "Acuerdo de 10 de diciembre. Reglamento de policía," 1862.
82. *Reglamento de policía de la República de Nicaragua, decretado por el poder ejecutivo en 25 de octubre de 1880 y mandado redactar por el señor presidente General D. Joaquín Zavala* (Managua: Tipografía Nacional, 1890).
83. Estelle Freedman, "Doing Time in Lesbian History," presentation at San Diego State University, September 20, 2017.
84. González-Rivera, *Before the Revolution*, 143.
85. Anne Hayes, *Female Prostitution in Costa Rica: Historical Perspectives, 1880–1930* (New York: Routledge, 2006).
86. Hayes, *Female Prostitution in Costa Rica*, 22.
87. *Reglamento de policía . . .*, 25.
88. "La policía de esta capital está persiguiendo activamente la vagancia, la ebriedad, y la prostitución . . . ," *El Comercio*, August 30, 1905.
89. "María Ordeñana de conducta viciada . . . ," *El Comercio*, December 31, 1905.
90. "Como una medida de moralidad . . . ," *El Comercio*, January 10, 1906.
91. "Como una medida de moralidad . . ."
92. "A Paula Aguilar se le decretaron . . . ," *El Comercio*, January 24, 1906.
93. "Y a María Zelaya de San Sebastián . . . ," *El Comercio*, March 11, 1906.
94. "Acuerdo aprobando la Ordenanza municipal de Santa Teresa," April 22, 1875.
95. "Como en las fiestas públicas suelen salir enmascarados, vestidos de sacerdotes, de militares o de alguna otra profesión de carácter público: asimismo hombres vestidos de mujer o cuasi desnudos o haciendo figuras obscenas a la vista del público, todos los empleados de policía deben empeñarse en que se destruya tan corruptela, conduciendo a la cárcel a toda persona así vestida." "Reglamento de policía decretado por el gobierno en 10 de diciembre, 1862."
96. "El que profiera malas palabras / El que cometiere acción deshonesta o inmoral. / El que exhiba o venda figuras o estampas que ofendan la moral y buenas costumbres." "Acuerdo aprobando el Reglamento interior del Mercado Central de Managua," 1882.
97. "Acuerdo aprobando el Reglamento," 1882.
98. "Acuerdo aprobando el Reglamento," 1882.

99. "El que usare excusado destinado a distinto sexo." "Acuerdo aprobando el Reglamento," 1882.
100. "Acuerdo aprobando el Reglamento de cárceles de la ciudad de Granada," August 9, 1883.
101. "Decreto de 29 de marzo, reformando varios artículos del Código penal," 1865.
102. Most of the victims of *rapto* were women and girls.
103. The difference between presidio and prisión is unclear from the sources. Perhaps there was a forced labor component to one and not the other. "Decreto legislativo de 7 de julio de 1851, declarando por delitos el rapto y el incesto."
104. "Acuerdo aprobando los estatutos de la sociedad filarmónica de Granada, 'La Juventud,'" 1883.
105. González-Rivera, *Before the Revolution*, 144.
106. Katherine Elaine Bliss, "Theater of Operations: Reform Politics and the Battle for Prostitutes' Redemption at Revolutionary Mexico City's Syphilis Hospital," in *The Women's Revolution in Mexico, 1910–1953*, ed. Stephanie Mitchell and Patience A. Schell (Lanham, Md.: Rowman and Littlefield, 2007), 125.
107. Teresa Cobo del Arco, *Políticas de género durante el liberalism: Nicaragua, 1893–1909* (Managua: UCA, 2000), 121.
108. "Decreto: Se reglamenta la Ley de Profilaxis en la República 1918"; Rafael Alvarado Sarria, *Breve historia hospitalaria de Nicaragua* (León, Nic.: Editorial Hospicio, 1969), 70; "Legislación nicaragüense sobre la prostitución," 1955.
109. "Decreto: Se reglamenta la Ley de Profilaxis en la República 1918"; Alvarado, *Breve historia*, 70; "Legislación nicaragüense sobre la prostitución"; and J. H. Robleto, *Memoria de Higiene y Beneficiencia Públicas* (Managua: n.p., 1933), 102–3.
110. Chad Allen Halvorson, "Padre Agustín Vigil and William Walker: Nicaragua, Filibustering, and the National War" (master's thesis, North Dakota State University, 2014), 66.
111. T. J. Stiles, "The Filibuster King: The Strange Career of William Walker, The Most Dangerous International Criminal of the Nineteenth Century," https://mrtomecko.weebly.com/uploads/1/3/2/9/13292665/walker.
112. Amy S. Greenberg, *Manifest Manhood and the Antebellum American Empire* (Cambridge: Cambridge University Press, 2005), 87.
113. "Fillibusterism: Walker Still Confident—And Twenty Thousand People to Hear Him: Speech of Gen. William Walker, Delivered at New Orleans, May 30," *New York Daily Times*, June 8, 1857, 2.
114. Robert E. May, *Manifest Destiny's Underworld: Filibustering in Antebellum America* (Chapel Hill: University of North Carolina, 2002), xi.
115. May, *Manifest Destiny's Underworld*, 20, 65.
116. "Fillibusterism."
117. Amy S. Greenberg, "A Gray-Eyed Man: Character, Appearance, and Filibustering," *Journal of the Early Republic* 20, no. 4 (Winter 2000): 674.
118. Greenberg, "Gray-Eyed Man," 674.
119. "Fillibusterism."

120. "Fillibusterism."
121. Richard Slotkin, *The Fatal Environment: The Myth of the Frontier in the Age of Industrialization* (Norman: University of Oklahoma Press, 1985), 252.
122. Slotkin, *Fatal Environment*, 251–52.
123. Greenberg, "Gray-Eyed Man," 699.
124. Townsend, "Burying the White Gods," 4.
125. Robert E. May, "Reconsidering Antebellum U.S. Women's History: Gender, Filibustering, and American's Quest for Empire," *American Quarterly* 57, no. 4 (December 2005): 1182.
126. William Oscar Scroggs, *Filibusters and Financiers: The Story of William Walker and His Associates* (New York: The MacMillan Company, 1916), 381.
127. Gámez, *Historia de Nicaragua*, 620–21.
128. Francisco Vijil, *El padre Vijil, su vida: Algunos episodios de nuestra historia nacional; comentarios relativos a los mismos. Juicios de diferentes autores. Algunos sermones fotograbados. Época comprendida entre 1801 y 1867; datos históricos y comprobantes manuscritos auténticos compilados por Francisco Vijil* (Granada, Nicaragua: Tipografía de "El Centro-americano," 1930), 154.
129. Gobat, *Confronting the American Dream*, 31.
130. Gobat, *Confronting the American Dream*, 31–32.
131. Gobat, *Empire by Invitation*.
132. Greenberg, "Gray-Eyed Man," 683.
133. May, "Reconsidering Antebellum U.S.," 1157.
134. May, "Reconsidering Antebellum U.S.," 1158.
135. John Slidell, "The Arrest of William Walker," speech delivered at the United States Senate on April 8,1858; May, "Reconsidering Antebellum U.S.," 1159.
136. William V. Wells, *Walker's Expedition to Nicaragua: A History of the Central American War; and the Sonora and Kinney Expeditions, Including All the Recent Diplomatic Correspondence, Together with a New and Accurate Map of Central America, and a Memoir and Portrait of General William Walker* (New York: Stringer and Townsend, 1856), 13; May, "Reconsidering Antebellum U.S.," 1159.
137. May, "Reconsidering Antebellum U.S.," 1159.
138. May, "Reconsidering Antebellum U.S.," 1159; Lowell Gudmundson and Héctor Lindo-Fuentes, *Central America, 1821–1871: Liberalism Before Liberal Reform* (Tuscaloosa: University of Alabama Press, 1995), 110.
139. May, "Reconsidering Antebellum U.S." See also Gobat, *Empire by Invitation*.
140. Orville Vernon Burton and Georganne Burton, *The Free Flag of Cuba: The Lost Novel of Lucy Holcombe Pickens* (Baton Rouge: Louisiana State University Press, 2002), 8.
141. Gámez, *Historia de Nicaragua*, 621. Gobat, *Empire by Invitation*, 152–54.
142. Gámez, *Historia de Nicaragua*, 621.
143. Greenberg, *Manifest Manhood*, 100.
144. Alejandro Bolaños Geyer, *William Walker, el predestinado* (St. Charles, Mo.: Self-published, 1995), 184.

145. Iván Molina Jiménez, "El extraño William Walker de Alejandro Bolaños Geyer," *Ciencias Sociales* I–II, nos. 103–4 (2004): 167.
146. William Walker, *The War in Nicaragua* (Mobile, Ala.: S. H. Goetzel and Co., 1860), 322.
147. Walker, *War in Nicaragua*, 333.
148. Walker, *War in Nicaragua*, 53.
149. Brady Harrison, *Agent of Empire: William Walker and the Imperial Self in American Literature* (Athens: University of Georgia Press, 2004), 8.
150. Harrison, *Agent of Empire*, 6.
151. Noel B. Gerson, *Sad Swashbuckler: The Life of William Walker* (Nashville, Tenn.: Thomas Nelson Inc., 1976), 16.
152. Cited in Greenberg, *Manifest Manhood*, 144.
153. Greenberg, "Gray-Eyed Man," 680, 697–99.
154. Harrison, *Agent of Empire*, 157.
155. Harrison, *Agent of Empire*, 62–63.
156. Harrison, *Agent of Empire*, 200.
157. Michael Williams, "The Filibusters of San Francisco," *Pearson's Magazine* 34, no. 1 (July 1915): 146–47.
158. Harrison, *Agent of Empire*, 157.
159. Harrison, *Agent of Empire*, 147.
160. Harrison, *Agent of Empire*, 158–59.
161. Harrison, *Agent of Empire*, 157.
162. Harrison, *Agent of Empire*, 158.
163. Discussed by Ernesto Mejía Sánchez, *Romances y corridos nicaragüenses* (Managua: Banco de América, 1976), 23, citing Ephraim Squier, *Nicaragua: Its People, Scenery, Monuments, Resources, Conditions, and Proposed Canal* (New York: Harper and Brothers, 1860), 189. The original in English can also be found in E. G. Squier, *Nicaragua: Its People, Scenery, Monuments, and the Proposed Interoceanic Canal with Numerous Original Maps and Illustrations*, vol. 1 (New York: D. Appleton and Co., Publishers, 1852), 213.
164. Mejía Sánchez, *Romances y corridos*, 116–17. The translation is mine.
165. Ernesto Mejía Sánchez, "Romances y corridos: Fuentes históricas para los romances y corridos nicaragüenses," *Revista Conservadora*, no. 74 (November 1966): 41–42. The translation is mine.
166. Squier, *Nicaragua: Its People, Scenery, Monuments, Resources, Conditions, and Proposed Canal*, 215.
167. Gámez, *Historia de Nicaragua*, 621.
168. Steve Rathje, "The Power of Framing: It's Not What You Say, It's How You Say It," *The Guardian*, July 20, 2017.
169. Pedro Rafael Gutiérrez, "William Walker y Ricarda Cerda, las huellas de un romance," *La Prensa*, February 13, 1977.
170. Arlen Cerda y Dora Luz Romero, "Los Hijos de Walker," *La Prensa Magazine*, August 12, 2012.

171. Scroggs, *Filibusters and Financiers*, 9.
172. Frederic Rosengarten, *William Walker y el ocaso del filibusterismo*, trans. Luciano Cuadra (Tegucigalpa, Hn.: Editorial Guaymuras, 2002), 207.
173. Rosalinda Fregoso, "'Fantasy Heritage': Tracking Latina Bloodlines," in *A Companion to Latina/o Studies*, ed. Juan Flores and Renato Rosaldo (Oxford: Wiley Blackwell, 2007), 452.
174. "Apuntes sobre el tío Sam," *La Prensa Magazine*, July 9, 2017.
175. Grupo Pancasán, "Apuntes del tío Sam."
176. Andreas Beer, "Martial Men in Virgin Lands? Nineteenth-Century Filibustering, Nation-Building, and Competing Forms of Masculinity in the United States and Nicaragua," in *Masculinities and the Nation in the Modern World: Between Hegemony and Marginalization*, ed. Pablo Dominguez Andersen and Simon Wendt (London: Palgrave Macmillan, 2015), 113–28. See also Andreas Beer, *A Transnational Analysis of Representations of the US Filibusters in Nicaragua, 1855–1857* (New York: Palgrave Macmillan, 2016).
177. Wolfe, *Everyday Nation-State*, 2–3.
178. Wolfe, *Everyday Nation-State*, 3.
179. Wolfe, *Everyday Nation-State*, 3.
180. "Decreto de 29 de marzo reformando . . . 1865"; "Código Penal de la República . . . 1873."
181. ANIT, *Informe de sondeo*, 48.
182. Banco Central de Nicaragua, *Cartografía digital y censo de edificaciones: Cabecera municipal de Managua*, January 2017, 23.
183. András Tilcsik, Michel Anteby, and Carly R. Knight, "Concealable Stigma and Occupational Segregation: Toward a Theory of Gay and Lesbian Occupations," *Administrative Science Quarterly* 60, no. 3 (2015): 447.

Chapter 3

Sections of chapter three were published earlier as "Nicaraguan Feminist Josefa Toledo de Aguerri (1866–1962). Her Life and Her Legacy," *Diálogos: Revista Electrónica de Historia* 5, nos. 1–2 (April–August 2005): 1–22.

1. Kampwirth, *LGBTQ Politics in Nicaragua*.
2. Steven B. Smith, *Modernity and Its Discontents: Making and Unmaking the Bourgeois from Machiavelli to Bellow* (New Haven, Conn.: Yale University Press, 2016), ix.
3. Aníbal Quijano, "Modernity, Identity, and Utopia in Latin America," *Boundary 2*, vol. 20, no. 3 (1993): 143.
4. Quijano, "Modernity, Identity," 145.
5. Quijano, "Modernity, Identity," 145, 146.
6. Quijano, "Modernity, Identity," 146.
7. Gobat, *Confronting the American Dream*, 49.
8. Arturo J. Cruz, *Nicaragua's Conservative Republic, 1858–1893* (New York: Palgrave, 2002).

9. Courtney Desiree Morris, "To Defend This Sunrise: Race, Place, and Creole Women's Political Subjectivity on the Caribbean Coast of Nicaragua" (PhD diss., University of Texas at Austin, 2012), 27, 28.
10. "La novedad de antier," *El Comercio*, June 11, 1906.
11. Sue Macy, *Wheels of Change: How Women Rode the Bicycle to Freedom (With a Few Flat Tires Along the Way)* (Washington, D.C.: National Geographic, 2011), 35, 36.
12. "Isidro J. Olivares vende bicicletas," *El Comercio*, June 11, 1906.
13. Juliet Hooker, "Race and the Space of Citizenship: The Mosquito Coast and the Place of Blackness and Indigeneity in Nicaragua," in *Blacks and Blackness in Central America. Between Race and Place*, ed. Lowell Gudmundson and Justin Wolfe (Durham, N.C.: Duke University Press, 2010), 263–64.
14. Cruz, *Nicaragua's Conservative Republic*, 150–52, 154.
15. Gobat, *Confronting the American Dream*, 49.
16. Gould, *To Die*, 38.
17. Mario Sandoval Aranda, "José Santos Zelaya: Apóstol y reformador," *La Prensa*, July 11, 2004.
18. Michael David Rice, "Nicaragua and the United States: Policy Confrontations and Cultural Interactions, 1893–1933" (PhD diss., University of Houston, 1995), 359.
19. Rice, "Nicaragua and the United States," 358.
20. Fabián Medina, "Los descendientes de Zelaya," *La Prensa Magazine*, October 10, 2004.
21. Rice, "Nicaragua and the United States," 357.
22. Frederick Palmer, *Central America and Its Problems: An Account of a Journey from the Rio Grande to Panama, with Introductory Chapters on Mexico and Her Relations to Her Neighbors* (New York: Moffat, Yard, and Company, 1913), 182.
23. Palmer, *Central America*, 182; Rice, "Nicaragua and the United States," 359.
24. "José Santos Zelaya o la astucia cruel del gallo de pelea," *El Nuevo Diario*, November 6, 2009.
25. José María Moncada, *Cosas de Centroamérica (Memorias de un testigo ocular de los sucesos)* (Madrid: Imprenta de Fortanet, 1908), 261, 262.
26. Moncada, *Cosas de Centroamérica*, 265.
27. Moncada, *Cosas de Centroamérica*, 265–67.
28. "Los Gallos: Una vieja pasión de los nicaragüenses," *El Nuevo Diario*, August 16, 2012.
29. Gobat, *Confronting the American Dream*, 64.
30. Margarita Vannini, "Las conflictivas memorias: La Revolución Sandinista," *Megafón: La Batalla de las Ideas*, no. 16/5 (September 2017), CLACSO.
31. Gratus Halftermeyer, *Managua a través de la historia, 1846–1946* (León, Nic.: Editorial Hospicio San Juan de Dios, nd), 108.
32. "Apoteosis de Zacarías Guerra," Memoria de Ocho Décadas, *La Prensa*.

33. Halftermeyer, *Managua a través*, 108.
34. Halftelmeyer, quoted in Jorge Eduardo Arellano, *Héroes sin fusil* (Managua: Hispamer, 1998), 322.
35. Francisco Javier Bautista Lara, *Manantial*, 2nd ed. (Managua: PAVSA, 2015).
36. "Estando en la puerta de su casa Don Zacarías Guerra . . . ," *El Comercio*, August 31, 1904.
37. Juan M. Mendoza, *Historia de Diriamba (ciudad del departamento de Carazo)* (Guatemala: Imprenta Electra, 1920), 353.
38. "José Zacarías Guerra," *La Prensa*, July 20, 2014.
39. Bautista Lara, *Manantial*, 185.
40. "Apoteosis de Zacarías Guerra."
41. Génesis Hernández, "100 Años del Zacarías Guerra," *La Prensa*, November 11, 2014.
42. "Apoteosis de Zacarías Guerra."
43. Hogar Zacarías Guerra, Facebook page, https://www.facebook.com/hogarzacariasguerraoficial/.
44. Lizandro Zambrana H., "Admiración," *El Comercio*, May 17, 1914.
45. "Dr. J. Carlos Serrano," *El Comercio*, July 24, 1906.
46. Bautista Lara, *Manantial*, 197.
47. "En actos de sodomía," *El 93*, no. 19, August 30, 1916.
48. "Antenoche a uno de los inspectores de la policía, especie de Sherlock Holmes . . . ," *El Comercio*, November 22, 1914.
49. Irwin, *Mexican Masculinities*, back cover.
50. Pablo Ben, "Male Sexuality, the Popular Classes, and the State: Buenos Aires, 1880–1955" (PhD diss., University of Chicago, 2009).
51. Irwin, *Mexican Masculinities*, 2.
52. Ben, "Male Sexuality," 7.
53. George Chauncey, *Gay New York: Gender, Urban Culture, and the Making of the Gay Male World, 1890–1940* (New York: Basic Books, 1994), 1–2.
54. Chauncey, *Gay New York*, 1–3.
55. Chauncey, *Gay New York*, 5–8.
56. Chauncey, *Gay New York*, 8.
57. Francisco Javier Bautista Lara, "El testamento de Zacarías un siglo después," *El Nuevo Diario*, May 5, 2014.
58. González-Rivera, *Before the Revolution*, 8–9.
59. González-Rivera, *Before the Revolution*, 22–84.
60. González-Rivera, *Before the Revolution*, 59–84.
61. Josefa Toledo de Aguerri, *Revista Femenina Ilustrada*, January 18, 1920, 1.
62. Fruto Montes, "Doña Josefa Toledo: Una dama ejemplar," *La Prensa*, June 19, 1995.
63. Margarita López Miranda, *Josefa Toledo de Aguerri: Una chontaleña en la educación nacional* (Juigalpa, Nic.: Asociación Ganadera de Chontales [ASOGACHO], 1988), 46–47.

64. López Miranda, *Josefa Toledo de Aguerri*, 72–73.
65. López Miranda, *Josefa Toledo de Aguerri*.
66. López Miranda, *Josefa Toledo de Aguerri*.
67. Vern Bullough, *Science in the Bedroom: A History of Sex Research* (New York: Basic Books, 1994), 50.
68. Bullough, *Science in the Bedroom*, 50.
69. Bullough, *Science in the Bedroom*, 50.
70. Bullough, *Science in the Bedroom*, 50.
71. López Miranda, *Josefa Toledo de Aguerri*, 73.
72. López Miranda, *Josefa Toledo de Aguerri*, 73.
73. López Miranda, *Josefa Toledo de Aguerri*, 74.
74. Gould, *To Die*, 1998.
75. Interview with Managua resident, 1997.
76. Josefa Toledo de Aguerri, *Educación y feminismo: Sobre enseñanza—Articulos varios Toledo de Aguerri* (Managua: Talleres nacionales, 1940), 9.
77. Toledo de Aguerri, *Educación y feminismo*, 29.
78. Toledo de Aguerri, *Educación y feminismo*, 13.
79. Toledo de Aguerri, *Educación y feminismo*, 30.
80. Toledo de Aguerri, *Educación y feminismo*, 20.
81. Toledo de Aguerri, *Educación y feminismo*, 11.
82. Toledo de Aguerri, *Educación y feminismo*, 12.
83. Toledo de Aguerri, *Educación y feminismo*, 12.
84. Toledo de Aguerri, *Educación y feminismo*, 12.
85. Toledo de Aguerri, *Educación y feminismo*, 12.
86. Toledo de Aguerri, *Educación y feminismo*, 11.
87. Toledo de Aguerri, *Educación y feminismo*, 27.
88. Toledo de Aguerri, *Educación y feminismo*, 6.
89. Toledo de Aguerri, *Educación y feminismo*, 15.
90. Toledo de Aguerri, *Educación y feminismo*, 15.
91. Carlos Tünnerman Bernheim, *Tendencias contemporáneas en la transformación de la educación superior* (Managua: Instituto Martin Luther King, UPOLI, 2002), 314.
92. Toledo de Aguerri, *Educación y feminismo*, 14.
93. Toledo de Aguerri, *Educación y feminismo*, 14.
94. Toledo de Aguerri, *Educación y feminismo*, 14–16.
95. "Distinguidas damas de Granada visitan al Presidente y le piden que no siga adelante la enseñanza sexual," *La Prensa*, December 18, 1934, 1.
96. "Contestación de la Directora de la Escuela Normal de Señoritas," *El Comercio*, November 18, 1910, 2.
97. "Ministerio de Instrucción Pública," 1910.
98. "Hay que alejarlas," *El Diario Nicaragüense*, November 18, 1910.
99. "Juana de Arco," *El Diario Nicaragüense*, November 24, 1910.
100. López Miranda, *Josefa Toledo de Aguerri*, 82.

101. López Miranda, *Josefa Toledo de Aguerri*, 83.
102. López Miranda, *Josefa Toledo de Aguerri*, 55–56.
103. Tünnerman Bernheim, *Tendencias contemporáneas*, 314.
104. Tünnerman Bernheim, *Tendencias contemporáneas*, 314–15.
105. Francisco Palma Martínez, *El siglo de los topos: Crítica y enseñanza en plan de ciencia: Filosofía del sexo, psicología, sociología, eugenesia, religión y artes* (León, Nic.: Editorial La Patria, 1949), 3.
106. Palma Martínez, *El siglo*, 3.
107. Palma Martínez, *El siglo*, 9.
108. Palma Martínez, *El siglo*, 120.
109. Palma Martínez, *El siglo*, 62.
110. Palma Martínez, *El siglo*, 61.
111. Palma Martínez, *El siglo*, 51.
112. Palma Martínez, *El siglo*, 25.
113. Carlos Cuadra Pasos, *Obras II* (Managua: Fondo de Promoción Cultural de Banco de América, 1977), 769.
114. José Antonio Lezcano y Ortega, *Predicación pastoral en las dominicas de un año litúrgico* (Managua: Tipografía Alemana, 1939), 195–96.
115. Briones, quoted in González-Rivera, *Before the Revolution*, 47.
116. Gobat, *Confronting the American Dream*, 196.
117. Quoted in Gobat, *Confronting the American Dream*, 197.
118. Palma Martínez, *El siglo*, 61, 66–67.
119. Gobat, *Confronting the American Dream*, 250.
120. Gobat, *Confronting the American Dream*, 251.
121. Gobat, *Confronting the American Dream*, 253.
122. Gobat, *Confronting the American Dream*, 254.
123. Gobat, *Confronting the American Dream*, 254, 255.
124. Sandino, quoted in José Román Román, *Maldito país* (Managua: Ediciones INPRHU-El Pez y la Serpiente, 1979), 89.
125. Sandino, quoted in Román, *Maldito país*, 80.
126. Gobat, *Confronting the American Dream*, 255.
127. Gobat, *Confronting the American Dream*, 255.
128. Erin Finzer, "Among Sandino's Girlfriends: Carmen Sobalvarro and the Gendered Poetics of a Nationalist Romance," *Latin American Research Review* 47, no. 1 (2012): 141.
129. José María Moncada, *El Gran Ideal* (Managua: Imprenta Nacional, 1929).
130. Moncada, *El Gran Ideal*.
131. González-Rivera, *Before the Revolution*.
132. Jorge Camacho,"El cirujano y la enferma: La representación de la mujer en la literatura modernista," *Revista canadiense de estudios hispánicos* 26, no. 1/2 (2001/2002): 58.
133. Jorge Camacho, "Rubén Darío y las feministas de New York," *Magazine Modernista: Revista Digital del Modernismo*, April 26, 2012.

134. Camacho, "Rubén Darío."
135. Rubén Darío, *Todo al Vuelo* (Madrid: Renacimiento, 1912), 34–36.
136. Darío, quoted in Camacho, "Rubén Darío."
137. Darío, quoted in Luis Sáinz de Medrano, "Rubén Darío ante la crisis europea de su tiempo," in *Rubén Darío y el arte de la prosa: Ensayo, retratos, y alegorías*, ed. Cristóbal Cuevas García (Málaga, Esp.: Congreso de Literatura Española Contemporánea, 1998), 50.
138. Camacho, "Rubén Darío."
139. Darío, *Todo al Vuelo*, 34–35.
140. Camacho, "Rubén Darío."
141. Darío, quoted in Frances England, "Latin Poet Suggests an International Thought Exchange to Help Spanish Women Free Themselves," *New York Tribune*, February 8, 1915, 5.
142. England, "Latin Poet Suggests."
143. López Miranda, *Josefa Toledo de Aguerri*, 33–34.
144. Carlos Fernando Álvarez, "La brillantez de la profesora Josefa Toledo y la nueva generación de excelencia educativa," El19digital.com, February 5, 2018.
145. J.Z. "La mujer y la política," *El Comercio*, September 2, 1905.
146. J. D. Mondragón, "Rebelión de la mujer," *La Tribuna*, August 14, 1921.
147. "Hasta ayer trabajaron las barrenderas de las calles en Managua," *La Prensa*, July 11, 1931.
148. "Contra la gente de mal vivir y las solteronas," *La Prensa*, May 4, 1926.
149. "Busca, Buscando," *El Comercio*, July 24, 1904.
150. "Disfraces nocturnos," *El Comercio*, November 25, 1904.
151. "Disfrazada de hombre," *El Comercio*, November 28, 1919.
152. "Alas cortadas," *El Comercio*, May 8, 1906.
153. "Antenoche como a las doce," *El Comercio*, 1906.
154. "En la policía," *El Comercio*, March 14, 1906.
155. "Disfrazado de mujer," *El Comercio*, November 11, 1919.
156. "Correcionales," *La Tribuna*, March 25, 1920.
157. "Un hombre disfrazado de mujer," *La Tribuna*, May 15, 1917, 2.
158. "El hombre-mujer en Managua," *La Noticia*, May 15, 1917, 3.
159. Francisco Javier Bautista Lara, "El legado inicial de Zacarías Guerra," *El Nuevo Diario*, July 17, 2013.
160. Bautista Lara, "El legado inicial."
161. Elia Martínez, death record. "Nicaragua Registro Civil, 1809–2023," Familysearch.org.
162. "Quedó organizado un nuevo club de golf," *La Prensa*, December 5, 1928, 8; "Don José Benito Ramírez, Campeón de Golf y dueño de Copa White Horse," *El eco de Managua*, no. 16, December 9, 1934, 2.
163. Gobat, *Confronting the American Dream*, 190.

164. Chester Urbina Gaitán, "Apuntes sobre la participación de la mujer nicaragüense en el deporte en la primera mitad del siglo XX," *EFDeportes.com, Revista Digital*, no. 209, 2015.
165. "Nota deportiva," *Faces y facetas: Semanario independiente*, no. 61, November 29, 1923, 4.
166. "Nota deportiva," 4.
167. Urbina Gaitán, "Apuntes sobre la participación," 2015.
168. Urbina Gaitán, "Apuntes sobre la participación," 2015.
169. "Deportes," *Nicaragua informativa*, no. 118, January 22, 1924, 4; Eddy Kühl Arauz, *Nicaragua: Historia de inmigrantes* (Managua: Hispamer, 2007), 326.
170. Jorge Eduardo Arellano, *El béisbol en Nicaragua: Rescate histórico y cultural—1889–1948* (Managua: Academia de Geografía e Historia de Nicaragua, 2007), 266.
171. Gobat, *Confronting the American Dream*, 190.
172. Gobat, *Confronting the American Dream*, 190.
173. Gobat, *Confronting the American Dream*, 185.
174. Gobat, *Confronting the American Dream*, 183.
175. Quoted in Gobat, *Confronting the American Dream*, 190.
176. "Esos trajes impúdicos," *La Prensa*, November 1940.
177. Palma Martínez, *El siglo*, 88.
178. Palma Martínez, *El siglo*, 88.
179. Palma Martínez, *El siglo*, 51, 61.
180. Palma Martínez, *El siglo*, 41.
181. Palma Martinez, *El siglo*, 34.
182. Dan Gordon, "Nicaragua: In Search of Diamonds," in *Baseball Beyond Our Borders: An International Pastime*, ed. George Gmelch and Daniel A. Nathan (Lincoln: University of Nebraska Press, 2017), 91.
183. Gordon, "Nicaragua: In Search," 91.
184. Gordon, "Nicaragua: In Search," 105.
185. "Entusiasmo por la serie de Béisbol Femenil que se inaugura el domingo en el Estadio," *La Prensa*, 1949.
186. Arellano, *El béisbol en Nicaragua*, 238.
187. Quoted in Arellano, *El béisbol en Nicaragua*, 238.
188. Arellano, *El béisbol en Nicaragua*, 275.
189. Arellano, *El béisbol en Nicaragua*, 276.
190. José Antonio Lezcano y Ortega, *Corazón de Padre: Exhortaciones a las Hijas de María* (Managua: Tipografía Alemana de Carlos Heuberger, 1938), 118.
191. Lezcano, *Corazón de Padre*, 116.
192. Lezcano, *Corazón de Padre*, 117.
193. Lezcano, *Corazón de Padre*, 46.
194. Arellano, *El béisbol en Nicaragua*, 277.

195. Orlando Ortega Reyes, "La Caja," *Ortega Reyes* (blog), October 20, 2010; Miguel Lira Rivera, "Historia de Managua: El Robo de la Caja Fuerte de la Ada Moncada," *Nicasoft*, edition 421, 2017, 11–13.
196. Ronald Hilton, *Hispanic American Report*, vol. 15, part 1 (Stanford University, 1962), 122.
197. Lira Rivera, "Historia de Managua," 2017.
198. Ortega Reyes, "La Caja," 2010.
199. Lira Rivera, "Historia de Managua," 2017.
200. Linda M. Callejas, "Donde estén mis hijos, ahí que me entierren: The Migration History of Aura Lila Callejas" (master's thesis, Florida International University, 1998), 19.
201. Callejas, "Donde estén mis hijos," 19.
202. Urbina Gaitan, "Apuntes sobre la participación"; "Sary Miranda Whitford," Salón de la Fama del Deporte Nicaragüense; and "Elogios de 'Los Angeles Examiner' a nuestra máxima deportista, la reina Sary Miranda Witford," *La Nueva Prensa*, no. 5024, February 8, 1946, 8.
203. Ortega Reyes, "La Caja."
204. "Una mujer monta un toro," *El Comercio*, 1904.
205. "Reglamento prohibe boxeo de mujeres," *La Prensa*, April 6, 1971, 1, 8; "Desagradable, antifemenino, muy repulsivo," *La Prensa*, April 5, 1971, 1, 16.
206. Don J. Odle, *Basketball Around the World* (Economy Printing Concern, 1961), 39.
207. Emiliano Chamorro, *El último caudillo*, 1983, 258, 259.
208. Brian G. Shellum, *African American Officers in Liberia: A Pestiferous Rotation, 1910–1942* (Omaha: University of Nebraska Press, 2018), 177.
209. Shellum, *African American Officers*, 176.
210. Shellum, *African American Officers*, 176.
211. Shellum, *African American Officers*, 177.
212. Zoraida Matus, marriage certificate, 1930.
213. Zoraida Matus, marriage certificate, 1930.
214. "Educación física es necesaria para la mujer," *La Prensa*, April 22, 1926, 8.
215. González-Rivera, *Before the Revolution*.
216. Toledo de Aguerri, *Revista Femenina Ilustrada*, 12.
217. Jennifer Ring, *Stolen Bases: Why American Girls Don't Play Baseball* (Urbana: University of Illinois Press, 2009), 16.
218. Ring, *Stolen Bases*.
219. Arellano, *El béisbol en Nicaragua*, 264.
220. Edgard Rodríguez, "¿Quién era Stanley Cayasso, el pelotero que da su nombre al viejo estadio de béisbol?," *La Prensa*, October 10, 2017.
221. Borgen, quoted in Arellano, *El béisbol en Nicaragua*, 143.
222. Borgen, quoted in Arellano, *El béisbol en Nicaragua*, 162, 163.
223. Hodgson, quoted in Arellano, *El béisbol en Nicaragua*, 164.
224. Rory Costello and Tito Rondón, "Stanley Cayasso," https://sabr.org/bioproj/person/cdceab6e.

225. Eduardo Cruz, "Keith Taylor, los Dantos y el general," *La Prensa*, July 10, 2016.
226. Cruz, "Keith Taylor."
227. Cruz, "Keith Taylor."
228. Gobat, *Confronting the American Dream*, 64.
229. Jorge Eduardo Arellano, "Años fundacionales de nuestro béisbol," *El Nuevo Diario*, May 27, 2012.
230. M. Ann Hall, *The Girl and the Game: A History of Women's Sport in Canada*, 2nd ed. (Toronto: University of Toronto Press, 2016), xv.
231. Costello and Rondón, "Stanley Cayasso."
232. Costello and Rondón, "Stanley Cayasso."
233. "Lady Baldwin," Findagrave.com, https://www.findagrave.com/memorial/21493136/charles-b-baldwin.
234. Hodgson, quoted in Arellano, *El béisbol en Nicaragua*, 164.

Chapter 4

Sections of chapter four were published earlier as "The Alligator Woman's Tale: Remembering Nicaragua's "First Self-Declared Lesbian," *Journal of Lesbian Studies* 18, no. 1 (2014): 75–87.

1. Marvin Saballos Ramírez, "80 años del terremoto de Managua," *La Prensa*, April 1, 2011.
2. Victoria González[-Rivera], "Somocista Women, Right-Wing Politics and Feminism in Nicaragua, 1936–1979," in *Radical Women in Latin America: Left and Right*, ed. Victoria González[-Rivera] and Karen Kampwirth (University Park: Penn State University Press, 2001).
3. "Nicaragua: La crisis económica de los años 30," *El Nuevo Diario*, May 26, 2009.
4. Luis Hernández Bustamante, "Aquella Managua de los años 40," *Managua en mis recuerdos*, 2012, 25.
5. Isolda Rodríguez Rosales, *Historia de la educación en Nicaragua: 50 años en el sistema educativo 1929–1979* (Managua: Editorial Hispamer, 2007), 28.
6. Rodríguez Rosales, *Historia de la educación*, 28.
7. González-Rivera, *Before the Revolution*.
8. "Managua a merced de la furia," *Managua en mis recuerdos*, 2012, 32.
9. González-Rivera, *Before the Revolution*, 176.
10. Although the use of *la* before a woman's name is seen by some as a sexist practice, I have chosen to use it before "Sebastiana" because that is how she is remembered and how she sometimes used it, perhaps because it emphasized her femininity. I also chose not to italicize her name.
11. Interview by Karen Kampwirth, December 9, 2015.
12. "Acto suicida de Rigoberto López Pérez," *La Prensa*, September 21, 2006.
13. "Acto suicida ..."
14. "Acto suicida ..."
15. Pablo Emilio Barreto Pérez, "Rigoberto López Pérez: Ajusticiador de Anastasio Somoza García y secreto familiar peligroso," *Pablo Emilio Barreto Pérez* (blog),

September 23, 2009, https://pabloemiliobarreto.wordpress.com/2009/09/23/secreto-peligroso-sobre-rigoberto-lopez-perez/.

16. Jairo Cajina, "Conmemoran heroica acción del revolucionario Rigoberto López Pérez," September 21, 2009, https://www.lavozdelsandinismo.com/nicaragua/2009-09-21/conmemoraron-heroica-accion-del-revolucionario-rigoberto-lopez-perez/; Ignacio Briones, "Notas para una biografía," *Bolsa de noticias*, September 26, 2002; "Acto suicida..." 2006.
17. "Acto suicida..." 2006; Alejandro Guevara, "Rigoberto López Pérez, 5 disparos que cambiaron a Nicaragua," Radio la Primerísima, September 21, 2014.
18. Wendy Jarquín, "¿Quién fue Rigoberto López Pérez? Habla el Comandante Carlos Fonseca," *Diario Barricada*, September 21, 2018, https://barricada.com.ni/fonseca-habla-rogiberto/.
19. Eduardo Cruz, "Adiós, viejo estadio nacional de Nicaragua," *La Prensa*, October 23, 2016.
20. Erika Gertsch Romero, "50 años de un polémico colegio," *La Prensa*, June 27, 2010.
21. "Rigoberto López Pérez, un heroe que cambió la historia," Radio La Primerísima, September 21, 2017.
22. Eduardo Pérez Valle, "Rigoberto López Pérez: Dopamina y heroismo en la verdad histórica (Cinco voces en el debate)," *Eduardo Pérez Valle* (blog), September 20, 2015, Eduardoperezvalle.blogspot.com.
23. Confidential U.S. State Department central files, Nicaragua, 1955–1959 [microform]: internal affairs, decimal numbers 717, 817, and 917; and foreign affairs, decimal numbers 617 and 611.17/ Reel 3. Unknown archive.
24. Unknown archive.
25. Arturo Wallace, "Por qué los nicaragüenses están convencidos de que el suyo es el país con mas poetas de América Latina," BBC Mundo, May 24, 2017.
26. Héctor Avellán, "Pánico en la granja," *El Nuevo Diario*, July 21, 2002.
27. "La sensibilidad modernista era manflorita y maricona, al margen de las costumbres sexuales de cada escritor." Blas Matamoro, "Parsifal y Ganimedes," *Página/12*, July 20, 2002.
28. Matamoro, "Parsifal y Ganimedes," 2002.
29. Lorenzo Helguero, "Transgresión y Modernidad: La Prosa de Rubén Darío" (PhD diss., Georgetown University, 2009), iii.
30. Nicasio Urbina, "La crítica dariana: Estado actual del arte," 2005, https://homepages.uc.edu/~urbinan/lacriticadariana.htm.
31. Avellán, "Pánico en la granja."
32. Avellán, "Pánico en la granja."
33. Alberto Acereda, "'Nuestro más profundo y sublime secreto': Los amores transgresores entre Rubén Darío y Amado Nervo," *Bulletin of Spanish Studies* 89, no. 6 (2012). See also Cinthia Membreño, "Las 'cartas privadas' de Rubén Darío a Nervo," *Confidencial*, November 13, 2012.
34. Acereda, "'Nuestro mas profundo."

35. Gunther Schmigalle, "El poeta de Nicaragua y el gran fraude de Arizona," *Temas nicaragüenses*, no. 56, (December 2012): 37.
36. See article by Sergio Ramírez Mercado, "El sencillo arte de dejarse engañar," *La Prensa*, November 22, 2012.
37. "ASU Libraries Acquires Rare Manuscripts of Nicaraguan Poet Ruben Darío," Arizona State University website, November 1, 2012, https://news.asu.edu/20220201-asu-libraries-acquires-rare-manuscripts-nicaraguan-poet-rub%C3%A9n-dar%C3%ADo.
38. "ASU Libraries Acquires."
39. Email communication, December 1, 2019.
40. Email communication, December 2, 2019.
41. Arizona Archives Online, Ruben Darío Papers, "Ruben Darío Papers 1882–1945 (bulk 1882–1915)," http://www.azarchivesonline.org/xtf/view?docId=ead/asu/dario.xml;query=Nicaragua;-brand=default
42. Arizona Archives Online, "Ruben Darío Papers 1882–1945."
43. Acereda, "'Nuestro más profundo,'" 896–97.
44. Alberto Acereda, "Los manuscritos darianos de Arizona: Autenticidad de la colección y apostillas a las cartas a Amado Nervo," *Siglo Diecinueve*, no. 19 (2013).
45. Roderick A. Molina, "Amado Nervo: His Mysticism and Franciscan Influence," *The Americas* 6, no. 2 (1949): 175.
46. Rafael Reig, "La Pérdida del reino," Eldiario.es, February 19, 2013.
47. *Nervo: Las Voces, Obras Completas*, vol. 3, 102–3, cited in Molina, "Amado Nervo," 176.
48. *La Prensa*, November 22, 2012.
49. "Por amor al arte dariano," *La Prensa*, February 3, 2014.
50. Francisco Aragón, "Translation as Activism," Poetry International website, May 25, 2018, http://poetryinternationalonline.com/translation-as-activism-francisco-aragon/.
51. Membreño, "Las 'cartas privadas.'"
52. Daniel Link, "Darío Queer," *Soy*, February 5, 2016.
53. Link, "Darío Queer."
54. Link, "Darío Queer."
55. Link, "Darío Queer."
56. Francisco Javier Bautista Lara, "Cuatro variaciones de un verso de Darío," *El Nuevo Diario*, March 20, 2015.
57. Avellán, "Pánico en la granja"; Marta Leonor González, "Miradas de Héctor Avellán," *La Prensa*, June 25, 2011.
58. Iván de Jesús Pereira, "Restauran en León la casa del magnicidio," *La Prensa*, August 10, 2013.
59. Pereira, "Restauran en León."
60. Ulises Huete Maltés, "Smith & Wesson No 74605," *La Prensa*, September 21, 2013.

61. Huete Maltés, "Smith & Wesson No 74605."
62. Rafael in the comment section on Jorge Eduardo Arellano, "La identidad sexual de Rigoberto," *El Nuevo Diario*, October 12, 2013.
63. Arellano, "La identidad sexual."
64. Absalón Pastora, "La identidad sexual de Rigoberto," *La Prensa*, October 22, 2013.
65. Jorge Eduardo Arellano, "La homofilia de Rigoberto López Pérez," *El Nuevo Diario*, November 2, 2013.
66. Davíd in the comment section of Arellano, "La homofilia."
67. Douglas in the comment section on Arellano, "La homofilia."
68. Douglas in the comment section on Arellano, "La homofilia."
69. Adriana in the comment section on Arellano, "La homofilia."
70. Adán in the comment section on Arellano, "La homofilia."
71. Orlando Morales Navarrete, "Huevos al estilo Rigoberto," November 20, 2013, porlaautonomia.wordpress.com.
72. Ramiro in the comment section on Arellano, "La homofilia."
73. Arellano, "La identidad sexual."
74. Rafael Casanova Fuertes, "Rigoberto mas allá de las preferencias," *El Nuevo Diario*, November 7, 2013.
75. Casanova Fuertes, "Rigoberto mas allá."
76. Roger Lancaster, *Life Is Hard: Machismo, Danger, and the Intimacy of Power in Nicaragua* (Berkeley: University of California Press, 1994).
77. Casanova Fuertes, "Rigoberto mas allá."
78. Pastora, "La identidad sexual."
79. Arellano, "La homofilia."
80. Arellano, "La identidad sexual."
81. Pastora, "La identidad sexual."
82. Rocha, *Crónicas de la ciudad*, 66.
83. Eduardo Cruz, "La furia tras los disparos contra Anastasio Somoza García," *La Prensa*, September 28, 2019.
84. Pastora, "La identidad sexual."
85. Pastora, "La identidad sexual."
86. Cruz, "La furia tras."
87. Cruz, "La furia tras."
88. Cruz, "La furia tras."
89. Huete Maltés, "Smith & Wesson No 74605."
90. "El Centroamericano escapó de desaparecer . . . ," *El Centroamericano*, no. 15831, September 29, 1971.
91. Casanova Fuertes, "Rigoberto mas allá."
92. Interview.
93. Interview.
94. Interview.
95. Interview.

96. Interview.
97. Interview.
98. Personal conversation with Hilda Scott, August 2012; "Managua presencia la vela mas extraña," *La Prensa*, August 1?, 1971; María Adelia Sandoval, "La Caimana: La primera lesbiana declarada," *7 Días*, no. 419, 2004, 3–7. Another source indicates that La Caimana might have been forty-seven years old at the time of his death. See "La Caimana: 28 casas a sus hijos; la fábrica a su amiga Hilda Scott," *La Prensa*, August 19, 1971, 16.
99. "Historia de la Caimana, punto de referencia en Managua," VOS TV, 2017.
100. Barbara Dröscher, "Travesía travesti y traducción posiciones in-between en la novela historiografía de América Central," *Revista de estudios sociales*, October 13, 2002, 87.
101. Amalia del Cid, "Las vidas de la Caimana," *La Prensa Magazine*, February 12, 2018.
102. Lisa Duggan, *The Twilight of Equality?: Neoliberalism, Cultural Politics, and the Attack on Democracy* (Boston: Beacon Press, 2003). See also the entire issue of *Radical History Review*, no. 100 (Winter 2008).
103. Elizabeth Lapovsky Kennedy and Madeline D. Davis, *Boots of Leather, Slippers of Gold: The History of a Lesbian Community* (New York: Routledge, 1993), 6.
104. del Cid, "Las vidas."
105. del Cid, "Las vidas."
106. Roger Lancaster, "Guto's Performace: Notes on the Transvestism of Everyday Life," in *Sex and Sexuality in Latin America*, ed. Daniel Balderston and Donna J. Guy (New York: New York University Press, 1997), 26.
107. Robert W. Kates et al., "Human Impact of the Managua Earthquake," *Science* 182, no. 7 (1973): 984.
108. "Managua presencia."
109. James Freeman, "From the Little Tree, Half a Block Toward the Lake: Popular Geography and Symbolic Discontent in Post-Sandinista Managua," *Antipode* 42, no. 2 (2010): 336.
110. Freeman quoting Erick Aguirre, in "From the Little Tree," 354.
111. González-Rivera, *Before the Revolution*.
112. Douglas Kellner, "Media Spectacle and the Triumph of the Spectacle," *Razón y Palabra*, no. 39 (April–May 2004).
113. Miguel Bolaños Garay, *Los Días de la Tortuga* (Managua: Anamá Ediciones, 1996), 132.
114. del Cid, "Las vidas."
115. González-Rivera, *Before the Revolution*.
116. González-Rivera, *Before the Revolution*; Consuelo Cruz Sequeira, "Mistrust and Violence in Nicaragua: Ideology and Politics," *Latin American Research Review* 30, no. 1 (1995): 218.
117. Sergio Ramírez Mercado, *Margarita, está linda la mar* (Madrid: Santillana, 1998), 365.

118. Ramírez Mercado, *Margarita*.
119. "'La Caimana' un popular personaje de Campo Bruce," *La Prensa*, June 26, 2006.
120. Ramírez Mercado, *Margarita*, 303.
121. Peter Sternberg, "Challenging Machismo: Promoting Sexual and Reproductive Health with Nicaraguan Men," *Gender and Development* 8, no. 1 (2000): 94.
122. *La Prensa*, April 21, 2001.
123. del Cid, "Las vidas."
124. Sandoval, "La Caimana," 6.
125. del Cid, "Las vidas."
126. Sandoval, "La Caimana," 3.
127. "La Caimana: 28 casas a sus hijos; la fábrica a su amiga Hilda Scott," *La Prensa*, August 19, 1971, 16.
128. Agustín Torres Lazo, *La Saga de los Somoza: Historia de un magnicidio* (Managua: Hispamer, 2000), 425.
129. González-Rivera, *Before the Revolution*; Amalia del Cid, "Deja vu: Así eran las turbas sandinistas en los años ochenta y noventa," *La Prensa*, June 29, 2019.
130. Lesbia Espinoza, "Mujeres empresarias con cupos rebasados," *El Nuevo Diario*, April 19, 2001.
131. Sandoval, "La Caimana."
132. del Cid, "Las vidas."
133. del Cid, "Las vidas."
134. González-Rivera, *Before the Revolution*.
135. Edgar Barberena "Hilda Rosa Scott Hernández: La heredera de la caimana. Un amor explosivo," *El Nuevo Diario*, December 6, 2008.
136. del Cid, "Las vidas."
137. del Cid, "Las vidas."
138. Sandoval, "La Caimana."
139. "La Caimana: 28 casas a sus hijos."
140. Sandoval, "La Caimana."
141. del Cid, "Las vidas."
142. del Cid, "Las vidas."
143. Sandoval, "La Caimana," 6.
144. del Cid, "Las vidas." Whenever I use the terms s/he or her/his in the English translation, it is because it is gender-neutral in the original Spanish.
145. Sandoval, "La Caimana," 6.
146. del Cid, "Las vidas."
147. del Cid, "Las vidas."
148. "Managua presencia."
149. del Cid, "Las vidas."
150. del Cid, "Las vidas."
151. del Cid, "Las vidas."
152. Sandoval, "La Caimana."
153. Palma Martínez, *El siglo*.

154. Roberto Sánchez Ramírez, "Puntos de referencia en al vieja Managua," *La Prensa*, July 25, 2005.
155. Dan Van Meter, "Rubén Darío and Vicente Huidobro: Two Views of Language as Impregnation," *Hispania* 75, no. 2 (1992): 295.
156. Van Meter, "Rubén Darío," 295.
157. Anuar Hassan, *Grandes crímenes del siglo XX en Nicaragua* (Managua, 2001), 93.
158. The Sacasa family is one of Nicaragua's old aristocratic families. They can trace their roots to the early colonial period. See Samuel Z. Stone, *The Heritage of the Conquistadors: Ruling Classes in Central America from the Conquest to the Sandinistas* (Lincoln: University of Nebraska Press, 1990), 38.
159. Cymene Howe, "Undressing the Universal Queer Subject: Nicaraguan Activism and Transnational Identity," *City and Society* (2002): 256.
160. Howe, "Undressing the Universal," 256.
161. Anuar Hassan and Emiliano Chamorro, "Andar por caminos torcidos no paga," *La Prensa*, August 26, 2000.
162. Hassan and Chamorro, "Andar por caminos."
163. Hassan and Chamorro, "Andar por caminos."
164. "The Huns: Original title—'La Regina dei Taitari,'" https://www.imdb.com/title/tt0056400/.
165. "Música, Drogas y Pólvora," *La Prensa*, August ?, 1971; "Managua presencia"; and "Increíble cantidad de gente en extraño funeral," *La Prensa*, August 20, 1971, 1.
166. Howe, "Undressing the Universal," 258.
167. Rocha, "Cartografías de homosocialización," 48.
168. Rocha "Cartografías de homosocialización," 106.
169. Rocha, "Cartografías de homosocialización," 133.
170. Rocha, "Cartografías de homosocialización," 134.
171. Rocha, "Cartografías de homosocialización," 135, 136.
172. Interview by Karen Kampwirth, December 9, 2015.
173. Interview by Karen Kampwirth, December 6, 2015.
174. Interview by Karen Kampwirth, December 6, 2015.
175. Interview by Karen Kampwirth, December 6, 2015.
176. Rocha, "Cartografías de homosocialización," 56.
177. Rocha, "Cartografías de homosocialización," 51.
178. Carol Tisch, "Who's in Store: Mission Avenue's Bernabé Somoza," Sarasota Magazine.com, 2013; "Mission Avenue Studio Offers 'Furniture with a Story,'" press release by Mission Avenue Studio in Woodworking, Network.com, February 17, 2014.
179. González-Rivera, *Before the Revolution*, 135, 140.
180. Hassan, *Grandes crímenes*, 93.
181. Hassan and Chamorro, "Andar por caminos."
182. Hassan, *Grandes crímenes*, 93.
183. Hassan, *Grandes crímenes*, 93.

184. Francisco J. Barbosa, "July 23, 1959: Student Protest and State Violence as Myth and Memory in León, Nicaragua," *Hispanic American Historical Review* 85, no. 2 (2005): 187–222.
185. Lillian Guerra, "Gender Policing, Homosexuality, and the New Patriarchy of the Cuban Revolution, 1965–1970," *Social History* 35, no. 3 (2010).
186. Lee Lockwood, *Castro's Cuba, Cuba's Fidel* (Boulder, Colo.: Westview Press, 1990).
187. Rocha, *Crónicas de la ciudad*, 66.
188. Rocha, *Crónicas de la ciudad*, 110.
189. Rocha, "Cartografías de homosocialización," 72.
190. Rocha, "Cartografías de homosocialización," 73.
191. *Novedades*, May 1969, 8, cited in Rocha, "Cartografías de homosocialización," 74.
192. Rocha, "Cartografías de homosocialización," 73.
193. Interview by Karen Kampwirth, December 6, 2015.
194. Rocha, "Cartografías de homosocialización," 116.
195. Rocha, "Cartografías de homosocialización," 117.
196. Richard Ward, "Print Culture, Moral Panic, and the Administration of the Law: The London Crime Wave of 1744," *Crime, Histoire and Sociétés/Crime, History and Societies* 16, no. 1 (2012): 7, 8.
197. Matthew Wills, "The First Moral Panic: London, 1774," JSTOR Daily, January 9, 2018.
198. Ward, "Print Culture, Moral Panic," 7.
199. "Gran Campaña Policial para sanear barrios orientales," *Novedades*, July 3, 1969.
200. Bosco León Báez, "Prostíbulos de los 70: De la Conga Roja al Baby Doll," October 17, 2017, originally viewed at http://www.lacalleonline.com/2017/10/17/prostibulos-de-los-70-de-la-conga-roja-al-baby-doll/; viewed on January 24, 2023, on a public Facebook post from June 6, 2021, on the Facebook page called Nicaragua y su historia.
201. Bosco León Báez, "Ni el terremoto cerró los prostíbulos de Managua," October 24, 2017, originally viewed at http://www.lacalleonline.com/2017/10/24/ni-el-terremoto-cerro-los-prostibulos-de-managua/; this website is no longer available.
202. Rocha, "Cartografías de homosocialización," 65.
203. *La Prensa*, April 8, 1969, 2, cited in Rocha, "Cartografías de homosocialización," 65–66.
204. "El Charco de los Patos Cerrará de Inmediato," *Novedades*, April 9, 1969, 9, cited in Rocha, "Cartografías de homosocialización," 66.
205. Rocha, "Cartografías de homosocialización," 65, 66, 59.
206. Orlando Ortega, "Le dicen: La Sebastiana," Los hijos de septiembre, *Ortega Reyes* (blog), February 4, 2012, ortegareyes.wordpress.com.
207. Amalia del Cid, "Salvadora Debayle: La matrona de los Somoza," *La Prensa Magazine*, December 13, 2015.

208. "Primeros testigos de la defensa de Zelaya: Tres declararon ayer," *Novedades*, July 1, 1969.
209. "Renuncia en balde: Diputados conocerán en el caso Zelaya," *La Prensa*, June 19, 1969.
210. "Cámara de Diputados no conocerá de la acusación: Resolución ajustada a derecho," *Novedades*, June 20, 1969.
211. "Mitómano considera la defensa a Real Espinales: Se basan en el historial clínico," *Novedades*, July 11, 1969.
212. "Niegan a Jarquín, Voto de confianza," *Novedades*, July 15, 1969, 1.
213. "Renuncia en balde...," 1.
214. "Renuncia en balde...," 1.
215. United Nations, *Delegations to the General Assembly*, issues 29–30, 1974, 211.
216. Unknown archive, August 11, 1969.
217. *La Gaceta Diario Oficial* 72, no. 67 (March 19, 1968): 909–10.
218. *La Gaceta Diario Oficial* 72, no. 70 (March 22, 1968): 937–38.
219. He was the father of Carlos Arroyo Pineda (1954–77), a member of the FSLN killed by the Somoza dictatorship. Carlos Arroyo Pineda is considered a hero and martyr of the leftist Sandinista revolution.
220. Franklin Villavicencio, "David Rocha: Cartógrafo de memorias," September 14, 2017, https://furiaca.com/david-rocha-cartografo-memorias/.
221. Ortega, "Le dicen"; interview by Karen Kampwirth, December 6, 2015.
222. Ortega, "Le dicen."

Conclusion

1. Gobat, *Empire by Invitation*, 11. Emphasis in the original.
2. Gobat, *Empire by Invitation*, 13.

BIBLIOGRAPHY

"80 preguntas hace a Real Espinales la defensa del Profesor Zelaya U." *Novedades*, July 8, 1969.
"A Paula Aguilar se le decretaron . . ." *El Comercio*, January 24, 1906.
Aburto, Ernesto. "El último mambo de Somoza." *El Nuevo Diario*, September 21, 2016.
Acereda, Alberto. "Los manuscritos darianos de Arizona: Autenticidad de la colección y apostillas a las cartas a Amado Nervo." *Siglo Diecinueve* 19 (2013): 7–37.
Acereda, Alberto. "'Nuestro más profundo y sublime secreto': Los amores transgresores entre Rubén Darío y Amado Nervo." *Bulletin of Spanish Studies* 89, no. 6 (2012): 895–924.
"Acto suicida de Rigoberto López Pérez." *La Prensa*, September 21, 2006.
"Acuerdo aprobando el Reglamento de cárceles de la ciudad de Granada." August 9, 1883. http://sajurin.enriquebolanos.org/vega/docs/CLAD-1883-090.pdf.
"Acuerdo aprobando el Reglamento interior del Mercado Central de Managua." 1882. http://sajurin.enriquebolanos.org/vega/docs/CLAD%20-%201882%20-%20365.pdf.
"Acuerdo aprobando la Ordenanza municipal de Santa Teresa." April 22, 1875. http://sajurin.enriquebolanos.org/vega/docs/CLAD%20-%201875%20-%20121.pdf.
"Acuerdo aprobando los estatutos de la sociedad filarmónica de Granada, 'La Juventud.'" 1883. http://sajurin.enriquebolanos.org/vega/docs/CLAD-1883-245.pdf.
"Acuerdo aprobando los siguientes estatutos de la 'Sociedad Filarmónica de León.'" 1883. http://sajurin.enriquebolanos.org/vega/docs/CLAD-1883-423.pdf.
"Acuerdo del 10 de diciembre. Reglamento de policía." 1862. http://sajurin.enriquebolanos.org/vega/docs/CLAD%20-%201862%20-%20180.pdf.

Adam, Barry. "In Nicaragua: Homosexuality Without a Gay World." *Journal of Homosexuality* 24, no. 3/4 (1993): 171–83.

ADESENI (Asociación por los derechos de la diversidad sexual Nicaragüense). "INFORME FINAL: Estudio línea de base con población TRANS y mujeres lesbianas de 4 municipios intervenidos." 2010. http://www.sidocfeminista.org/buscar/13977-informe-final—estudio-linea-de-base-con-poblacion-trans-y-mujeres-lesbianas-de-4-municipios-intervenidos.

"Al policial del mercado se le hará responsable . . ." *El Comercio*, March 2, 1906.

"Alas cortadas . . ." *El Comercio*, May 8, 1906.

Alcoff, Linda Martín. "Philosophy, the Conquest, and the Meaning of Modernity: A Commentary on 'Anti-Cartesian Meditations: On the Origin of the Philosophical Anti-Discourse of Modernity' by Enrique Dussel." *Human Architecture: Journal of the Sociology of Self-Knowledge* 11, no. 1 (2013).

Alemán, Filadelfo. "'La caimana,' por fin, revela su secreto." *La Prensa*, December 20, 1969.

Alemay Bay, Carmen. "Versiones, revisiones, y subversiones de la poesía de Rubén Darío en el siglo veinte." *Anales de Literatura Hispanoamericana* 3 (2007): 137–52.

Allen, Ann Taylor. "Feminism and Eugenics in Germany and Britain, 1900–1940: A Comparative Perspective." *German Studies Review* 23, no. 3 (2000): 477–505.

Allen, Ann Taylor. "German Radical Feminism and Eugenics, 1900–1908." *German Studies Review* 11, no. 1 (1988): 31–56.

Altamirano Montoya, Álvaro José, and Karla María Damiano Texteira. "Multidimensional Poverty in Nicaragua: Are Female-Headed Households Better Off?" *Social Indicators Research* 132, no. 3 (2017): 1037–63.

Alvarado Sarria, Rafael. *Breve historia hospitalaria de Nicaragua*. León, Nic.: Editorial Hospicio, 1969.

Álvarez, Carlos Fernando. "La brillantez de la profesora Josefa Toledo y la nueva generación de excelencia educativa." El19digital.com, February 5, 2018. https://www.el19digital.com/articulos/ver/titulo:66247-la-brillantez-de-la-profesora-josefa-toledo-y-la-nueva-generacion-de-excelencia-educativa.

Andagoya, Pascual de. "Relación de los sucesos de Pedrarias Dávila en las Provincias de Tierra Firme o Castilla del Oro, y de lo ocurrido en el descubrimiento de la mar del Sur y costa del Perú y Nicaragua." *Revista de Temas Nicaragüenses*, no. 38 (July 2011): 184–99. Reprint from *Colección de los viages y descubrimientos que hicieron por mar los españoles desde fines del siglo XV*, edited by Martín Fernández de Navarrete, no. 7, 3rd sec.: Establecimientos o primeras poblaciones de los españoles en el Darién, vol. 3, 393–456. Madrid: Imprenta Real, 1829.

Andradi, Esther. "La mujer en las crónicas de Rubén Darío." *La Jornada Semanal*, December 2, 2016.

ANIT (Asociación Nicaragüense de Transgénero). *Informe de sondeo de percepción de personas transgéneros sobre discriminación en el departamento de Managua*. August 5, 2016. https://issuu.com/mv.86/docs/informe-final-sondeo-de-percepcion.

Anonymous. "The U.S.-Orchestrated Overthrow of the Nicaraguan Government, 1910." Libcom.org, December 14, 2016. https://libcom.org/history/us-orchestrated-overthrow-nicaraguan-government-1910.

"Antenoche a uno de los inspectores de la policía, especie de Sherlock Holmes . . ." *El Comercio*, November 22, 1914.

"Antenoche como a las doce." *El Comercio*, 1906.

"Apoteosis de Zacarías Guerra." Memoria de Ocho Décadas. *La Prensa*, nd.

"Apuntes sobre el Tío Sam." *La Prensa Magazine*, July 9, 2017.

Aragón, Alba F. "The Rhetoric of Fashion in Latin America." PhD diss., Harvard University, 2012.

Aragón, Francisco. "Translation as Activism." Poetry International. May 25, 2018. http://poetryinternationalonline.com/translation-as-activism-francisco-aragon/.

Arauz Henríquez, María José. "De la patria potestad a la autoridad parental de tránsito hacia la humanización de los derechos de la niñez y la adolescencia." Master's thesis, Universidad Centroamericana, April 13, 2017.

Arboleda, Manuel G. "On Some of Lancaster's Misrepresentations." *American Ethnologist* 24, no. 4 (November 1997): 931–34.

Arellano, Jorge Eduardo. "Acepciones y etimología de la palabra cochón." *La Prensa*, March 14, 2004.

Arellano, Jorge Eduardo. "Años fundacionales de nuestro béisbol." *El Nuevo Diario*, May 27, 2012.

Arellano, Jorge Eduardo. "Del léxico sexual en Nicaragua." *La Prensa*, October 8, 2006.

Arellano, Jorge Eduardo. *El béisbol en Nicaragua: Rescate histórico y cultural: 1889–194*. Managua: Academia de Geografía e Historia de Nicaragua, 2007.

Arellano, Jorge Eduardo. "El movimiento nicaragüense de vanguardia." *Cuadernos Hispanoamericanos*, no. 468 (June 1989): 7–44.

Arellano, Jorge Eduardo. *Héroes sin fusil*. Managua: Hispamer, 1998.

Arellano, Jorge Eduardo. *Historia básica de Nicaragua*. Vol. 1. Managua: Fondo editorial CIRA, 1993.

Arellano, Jorge Eduardo. "La homofilia de Rigoberto López Pérez." *El Nuevo Diario*, November 2, 2013.

Arellano, Jorge Eduardo. "La identidad sexual de Rigoberto." *El Nuevo Diario*, October 12, 2013.

Arellano, Jorge Eduardo. "Nicaragua: 500 años de historia." *Temas Nicaragüenses*, no. 35 (March 2011): 46–65.

Arellano, Jorge Eduardo. "Poesía y testamento: Juan Iribarren—Introducción, recopilación y notas." *Revista Conservadora*, no. 69 (June 1966).

Arellano, Jorge Eduardo. "Una hermana en ideales patrios." *El Nuevo Diario*, December 24, 2017.

Arizona Archives Online. "Rubén Darío Papers 1882–1945 (bulk 1882–1915)." http://www.azarchivesonline.org/xtf/view?docId=ead/asu/dario.xml;query=dario;brand=default.

Argüello, Alfonso. *Historia de León Viejo*. León, Nic.: Editorial Antorcha, 1969.
Argüello Gómez, José. "Plano esquemático de León Viejo." *Revista de Temas Nicaragüense*, no. 14 (July 2009): 40–60.
Arvey, Sarah R. "Sex and the Ordinary Cuban: Cuban Physicians, Eugenics, and Marital Sexuality, 1933–1958." *Journal of the History of Sexuality* 21, no. 1 (January 2012): 93–120.
Asamblea Nacional de la República de Nicaragua. "Ley de Reformas al Código Penal." *La Gaceta*, no. 174, September 9, 1992.
"ASU Libraries Acquires Rare Manuscripts of Nicaraguan Poet Ruben Darío." Arizona State University website. November 1, 2012. https://news.asu.edu/20220201-asu-libraries-acquires-rare-manuscripts-nicaraguan-poet-rub%C3%A9n-dar%C3%ADo.
Avellán, Héctor. "Pánico en la granja." *El Nuevo Diario*, July 21, 2002.
Ayón, Tomás. *Historia de Nicaragua: Desde los tiempos más remotos hasta el año de 1852*. Vol. 1. Granada, Nic.: Tipografía de "El Centro Americano," 1882.
Ayón, Tomás. "Viajes de Cristóbal Colón y descubrimiento de Nicaragua por el lado del Atlántico." Chap. 1 of book 2 of *Historia de Nicaragua*. Managua: Colección Cultural Banco de América, 1977.
Badenes, José Ignacio. "Modernismos, masculinidades, y nacionalismos: Rubén Darío y Federico García Lorca ante Walt Whitman." *Chasqui: Revista de literatura latinoamericana* 43, no. 1 (2014): 92–102.
Banco Central de Nicaragua. *Cartografía digital y censo de edificaciones: Cabecera municipal de Managua*. January 2017. http://www.bcn.gob.ni/publicaciones/cartografia/documentos/Managua.pdf.
Barberena, Edgard. "Hilda Rosa Scott Hernández. La heredera de 'la caimana' y un amor explosivo." *El Nuevo Diario*, December 6, 2020.
Barbosa, Francisco J. "July 23, 1959: Student Protest and State Violence as Myth and Memory in León, Nicaragua." *Hispanic American Historical Review* 85, no. 2 (2005): 187–222.
Barnhart, Terry A. *Ephraim George Squier and the Development of American Anthropology*. Omaha: University of Nebraska Press, 2005.
Barreto Pérez, Pablo Emilio. "93 siniestros en siete años: Incendios—tragedias reiteradas en Mercado Oriental." *Pablo Emilio Barreto Pérez* (blog), October 28, 2009. https://pabloemiliobarreto.wordpress.com/2009/10/28/93-siniestros-en-siete-anos-incendios-tragedias-reiteradas-en-mercado-oriental/.
Barreto Pérez, Pablo Emilio. "Rigoberto López Pérez: Ajusticiador de Anastasio Somoza García y secreto familiar peligroso." *Pablo Emilio Barreto Pérez* (blog), September 23, 2009. https://pabloemiliobarreto.wordpress.com/2009/09/23/secreto-peligroso-sobre-rigoberto-lopez-perez/.
Bautista Lara, Francisco Javier. "Cuatro variaciones de un verso de Darío." *El Nuevo Diario*, March 20, 2015.
Bautista Lara, Francisco Javier. "El legado inicial de Zacarías Guerra." *El Nuevo Diario*, July 17, 2013.

Bautista Lara, Francisco Javier. "El testamento de Zacarías un siglo después." *El Nuevo Diario*, May 5, 2014.
Bautista Lara, Francisco Javier. *Manantial*. 2nd ed. Managua: PAVSA, 2015.
Becker, Mark. "Race, Gender, and Protest in Ecuador." In *Work, Protest and Identity in Twentieth Century Latin America*, edited by Vincent C. Peloso, 125–42. Wilmington, Del.: Scholarly Resources, 2003.
Beer, Andreas. "Martial Men in Virgin Lands? Nineteenth-Century Filibustering, Nation-Building, and Competing Forms of Masculinity in the United States and Nicaragua." In *Masculinities and the Nation in the Modern World: Between Hegemony and Marginalization*, edited by Pablo Dominguez Andersen and Simon Wendt, 113–28. London: Palgrave Macmillan, 2015.
Beer, Andreas. *A Transnational Analysis of Representations of the US Filibusters in Nicaragua, 1855–1857*. New York: Palgrave Macmillan, 2016.
Ben, Pablo. "Male Sexuality, the Popular Classes, and the State: Buenos Aires, 1880–1955." PhD diss., University of Chicago, 2009.
Bendaña, Alejandro. *Buenas al pleito: Mujeres en la rebelión de Sandino*. Managua: Anamá Editores, 2019.
Binyon, Kristin Danell. "American Imperialism? The United States Interventions in Nicaragua, 1909–1933." Master's thesis, Texas Woman's University, 2013.
Blandón, Erick. *Barroco descalzo: Colonialidad, sexualidad, género y raza en la construcción de la hegemonía cultural en Nicaragua*. Managua: URACCAN, 2003.
Bliss, Katherine Elaine. "Theater of Operations: Reform Politics and the Battle for Prostitutes' Redemption at Revolutionary Mexico City's Syphilis Hospital." In *The Women's Revolution in Mexico, 1910–1953*, edited by Stephanie Mitchell and Patience A. Schell, 125–40. Lanham, Md.: Rowman and Littlefield, 2007.
"Bluefields, cuna de las primeras glorias del deporte rey." *La Costeñísima*, January 31, 2017.
Bolaños, Pío. "Memorias de Pío Bolaños." *Revista Conservadora*, no. 69 (1966).
Bolaños Garay, Miguel. *Los Días de la Tortuga*. Managua: Anamá Ediciones, 1996.
Bolaños Geyer, Alejandro. *William Walker, el predestinado*. St. Charles, Mo.: Self-published, 1995.
Bolaños Geyer, Enrique. "Discurso en homenaje al Doctor Eduardo Montealegre Callejas." Masaya, December 17, 1976. http://sajurin.enriquebolanos.org/vega/docs/Homenaje%20de%20Masaya%20al%20Dr.E.%20Montealegre%20C.%20-%2017%20Dic%2076.pdf.
Borland, Katherine. *Unmasking Class, Gender, and Sexuality in Nicaraguan Festival*. Tucson: University of Arizona Press, 2006.
Brenes Flores, María Haydee. "¿Rubén Darío Homosexual?" *El Nuevo Diario*, July 6, 2002.
Brenes, María Haydée. "La lesbiana más pública de Nicaragua." DiarioMetro.Com.ni, November 17, 2014. https://issuu.com/metro_nicaragua/docs/20141117_ni_metronicaragua.
Briones Torres, Ignacio. "Alejandro Dávila Bolaños." *El Nuevo Diario*, November 26, 1999.

Briones, Ignacio. "Notas para una biografía." *Bolsa de noticias*, September 26, 2002.
Bronski, Michael. *A Queer History of the United States*. Boston: Beacon Press, 2011.
Bullough, Vern. *Science in the Bedroom: A History of Sex Research*. New York: Basic Books, 1994.
Burkhart, Louise. *The Slippery Earth: Nahua-Christian Moral Dialogue in Sixteenth-Century Mexico*. Tucson: The University of Arizona Press, 1989.
Burns, Bradford. *Patriarch and Folk: The Emergence of Nicaragua, 1798–1858*. Cambridge, Mass.: Harvard University Press., 1991
Burton, Orville Vernon, and Georganne Burton. *The Free Flag of Cuba: The Lost Novel of Lucy Holcombe Pickens*. Baton Rouge: Louisiana State University Press, 2002.
"Busca, Buscando." *El Comercio*, July 24, 1904.
Cáceres Gómez, Rina. "Indígenas y africanos en las redes de la esclavitud en Centroamérica." In *Rutas de la esclavitud en África y América Latina*, edited by Rina Cáceres Gómez, 83–100. San José, C.R.: Editorial de la Universidad de Costa Rica, 2001.
Cajina Vega, Mario. "Masaya: Un departamento con sus alforjas al hombro." *Revista Conservadora*, no. 28 (1963).
Cajina, Jairo. "Conmemoran heroica acción del revolucionario Rigoberto López Pérez." September 21, 2009. Originally accessed at https://www.lavozdelsandinismo.com/nicaragua/2009-09-21/conmemoraron-heroica-accion-del-revolucionario-rigoberto-lopez-perez/. URL no longer works.
Calero Sequeira, Antonia. "Mujeres Trans de Jalapa Se Organizan." *La Boletina*, no. 98 (September 2015): 51.
Callejas, Linda M. "Donde estén mis hijos, ahí que me entierren: The Migration History of Aura Lila Callejas." Master's thesis, Florida International University, 1998.
Calvo Maturana, Antonio. *Impostores: Sombras en la España de las luces*. Madrid: Cátedra, 2015.
Camacho, Jorge. "El cirujano y la enferma: La representación de la mujer en la literatura modernista." *Revista canadiense de estudios hispánicos* 26, no. 1/2 (2001/2002): 351–60.
Camacho, Jorge. "Rubén Darío y las feministas de New York." *Magazine Modernista: Revista Digital del Modernismo*, April 26, 2012.
"Cámara de Diputados no conocerá de la acusación: Resolución ajustada a derecho." *Novedades*, June 20, 1969.
Campaña Somos Iguales a Vos. "Historias de éxito: Doctora René Villalobos." Facebook, November 16, 2016. https://www.facebook.com/SOMOSIGUALESAVOS/videos/1316743465002860/.
Campaña Somos Iguales a Vos. "Historia de Éxito de Mujeres Trans en Nicaragua (Mística Guerrero)." Facebook, December 21, 2015. https://www.facebook.com/SOMOSIGUALESAVOS/videos/1076903515653524/.
Cardenal, Ernesto. *In Cuba*. Translated by Donald Walsh. New York: New Directions Books, 1974.

Carrillo, Héctor. *The Night Is Young: Sexuality in Mexico in the Time of AIDS.* Chicago: University of Chicago Press, 2001.

Carrillo, Héctor. *Pathways of Desire: The Sexual Migration of Mexican Gay Men.* Chicago: University of Chicago Press, 2017.

"Carta de la Audiencia de Santo Domingo al Rey transmitiendo la información dada por el licenciado Francisco Castañeda. Ciudad de Santo Domingo, 28 de mayo de 1537." http://sajurin.enriquebolanos.org/vega/docs/AVB-CS-T5-DOCUMENTO%20331.pdf.

"Carta del licenciado Francisco de Castañeda, informando de la situación de la provincia, del estado de vejez de Pedrarias y de sus disensiones con éste. Pide, no se dé crédito a lo que llega a informar el veedor Alonso Pérez de Valer. León, 5 de octubre de 1529." Archivo General de Indias, Sevilla, Patronato, Legajo 26, Ramo 5.

Carranza. "Código de la Familia en vigor en 180 días." *El Nuevo Diario*, October 16, 2014.

Casanova Fuertes, Rafael. "Rigoberto: Más allá de la homofilia y la homofobia." *El Nuevo Diario*, October 22, 2013.

Casanova Fuertes, Rafael. "Rigoberto: Más allá de las preferencias." *El Nuevo Diario*, November 7, 2013.

Caudwell, Jayne, ed. *Sports, Sexualities and Queer Theory.* New York: Routledge, 2006.

Caulfield, Sueann, Sarah C. Chambers, and Lara Putnam, eds. *Honor, Status and Law in Modern Latin America.* Durham, N.C.: Duke University Press, 2006.

Cerda, Arlen y Dora Luz Romero. "Los Hijos de Walker." *La Prensa Magazine*, August 12, 2012.

"Certificación librada por el Secretario de Gobernación y Residencia de las demandas en residencia que opuso el Tesorero Pedro de los Ríos. León, 12 de febrero de 1536." http://sajurin.enriquebolanos.org/vega/docs/AVB-CS-T4-DOCUMENTO%20312%20-%20087.pdf.

Cerutti, Franco, ed. *Obras de Don Pío Bolaños.* Managua: Banco de América, 1976.

CEJIL (Coordinación del Centro por la Justicia y el Derecho Internacional). *Diagnóstico sobre los crímenes de odio motivados por la orientación sexual e identidad de género en Costa Rica, Honduras y Nicaragua.* San José, C.R.: CEJIL, 2013.

Chamorro, Carlos Fernando. "Diversidad Sexual en Nicaragua y el Código de la Familia." Programa "Esta Noche" en Canal 12, 2012. https://vimeo.com/42982082.

Chamorro, Emiliano. *El último caudillo*, 1983. http://sajurin.enriquebolanos.org/docs/El%20ultimo%20caudillo,%20autobiograf%C3%ADa%20Emiliano%20Chamorro%2003.pdf.

Chamorro, Pedro Joaquín. *Estirpe sangrienta: Los Somoza.* 2nd ed. Mexico: Editorial Diógenes, S.A, 1980 (1957).

Chauncey, George. *Gay New York: Gender, Urban Culture, and the Making of the Gay Male World, 1890–1940.* New York: Basic Books, 1994.

Cobo del Arco, Teresa. *Políticas de género durante el liberalismo: Nicaragua, 1893–1909.* Managua: UCA, 2000.

"Código Civil de la República de Nicaragua." 1867. http://digesto.asamblea.gob.ni/consultas/util/pdf.php?type=rdd&rdd=%2Bi4zB3KvgHs%3D.

"Código Civil de la República de Nicaragua." 1904. http://digesto.asamblea.gob.ni/consultas/util/pdf.php?type=rdd&rdd=vFJ34wip4oU%3D.

"Código de Comercio de la República de Nicaragua." 1914. https://www.registropublico.gob.ni/Files/PDF/MarcoLegal/Codigos/Codigo-Comercio.pdf.

"Código de Comercio de la República de Nicaragua." 1869. http://legislacion.asamblea.gob.ni/Normaweb.nsf/xpNorma.xsp?documentId=E94BBFB891EBD7F4062578540052AC78&action=openDocument.

"Código Penal de la República decretado por la legislatura de 27 de abril de 1837 [should read 1873]." http://sajurin.enriquebolanos.org/vega/docs/CodigosLegislacion%20-%20Jesus%20de%20la%20Rocha%20-%20511.pdf.

Collinson, Helen, comp. *Women and Revolution in Nicaragua*. New Jersey: Zed Books, 1990.

"Colocación de la primera piedra." *La Noticia*, July 25, 1906.

Colquhoun, Archibald Ross. *The Key of the Pacific: The Nicaraguan Canal*. New York: Longmans, Green and Co., 1898.

"Como una medida de moralidad . . ." *El Comercio*, January 10, 1906.

"Conservador, no más!" *La Noticia*, November 27, 1917.

"Con especial placer enviamos . . . saludo . . . a . . . María Gámez." *El Comercio*, 1906.

"Constancia de irregularidades en juicios por no aparecer pagadas las multas que se imponían en diferentes juicios y casos. León, el 9 de mayo [1536?]." http://sajurin.enriquebolanos.org/vega/docs/AVB-CS-T4-DOCUMENTO%20312%20-%20010.pdf.

"Constitución Política de Nicaragua." 1858. http://enriquebolanos.org/context.php?item=constitucion-1858-item.

"Constitución Política de Nicaragua 1893 'Libérrima' + Reforma." 1896. http://enriquebolanos.org/context.php?item=constitucion-1893-item.

"Constitución de la República Federal de Centroamérica." 1824. http://enriquebolanos.org/context.php?item=constitucion-1824-item.

"Constitución Política de Nicaragua 1848 Non Nata." http://enriquebolanos.org/context.php?item=constitucion-1848-item.

"Contestación de la Directora de la Escuela Normal de Señoritas." *El Comercio*, November 18, 1910.

"Contra la gente de mal vivir y las solteronas." *La Prensa*, May 4, 1926.

Córdoba, Matilde. "Mayoría de nicas contra el matrimonio homosexual." *El Nuevo Diario*, June 25, 2015.

Coronel Urtecho, José. *Oda a Rubén Darío: Poemas selectos*. Caracas: Biblioteca Ayacucho, 2005.

Coronel Urtecho, José y Ernesto Mejía Sánchez. "La mujer nicaragüense en los cronistas y viajeros." *Revista Conservadora*, no. 72 (September 1966).

Corrales, Javier, and Mario Pecheny, comps. *The Politics of Sexuality in Latin America: A Reader on Lesbian, Gay, Bisexual, and Transgender Rights*. Pittsburgh: University of Pittsburgh Press, 2010.
"Correcionales." *La Tribuna*, March 25, 1920.
Cortés, Eladio, and Mirta Barrea-Marlys, eds. *Encyclopedia of Latin American Theater*. Westport, Conn.: Greenwood Press, 2003.
Costello, Rory and Tito Rondón. "Eduardo Green." https://sabr.org/bioproj/person/8544593e.
Costello, Rory and Tito Rondón. "Stanley Cayasso." https://sabr.org/bioproj/person/cdceab6e.
Cowan, Benjamin. *Securing Sex: Morality and Repression in the Making of Cold War Brazil*. Chapel Hill: University of North Carolina Press, 2016.
"Crónica Policiaca . . . mujeres de vida alegre fueron arrestadas . . ." *El Comercio*, December 13, 1904.
Cruz, Arturo J. *Nicaragua's Conservative Republic, 1858–1893*. New York: Palgrave, 2002.
Cruz, Eduardo. "Adiós, viejo estadio nacional de Nicaragua." *La Prensa*, October 23, 2016.
Cruz, Eduardo. "Keith Taylor, los Dantos y el general." *La Prensa*, July 10, 2016.
Cruz, Eduardo. "La furia tras los disparos contra Anastasio Somoza García." *La Prensa*, September 28, 2019.
Cruz, Eduardo. "¿Quién es Pedro Reyes?" *La Prensa*, June 9, 2016.
Cruz Sequeira, Consuelo. "Mistrust and Violence in Nicaragua: Ideology and Politics." *Latin American Research Review* 30, no. 1 (1995): 212–25.
Cuadra Pasos, Carlos. *Obras II*. Managua: Fondo de Promoción Cultural de Banco de America, 1977.
Cuadra, Pablo Antonio. *El nicaragüense*. San José, C.R.: Libro Libre, 1987.
"¿Cuánto se acepta diversidad sexual en Nicaragua?" *El Nuevo Diario*, March 21, 2010.
Cuarezma, Lola. "El feminismo liberal." *La Noticia*, no. 221, July 19, 1916.
Darío, Rubén. *Todo al Vuelo*. Madrid: Renacimiento, 1912.
Davis, Richard Harding. *Real Soldiers of Fortune*. New York: Charles Scribner's Sons, 1911.
De Bry, Theodore. "Valboa throws some Indians, who had committed the terrible sin of sodomy, to the dogs to be torn apart." 1594. Copper engraving. University of Houston Libraries Special Collection, Rare Books and Maps Collection.
de Cordova, Juan. *Vocabulario en Lengua Zapoteca*. Mexico, 1578.
"Declaración de Benito de Prado." http://sajurin.enriquebolanos.org/vega/docs/AVB-CS-T4-DOCUMENTO%20312%20-%20017.pdf.
"Declaración del escribano Diego Sánchez." http://sajurin.enriquebolanos.org/vega/docs/AVB-CS-T4-DOCUMENTO%20312%20-%20014.pdf.
"Decreto: Se reglamenta la Ley de Profilaxis en la República 1918." http://sajurin.enriquebolanos.org/vega/docs/CLAD%20-%201917-1919%20-%20207.pdf.
"Decreto de 1ero de marzo de 1852 creando los Gobernadores de policía." http://sajurin.enriquebolanos.org/vega/docs/CLAD%20-%201851-53%20-%20215.pdf.

"Decreto de 20 de febrero, aclarando la ley de 20 de febrero de 1875, sobre mayoría de edad." 1875. http://sajurin.enriquebolanos.org/vega/docs/CLAD%20-%20CR%20-%201881-82%20-%20020.pdf.

"Decreto de 29 de marzo reformando varios artículos del código penal." 1865. http://sajurin.enriquebolanos.org/vega/docs/CLAD%20-%20CR%20-%201865%20-%2052.pdf.

"Decreto ejecutivo de 28 de abril de 1852, estableciendo Jueces de policía en el departamento Meridional y en los distritos de Granada y San Fernando." http://sajurin.enriquebolanos.org/vega/docs/CodigosLegislacion%20-%20Jesus%20de%20la%20Rocha%20-%20316.pdf.

"Decreto estableciendo la pena de tres años de presidio para los que cometan los delitos de bestialidad o sodomía. 27 de enero de 1826." http://sajurin.enriquebolanos.org/vega/docs/CL-JDR-1825-1840-019.pdf.

"Decreto indultando a Simón Corea. 1ero de marzo de 1882." http://sajurin.enriquebolanos.org/docs/CLAD%20-%20CR%20-%201881-82%20-%20075.pdf.

"Decreto legislativo de 7 de julio de 1851, declarando por delitos el rapto y el incesto." http://sajurin.enriquebolanos.org/vega/docs/CodigosLegislacion%20-%20Jesus%20de%20la%20Rocha%20-%20514.pdf.

Deer, Carmen Diana, and Magdalena de León. "Liberalism and Married Women's Property Rights in 19th Century Latin America." *Hispanic American Historical Review* 85, no. 4 (2005): 627–78.

De la Dehesa, Rafael. *Queering the Public Sphere in Mexico and Brazil*. Durham, N.C.: Duke University Press, 2010.

del Cid, Amalia. "Deja vu: Así eran las turbas sandinistas en los años ochenta y noventa." *La Prensa*, June 29, 2019.

del Cid, Amalia. "Las vidas de la Caimana." *La Prensa Magazine*, February 12, 2018.

del Cid, Amalia. "Salvadora Debayle: La matrona de los Somoza." *La Prensa Magazine*, December 13, 2015.

D'Emilio, John. "Capitalism and Gay Identity." In *Culture, Society and Sexuality: A Reader*, compiled by Richard Parker and Peter Aggleton, 250–58. New York: Routledge, 2007.

D'Emilio, John, and Estelle B. Freedman. *Intimate Matters: A History of Sexuality in America*. 3rd ed. Chicago: University of Chicago Press, 2012.

"Deportes." *Nicaragua informativa*, no. 118, January 22, 1924.

"Derechos de la Iglesia Católica." *La Prensa*, January 13, 1939.

"Desagradable, antifemenino, muy repulsivo." *La Prensa*, April 5, 1971.

Díaz, Mónica. *Indigenous Writings from the Convent: Negotiating Ethnic Autonomy in Colonial Mexico*. Tucson: University of Arizona Press, 2013.

Dirección General del Digesto Jurídico Nicaragüense. Antecedentes históricos de la codificación del derecho civil de la república de Nicaragua. 2016. http://digesto.asamblea.gob.ni/wp-content/uploads/2016/02/historia-codigo-civil.pdf.

"Disfraces nocturnos." *El Comercio*, November 25, 1904.

"Disfrazada de hombre." *El Comercio*, November 28, 1919.
"Disfrazado de mujer." *El Comercio*, November 11, 1919.
"Distinguidas damas de Granada visitan al Presidente y le piden que no siga adelante la enseñanza sexual." *La Prensa*, December 18, 1934.
d'Olwer, Luis Nicolau. *Cronistas de las culturas precolombinas*. 1963. Mexico City: Fondo de cultura económica, 2010.
"Don José Benito Ramírez, campeón de golf y dueño de Copa White Horse." *El eco de Managua*, no. 16, December 9, 1934.
"Don Zacarías Guerra en Managua." *El Comercio*, May 7, 1914.
"Doña María Gámez de Mercury . . . hoy se embarcará . . . con destino a los Estados Unidos . . ." *El Comercio*, December 8, 1903.
Dore, Elizabeth. *Myths of Modernity: Peonage and Patriarchy in Nicaragua*. Durham, N.C.: Duke University Press, 2006.
Dore, Elizabeth. "Property, Households, and the Public Regulation of Domestic Life: Diriomo, Nicaragua, 1840–1900." In *Hidden Histories of Gender and the State in Latin America*, edited by Elizabeth Dore and Maxine Molyneaux, 147–71. Durham, N.C.: Duke University Press, 2000.
Dore, Elizabeth. "Property, Households, and Public Regulation of Domestic Life: Diriomo, Nicaragua, 1840–1900." *Journal of Latin American Studies* 29, no. 3 (October 1997): 591–611.
Dirección General del Digesto Jurídico Nicaragüense. *Antecedentes históricos de la codificación del derecho civil de la república de Nicaragua*. 2016. http://digesto.asamblea.gob.ni/wp-content/uploads/2016/02/historia-codigo-civil.pdf.
"Diversidad sexual pide acceso a empleo sin discriminación." Radio La Primerísima, June 16, 2017. diversidad-sexual-pide-acceso-a-empleo-sin-discriminación.
"Dr. J. Carlos Serrano." *El Comercio*, July 24, 1906.
Droscher, Barbara. "Travesía, Travestí, y Traducción: Posiciones In-Between en la Nueva Novela Historiográfica de América Central." *Revista de Estudios Sociales* 13 (2002): 81–89.
Drucker, Peter. "In the Tropics There Is No Sin: Sexuality and Gay-Lesbian Movements in the Third World." *New Left Review* 218 (1996): 75–101.
Duggan, Lisa. *The Twilight of Equality?: Neoliberalism, Cultural Politics, and the Attack on Democracy*. Boston, Mass.: Beacon Press, 2003.
Dussel, Enrique. "Europa, modernidad y eurocentrismo." In *La colonialidad del saber: eurocentrismo y ciencias sociales. Perspectivas Latinoamericanas*, edited by E. Lander, 41–53. Buenos Aires: CLACSO, 2005.
"Educación física es necesaria para la mujer." *La Prensa*, April 22, 1926.
"El Centroamericano escapó de desaparecer del escenario periodístico cuando se perpetró atentado a Presidente Somoza." *El Centroamericano*, September 29, 1971. Reprinted in "Nicaragua desde el mirador de nuestra historia." *Eduardo Pérez Valle* (blog), October 25, 2014. https://eduardoperezvalle.blogspot.com/2014/10/el-centroamericanoescapo-de-desaparecer.html.

"El hombre-mujer en Managua." *La Noticia*, May 15, 1917.

"El Loco Desiderio de la Quadra." *Revista Conservadora del Pensamiento Centroamericano* 26, no. 129 (1971): 32–41.

"El Mañana. Asuntos sociales. A partir del año de 1882 . . . en que se hicieron venir al país profesoras norteamericanas . . ." *El Comercio*, August 1, 1905.

"Elogios de 'Los Angeles Examiner' a nuestra máxima deportista, la reina Sary Miranda Witford." *La Nueva Prensa*, no. 5024, February 8, 1946.

Elsey, Brenda, and Joshua Nadel. *Futbolera: A History of Women and Sports in Latin America*. Austin: University of Texas Press, 2019.

"Rubén Darío: El varón incorrecto que algunos nicaragüenses no quieren ver." *El Nuevo Diario*, January 7, 2013.

"En actos de sodomía." *El 93*, no. 19, August 30, 1916.

"En la policía." *El Comercio*, March 14, 1906.

England, Frances. "Latin Poet Suggests an International Thought Exchange to Help Spanish Women Free Themselves." *New York Tribune*, February 8, 1915.

Ennis, Dawn. "Study: 55% of Americans O.K. with Gay, Lesbian, and Trans Coworkers." NewNowNext, June 6, 2018. http://www.newnownext.com/study-55-of-americans-ok-with-gay-lesbian-and-trans-coworkers/06/2018/.

"Entusiasmo por la serie de Béisbol Femenil que se inaugura el domingo en el Estadio." *La Prensa*, 1949.

"Era hombre . . ." *El Comercio*, September 20, 1903.

"Esos trajes impúdicos." *La Prensa*, November 1940.

Espinoza, Lesbia. "Mujeres empresarias con cupos rebasados." *El Nuevo Diario*, April 19, 2001.

"Estadística Rivas . . . 397 nacimientos . . ." *El Comercio*, July 24, 1906.

"Estando en la puerta de su casa Don Zacarías Guerra . . ." *El Comercio*, August 31, 1904.

"Exposición que las mujeres of Bluefields lanzan ante el mundo con motivo de la intervención americana en su patria. De Diario de Panamá, 17 de febrero de 1927." *La Tribuna*, February 2, 1929.

Faderman, Lillian. *Odd Girls and Twilight Lovers: A History of Lesbian Life in Twentieth-Century America*. New York: Penguin, 1991.

Fêo Rodrigues, Isabel P. B. "Islands of Sexuality: Theories and Histories of Creolization in Cape Verde." *The International Journal of African Historical Studies*, Special Issue: Colonial Encounters between Africa and Portugal, 36, no. 1 (2003): 83–103.

Ferguson, Ann. "Lesbianism, Feminism, and Empowerment in Nicaragua." *Socialist Review* 21, no. 3/4 (1991): 75–97.

Fernández Vílches, Manuel. "Lo femenino indio en la cultura nicaragüense, crítica de *El nicaragüense* de Pablo Antonio Cuadra." *Revista de Temas Nicaragüense*, no. 64 (2013): 18–28.

Ferrero Blanco, María Dolores. *La Nicaragua de los Somoza 1936–1979*. Huelva, Esp.: Universidad de Huelva, 2010.

Few, Martha. "'That Monster of Nature': Gender, Sexuality, and the Medicalization of a 'Hermaphrodite' in Late Colonial Guatemala." *Ethnohistory* 54, no. 1 (2007): 159–76.

Field, Les W. *The Grimace of Macho Ratón. Artisans, Identity, and Nation in Late-Twentieth-Century Western Nicaragua.* Durham, N.C.: Duke University Press, 1999.

"Fillibusterism: Walker Still Confident—And Twenty Thousand People to Hear Him: Speech of Gen. William Walker, Delivered at New Orleans, May 30." *New York Daily Times*, June 8, 1857.

Finzer, Erin. "Among Sandino's Girlfriends: Carmen Sobalvarro and the Gendered Poetics of a Nationalist Romance." *Latin American Research Review* 47, no. 1 (2012).

Finzer, Erin. "Poetisa Chic: Fashioning the Modern Female Poet in Central America, 1929–1944." PhD diss., University of Kansas, 2008.

Fletes, Pablo. "Plath optimista." *La Prensa*, September 16, 2002.

Francis, Hilary. "¡Que se rinda tu madre!: Leonel Rugama and Nicaragua's Changing Politics of Memory." *Journal of Latin American Cultural Studies* 21, no. 2 (2012): 235–52.

Freedman, Estelle. "Doing Time in Lesbian History." Presentation at San Diego State University, September 20, 2017.

Freeman, James. "From the Little Tree, Half a Block Toward the Lake: Popular Geography and Symbolic Discontent in Post-Sandinista Managua." *Antipode* 42, no. 2 (2010).

Fregoso, Rosalinda. "'Fantasy Heritage': Tracking Latina Bloodlines." In *A Companion to Latina/o Studies*, edited by Juan Flores and Renato Rosaldo, 452–60. Oxford: Wiley Blackwell, 2007.

Gámez, José Dolores. *Historia de Nicaragua: Desde los tiempos prehistóricos hasta 1860, en sus relaciones con España, México, y Centroamérica.* Managua: Tipografía del País, 1889.

García, Gregorio. *Origen de los Indios de el Nuevo Mundo e Indias Occidentales.* Valencia, Esp.: Casa de Pedro Patricio Mey, 1607.

García, Melissa. "Las Mujeres Transgéneras: Creando Espacios y una identidad Colectiva para combatir la discriminación y la Violencia." Colección ISP. Trabajo Escrito 1041. 2011.

García Castillo, Juan. "El suicidio de un hijo del General José Santos Zelaya." *El Centroamericano*, November 23, 1967.

García Peláez, Francisco de Paula. *Memorias para la historia del antiguo reyno de Guatemala.* Vol. 1. Guatemala: Establecimiento tipográfico de L. Luna, 1851.

Garza Carvajal, Federico. *Butterflies Will Burn: Prosecuting Sodomites in Early Modern Spain and Mexico.* Austin: University of Texas Press, 2003.

Gerson, Noel B. *Sad Swashbuckler: The Life of William Walker.* Nashville, Tenn.: Thomas Nelson, 1976.

Gertsch Romero, Erika. "50 años de un polémico colegio." *La Prensa*, June 27, 2010.

Gobat, Michel. *Confronting the American Dream: Nicaragua Under U.S. Imperial Rule.* Durham, N.C.: Duke University Press, 2005.

Gobat, Michel. *Empire by Invitation: William Walker and Manifest Destiny in Central America.* Cambridge, Mass.: Harvard University Press, 2018.

Goett, Jennifer. *Black Autonomy, Race, Gender, and Afro-Nicaraguan Activism.* Redwood City, Calif.: Stanford University Press, 2017.

Gómez Arévalo, Amaral Palevi. "Del *cuiloni* al homosexual: Sexualidades masculinas disidentes en El Salvador entre 1932–1992." *Cultura, Lenguage y Representacion: Revista de Estudios Culturales de la Universidat Jaume* 1, no. 15 (2016): 119–37.

Gómez, Juan Pablo. *Autoridad/Cuerpo/Nación. Batallas culturales en Nicaragua (1930–1943).* Managua: IHNCA, 2015.

Gonzalez, Chris. "Frida Kahlo and Appropriation of Indigenous Cultures." OPB, March 7, 2022. https://www.opb.org/article/2022/02/28/frida-kahlo-and-cultural-appropriation/.

González, Deena. *Refusing the Favor: The Spanish-Mexican Women of Santa Fe, 1820–1880.* Oxford: Oxford University Press, 1999.

González, Marta Leonor. "Miradas de Héctor Avellán." *La Prensa*, June 25, 2011.

González-Rivera, Victoria. "The Alligator Woman's Tale: Remembering Nicaragua's 'First Self-Declared Lesbian.'" *Journal of Lesbian Studies* 18, no. 1 (2014): 75–87.

González-Rivera, Victoria. *Before the Revolution: Women's Rights and Right-Wing Politics in Nicaragua, 1821–1979.* University Park: Pennsylvania State University Press, 2011.

González[-Rivera], Victoria. "'El Diablo se la llevó': Política, sexualidad femenina y trabajo en Nicaragua, 1855–1979." In *Un siglo de luchas femeninas en América Latina*, edited by Eugenia Rodríguez Sáenz, 53–70. San José, C.R.: Editorial de la Universidad de Costa Rica, 2002.

González[-Rivera], Victoria. "Somocista Women, Right-Wing Politics and Feminism in Nicaragua, 1936–1979." In *Radical Women in Latin America: Left and Right*, edited by Victoria González[-Rivera] and Karen Kampwirth, 41–78. University Park: Penn State University Press, 2001.

González-Rivera, Victoria. "Writing Western Nicaragua's LGBTQIA+ History: *Tiangues*, Indigeneity, and Survivance." In *Feminisms in Movement: Theories and Practices from the Americas*, edited by Livia De Souza Lima, Edith Otero Quezada, and Julia Roth, 215–26. Bielefield, Germany:Transcript, 2024.

Gordon, Dan. "Nicaragua: In Search of Diamonds." In *Baseball Beyond Our Borders: An International Pastime*, edited by George Gmelch and Daniel A. Nathan, 85–109. Lincoln: University of Nebraska Press, 2017.

Gordon, Edmund T. *Disparate Diaspora: Identity and Politics in an African Nicaraguan Community.* Austin: University of Texas Press, 1998.

Gould, Jeffrey L. *To Die in This Way: Nicaraguan Indians and the Myth of Mestizaje, 1880–1965.* Durham, N.C.: Duke University Press, 1998.

"Gran Campaña Policial para sanear barrios orientales." *Novedades*, July 3, 1969.

Greenberg, Amy S. "A Gray-Eyed Man: Character, Appearance, and Filibustering." *Journal of the Early Republic* 20, no. 4 (Winter 2000): 673–99.
Greenberg, Amy S. *Manifest Manhood and the Antebellum American Empire*. Cambridge: Cambridge University Press, 2005.
Grupo Pancasán. "Apuntes del Tío Sam."
Grupo Safo. "Quienes Somos." 2005. http://gruposafo.doblementemujer.org/inicio/acerca-de/.
Gudmundson, Lowell, and Héctor Lindo-Fuentes. *Central America, 1821–1871: Liberalism Before Liberal Reform*. Tuscaloosa: University of Alabama Press, 1995.
Gudmundson, Lowell, and Justin Wolfe. *Blacks and Blackness in Central America: Between Race and Place*. Durham, N.C.: Duke University Press, 2010.
Guerra, Lillian. "Gender Policing, Homosexuality, and the New Patriarchy of the Cuban Revolution, 1965–70." *Social History* 35, no. 3 (2010): 268–89.
Guevara, Alberto. *Performance, Theater, and Society in Contemporary Nicaragua: Spectacles of Gender, Sexuality and Marginality*. Amherst, N.Y.: Cambria Press, 2014.
Guevara, Alejandro. "Rigoberto López Pérez, 5 disparos que cambiaron a Nicaragua." Radio la Primerísima, September 21, 2014.
Guido Martínez, Clemente. *Valdivieso: El obispo que murió por los chorotegas*. Managua: Alcaldía de Managua, 2010.
Gutiérrez, Pedro Rafael. "William Walker y Ricarda Cerda, las huellas de un romance." *La Prensa*, February 13, 1977.
Hale, Charles R. *Resistance and Contradiction: Miskitu Indians and the Nicaraguan State, 1894–1987*. Redwood City, Calif.: Stanford University Press, 1994.
Hall, M. Ann. *The Girl and the Game: A History of Women's Sport in Canada*. 2nd ed. Toronto: University of Toronto Press, 2016.
Hassan, Anuar. *Grandes crímenes del siglo XX en Nicaragua*. Managua: n.p., 2001.
Hassan, Anuar, and Emiliano Chamorro. "Andar por caminos torcidos no paga." *La Prensa*, August 26, 2000.
Halftermeyer, Gratus. *Historia de Managua: Data desde el siglo XVIII hasta hoy*. Managua: Taller de la Imprenta Nacional, 1971.
Halftermeyer, Gratus. *Managua a través de la historia, 1846–1946*, León, Nic.: Editorial Hospicio San Juan de Dios, n.d.
Halvorson, Chad Allen. *Padre Agustín Vijil and William Walker: Nicaragua, Filibustering, and the National War*. Master's thesis, North Dakota State University, 2014.
Harrison, Brady. *Agent of Empire: William Walker and the Imperial Self in American Literature*. Athens: University of Georgia Press, 2004.
"Hasta ayer trabajaron las barrenderas de las calles en Managua." *La Prensa*, July 11, 1931.
"Hasta el presente no ha tenido efecto la disposición de la policía . . ." *El Comercio*, March 15, 1906.
"Hay que alejarlas." *El Diario Nicaragüense*, November 18, 1910.

Hayes, Anne M. *Female Prostitution in Costa Rica: Historical Perspectives, 1880–1930.* New York: Routledge, 2006.

Healy, Paul F. *Archeology of the Rivas Region: Nicaragua.* Waterloo, Ont.: Wilfrid Laurier University Press, 1980.

Helguero, Lorenzo. "Transgresión y Modernidad: La Prosa de Rubén Darío." PhD diss., Georgetown University, 2009.

Hernández, Génesis. "100 Años del Zacarías Guerra." *La Prensa*, November 11, 2014.

Hernández Bustamante, Luis. "Aquella Managua de los años 40." *Managua en mis recuerdos*, 2012.

Hilton, Ronald. *Hispanic American Report.* Vol. 15, part 1. Stanford, Calif: Stanford University, 1962.

Hirth, Kenneth G. *The Aztec Economic World: Merchants and Markets in Ancient Mesoamerica.* Cambridge: Cambridge University Press, 2016.

"Historia de la Caimana, punto de referencia en Managua." VOS TV, 2017.

Hogar Zacarías Guerra. Facebook page. https://www.facebook.com/hogarzacariasguerraoficial/.

Hooker, Juliet. "'Beloved Enemies': Race and Official Mestizo Nationalism in Nicaragua." *Latin American Research Review* 40, no. 3 (October 2005): 14–39.

Hooker, Juliet. "Race and the Space of Citizenship: The Mosquito Coast and the Place of Blackness and Indigeneity in Nicaragua." In *Blacks and Blackness in Central America: Between Race and Place*, edited by Lowell Gudmundson and Justin Wolfe, 246–77. Durham, N.C.: Duke University Press, 2010.

Horswell, Michael J. *Decolonizing the Sodomite: Queer Tropes of Sexuality in Colonial Andean Culture.* Austin: University of Texas Press, 2005.

Howe, Cymene. *Intimate Activism: The Struggle for Sexual Rights in Postrevolutionary Nicaragua.* Durham, N.C.: Duke University Press, 2013.

Howe, Cymene. "Undressing the Universal Queer Subject: Nicaraguan Activism and Transnational Identity." *City and Society* (2002): 237–79.

Huete Maltés, Ulises. "Smith & Wesson No 74605." *La Prensa*, September 21, 2013.

"The Huns: Original title—'La Regina dei Taitari.'" https://www.imdb.com/title/tt0056400/.

Incer Barquero, Jaime. *Descubrimiento, conquista y exploraciones de Nicaragua.* Crónicas de fuentes originales seleccionadas y comentadas por Jaime Incer Barquero. Serie Cronistas, no. 6. Managua: Colección Cultural de Centro América, 2002.

Incer Barquero, Jaime. *Nicaragua: Viaje, rutas y encuentros, 1502–1838.* San José, C.R.: Libro Libre, 1989.

"Increíble cantidad de gente en extraño funeral." *La Prensa*, August 20, 1971.

"Información iniciada en León contra Hernando Bachicao, denunciado de blasfemia, por cuyo delito fue condenado el 12 de marzo de 1530." http://sajurin.enriquebolanos.org/vega/docs/AVB-CS-T4-DOCUMENTO%20312%20-%20116.pdf.

"Información seguida en León ante el alcalde de aquella ciudad, Alvaro de Peñalver, a solicitud del alcalde mayor Francisco de Castañeda, con el objeto de establecer los motivos de su enemistad con el gobernador Pedrarias Dávila, el tesorero Diego de la Tobilla y el veedor Alonso Pérez de Valer. Se inició el 17 de septiembre de 1529." Archivo General de Indias, Sevilla, Justicia, Legajo 1.030, Ramo 2.

INN. "Agapito Díaz y la melcocha a peso." YouTube, 2016. https://www.youtube.com/watch?v=6zmjEhGjv1A.

Irwin, Robert McKee. *Mexican Masculinities*. Minneapolis: University of Minnesota Press, 2003.

Irwin, Robert McKee, Edward J. McCaughan, and Michelle Rocío Nasser, eds. *The Famous 41: Sexuality and Social Control in Mexico, 1901*. New York: Palgrave Macmillan, 2003.

"Isidro J. Olivares vende bicicletas." *El Comercio*, June 11, 1906.

Islas, Alejandra, dir. *Muxes: Auténticas, intrépidas y buscadoras de peligro*. Mexico City: Instituto Mexicano de Cinematografía, 2005.

Jarquín, Wendy. "¿Quién fue Rigoberto López Pérez? Habla el Comandante Carlos Fonseca." *Diario Barricada*, September 21, 2018.

"José Santos Zelaya o la astucia cruel del gallo de pelea." *El Nuevo Diario*, November 6, 2009.

"José Zacarías Guerra." *La Prensa*, July 20, 2014.

"Juan Miguel Robleto estuvo detenido por impertenencias con el mesonero, hombre muy delicado, como todos los de su oficio." *El Comercio*, February 27, 1906.

"Juana de Arco." *El Diario Nicaragüense*, November 24, 1910.

J. Z. "La mujer y la política." *El Comercio*, September 2, 1905.

Kampwirth, Karen. *LGBTQ Politics in Nicaragua: Revolution, Dictatorship and Social Movements*. Tucson: University of Arizona Press, 2022.

Kate, Robert W., Eugene Haas, Daniel J. Amaral, Robert A. Olson, Reyes Ramos, and Richard Olson. "Human Impact of the Managua Earthquake." *Science* 182, no. 7 (1973): 984.

Kellner, Douglas. "Media Spectacle and the Triumph of the Spectacle." *Razón y Palabra*, no. 39 (April–May 2004).

Kennedy, Elizabeth Lapovsky, and Madeline D. Davis. *Boots of Leather, Slippers of Gold: The History of a Lesbian Community*. New York: Routledge, 1993.

Kinloch Tijerino, Frances. *Identidad y Cultura Política, 1821–1858*. Managua: Banco Central de Nicaragua, 1999.

Kinzer, Stephen. *Overthrow: America's Century of Regime Change—From Hawaii to Iraq*. New York: Times Books, 2007.

Kirk, Stephanie. "Illicit Passions: 'Mala Amistad' in the Eighteenth Century Mexican Convent." *Latin American Literary Review* 33, no. 66 (July–December 2005): 5–30.

Kirk, Stephanie. *Sor Juana Inés de la Cruz and the Gender Politics of Knowledge in Colonial Mexico*. New York: Routledge, 2016.

Klor de Alva, Jorge. "Colonizing Souls: The Failure of the Indian Inquisition and the Rise of Penitential Discipline." In *Cultural Encounters: The Impact of the Inquisition in Spain and the New World*, edited by Mary Elizabeth Perry and Anne J. Cruz, 3–22. Berkeley: University of California Press, 1991.

Krane Vikki. "We Can Be Athletic and Feminine, But Do We Want To? Challenging Hegemonic Femininity in Women's Sport." *Quest* 53, no. 1 (2001): 115–33.

Kühl Arauz, Eddy. *Nicaragua: Historia de inmigrantes*. Managua: Hispamer, 2007.

"La Caimana: 28 casas a sus hijos; la fábrica a su amiga Hilda Scott." *La Prensa*, August 19, 1971.

"'La Caimana' un popular personaje de Campo Bruce." *La Prensa*, June 26, 2006.

La Gaceta. Diario Oficial. No. 67 (March 19, 1968), 909–10.

La Gaceta. Diario Oficial. No. 70 (March 22, 1968), 937–938.

La Gaceta. Diario Oficial. No. 242 (October 25, 1967).

"La esclavitud colonial en la Nicaragua del pacífico." *El Nuevo Diario*, May 29, 2010.

"La novedad de antier." *El Comercio*, June 11, 1906.

"La policía de esta capital está persiguiendo activamente la vagancia, la ebriedad, y la prostitución . . ." *El Comercio*, August 30, 1905.

"La sesión de ayer de la Asamblea Nacional Constituyente." *La Prensa*, January 13, 1939.

"Lady Baldwin." Findagrave.com. https://www.findagrave.com/memorial/21493136/charles-b-baldwin.

Lancaster, Roger. "Guto's Performace: Notes on the Transvestism of Everyday Life." In *Sex and Sexuality in Latin America*, edited by Daniel Balderston and Donna J. Guy, 26. New York: New York University Press, 1997.

Lancaster, Roger. *Life Is Hard: Machismo, Danger, and the Intimacy of Power in Nicaragua*. Berkeley: University of California Press, 1994.

Lancaster, Roger. "Sexual Positions: Caveats and Second Thoughts on 'Categories.'" *The Americas* 54, no. 1 (1997): 1–16.

Lee, David Johnson. "The Ends of Modernization: Development, Ideology, and Catastrophe in Nicaragua after the Alliance for Progress." PhD diss., Temple University Press, 2015.

Lee, Joongsoo. *The Allure of Nezahualcoyotl: Prehispanic History, Religion, and Nahua Poetics*. Albuquerque: University of New Mexico Press, 2008.

"Legislación nicaragüense sobre la prostitución." 1955.

León Báez, Bosco. "Ni el terremoto cerró los prostíbulos de Managua." *La Calle Semanario*. October 24, 2017. Originally viewed at http://www.lacalleonline.com/2017/10/24/ni-el-terremoto-cerro-los-prostibulos-de-managua/. This website is no longer available.

León Báez, Bosco. "Prostíbulos de los 70: De la Conga Roja al Baby Doll." October 17, 2017. Originally viewed at http://www.lacalleonline.com/2017/10/17/prostibulos-de-los-70-de-la-conga-roja-al-baby-doll/. Viewed on January 24, 2023, on a public Facebook post from June 6, 2021, on the Facebook page called Nicaragua y su historia.

León-Portilla, Miguel. *Religión de los Nicaraos: Análisis y comparación de tradiciones culturales nahuas*. Mexico City: Universidad Nacional Autónoma de México, Instituto de Investigaciones Históricas, 1972.

"Ley de Código Penal." 1974. http://legislacion.asamblea.gob.ni/Normaweb.nsf/164aa15ba012e567062568a2005b564b/643cc814a8e2e2c4062570a600648d01.

"Ley de extranjería." 1894. http://sajurin.enriquebolanos.org/docs/CLR%20-%201893-1895%20-%2016.pdf.

"Ley de higiene y saneamiento de los mercados de Managua." June 19, 1911. http://sajurin.enriquebolanos.org/docs/CLAD%20-%201914%20-%2075.pdf.

"Ley reglamentaria del matrimonio." July 9, 1894. http://sajurin.enriquebolanos.org/docs/CLR%20-%201893-1895%20-%2009.pdf.

"Ley reglamentaria para los tribunales y juzgados de la República." http://sajurin.enriquebolanos.org/vega/docs/CodigosLegislacion%20-%20Jesus%20de%20la%20Rocha%20-%20444.pdf.

Lezcano y Ortega, José Antonio. *Corazón de Padre: Exhortaciones a las Hijas de María*. Managua: Tipografía Alemana de Carlos Heuberger, 1939.

Lezcano y Ortega, José Antonio. *Predicación pastoral en las dominicas de un año litúrgico*. Managua: Tipografía Alemana, 1939.

Link, Daniel. "Darío Queer." *Soy*, February 5, 2016.

Lira Rivera, Miguel. "Historia de Managua." *Nicasoft*, edition 390, 2014.

Lira Rivera, Miguel. "Historia de Managua: El Robo de la Caja Fuerte de la Ada Moncada." *Nicasoft*, edition 421, 2017.

Lockhart, James. *The Nahuas After the Conquest: A Social and Cultural History of the Indians of Central Mexico, Sixteenth Through Eighteenth Centuries*. Redwood City, Calif.: Stanford University Press, 1992.

Lockwood, Lee. *Castro's Cuba, Cuba's Fidel*. Boulder, Colo.: Westview Press, 1990.

López Miranda, Margarita. *Josefa Toledo de Aguerri: Una chontaleña en la educación nacional*. Juigalpa, Nic.: Asociación Ganadera de Chontales (ASOGACHO), 1988.

"Los gallos: Una vieja pasión de los nicaragüenses." *El Nuevo Diario*, August 16, 2012.

Loveman, Mara. *National Colors: Racial Classification and the State in Latin America*. New York: Oxford University Press, 2014.

Macy, Sue. *Wheels of Change: How Women Rode the Bicycle to Freedom (With a Few Flat Tires Along the Way)*. Washington, D.C.: National Geographic, 2011.

"Managua a merced de la furia." *Managua en mis recuerdos*, 2012. https://issuu.com/abdulsirker/docs/managua_en_mis_recuerdos.

Managua a traves de la historia, 1846–1946. Editorial Hospicio San Juan de Dios.

"Managua presencia la vela mas extraña." *La Prensa*, August 1?, 1971.

Mangipano, John. "William Walker and the Seeds of Progressive Imperialism: The War in Nicaragua and the Message of Regeneration, 1855–1860." PhD diss., University of Southern Mississippi, 2017.

Mántica, Carlos. *El habla nicaragüense y otros ensayos*. San José, C.R.: Libro Libre, 1989.

"María Ordeñana de conducta viciada . . ." *El Comercio*, December 31, 1905.

Marshall, Sydney. "Sandinistas and Prostitutas: Reeducation and Rehabilitation of Prostitutes in Revolutionary Nicaragua, 1980–1987." Master's thesis, Iowa State University, 2018.

Martínez, María Elena. "Archives, Bodies, and Imagination: The Case of Juana Aguilar and Queer Approaches to History, Sexuality, and Politics." *Radical History Review* 120 (2014): 159–82.

Martínez, María Elena. "Sex and the Colonial Archive: The Case of 'Mariano' Aguilera." *Hispanic American Historical Review* 96, no. 3 (2016): 421–43.

Martínez Peláez, Severo. *La patria del criollo: Ensayo de interpretación de la realidad colonial guatemalteca.* Guatemala: Editorial Universitaria, 1971.

Matamoro, Blas. "Parsifal y Ganimedes." *Página/12*, July 20, 2002.

Matus, Zoraida. Marriage certificate, 1930.

May, Robert E. *Manifest Destiny's Underworld: Filibustering in Antebellum America.* Chapel Hill: University of North Carolina Press, 2002.

May, Robert E. "Reconsidering Antebellum U.S. Women's History: Gender, Filibustering, and American's Quest for Empire." *American Quarterly* 57, no. 4 (December 2005): 1155–88.

Medina, Fabián. "Los descendientes de Zelaya." *La Prensa Magazine*, October 10, 2004.

Medina, Julia. "The Poet, the Journalist, and the Politician: Critical Intervention of Rubén Darío, Enrique Guzmán, and Augusto C. Sandino." PhD diss., U.C. Davis, 2005.

Mejía Lacayo, José. "Cleto Ordóñez y la Guerra Civil de 1824." *Revista de Temas Nicaragüense*, no. 43 (November 2011): 150–70.

Mejía Lacayo, José. "La conquista, 1522–1572." *Revista de Temas Nicaragüense*, no. 40 (August 2011): 96–130.

Mejía Sánchez, Ernesto. "Romances y corridos: Fuentes históricas para los romances y corridos nicaragüenses." *Revista Conservadora*, no. 74 (November 1966): 29–43.

Mejía Sánchez, Ernesto. *Romances y corridos nicaragüenses.* Managua: Banco de América, 1976.

Membreño, Cinthia. "Las 'cartas privadas' de Rubén Darío a Nervo." *Confidencial*, November 13, 2012.

Mendiola, Daniel. 2019. "The Founding and Fracturing of the Mosquito Confederation: Zambos, Tawiras, and New Archival Evidence, 1711–1791." *Hispanic American Historical Review* 99, no. 4 (November 2019): 619–47.

Mendoza, Juan M. *Historia de Diriamba (ciudad del departamento de Carazo).* Guatemala: Imprenta Electra, 1920.

Miller, Claire Cain. "The Search for the Best Estimate of the Transgender Population." *The New York Times*, June 8, 2015.

Miller, Michael B. "El burdel de las Pedrarias de Ricardo Pasos Marciaq." *El Nuevo Diario*, May 14, 1999.

"Ministerio de Instrucción Pública." 1910.

Mirandé, Alfredo. *Behind the Mask: Gender Hybridity in a Zapotec Community.* Tucson: University of Arizona Press, 2019.

"Mission Avenue Studio Offers 'Furniture with a Story.'" Press Release by Mission Avenue Studio in Woodworking Network.com, February 17, 2014.

"Mitómano considera la defensa a Real Espinales: Se basan en el historial clínico." *Novedades*, July 11, 1969.

Molina, Roderick A. "Amado Nervo: His Mysticism and Franciscan Influence." *The Americas* 6, no. 2 (1949): 175.

Molina Jiménez, Iván. "El extraño William Walker de Alejandro Bolaños Geyer." *Revista de Ciencias Sociales* 1–2, nos. 103–4 (2004): 165–67.
"Molieron a palos a un guardia." *La Tribuna*, February 9, 1929.
Moncada, José María. *Cosas de Centroamérica (Memorias de un testigo ocular de los sucesos)*. Madrid: Imprenta de Fortanet, 1908.
Moncada, José María. *El Gran Ideal*. Managua: Imprenta Nacional, 1929.
Moncada Fonseca, Manuel. "Las tribus que habitaban Nicaraguas según diversos autores." *Libre Pensamiento*, March 3, 2012.
Mondragón, J. D. "Rebelión de la mujer." *La Tribuna*, August 14, 1921.
Montero, Oscar. "Modernismo y 'degeneración': Los raros de Darío." *Revista iberoamericana* LXII, nos. 176–77 (1996): 821–34.
Montes, Fruto. 1995. "Doña Josefa Toledo: Una dama ejemplar." *La Prensa*, June 19, 1995.
Mora Chinchilla, Carolina. "El nacimiento del Registro Civil como parte de un proyecto estatal (1888) y su aporte a la vida política democrática costarricense." *Revista Derecho Electoral*, no. 16 (July–December 2013).
Morales Navarrete, Orlando. "Huevos al estilo Rigoberto." November 20, 2013. porlaautonomia.wordpress.com.
Morris, Courtney Desiree. *To Defend This Sunrise: Black Women's Activism and the Authoritarian Turn in Nicaragua*. New Brunswick, N.J.: Rutgers University Press, 2023.
Morris, Courtney Desiree. "To Defend This Sunrise: Race, Place, and Creole Women's Political Subjectivity on the Caribbean Coast of Nicaragua." PhD diss., University of Texas at Austin, 2012.
"Música, Drogas y Pólvora." *La Prensa*, August ?, 1971.
"Mr. Chester Mercury . . ." *El Comercio*, June 9, 1906.
Myers, Kathleen Ann. *Fernández de Oviedo's Chronicle of America: A New History for a New World*. Austin: University of Texas Press, 2017.
Newson, Linda. *Indian Survival in Colonial Nicaragua*. Norman: University of Oklahoma Press, 1987.
"Nicaragua: La crisis económica de los años 30." *El Nuevo Diario*, May 26, 2009.
"Niegan a Jarquín, Voto de confianza." *Novedades*, July 15, 1969.
"Nota deportiva." *Faces y facetas: Semanario independiente*, no. 61, November 29, 1923.
"Notas de la primera piedra." *La Noticia*, no. 225, July 23, 1916.
"Noticia confirmada. Por cablegrama de nuestro ministro en Washington . . . nombramiento de Mr. Chester Mercury . . ." *El Comercio*, January 12, 1906.
"Nuevo Cónsul de los Estados Unidos en Nicaragua." *El Comercio*, January 11, 1906.
Núñez Becerra, Fernanda. "El agridulce beso de Safo: discursos sobre las lesbianas a fines del siglo XIX mexicano." In *Historia y Grafía*, no. 31, 49–75. Mexico City: Universidad Iberoamericana, 2008.
Obando Somarriba, Francisco. *Doña Angélica Balladares de Argüello: La primera dama del liberalism—Su vida, sus hechos, episodios de la historia de Nicaragua*. Managua: Tipografía Comercial, 1969.

Odle, Don J. 1961. *Basketball Around the World*. Economy Printing Concern, 1961.
Ortega, Orlando. "Le dicen: La Sebastiana." Los Hijos de septiembre. *Ortega Reyes* (blog), February 4, 2012. ortegareyes.wordpress.com.
Ortega Reyes, Orlando. "La Caja." *Ortega Reyes* (blog), October 20, 2010. https://ortegareyes.wordpress.com/2010/10/20/la-caja/#comments.
"¿Otro testamento?" *El Comercio*, May 14, 1914.
Oviedo y Valdés, Gonzalo Fernández de. *Historia general y natural de las Indias*. 3rd part. Vol. 4. Madrid: Imprenta de la Real Academia de la Historia, 1855.
Palafox Menegazzi, Alejandra. "Sodomía y masculinidad en la ciudad de México (1821–1870)." *Anuario de Estudios Americanos* 72, no. 1 (January–June 2015): 289–320.
Palma Martínez, Francisco. *El siglo de los topos: Crítica y enseñanza en plan de ciencia: Filosofía del sexo, psicología, sociología, eugenesia, religión y artes*. León, Nic.: Editorial La Patria, 1949.
Palmer, Frederick. *Central America and Its Problems: An Account of a Journey from the Rio Grande to Panama, with Introductory Chapters on Mexico and Her Relations to Her Neighbors*. New York: Moffat, Yard, and Company, 1913.
Pasos Marciaq, Ricardo. *El burdel de las Pedrarias*. 4th ed. Managua: Hispamer, 1997.
Pastora Absalón. "La identidad sexual de Rigoberto." *La Prensa*, October 22, 2013.
Pereira, Iván de Jesús. "Restauran en León la casa del magnicidio." *La Prensa*, August 10, 2013.
Pérez Valle, Eduardo. *Centroamérica en los cronistas de indias. Oviedo*. Serie Cronistas, no. 5. Managua: Banco de América, 1977.
Pérez Valle, Eduardo. "¿Martín Estete y el Gobernador Castañeda eran Homosexuales?" *Eduardo Pérez Valle* (blog), 1971. https://eduardoperezvalle.blogspot.com/2014/01/puntos-oscuros-en-la-historia-de.html.
Pérez Valle, Eduardo. "Rigoberto López Pérez: Dopamina y heroismo en la verdad histórica. (Cinco voces en el debate)." *Eduardo Pérez Valle* (blog), September 20, 2015. eduardoperezvalle.blogspot.com.
"Petición de Diego Núñez de Mercado al Consejo de las Indias el 16 de noviembre de 1541, Acompaña diligencias del Teniente Gobernador de la conducta de Francisco de Castañeda." http://sajurin.enriquebolanos.org/vega/docs/AVB-CS-T7-DOCUMENTO%20507.pdf.
Petrus, John. "International News Network: Un análisis de transgresiones de género en la producción audio-visual nicaragüense." *Revista de Historia*, no. 29 (September–December 2013): 111–26.
Pineda, Baron L. *Shipwrecked Identities: Navigating Race on Nicaragua's Mosquito Coast*. New Brunswick, N.J.: Rutgers University Press, 2006.
"Poetas y locos invaden Managua." *La Prensa*, Memoria de ocho décadas, Parte dos de diez, nd.
"Por amor al arte dariano." *La Prensa*, February 3, 2014.
"Por creerse mujer y haberse puesto en las orejas un par de chapitas de oro . . ." *El Comercio*, March 14, 1906.

Premo, Bianca. *Children of the Father King: Youth, Authority, and Legal Minority in Colonial Lima.* Chapel Hill: University of North Carolina Press, 2005.

"Primeros testigos de la defensa de Zelaya: Tres declararon ayer." *Novedades,* July 1969.

"Proceso ante el gobernador Contreras, contra Alonso de León, acusado de pronunciar palabras difamatorias contra el honor de señoras de León. León, el 22 de febrero de 1541." http://sajurin.enriquebolanos.org/vega/docs/AVB-CS-T9-DOCUMENTO%20608%20-%2034.pdf.

"Promulgación del Código de Comercio de Nicaragua." http://legislacion.asamblea.gob.ni/Normaweb.nsf/xpNorma.xsp?documentId=F4448F23AACAAB87062574280077CE2C&action=openDocument.

"Proyecto Constitución Política Nicaragua 1854." http://enriquebolanos.org/context.php?item=constitucion-1854-item.

Puar, Jasbir K. "Feminists and Queers in the Service of Empire." In *Feminism and War: Confronting U.S. Imperialism,* edited by Robin Riley, Chandra Talpade Mohanty, and Minnie Bruce Pratt, 47–55. New York: Zed Books, 2013.

Puar, Jasbir K. *Terrorist Assemblages: Homonationalism in Queer Times.* Durham, N.C.: Duke University Press, 2017.

"Quedó organizado un nuevo club de golf." *La Prensa,* December 5, 1928.

Quijano, Aníbal. "Modernity, Identity, and Utopia in Latin America." *Boundary 2,* vol. 20, no. 3 (1993): 140–55.

Radell, David R. "The Indian Slave Trade and Population of Nicaragua During the Sixteenth Century." In *The Native Population of the Americas in 1492,* 2nd ed., edited by William M. Deneven, 67–76. Madison: University of Wisconsin Press, 1992.

Ramírez Mercado, Sergio. "El sencillo arte de dejarse engañar." *La Prensa,* November 22, 2012.

Ramírez Mercado, Sergio. *Margarita está linda la mar.* Madrid: Santillana, 1998.

Rathje, Steve. "The Power of Framing: It's Not What You Say, It's How You Say It." *The Guardian,* July 20, 2017.

Reig, Rafael. "La Pérdida del reino." Eldiario.es, February 19, 2013.

"Reglamento prohíbe boxeo de mujeres." *La Prensa,* April 6, 1971.

"Reglamento sobre la Prostitución y Profilaxia Venérea." 1955. *La Gaceta Diario Oficial,* no. 120.

"Reglamento de policía decretado por el gobierno en 10 de diciembre." 1862. https://sajurin.enriquebolanos.org/docs/CodigosLegislacion%20-%20Jesus%20de%20la%20Rocha%20-%20312.pdf.

Reglamento de policía de la República de Nicaragua, decretado por el poder ejecutivo en 25 de octubre de 1880 y mandado redactar por el señor presidente General D. Joaquín Zavala. Managua: Tipografía Nacional, 1890.

"Renuncia en balde. Diputados conocerán en el caso Zelaya." *La Prensa,* June 19, 1969.

"Renuncia del Dr. Cabrera." *El Comercio,* November 5, 1914.

Rice, Michael David. "Nicaragua and the United States: Policy Confrontations and Cultural Interactions, 1893–1933." PhD diss., University of Houston, 1995.

Ring, Jennifer. *Stolen Bases: Why American Girls Don't Play Baseball*. Urbana: University of Illinois Press, 2009.

Richardson, Angelique. *Love and Eugenics in the Late Nineteenth Century: Rational Reproduction and the New Woman*. New York: Oxford University Press, 2003.

"Rigoberto López Pérez, un heroe que cambió la historia." Radio La Primerísima, September 21, 2017.

Robleto, J. H. *Memoria de Higiene y Beneficencia Públicas*. Managua: n.p., 1933.

Rocha Cortez, David J. *Cartografías de espacios en fuga: Managua 1968–1975*. Managua: Anamá ediciones, 2022.

Rocha Cortez, David. "Cartografías de homosocialización, espacios en fuga: Managua 1968–1975." Master's thesis, Universidad Centroamericana, 2016.

Rocha Cortez, David. *Crónicas de la Ciudad*. Managua: Soma Editores, 2019.

Rodríguez, Edgard. "¿Quién era Stanley Cayasso, el pelotero que da su nombre al viejo estadio de béisbol?" *La Prensa*, October 10, 2017.

Rodríguez, Francisco. "La Valoración Histórica como corriente formadora de género en la narrativa centroamericana." In *Actas del simposio hacia la comprensión del 98: Representaciones finiseculares en España e Hispanoamérica*, edited by Jorge Chen Sham, 213–28. 1st ed. San José, C.R.: Editorial Universidad de Costa Rica, 2001.

Rodríguez, Ileana. *Primer inventario del invasor*. Managua: Editorial Nueva Nicaragua, 1984.

Rodríguez Rosales, Isolda. *Historia de la educación en Nicaragua: 50 años en el sistema educativo 1929–1979*. Managua: Editorial Hispamer, 2007.

Román, José. *Maldito país*. Managua: Ediciones INPRHU-El Pez y la Serpiente, 1979.

Romero Vargas, Germán. "La presencia africana en el pacífico y el centro de Nicaragua." *Revista WANI*, no. 13, 1992.

Romero Vargas, Germán. *Las estructuras sociales de Nicaragua*. Managua: Editorial Vanguardia, 1988.

Rosengarten, Frederic. *William Walker y el ocaso del filibusterismo*. Translated by Luciano Cuadra. Tegucigalpa, Hn.: Editorial Guaymuras, 2002.

Rubio Sánchez, Manuel. *Status de la mujer en centroamérica*. Guatemala: Editorial "José de Pineda Ibarra," 1976.

Ruiz y Torres, Josefina Edith. *A puerta cerrada: Inquisición y lectura en el siglo xvi novohispano*. Mexico City: Ediciones Clandestino, 2014.

Saballos Ramírez, Marvin. "80 años del terremoto de Managua." *La Prensa*, April 1, 2011.

Sáinz de Medrano, Luis. "Rubén Darío ante la crisis europea de su tiempo." *Rubén Darío y el arte de la prosa: Ensayo, retratos, y alegorías*, edited by Cristóbal Cuevas García, 31–54. Málaga, Esp.: Congreso de Literatura Española Contemporánea, 1998.

Sánchez Ramírez, Roberto. "Puntos de referencia en la vieja Managua." *La Prensa*, July 25, 2005.

Sánchez Rodríguez, Susy Mariela. "From the Father to the Mother of the Nation: The Metamorphosis of the Politics of Commemoration in Nicaragua." PhD diss., University of Notre Dame, 2014.

Sandoval, María Adelia. "La Caimana: La primera lesbiana declarada." *7 Días*, no. 419, 2004.

Sandoval Aranda, Mario. "José Santos Zelaya: apóstol y reformador." *La Prensa*, July 11, 2004.

Sandoval Aranda, Mario. "Zelaya y Darío: Amigos por el liberalismo." *La Prensa*, July 11, 2017.

"Sary Miranda Whitford." Salón de la Fama del Deporte Nicaragüense. http://salondelafama-nicaragua.com/sary-mirando-whitford/.

Schmigalle, Gunther. "El poeta de Nicaragua y el gran fraude de Arizona." *Temas nicaragüenses*, no. 56 (December 2012): 7.

Schott, Cory L. "Frontiers and Fandangos: Reforming Colonial Nicaragua, 1759–1814." PhD diss., University of Arizona, 2014.

Scolieri, Paul. *Dancing in the New World: Aztecs, Spaniards, and the Choreography of Conquest*. Austin: University of Texas Press, 2013.

Scroggs, William Oscar. *Filibusters and Financiers: The Story of William Walker and His Associates*. New York: The MacMillan Company, 1916.

Selva, Buenaventura. *Instituciones de derecho civil nicaragüense*. Managua: Tipografía de Managua, 1883.

Shellum, Brian G. *African American Officers in Liberia: A Pestiferous Rotation, 1910–1942*. Omaha: University of Nebraska Press, 2018.

Sigal, Pete. "The *Cuiloni*, the *Patlache*, and the Abominable Sin: Homosexualities in Early Colonial Nahua Society." *Hispanic American Historical Review* 85, no. 4 (2005): 555–594.

Sigal, Pete. *The Flower and the Scorpion: Sexuality and Ritual in Early Nahua Culture*. Durham, N.C.: Duke University Press, 2011.

Sigal, Pete. *From Moon Goddesses to Virgins: The Colonization of Yucatecan Maya Sexual Desire*. Austin: University of Texas Press, 2000.

Sigal, Pete, ed. *Infamous Desire. Male Homosexuality in Colonial Latin America*. Chicago: University of Chicago Press, 2003.

Sinha, Mrinalini. *Colonial Masculinity: The "Manly Englishman" and the "Effeminate Bengali" in the Late Nineteenth Century*. Manchester, U.K.: Manchester University Press, 1995.

Silver, Peter. "Unreliable Sources." *Harvard Review*, no. 37 (2009): 104–16.

Slotkin, Richard. *The Fatal Environment: The Myth of the Frontier in the Age of Industrialization*. Norman: University of Oklahoma Press, 1985.

Slidell, John. "The Arrest of William Walker." Speech delivered at the United States Senate on April 8, 1858.

Smith, Steven B. *Modernity and Its Discontents: Making and Unmaking the Bourgeois from Machiavelli to Bellow*. New Haven, Conn.: Yale University Press, 2016.

Soza Chavarría, Rafael Antonio. "Las plumas y los modistas de la virgen. Un secreto público para la familia y la iglesia católica. La construcción y expresión de la homosexualidad en personas que pertenecen a familias heteroparentales y comunidades de fe católicas." Bachelor's thesis, Universidad Centroamericana, 2015.

Stanislawski, Dan. *The Transformation of Nicaragua, 1519–1548*. Vol. 54 of *Ibero-Americana*. Berkeley: University of California Press, 1983.

Starr, Frederick. *In Indian Mexico: A Narrative of Travel and Labor*. Chicago: Forbes and Company, 1908.

Starr, Frederick. *Notes upon the Ethnography of Southern Mexico*, Part 1. P. Putnam Memorial Publication Fund, 1900.

Stepan, Nancy Leys. *"The Hour of Eugenics": Race, Gender, and Nation in Latin America*. Ithaca, N.Y.: Cornell University Press, 1991.

Stiles, T. J. "The Filibuster King: The Strange Career of William Walker, The Most Dangerous International Criminal of the Nineteenth Century." https://mrtomecko.weebly.com/uploads/1/3/2/9/13292665/walker.

Stephen, Lynn. "Sexualities and Genders in Zapotec Oaxaca." *Latin American Perspectives* 29, no. 2 (2002): 41–59.

Sternberg, Peter. "Challenging Machismo: Promoting Sexual and Reproductive Health with Nicaraguan Men." *Gender and Development* 8, no. 1, (2000): 89–99.

Stockett, Miranda K. "On the Importance of Difference: Re-envisioning Sex and Gender in Ancient Mesoamerica." *World Archaeology* 37, no. 4 (2005): 566–78.

Stone, Samuel Z. *The Heritage of the Conquistadors: Ruling Classes in Central America from the Conquest to the Sandinistas*. Lincoln: University of Nebraska Press, 1990.

Streeby, Shelley. *American Sensations: Class, Empire, and the Production of Popular Culture*. Berkeley: University of California Press, 2002.

Squier, Ephraim. *Nicaragua: Its People, Scenery, Monuments, Resources, Conditions, and Proposed Canal*. New York: Harper and Brothers, 1860.

Squier, E. G. *Nicaragua: Its People, Scenery, Monuments, and the Proposed Interoceanic Canal with Numerous Original Maps and Illustrations*. Vol. 1. New York: D. Appleton and Co., Publishers, 1852.

Taylor, Analisa. *Indigeneity in the Mexican Cultural Imagination: Thresholds of Belonging*. Tucson: University of Arizona Press, 2009.

Taylor, Analisa. "Malinche and Matriarchal Utopia: Gendered Visions of Indigeneity in Mexico." *Signs* 31, no. 3 (2006): 815–40.

Taylor, William B. *Magistrates of the Sacred: Priests and Parishioners in Eighteenth-Century Mexico*. Redwood City, Calif.: Stanford University Press, 1996.

Téllez, Dora María. *Muera la gobierna!: Colonización en Matagalpa y Jinotega (1820–1890)*. Managua: URACCAN, 1999.

"Testimonio de las diligencias iniciado en León, el 31 de diciembre de 1530, para elegir alcaldes y regidores de su ayuntamiento mediante el voto de los respectivos funcionarios. Figura expediente en que se explica la conducta observada por el gobernador Pedrarias Dávila." Archivo General de Indias, Sevilla, Patronato, Legajo 185, Ramo 3.

Tilcsik, András, Michel Anteby, and Carly R. Knight. "Concealable Stigma and Occupational Segregation: Toward a Theory of Gay and Lesbian Occupations." *Administrative Science Quarterly* 60, no. 3 (2015): 446–81.

Tisch, Carol. "Who's in Store: Mission Avenue's Bernabé Somoza." Sarasota Magazine .com, October 1, 2013.
Toledo de Aguerri, Josefa. *Educación y feminismo: Sobre enseñanza—Artículos varios Toledo de Aguerri.* Managua: Talleres nacionales, 1940.
Toledo de Aguerri, Josefa. *Revista femenina ilustrada.* January 18, 1920.
Torres Lazo, Agustín. *La saga de los Somoza: Historia de un magnicidio.* Managua: Hispamer, 2000.
Townsend, Camilla. "Burying the White Gods: New Perspectives on the Conquest of Mexico." *The American Historical Review* 108, no. 3 (2003): 659–87.
Trexler, Richard C. *Sex and Conquest: Gendered Violence, Political Order, and the European Conquest of the Americas.* Ithaca, N.Y.: Cornell University Press, 1995.
Tünnerman Bernheim, Carlos. "Ruben Darío y las mujeres en su vida." http://salgadoperiodismo.blogspot.com/2013/01/ruben-dario-y-las-mujeres-en-su-vida .html.
Tünnerman Bernheim, Carlos. *Tendencias contemporáneas en la transformación de la educación superior.* Managua: Instituto Martin Luther King, UPOLI, 2002.
Twinam, Ann. *Public Lives, Private Secrets: Gender, Honor, Sexuality and Illegitimacy in Colonial Spanish America.* Redwood City, Calif.: Stanford University Press, 1999.
"Una mujer monta un toro." *El Comercio,* 1904.
United Nations. *Delegations to the General Assembly.* Issues 29–30. 1974.
Unruh, Vicky. *Latin American Vanguards: The Art of Contentious Encounters.* Berkeley: University of California Press, 1994.
"Un hombre disfrazado de mujer." *La Tribuna,* May 15, 1917.
Urbina, Nicasio. "La crítica dariana. Estado actual del arte." 2005. https://homepages .uc.edu/~urbinan/lacriticadariana.htm.
Urbina Gaitán, Chester. "Apuntes sobre la participación de la mujer nicaragüense en el deporte en la primera mitad del siglo XX." *EFDeportes.com, Revista Digital,* no. 209, 2015.
Urbina Gaitán, Chester. "Béisbol y estado en Nicaragua, 1915–1957." *EFDeportes.com, Revista Digital,* no. 194, 2014.
Van Meter, Dan. "Rubén Darío and Vicente Huidobro: Two Views of Language as Impregnation." *Hispania* 75, no. 2 (1992).
Vannini, Margarita. "Las conflictivas memorias: La Revolución Sandinista." *Megafón: La Batalla de las Ideas,* no. 16/5 (September 2017). CLACSO.
Various authors. *Recuerdos de Navidad en Nicaragua.* Managua: Alcaldía de Managua, 2012.
Vicente, Marta V. *Debating Sex and Gender in Eighteenth-Century Spain.* Cambridge: Cambridge University Press, 2017.
Vijil, Francisco. *El padre Vijil, su vida: Algunos episodios de nuestra historia nacional; comentarios relativos a los mismos. Juicios de diferentes autores. Algunos sermones fotograbados. Época comprendida entre 1801 y 1867; datos históricos y comprobantes manuscritos auténticos compilados por Francisco Vijil.* Granada, Nic.: Tipografía de "El Centro-americano," 1930.

Vizenor, Gerald. *Native Liberty: Natural Reason and Cultural Survivance*. Lincoln: University of Nebraska Press, 2009.

Velasco, Sherry. *Lesbians in Early Modern Spain*. Nashville, Tenn.: Vanderbilt University Press, 2011.

Velásquez Villatoro, Antonio. "Miradas sobre la representación de la homosexualidad en la literatura centroamericana y el caso de *Trágame Tierra* de Lisandro Chávez Alfaro." *The Latin Americanist* 59, no. 2 (2015): 51–66.

Velásquez, Uriel. "Nicas son más tolerantes a la diversidad sexual." *El Nuevo Diario*, July 27, 2017.

Villavicencio, Franklin. "David Rocha: Cartógrafo de memorias." September 14, 2017. https://furiaca.com/david-rocha-cartografo-memorias/.

Von Tempsky, G. F. *Mitla: A Narrative of Incidents and Personal Adventures on a Journey in Mexico, Guatemala, and Salvador in the Years 1853 to 1855—Observations on the Modes of Life in Those Countries*. London: Longman, Brown, Green, Longmans, and Roberts, 1858.

Walker, William. *The War in Nicaragua*. Mobile, Ala.: S. H. Goetzel and Co., 1860.

Wallace, Arturo. "Por qué los nicaragüenses están convencidos de que el suyo es el país con más poetas de América Latina." BBC Mundo, May 24, 2017.

Ward, Richard. "Print Culture, Moral Panic, and the Administration of the Law: The London Crime Wave of 1744." *Crime, Histoire and Sociétés/Crime, History and Societies* 16, no. 1 (2012).

Wardlow, Holly. "Anger, Economy, and Female Agency: Problematizing 'Prostitution' and 'Sex Work' Among the Huli of Papua New Guinea." *Signs* 29, no. 4 (Summer 2004): 1017–40.

Wardlow, Holly. *Wayward Women: Sexuality and Agency in a New Guinea Society*. Berkeley: University of California Press, 2006.

Wells, William V. *Walker's Expedition to Nicaragua: A History of the Central American War; and the Sonora and Kinney Expeditions, Including All the Recent Diplomatic Correspondence, Together with a New and Accurate Map of Central America, and a Memoir and Portrait of General William Walker*. New York: Stringer and Townsend, 1856.

Werner, Patrick S. *Época temprana de León Viejo: Una historia de la primera capital de Nicaragua*. Managua: Fondo Editorial Instituto Nicaragüense de Cultura-ASDI, 2000.

Williams, Michael. "The Filibusters of San Francisco." *Pearson's Magazine* 34, no. 1. (July 1915): 144–51.

Wills, Matthew. "The First Moral Panic: London, 1774." *JSTOR Daily*, January 9, 2018.

Wolfe, Justin. "'The Cruel Whip': Race and Place in Nineteenth Century Nicaragua." In *Blacks and Blackness in Central America: Between Race and Place*, edited by Lowell Gudmundson and Justin Wolfe, 177–208. Durham, N.C.: Duke University Press, 2010.

Wolfe, Justin. *The Everyday Nation-State: Community and Ethnicity in Nineteenth-Century Nicaragua*. Lincoln: University of Nebraska Press, 2007.

"Y a María Zelaya, de San Sebastián . . ." *El Comercio*, March 11, 1906.

"Ya está al servicio del publico el excusado que dicho Comité [Comité del Mercado] mandó construir al Sur del Mercado. Hay un policía encargado de la vigilancia y aseo de él." *El Comercio*, September 5, 1903.

Yeager, Timothy J. "Encomienda or Slavery? The Spanish Crown's Choice of Labor Organization in Sixteenth-Century Spanish America." *The Journal of Economic History* 55, no. 4 (1995): 842–59.

Zambrana H., Lizandro. "Admiración." *El Comercio*, May 17, 1914.

Zapata, Nemesio de la Concepción. "Vida del guerrero bárbaro Nicaroguan." *Revista de Temas Nicaragüense*, no. 64 (August 2013): 186–96.

INDEX

abusos deshonestos, 248
Acereda, Alberto, 198, 204
Ada. *See* Moncada, Ada
afeminado/s, 17, 105
Afro-mestizos, 72, 142
Afro-Nicaraguans, 7, 18, 20, 23, 256; in baseball, 173, 180–83
Agapito. *See* Díaz, Agapito
agro-export economic model, 129
Aguirre, Carmelo. *See* La Caimana
Aguirre, Carmen. *See* La Caimana
Aguirre, José Dolores, 229
Alfaguara Prize, 219
Álvarez Montalbán, Emilio, 190
amancebados, 32
Andagoya, Pascual de, 26–27
Anti-American (U.S.), 152, 154–55, 170, 172
anti-Black racism, 18, 126, 180, 182–83
anti-communism, 109, 191
anti-Indigenous racism, 20, 73, 117
anti-LGBTQIA+, 11, 119 193, 241, 249; anti-gay, 137; anti-lesbian, 147, 149, 156
anti-sodomy law, 46, 81, 93, 250, 254
anti-Somocista, 176, 191, 193, 223, 226, 239, 241, 246, 248, 250

Aragón, Francisco, 203
Arellano, Jorge Eduardo, 11, 35–36, 40–42, 50–51, 53, 70, 132, 173, 180, 198, 201, 206–9
Argüello Gómez, José, 36
Arizona State University (ASU), 198–202; ASU Special Collections, 200
Arroyo Buitrago (*Diputado*), 250
Atlantic coast (of Nicaragua), 123–26, 181. *See also* Caribbean Coast
Audiencia, 63
autoridad marital, 87, 89
Avellán, Hector, 198, 205
Ayón, Tomas, 64

Baby Dolls (brothel), 223
Bachicao, Fernando (Machicao, Hernando), 32
Baldwin, Charles, 186
Balmaceda Toro, Pedro, 197
Barberena, Edgar, 229
Barbosa, Francisco J., 53, 240
Barquero, Ramona, 110–11
Bautista Lara, Francisco Javier, 132, 135, 139

Bautista Sacasa, Juan, 190
Beatles the, 222
Beer, Andreas, 115
Ben, Pablo, 137
Benavente, Toribio "Motolinía," 33
Bendaña, Juana, 113
bisexual, 8, 13, 232, 234; Somoza, Bernabé, 213, 215, 251
Black (race), 71–72, 124–28, 181
Blandón, Erick, 9–11, 35, 47, 49, 50
Blandón, Jesus Miguel "Chuno," 206
Bluefields, 173, 180, 183
Bobadilla, Francisco de, 26, 30, 34–35, 46–48, 56
Boer, El (baseball team), 182
Bolaños, Pío, 74
Bolaños Geyer, Alejandro, 105–6
Bolaños Geyer, Enrique, 56
Bolivar Coronado, Rafael, 55
Bone Prado, Ana, 130
Borgen, José Francisco "Chepe Chico," 181
Bourbon Reforms, 43, 45, 61–62, 116
Briones, Ignacio, 151
Bullough, Vern, 142
Burkhart, Louise, 30
Burns, Bradford, 88
Burns, Muriel, 169
butch–femme roles, 218

Caballero, Andrés, 3, 11, 32–33, 36–44, 63, 65, 209, 212
Cabello y Robles, Domingo (Governor Cabello), 62–64
caciques, 15, 30
Camacho, Jorge Luis, 156–57
campechana, 150
campechano, 215
cargabates, 182
Caribbean Coast (of Nicaragua), 6–7, 22, 51, 125–28; and baseball, 173, 180–81, 183, 187, 258
Carretera Norte (the Northern Freeway), 177

Carroll, Anna, 101
Casanova Fuertes, Rafael, 209, 212
Casco, Aura Lila, 175–76
Casco sisters, the (Castalia, Lila, and Tere), 175
Castañeda, Francisco de, 3, 36–44
Castillo, Emelina, 169
Castro, Fidel, 241
Catholic Gentlemen (*Caballeros Católicos*; *Caballeros*), 154, 170
Cayasso, Stanley, 180, 186–87
Cedeño, Francisco, 114
Central American Allied Army (*Ejército Aliado Centroaméricano*), 68
Central American Confederation, 68
Central American Federation (*República Federal de Centroamérica*), 68, 81
Central Bank, 198, 217
Central Managua Market (Central Market), 93–94
central Mexico, 14
Cerda, Pío, 113
Cerda, Ricarda, 113
Chamber of Deputies, 249
Chamorro, Emiliano, 169, 178
Chamorro, Fruto, 68
Chamorro Zelaya, Pedro Joaquín, 152–53
Charco de los Patos, El (The Puddle of the Ducks), 193, 215, 232–37, 245, 246, 251
Chauncey, George, 137–38
Chepes, Los, 32
chinvaronismo, 111
Chorotega, 14–16, 19, 255
Church of the Sacred Heart, 178
cocheche, 52. See also *cochón*
cochón, 8, 10–11, 18, 25, 49–53, 65, 207, 209, 215, 233, 238, 239, 242, 250–51
cochona, 8, 50, 51
Código de la familia (family code), 86
Colegio de Señoritas de Managua, 179
Cole, Byron, 68
Columbus, Christopher, 26
comerciantes, 79

comiderías, 58
Comunidades Indígenas, 72, 80
concúbito, 250
conquistadors, 3, 7, 17, 26, 33, 35–37, 41, 43, 45, 101
Conservative Party, 98, 152, 172
Conservatives (political party), 68, 102, 123, 128, 147, 148, 152, 154–55, 179, 251
Constitutional Assembly, 151
Contra War, 5
Contras, the, 208
Contreras, Rodrigo de, 32, 36, 41–42
Córdoba, Hernández de, 33
córdobas (Nicaraguan currency), 176, 226, 231
Cordova, Juan de, 17
Corea, Simón, 87
Corn Island, 182
Coronel Urtecho, José, 52
Corrales Rojas, Rafael, 206, 209–12
Costello, Rory, 182, 186
cotzoani, 50
Council of Indies, 38
Cousin, Rosa, 169
Cristo del Rosario (Managua neighborhood), 232
Crocker, Captain, 106–8
cross-dressing, 48, 65, 93, 108, 235, 242
Cruz, Arturo, Jr., 128
Cruz, Eduardo, 211
Cuadra, Pablo Antonio, 15–17, 56
cuilon, 8, 51. See also *cuylon*
cuiloni, 48, 50. See also *cuylon*
cuir, 8
cuylon, 8, 11, 14, 47, 49–51, 65; cuylon-turned-cochón, 50. See also *cuilon*

Dance of the Forty-One, 136
Dantos, Los (baseball team), 182–83
Darío, Rubén, 119, 156–58, 192, 196–206, 233, 236
Darwin, Charles, 142
Daughters of Mary (*Hijas de María*), 174

Dávila, Pedrarias, 26–27, 35–36, 40–42, 44
Davis, Madeline D., 218
de Andagoya, Pascual, 26–27
Debayle, Luis H., 222
Debayle, Salvadora, 222–23, 244, 247, 251
de Bry, Theodore, 46
decolonial, 255
de conducta viciada, 92
de la diversidad, 8, 60
de la Quadra, José Desiderio, 52
del Cid, Amalia, on Debayle, Salvadora, 247; on La Caimana, 228–31
de León, Alonso, 32
de los Ríos, Pedro, 39–41
de Noguera, Florentina, 169
department of Rivas. See Rivas
Department of State, 195, 249
de Prado, Benito, 39
de Tapia, Diego, 36, 39, 41–49
Díaz, Agapito, 58–59
Díaz, Porfirio, 64, 136
Díaz Figueroa, Alejandro, 242–43
Diriamba, 228
Diriomo, 80
diversidad sexual, 8, 60
Dore, Elizabeth, 65, 69, 80, 129
Dussel, Enrique, 121

el bajo pueblo, 132
El Comercio (Managua), 75–76, 92, 125–26, 134–35, 161–64, 177
El Cronista (Nicaragua), 193, 211, 212
Elizondo, Francisco Javier, 87
El Nuevo Diario (Managua), 194, 195
estado de sitio, 191
Estete, Captain Martín, 44
Euroamerican, 12, 15, 103, 106, 109, 112, 254; about Walker, William, 68, 98–100
excusado (latrine), 94–96

Faderman, Lillian, 76
Famous 41, 64

Federal Republic of Central America. *See* Central American Federation.
Federation of Liberal Students (*Federación de Estudiantes Liberales* or FEL), 248
Feminine School for Journalism (*Escuela Femenina de Prensa*), 142
Fernández, Francisco, 35
Finzer, Erin, 155
First Congress of Female Business Owners, 228
first wave feminism, 12, 118, 120, 139, 140, 149, 152, 158, 187
Flores, Concepción, 163
Fonseca Amador, Carlos, 194
Franco, Francisco, 150
Fregoso, Rosalinda, 114
Friends of Progress, 88

gallo ennavajado, 131
Galton, Francis, 142
Gámez, José Dolores, 101, 112
García, Alvar, 39
García, Gregorio, 54
García, Luciano, 160
Garza Carvajal, Federico, 43–44
gay, 6, 8, 9, 13, 17, 50, 51, 60, 108, 135, 143, 197, 203, 205, 208–9, 212–14, 221, 232–34, 247; about Darío, Rubén, 203–4; about New York, 137, 138
General Archive of Central America, 63
Gerson, Noel B., 107
Gertrudis Rodríguez, María, 54
Global North, 6
Gobat, Michel, 102–3, 128–29, 152, 154–55, 168–70, 253–54
gobernadores de policías, 90
Gómez, Juan Pablo, 129
Gómez Martínez, Gerardo, 239–40
González, Benito, 164
González Dávila, Gil, 34–35
Good Neighbor Policy, 189
Gordon, Dan, 172
Gould, Jeffrey, 71–72, 129

Granada (city), 17, 52, 58, 70, 74, 96, 99, 101–11, 113, 125–27, 147, 152, 165–66, 169–70, 172, 175, 183, 190, 208
granadina, 126–27
Greenberg, Amy S., 99–100, 103, 105, 108
Guadamuz, Carlos Alberto, 160
Guardia Nacional (National Guard), 214, 216, 240. *See also* National Guard
Gudmundson, Lowell, 103
Guerrero, Lorenzo, 147
Gutiérrez, Pedro Rafael, 113
Guy, Donna, 96
Guzmán, Domingo de (Saint), 220

Halftelmeyer Gómez, Gratus, 132
Harrison, Brady, 107–10
Hassan, Anuar, 233–35, 239–40
Helguero, Lorenzo, 197–98
Hernández, Agustín, 193
Hernández, María Magdalena, 229
Herrera y Tordesillas, Antonio de, 16, 28
heteromasculinity, 87, 119, 129, 168, 175, 185
heteroperformances, 219
heterostate, 25, 81
Hodgson, Anita, 173
Hodgson, Frank, 181
homonormativity, 13, 217, 232
Hospicio San Juan de Dios, 193
Hospital Bautista, 229
Hotel Montelimar, 227
Howe, Cymene, 233
Huembes market, 58
Huete Maltés, Ulises, 206, 211

Ibarra, Joseph Gregorio, 32
Imbita, 33–34
Immaculate Conception of the Virgin Mary, 220. *See also* Virgin Mary
Incer, Jaime, 33
Indies, Council of, 38; Chronicler(s) of, 46, 56
Indigeneity, 11, 17, 44, 73, 117, 120, 241, 255. *See also* Indigenous
indigenismo, 16

INDEX   327

Indigenous, 5, 7–8, 12, 14–17, 20–31, 33–34, 37, 44–49, 51, 56, 64–66, 71–75, 80–81, 90, 100, 116–17, 120, 124, 128, 142–43, 166–67, 169, 180–82, 184, 255–66; baptisms of, 35; land, 80; and markets, 11, 18–19, 55, 57, 73–74; survivance and resistance, 5, 11, 72–73, 255
Indigenous Communities (*Comunidades Indígenas*), 72, 80
Infante, Pedro, 222
INN (group), 58–61
Inquisition, the, 3, 31–33, 36, 47, 54, 116, 150, 160
Irwin, Robert McKee, 81–82, 136
Iturbide, Graciela, 16
Iván Montenegro market, 54

Jalteva, 17
Jinotega, 169
Jinotepe, 169
Jirón Terán, José, 201
Juchitán, 14–15, 17
Juigalpa, Chontales, 141

Kahlo, Frida, 16
Kampwirth, Karen, 64
Kellner, Douglas, 221
Kennedy, Elizabeth Lapovsky, 218
King, Peter, 243
Kingdom of Guatemala/Captaincy General of Guatemala, 32
Kirk, Stephanie, 54
Kühl, Eddy, 201

La Caimana, 13–14, 192, 213–35
Lakoff, George, 113
Lancaster, Roger, 50, 209
La Noticia (Nicaragua), 165, 166, 173
La Prensa (Managua), 10, 113, 152, 160, 170, 172, 178, 194, 205–6, 226, 229, 245–46, 248–49, 251
La Reina de los Tártaros (the Queen of the Tartars), 193, 235–37, 250

Las Casas, Bartolomé de, 37, 45–46, 48–49
La Sebastiana, 13–14, 193, 213, 236–38, 243, 247, 252
La Tribuna (Nicaragua), 159, 165
Lauderdale Graham, Sandra, 91
León (city), 17, 32–33, 36, 38–39, 68, 70, 171–72, 194, 206–9, 211–12, 240
León Viejo (city), 3, 36
León Báez, Bosco (León Báez), 243–45, 247
lesbophobia, 152
Lewis, George W., 178
Lezcano y Ortega, José Antonio (*Monseñor* Lezcano), 150–51, 167, 174–75, 179
Liberals (political party), 68, 98, 102, 129, 172, 190, 213, 238, 244, 253
Library of the Central Bank in Managua, 198
limpieza de sangre, 22, 71
Lindo-Fuentes, Hector, 103
Link, Daniel, 204
locas, 9, 242
lo nuestro, 220
López, Amanda, 169
López, Soledad, 193
López de Salceda, Diego, 35
López Pérez, Rigoberto, 192–97, 205–12, 222, 224–25
lucha libre, 176

magnicide, 192, 211
Managua, 13, 52, 58, 92–93, 131, 134, 139, 148, 150, 160, 163, 166–67, 169, 172, 174–76, 179, 183–84, 187, 189, 191, 193–95, 198, 201–2, 213, 216, 219, 220–21, 225, 229, 232, 235, 236, 238–39, 242, 244–47
Mann, Thomas C. (Ambassador Mann), 195–96
Mántica, Carlos, 50
manutención de alimentos, 86

marimacha, 151–53, 188, 218
marimacho, 150, 158, 171
Marines (U.S.), 3, 5, 97, 131, 138, 152–54, 168, 182–83, 189, 224
marivarones, 152, 157
Martí, José, 204–5
Martin, Ellen, 107
Martín Breño, Martín, 38
Martínez, Bartolomé, 51
Martínez, Celso, 165
Martínez, Elia, 165–67
Martínez, José Dolores, 167
Masatepe, 237
Masaya, 17, 19, 56, 110, 237
Matagalpa, 52, 153
Matamoro, Blas, 197–98
Matus, Juan de Dios, 172
Matus, Zoraida M., 178
May, Robert E., on filibusters, 99–100, 103–4
Maya, 29, 31
McCaughan, Edward J., 136
Medal, Xinda, 175
Medina, Emilio, 113
Mejía Godoy, Carlos, 182
Mejía Lacayo, José, 42
melcochas, 58–59
Mercado Oriental. See *Oriental* market
mesones, 75
mestizaje, 17–20
Mexican revolution, 141
Mexicas, 14–15, 30
Ministry of Public Education, 179
Miranda, Sary and Gloria, 176
Misesboy, 34–35
Miss Gay Nicaragua pageants, 233, 235
Molina Jiménez, Iván, 105
Moncada, Ada, 175–77
Moncada de Inestroza, Elsa, 155
Moncada Fonseca, Manuel, 16
Moncada Tapia, José María, 130, 155–56; and Ada Moncada, 175
Mondragón, J. D., 159

Monimbó, 17
Monrovia, 178
Morales Navarrete, Orlando, 208
Moreira, Mercedes, 163
Morris, Courtney, 123–24, 126
mujer honrada (honest woman), 83, 84, 270
Muxe (Muxe'), 9, 17

Nahua (peoples), 11, 14, 20, 46, 49–50, 51
Nahuat (language spoken by Nahua peoples in Nicaragua before the conquest), 8, 11, 51, 250
Nahuatl (language of the Nahua peoples in Mexico), 14, 20
Nasser, Michelle Rocío, 136
National Guard (*Guardia Nacional*), 12–13, 53–54, 177, 190–92, 195–96, 210, 212, 214, 216, 222, 227, 239–43, 245–47, 251–52
National Hero (*Héroe Nacional*), 194
Nationalist Liberal Party, 238, 245
Navy (baseball team), 181–82
Nervo, Amado, 198–205
Newson, Linda A., 72
New Spain, 32, 43, 50, 54
Nicaraguan Sports Hall of Fame, 177
Nicarao, 8, 14–16, 19, 46, 65, 255
non-heteronormative, 46, 129, 139, 161, 198, 212
non-moralistic, 98
non-Somocistas, 241
Normal School for Indigenous peoples (*Escuela Normal de Indígenas*), 142–43
Normal School for Señoritas (*Escuela Normal de Señoritas*), 147–48, 151
Novedades (Managua), 242, 245–47
Nuñez, José, 82
Núñez de Mercado, Diego, 38, 40–41
Núnez de Saballos, Olga, 250

Oaxaca, 14–19
Odle, Don, 177

Omier, Erika, 174
Orden de Alfonso el Sabio (Order of Alfonso X the Wise), 150
Oriental market, 58, 117, 236, 242
Ortega, Daniel, 6, 131, 195, 202, 207–8
Ortega, Orlando, 246–47
Oto-Manguean, 15, 19, 34
over-heterosexualization, 170
Oviedo y Valdés, Gonzalo Fernández de, 16, 27–29, 31, 34, 35, 46–48, 51, 55–56

Pacific coast (of Nicaragua), 6–8, 11, 16, 18–20, 22–23, 26, 30, 51, 55, 57, 70, 72, 78, 124–26, 141, 173, 180–84, 187, 255
Pacific Ocean, 3
Palafox, Alejandra, 53
Palma Martínez, Francisco, 149–50, 153, 171, 175, 179, 232
Pancasán, 114
Paniagua, Félix P., 135
Pasadena Ramblers (softball team), 176
Pasos, María, 113
Pasos Argüello, Joaquín, 36, 52
Pasos Marciaq, Ricardo, 37
Pastora, Joaquín Absalón, 207, 209–10
Patino sisters, the, 175
patria potestad, 85, 87, 89
Pearson, Karl, 142
pecado nefando, 7, 45
pena del último suplicio, 81
Peralta, Ignacio, 164
Pereira, Iván de Jesús, 205–6
Pérez, Isaura, 92
Pérez Valle, Eduardo, Jr., 42, 44, 113, 194–95
performances de travestismo, 235. *See also* cross-dressing
Perlongher, Nestor, 10
Period of the Directorate, 68
Pertz, Alfredo, 169
Pertz, Argentina, 169
Petrus, John, 60
Pizarro, Francisco, 41

placemark, 232
pobrecitos, 253
por andar de chinvarona, 111
Portillo, Domingo, 51
Portocarrero, Haydee, 169
postizos, 166
post-1979 era (in Nicaragua), 97, 241
post-WWII, 191
potestad marital, 79
prepolitical, 218
presidio, 95
Productores de la UNAG, Los (baseball team), 183
Puar, Jasbir K., 12
Puntarenas, Costa Rica, 178

Queen of the *Torovenado* Carnival. See *Torovenado*
queer, 6, 8; about Walker, William, 12, 105, 108–9, 118; about Guerra, Zacarías, 135; about Darío, Rubén, 203–4
Quetzalcoatl, 100
Quijano, Anibal, on Latin American modernism, 121–22
quinta, 177
Quintanilla, *Diputado*, 250
Quintanilla, José Ramón "JR," 58–59, 61

Radio Colonial, 193
Ramírez Mercado, Sergio, 199, 202, 204, 217, 219, 222–25
Rappaciolli, Roberto, 221
rapto for fuerza, 95
rapto por seducción, 95–96
raro, 133–35, 204
Rathje, Steve, 112
Real Espinales, Anastacio, 247–49
Reñazco, Francisco, 166–67
Rice, Michael, 129
Ring, Jennifer, 180
Rivas, 32, 46–47, 113
Rivas, Juliana, 177
Rivera, Diego, 16

Robleto, J. Filadelfo, 160
Rocha, David, 9–11, 193, 209, 235–38, 241–43, 245–47, 251
Rodríguez, Francisco, 37
Rondón, Alberto "Tito" (Tito Rondón), 182, 186
Rolling Stones, 222

Saballos, Anita, 175
Sacasa, Crisanto (Colonel) 52
Sala Cunas, 142, 148
Sánchez, Diego, 40, 42
Sánchez del Pozo, Francisca, 202
Sandinismo, 187
Sandinista, 5–6, 97, 135, 155, 191, 194, 208, 212–14, 221–22, 227, 234, 241, 252; revolution, 5, 10, 85, 97, 114, 139, 192, 213, 223, 233, 238, 241
Sandinista National Liberation Front (FSLN), 194, 214, 241, 252
Sandino, Augusto C., 5, 114, 154–55, 187, 189–90, 208, 231
Santana (artist), 222
Schmigalle, Gunther, 198
Schott, Cory L., 62–63
Scott, Carlos Eduardo, 228
Scott Hernández, Hilda Rosa, 214, 218, 220, 225–26, 228–32
semi-homosocial, 186
señoritas, 184
Serrano, J. Carlos, 134
settler colonialism, 254
Sevilla, Nicolasa, 223–24, 227
Sevilla Sacasa, Guillermo, 151
sexualized political correctives, 210
sexualmente diversos, 8
Shellum, Brian, 178
Sigal, Pete, 29, 31, 48, 50
Siles, Freddy, 182
Smith, Steven B., 121
Squier, Ephraim George, 110, 112
Social Christian Party, 248
Social Club, 135

sociedad conyugal, 78
sodometico, 7
sodomitas, 7
Solis, Manuel, 125, 127–28
solterón, 135
solteronas, 160
sometico, 7, 17, 38–39
Somocismo, 192, 212, 218, 241, 248, 252
Somocista, 13, 190–92, 194, 206, 210, 213–15, 217, 223–24, 226–28, 234–35, 239, 241, 246, 248, 251; elites, 234–35, 239, 241; Liberalism, 239; rule, 13, 242, 251
Somocista Popular Fronts, 223
Somoza Debayle, Anastasio "Tachito," 191, 196, 226, 244, 247
Somoza Debayle, Lillian, 247
Somoza Debayle, Luis, 191, 232, 245
Somoza dictatorship, 5, 12–13, 17, 20, 114, 176, 191–94, 210, 213–19, 223–24, 232–33, 240, 242, 251–52. See also Somocista
Somoza family, 12, 196, 213, 219, 223, 226, 238–39, 246–47
Somoza García, Anastasio, 148, 151, 154, 190–92, 222, 226, 231; assassination of, 194, 205, 210, 211, 212, 224
Somoza regime, 97, 138, 190, 213, 217
Somoza Urcuyo, Bernabé (Bernabé Somoza; Bernabé), 213, 215–16, 232–33, 238, 245–47, 251
Starr, Frederick, 15–16
Stephen, Lynn, 18
Stiles, T. J., 99
Streeby, Shelley, 103
Stockett, Miranda, 19
su calidad de mengala, 125
Sutiava, 17

Taylor, Keith, 182–83
Taylor, William B., 61
Tazoteyda, 30–31
Technical Council for Education (*Consejo Técnico de Educación*), 149

Tehuantepec, 14–16
Teilhet, Darwin, 108–9
Tellería, Clementina, 169
tiangue, 11, 14–15, 17–19, 23, 56–57, 65, 73, 74–75, 255
tijera, 162
tijeras de lona, 50
tintes homófilos, 197
tlacacolli, 30
Toledo de Aguerri, Josefa, (Doña Chepita), 140–52, 158, 160, 178
Torovenado, 193, 237, 252
Torquemada, Juan de, 33
Torres de Sola, Lolita, 170
Torres Espinoza, Edelberto, 149, 160
Tortuga Morada, La, 221
Townsend, Camilla, 100–101
trans, 8–9, 11, 13, 18, 57–58, 65, 67, 72–73, 75–76, 91, 94, 97, 117, 187, 228, 251, 255
travestismo. *See* cross-dressing

un campechano nato, 215
United Provinces of Central America, 67
University of Pennsylvania, 99
un oficio, 91
Unruh, Vicky, 52
Urbina, Nicasio, 197
Urbina Gaitán, Chester, 169
U.S.: Americans, 5, 12, 15, 104, 254; feminism, 157; imperialism, 19–20, 97, 104, 109–10, 112, 115, 154, 171, 180, 183, 253–54; intervention, 119–21, 129, 142, 168; Marines, 3, 5, 97, 131, 138, 152, 154, 169, 183, 187, 189, 224; military, 4–5, 12, 155, 170, 182–83, 189, 190

vago, 209
Valdivieso, Antonio (Bishop), 37
Valle, Alfonso, 53
van Meter, Dan A., 233
varonil, 214
Vatican II, 79
Vega, Ludwika, 58, 67

Vélez, Manuela, 169
Vijil, Agustín, 88; on William Walker, 101–2
Vílchez y Carrera, Juan Carlos, 62–64
Virgin Mary, 103, 220
Virto, Joseph Manuel, 32
Von Berswodt Wallrabe, Berta, 169
Von Tempsky, Gustavus Ferdinand, 15

Walker, William, 3, 5, 12, 98–115, 118, 129, 131, 253–54; on his defeat, 67–68
Ward, Richard, 243
Wardlow, Holly, 28
Werner, Patrick S., 35–36
western Nicaragua, 4–6, 8, 10–12, 14–20, 23, 25–26, 28, 30, 51, 57–58, 65, 72–73, 75, 84, 126, 141, 250, 254–56
white (race), 5, 12, 15, 17, 22, 77, 99–100, 103–4, 124, 131, 180, 182, 252–54; masculinity, 109, 115, 118
Whitford, Sary Miranda, 176
Wilson, Emely, 173
Wolfe, Justin, 82, 115–16
Workers' Hall, 194, 205–6
World War II, 122, 137–38, 190

Xochiquetzal, 233; pageants, 233, 235

Zacarías Guerra Home, 134, 167
Zacarías Guerra, José, 119, 131–35, 138, 176
Zambrana H., Lisandro, 134
Zapata, Nemesio de la Concepción, (Fray Nemesio), 55
Zapotec, 14–17, 19
Zelaya, Armando, 194
Zelaya, José Santos, 68–69, 85, 119, 123–25, 128–31, 148, 169, 172
Zelaya, María, 93
Zelaya Bolaños, Dominga, 169
Zelaya case, 247–48
Zelaya Castro, Amparo, 194
Zelaya Úbeda, José María, 247–48

ABOUT THE AUTHOR

Victoria González-Rivera holds a PhD in Latin American history from Indiana University. Her book, *Before the Revolution: Women's Rights and Right-Wing Politics in Nicaragua, 1821–1979,* was published by Penn State University Press (2011). She is the author of the 2020 essay "Why My Nicaraguan Father Did Not 'See' His Blackness and How Latinx Anti-Black Racism Feeds on Racial Silence." She is an associate professor in the Department of Chicana/o Studies at San Diego State University.